HAJIME KOMOTO

Thank you so much for picking up this book.
I'll work hard.

Hajime Komoto made his manga debut with the
hit series *Mashle: Magic and Muscles*, which
began serialization in *Weekly Shonen Jump* in
January 2020.

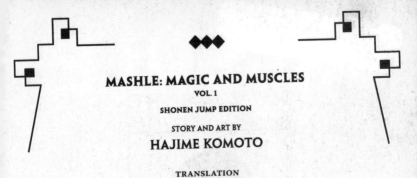

MASHLE: MAGIC AND MUSCLES
VOL. 1
SHONEN JUMP EDITION

STORY AND ART BY
HAJIME KOMOTO

TRANSLATION
NOVA SKIPPER

TOUCH-UP ART & LETTERING
EVE GRANDT

DESIGN
JIMMY PRESLER

EDITOR
KARLA CLARK

MASHLE © 2020 by Hajime Komoto
All rights reserved.
First published in Japan in 2020 by SHUEISHA Inc., Tokyo.
English translation rights arranged by SHUEISHA Inc.

The stories, characters and incidents mentioned
in this publication are entirely fictional.

Printed in Canada

Published by VIZ Media, LLC
P.O. Box 77010
San Francisco, CA 94107

10 9 8 7 6 5 4 3 2 1
First printing, July 2021

VIZ MEDIA

SHONEN JUMP

viz.com

AUG 1 8 2021

MASHLE

MAGIC AND MUSCLES

STORY AND ART BY

HAJIME KOMOTO

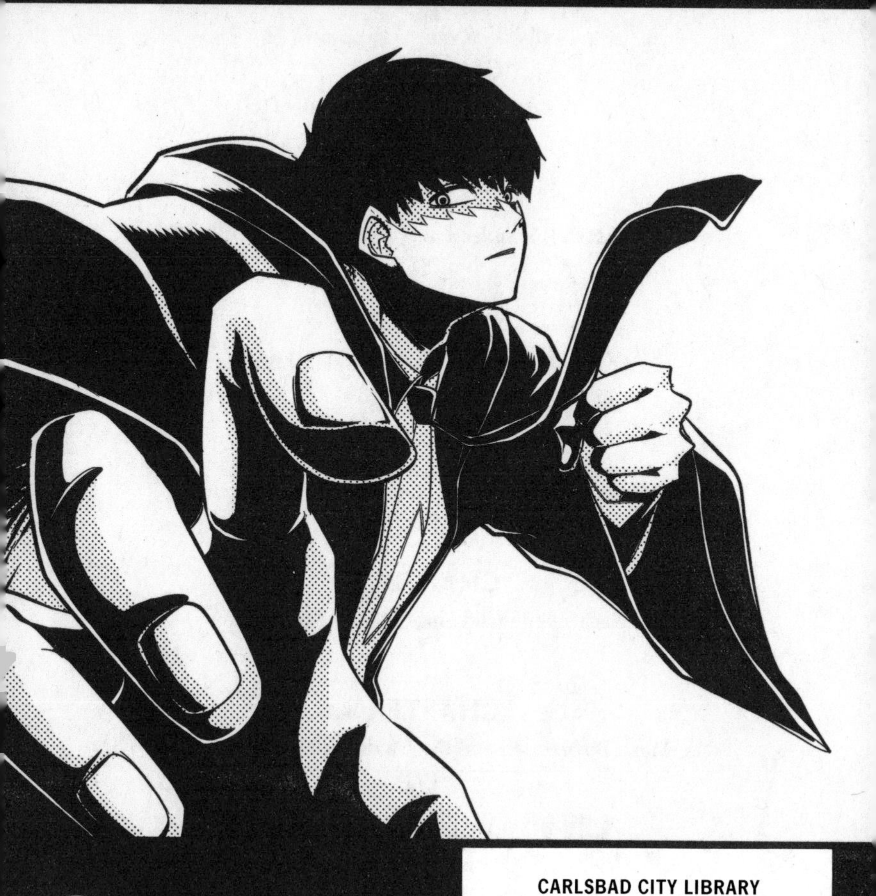

1 MASH BURNEDEAD

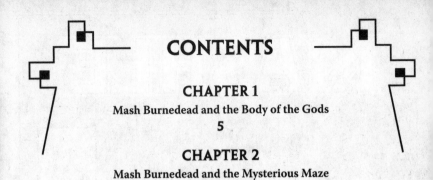

CONTENTS

CHAPTER 1
Mash Burnedead and the Body of the Gods
5

CHAPTER 2
Mash Burnedead and the Mysterious Maze
61

CHAPTER 3
Mash Burnedead and the Deadly Doll
87

CHAPTER 4
Mash Burnedead and the Clean Sweep
111

CHAPTER 5
Mash Burnedead and the Baleful Bully
131

CHAPTER 6
Mash Burnedead and the Academy Hierarchy
151

CHAPTER 7
Mash Burnedead and the Game of Brooms
171

CHAPTER 8
Mash Burnedead and the Challenging Magic User
191

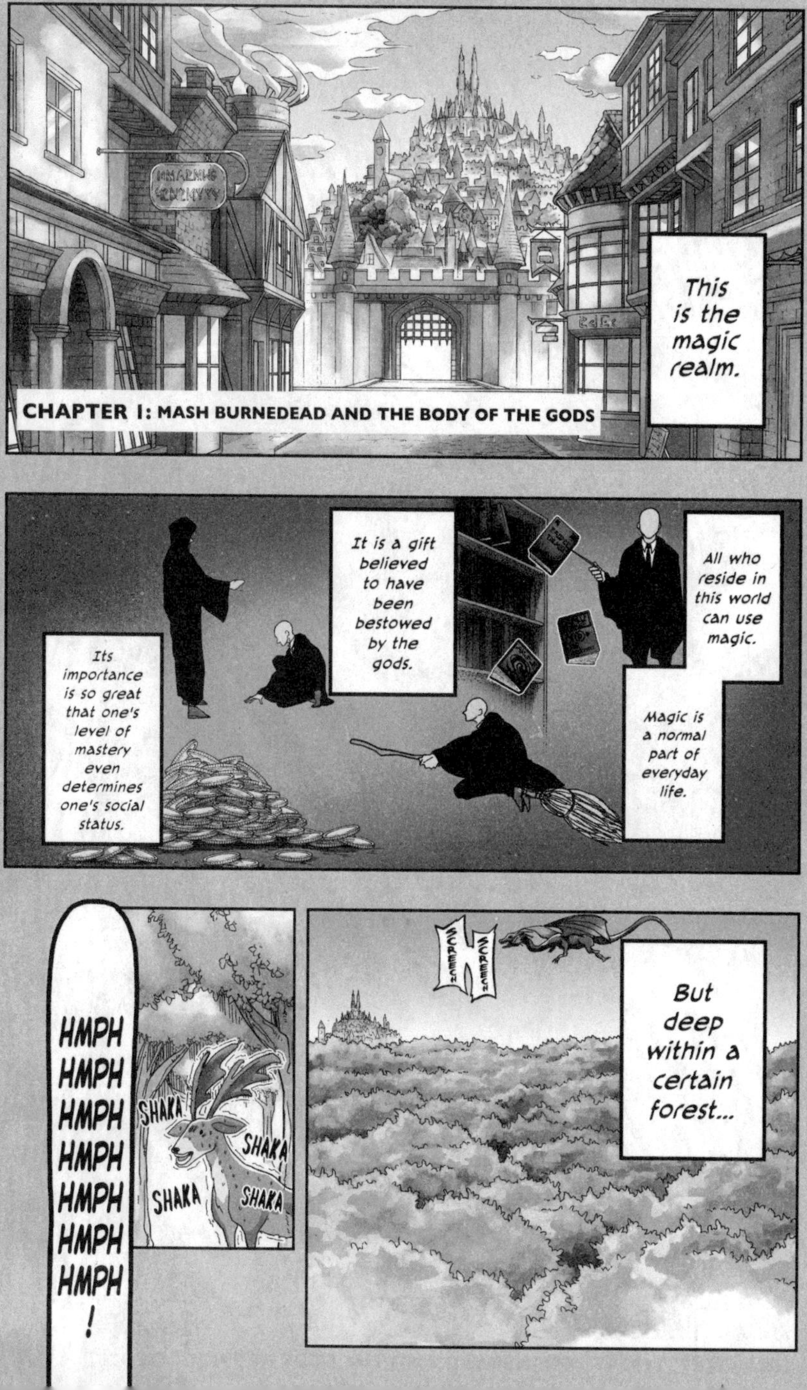
This is the magic realm.
CHAPTER 1: MASH BURNEDEAD AND THE BODY OF THE GODS
All who reside in this world can use magic.
It is a gift believed to have been bestowed by the gods.
Magic is a normal part of everyday life.
Its importance is so great that one's level of mastery even determines one's social status.
SCREECH
SCREECH
But deep within a certain forest...
SHAKA
SHAKA
SHAKA
SHAKA
HMPH HMPH HMPH HMPH HMPH HMPH HMPH !

CHAPTER 1: MASH BURNEDEAD AND THE BODY OF THE GODS

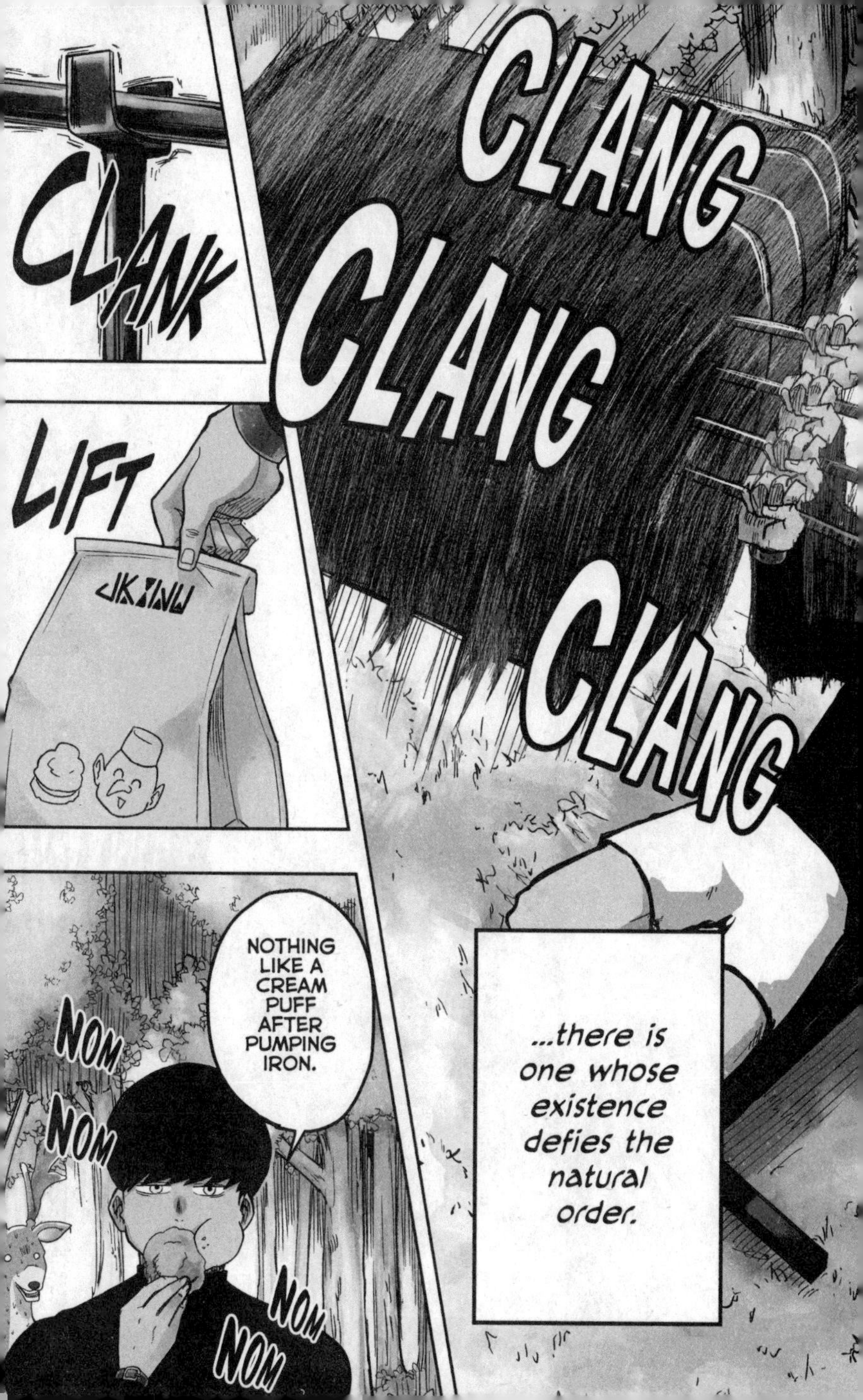
CLANG
CLANG
CLANG
...there is one whose existence defies the natural order.
CLANK
LIFT
NOTHING LIKE A CREAM PUFF AFTER PUMPING IRON.
NOM
NOM
NOM
NOM

MASHLE

MAGIC AND MUSCLES

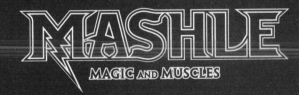

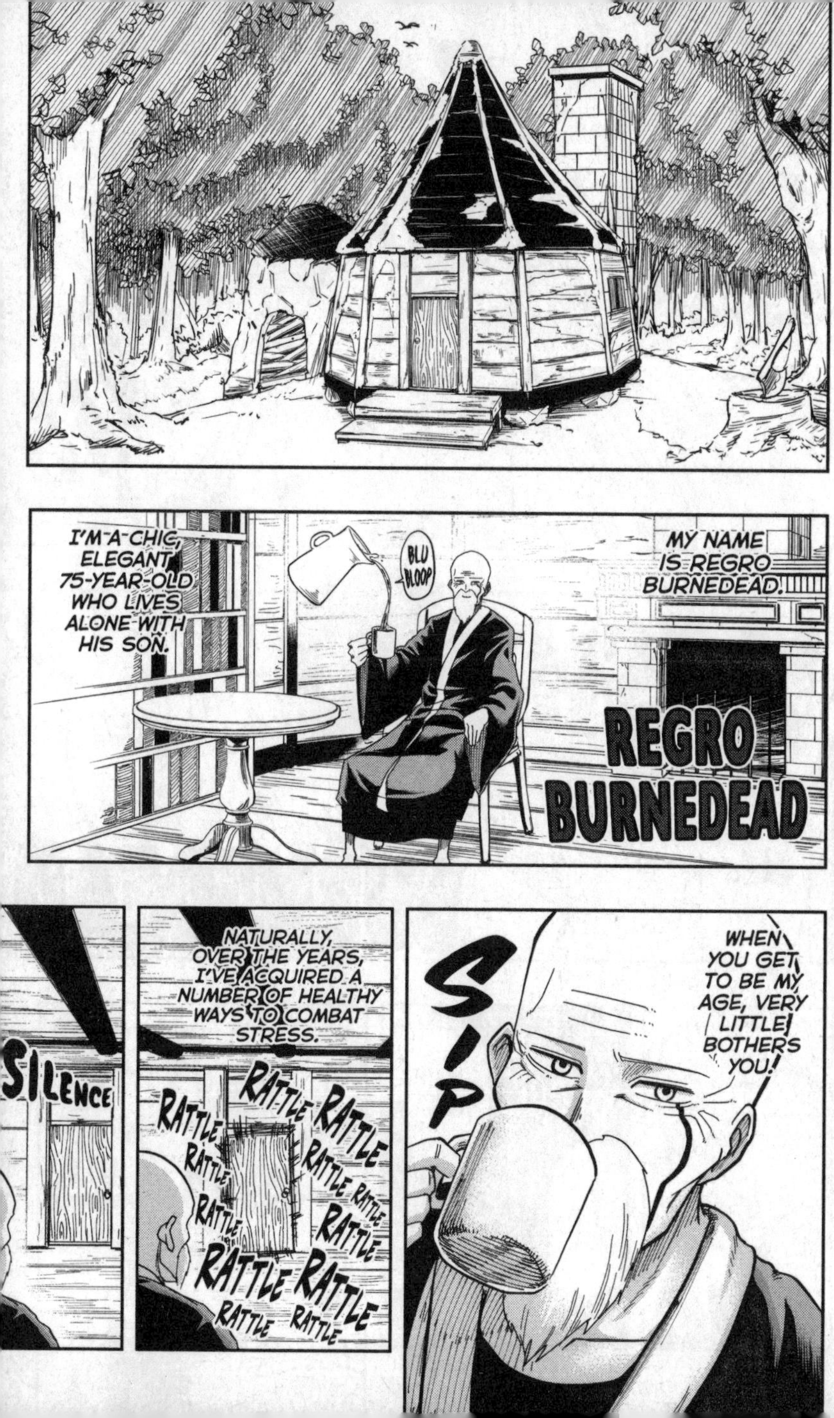
MY NAME IS REGRO BURNEDEAD.
REGRO BURNEDEAD
BLU BLOOP
I'M A CHIC, ELEGANT 75-YEAR-OLD WHO LIVES ALONE WITH HIS SON.
WHEN YOU GET TO BE MY AGE, VERY LITTLE BOTHERS YOU!
SIP
NATURALLY, OVER THE YEARS, I'VE ACQUIRED A NUMBER OF HEALTHY WAYS TO COMBAT STRESS.
RATTLE RATTLE RATTLE RATTLE RATTLE RATTLE RATTLE RATTLE RATTLE RATTLE RATTLE RATTLE RATTLE RATTLE
SILENCE

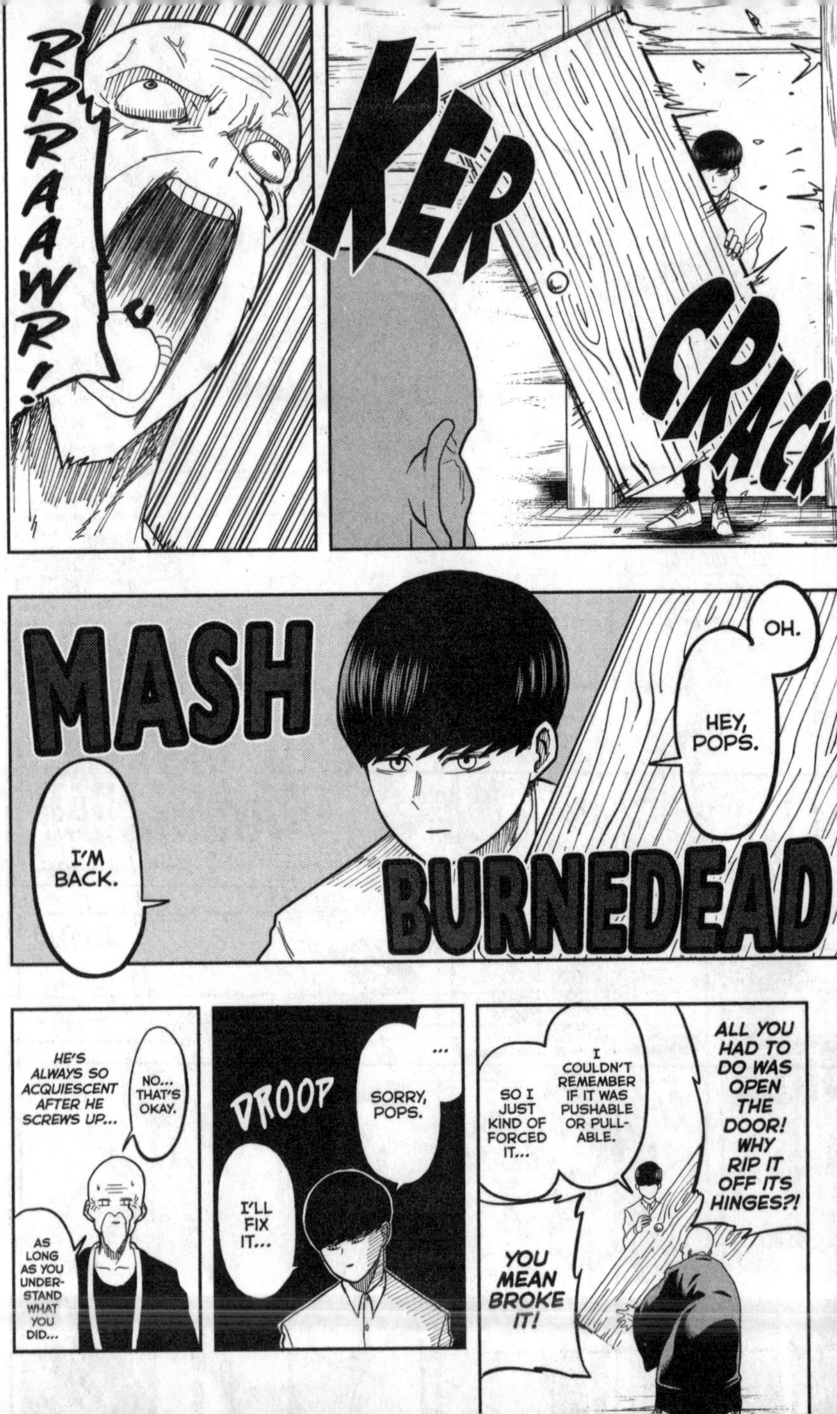

KER
CRACK
RRRAAWR!
OH.
HEY, POPS.
MASH
BURNEDEAD
I'M BACK.
ALL YOU HAD TO DO WAS OPEN THE DOOR! WHY RIP IT OFF ITS HINGES?!
I COULDN'T REMEMBER IF IT WAS PUSHABLE OR PULL-ABLE.
SO I JUST KIND OF FORCED IT...
YOU MEAN BROKE IT!
...
SORRY, POPS.
DROOP
I'LL FIX IT...
NO... THAT'S OKAY.
HE'S ALWAYS SO ACQUIESCENT AFTER HE SCREWS UP...
AS LONG AS YOU UNDERSTAND WHAT YOU DID...

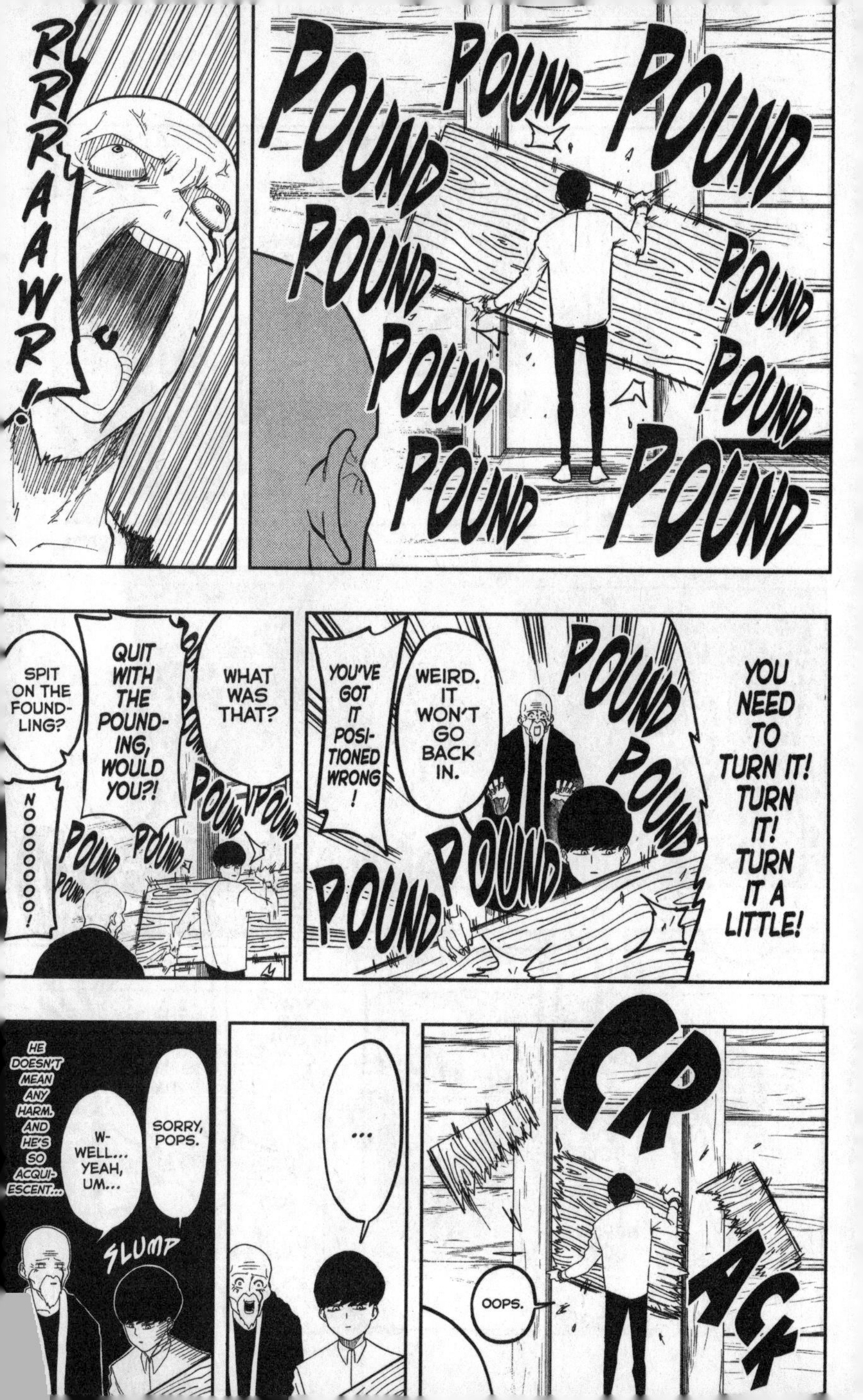
POUND POUND POUND
POUND POUND POUND
POUND POUND POUND
POUND POUND
RRRAAWR!
YOU NEED TO TURN IT! TURN IT! TURN IT A LITTLE!
POUND POUND
WEIRD. IT WON'T GO BACK IN.
YOU'VE GOT IT POSITIONED WRONG!
POUND POUND
WHAT WAS THAT?
QUIT WITH THE POUNDING, WOULD YOU?!
SPIT ON THE FOUNDLING?
POUND POUND POUND POUND POUND
NOOOOOOOO!
CRACK
OOPS.
...
SORRY, POPS.
W-WELL... YEAH, UM...
HE DOESN'T MEAN ANY HARM. AND HE'S SO ACQUIESCENT...
SLUMP

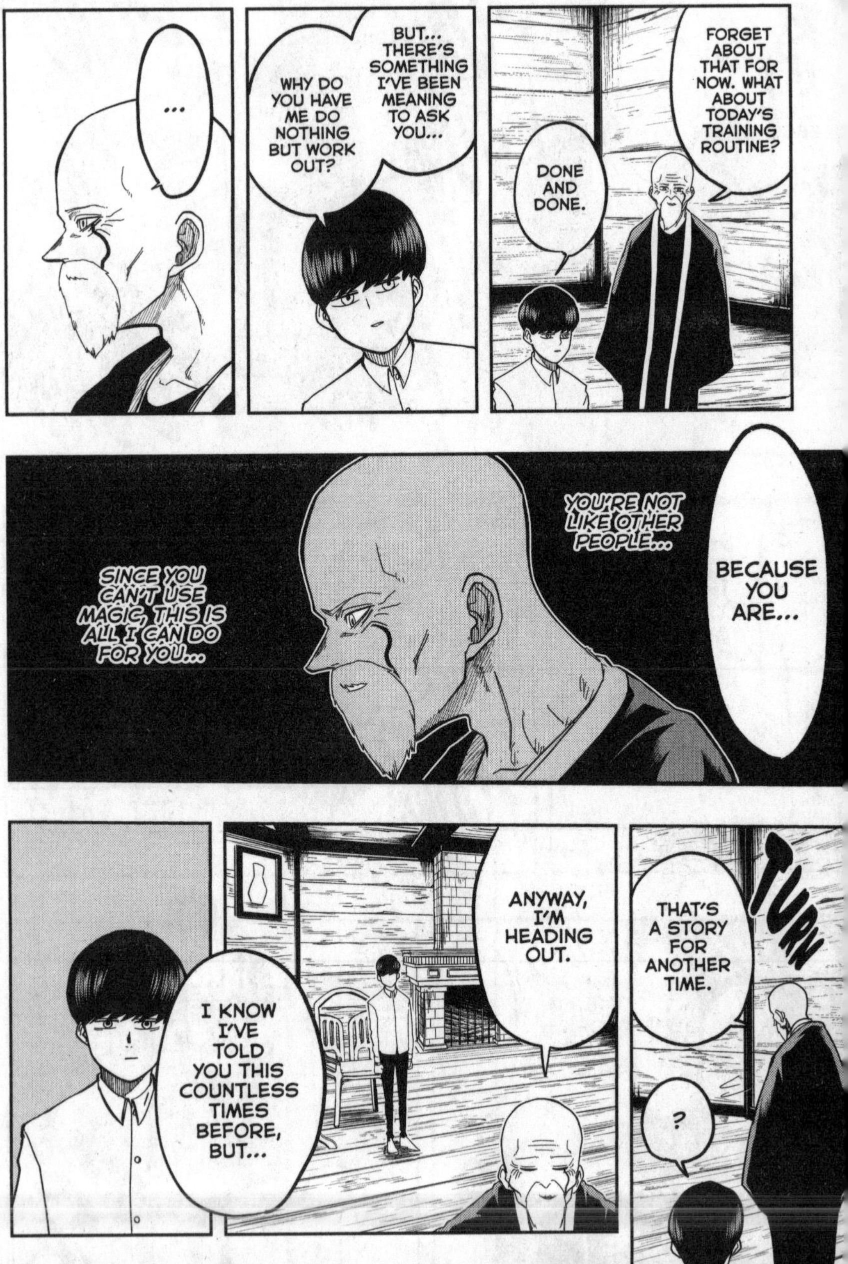
FORGET ABOUT THAT FOR NOW. WHAT ABOUT TODAY'S TRAINING ROUTINE?
DONE AND DONE.
BUT... THERE'S SOMETHING I'VE BEEN MEANING TO ASK YOU...
WHY DO YOU HAVE ME DO NOTHING BUT WORK OUT?
...
BECAUSE YOU ARE...
YOU'RE NOT LIKE OTHER PEOPLE...
SINCE YOU CAN'T USE MAGIC, THIS IS ALL I CAN DO FOR YOU...
TURN
THAT'S A STORY FOR ANOTHER TIME.
?
ANYWAY, I'M HEADING OUT.
I KNOW I'VE TOLD YOU THIS COUNTLESS TIMES BEFORE, BUT...

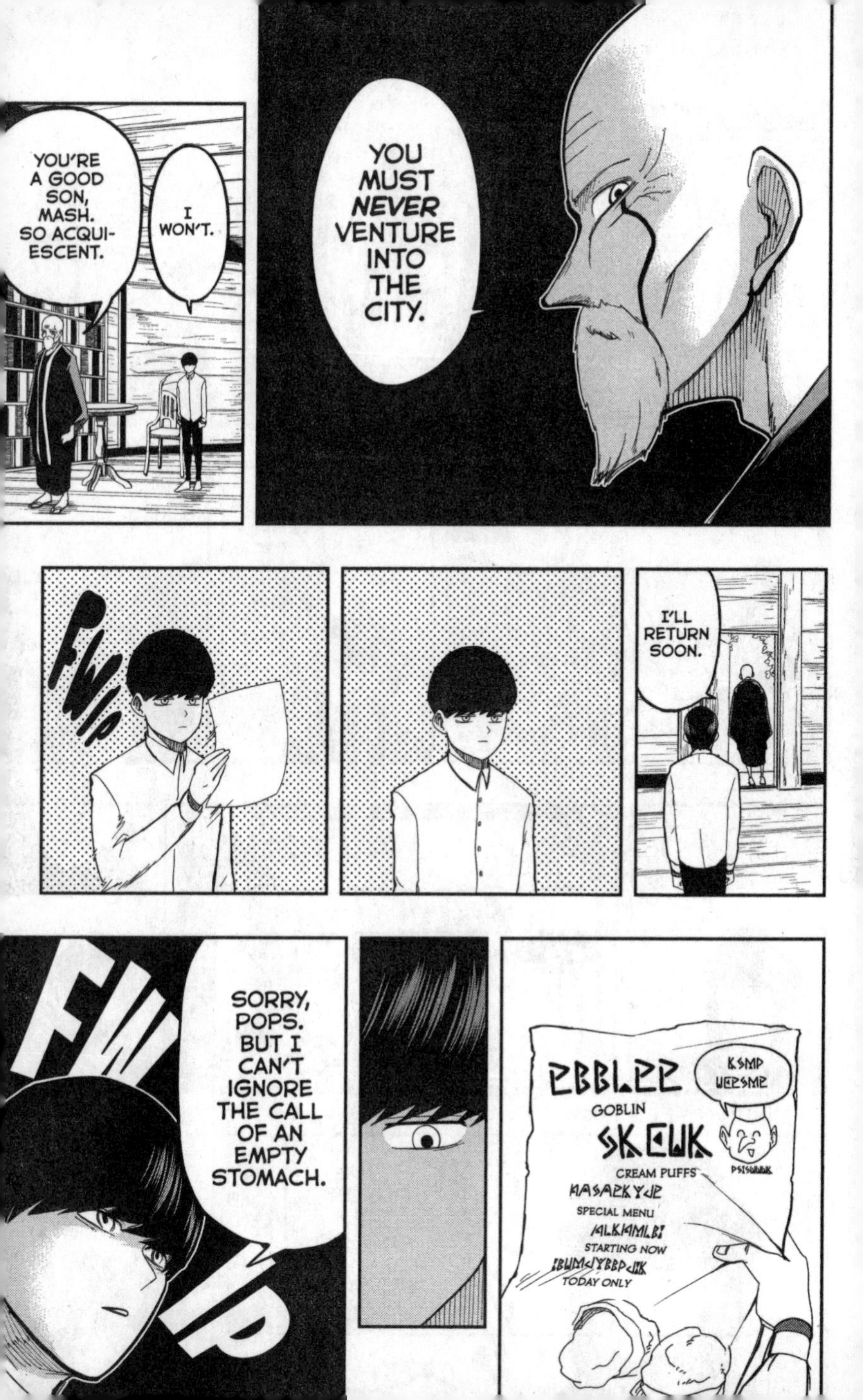
YOU MUST NEVER VENTURE INTO THE CITY.
I WON'T.
YOU'RE A GOOD SON, MASH. SO ACQUI-ESCENT.
I'LL RETURN SOON.
FWIP
GOBLIN
CREAM PUFFS
SPECIAL MENU
STARTING NOW
TODAY ONLY
SORRY, POPS. BUT I CAN'T IGNORE THE CALL OF AN EMPTY STOMACH.
FWIP

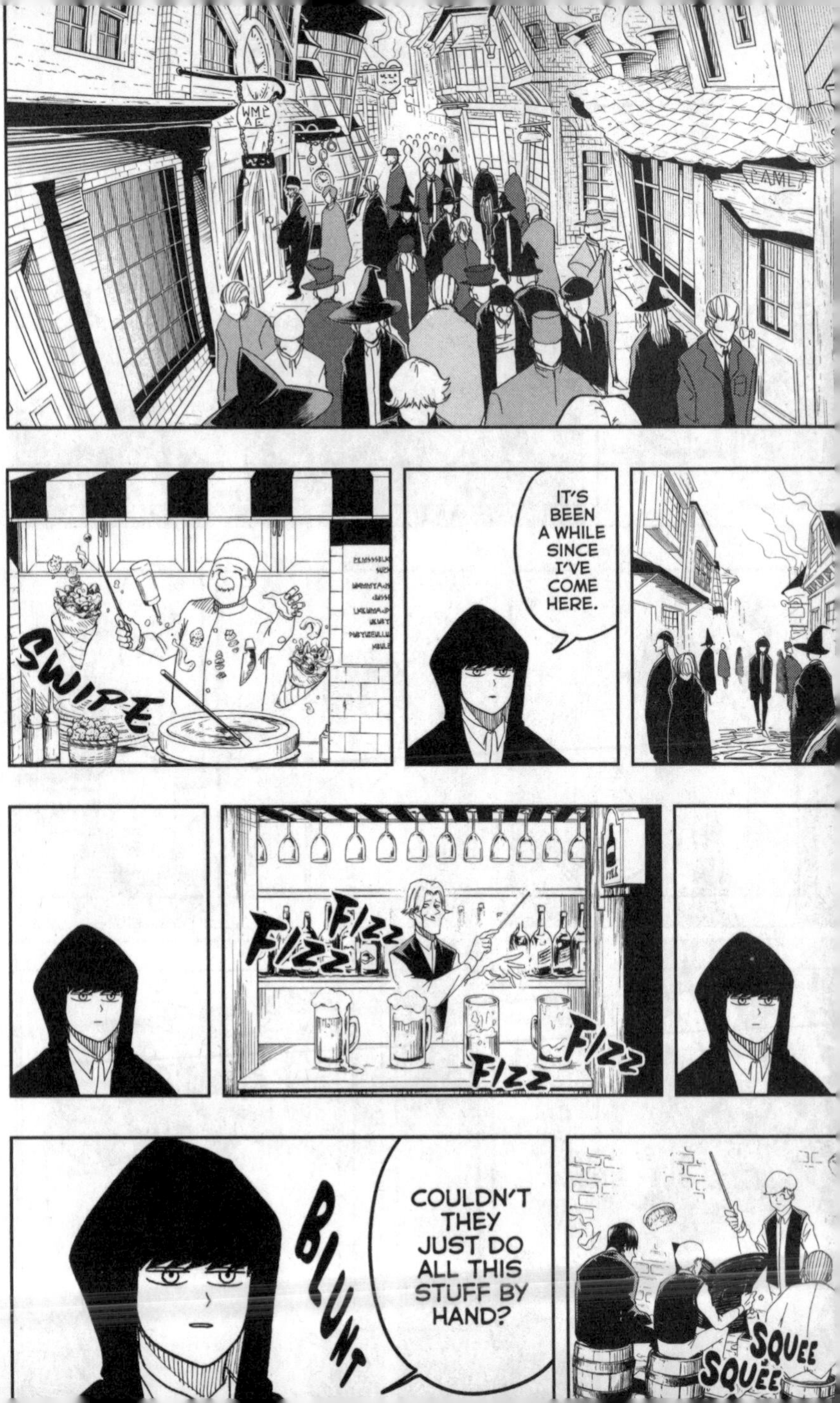
IT'S BEEN A WHILE SINCE I'VE COME HERE.
SWIPE
FIZZ
FIZZ
FIZZ
FIZZ
SQUEE
SQUEE
COULDN'T THEY JUST DO ALL THIS STUFF BY HAND?
BLUNT

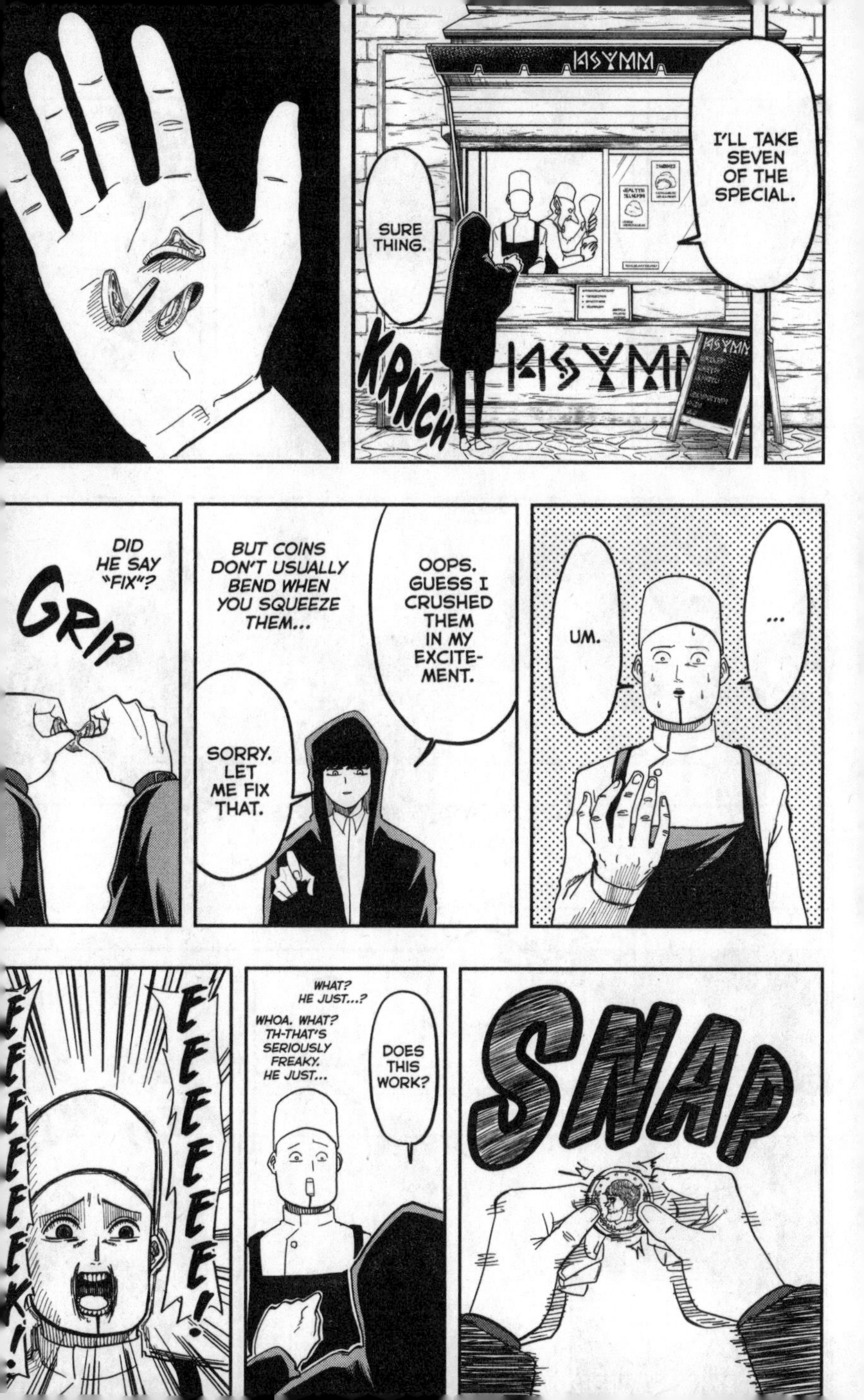
I'LL TAKE SEVEN OF THE SPECIAL.
SURE THING.
KRNCH
...
UM.
OOPS. GUESS I CRUSHED THEM IN MY EXCITE-MENT.
BUT COINS DON'T USUALLY BEND WHEN YOU SQUEEZE THEM...
SORRY. LET ME FIX THAT.
DID HE SAY "FIX"?
GRIP
SNAP
DOES THIS WORK?
WHAT? HE JUST...?
WHOA. WHAT? TH-THAT'S SERIOUSLY FREAKY. HE JUST...
EEEEEEEEEEK!
EEEEEEEEEEK!

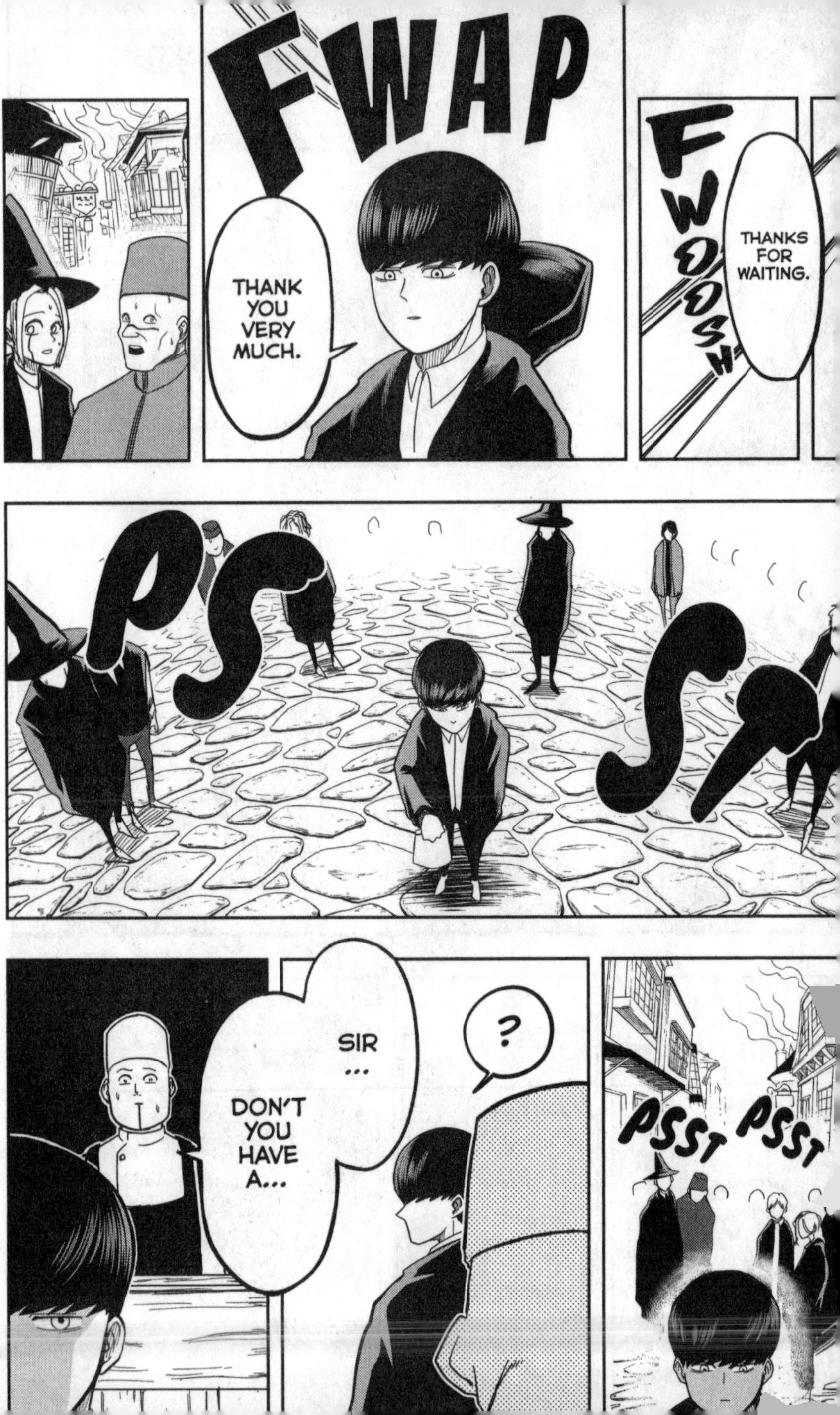
FWOOSH
THANKS FOR WAITING.
FWAP
THANK YOU VERY MUCH.
PSST
PSST
PSST
PSST
?
SIR ... DON'T YOU HAVE A...

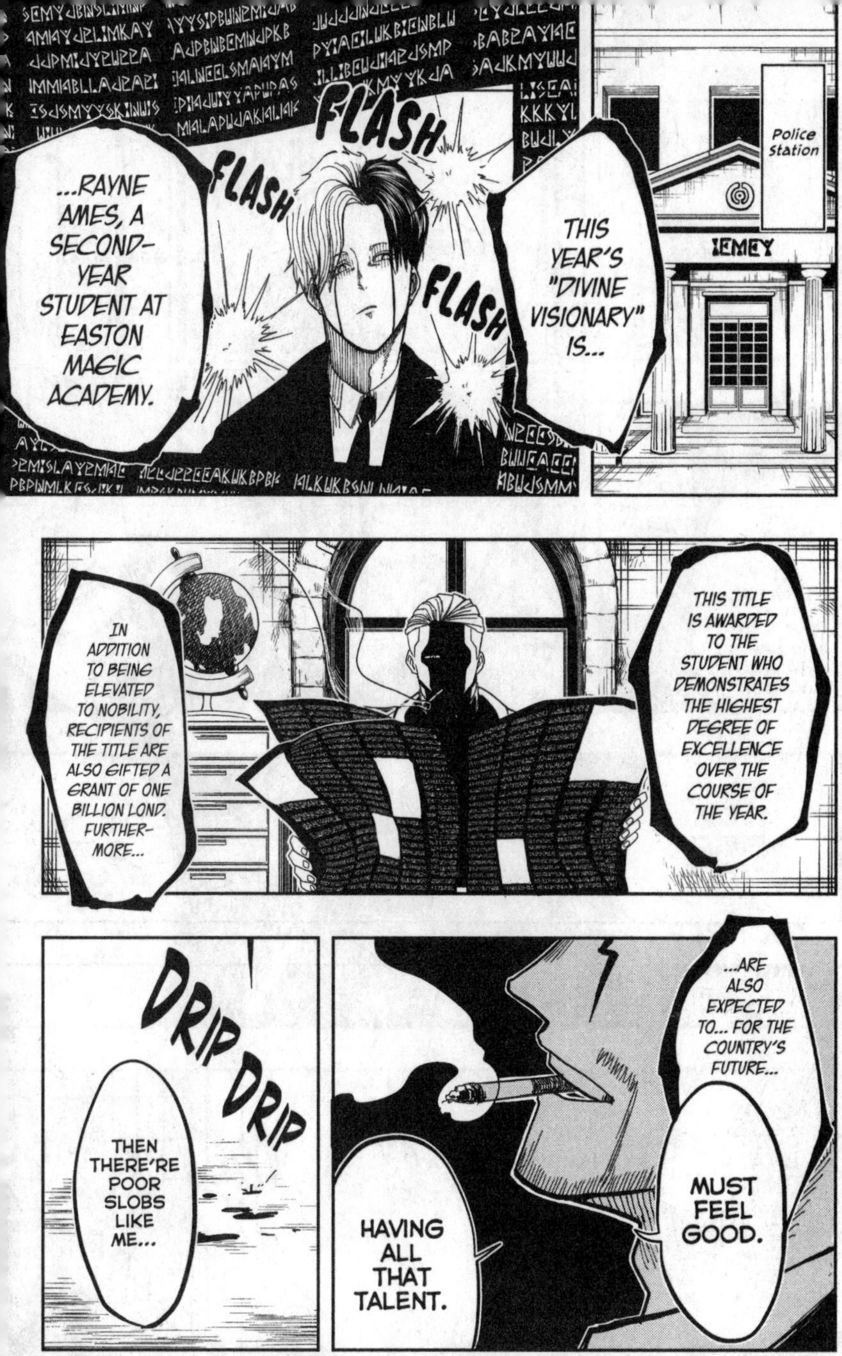
Police Station
THIS YEAR'S "DIVINE VISIONARY" IS...
FLASH
FLASH
FLASH
...RAYNE AMES, A SECOND-YEAR STUDENT AT EASTON MAGIC ACADEMY.
THIS TITLE IS AWARDED TO THE STUDENT WHO DEMONSTRATES THE HIGHEST DEGREE OF EXCELLENCE OVER THE COURSE OF THE YEAR.
IN ADDITION TO BEING ELEVATED TO NOBILITY, RECIPIENTS OF THE TITLE ARE ALSO GIFTED A GRANT OF ONE BILLION LOND. FURTHER-MORE...
...ARE ALSO EXPECTED TO... FOR THE COUNTRY'S FUTURE...
MUST FEEL GOOD.
HAVING ALL THAT TALENT.
DRIP DRIP
THEN THERE'RE POOR SLOBS LIKE ME...

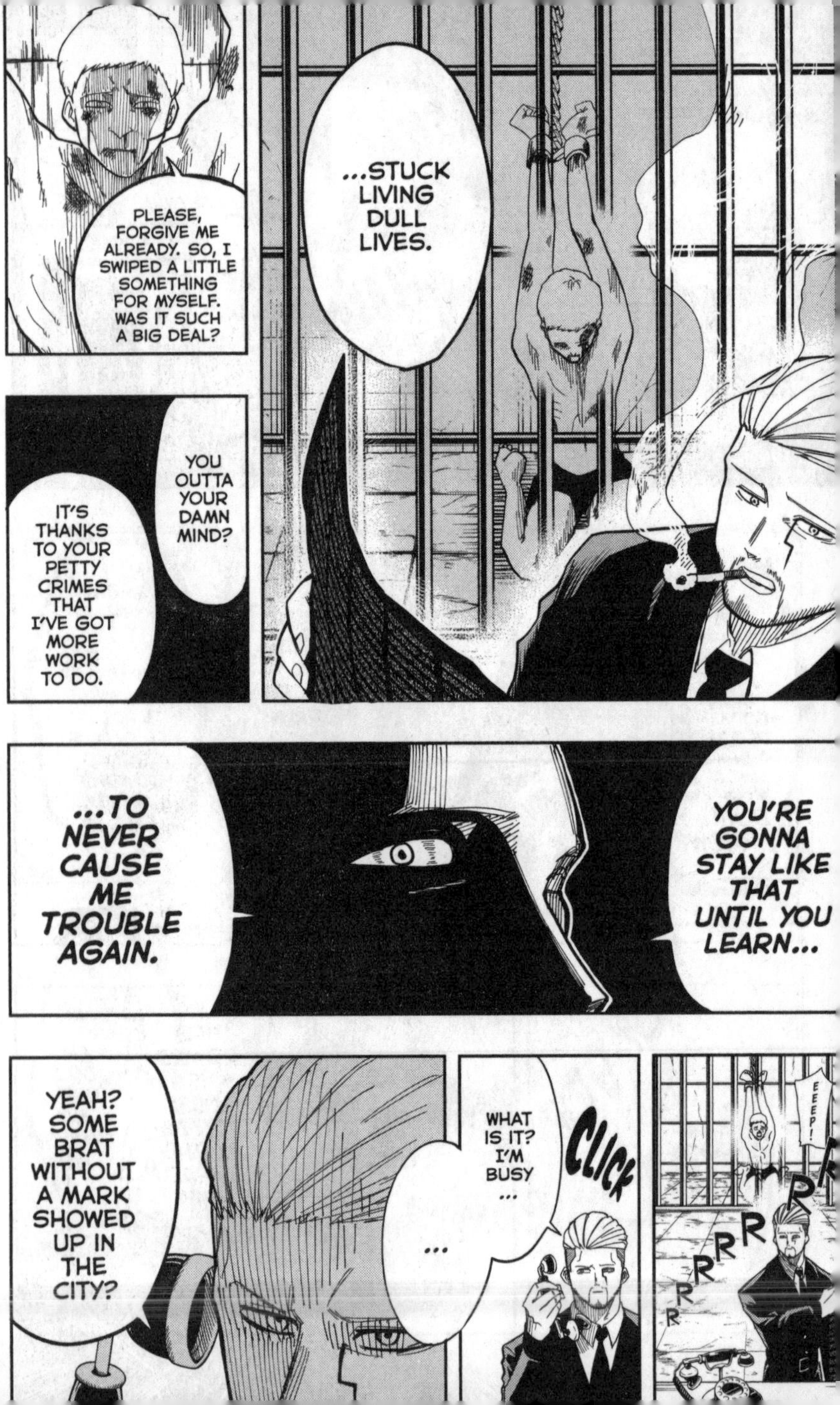
...STUCK LIVING DULL LIVES.
PLEASE, FORGIVE ME ALREADY. SO, I SWIPED A LITTLE SOMETHING FOR MYSELF. WAS IT SUCH A BIG DEAL?
YOU OUTTA YOUR DAMN MIND?
IT'S THANKS TO YOUR PETTY CRIMES THAT I'VE GOT MORE WORK TO DO.
YOU'RE GONNA STAY LIKE THAT UNTIL YOU LEARN...
...TO NEVER CAUSE ME TROUBLE AGAIN.
EEEP!
RRRRRRR
CLICK
WHAT IS IT? I'M BUSY...
...
YEAH? SOME BRAT WITHOUT A MARK SHOWED UP IN THE CITY?

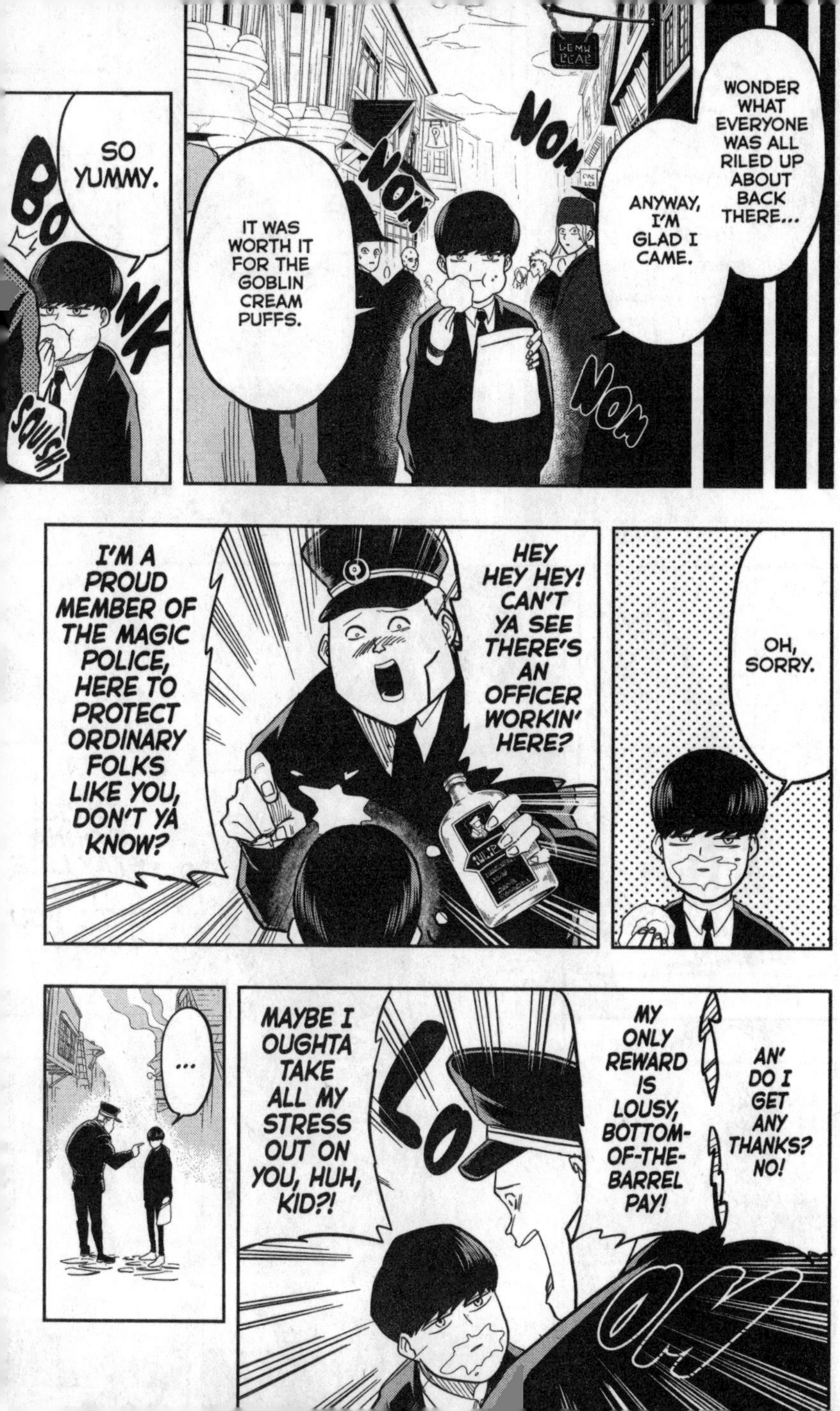
WONDER WHAT EVERYONE WAS ALL RILED UP ABOUT BACK THERE...
ANYWAY, I'M GLAD I CAME.
NOM
NOM
IT WAS WORTH IT FOR THE GOBLIN CREAM PUFFS.
NOM
BONK
SO YUMMY.
SQUISH
OH, SORRY.
HEY HEY HEY! CAN'T YA SEE THERE'S AN OFFICER WORKIN' HERE?
I'M A PROUD MEMBER OF THE MAGIC POLICE, HERE TO PROTECT ORDINARY FOLKS LIKE YOU, DON'T YA KNOW?
AN' DO I GET ANY THANKS? NO!
MY ONLY REWARD IS LOUSY, BOTTOM-OF-THE-BARREL PAY!
MAYBE I OUGHTA TAKE ALL MY STRESS OUT ON YOU, HUH, KID?!
...

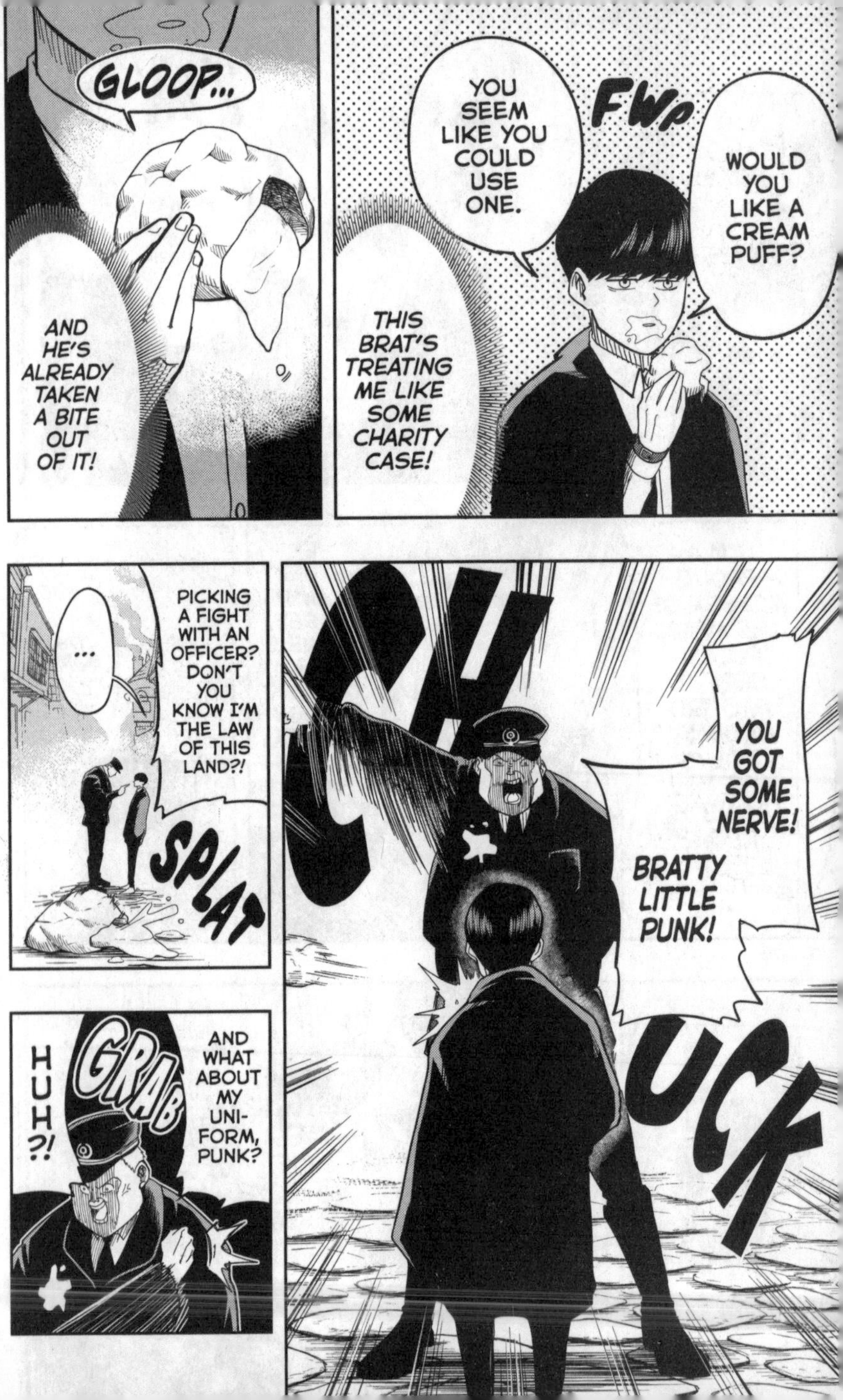
WOULD YOU LIKE A CREAM PUFF?
FWP
YOU SEEM LIKE YOU COULD USE ONE.
THIS BRAT'S TREATING ME LIKE SOME CHARITY CASE!
GLOOP...
AND HE'S ALREADY TAKEN A BITE OUT OF IT!
YOU GOT SOME NERVE!
CHUCK
BRATTY LITTLE PUNK!
PICKING A FIGHT WITH AN OFFICER? DON'T YOU KNOW I'M THE LAW OF THIS LAND?!
...
SPLAT
AND WHAT ABOUT MY UNI-FORM, PUNK?
GRAB
HUH?!

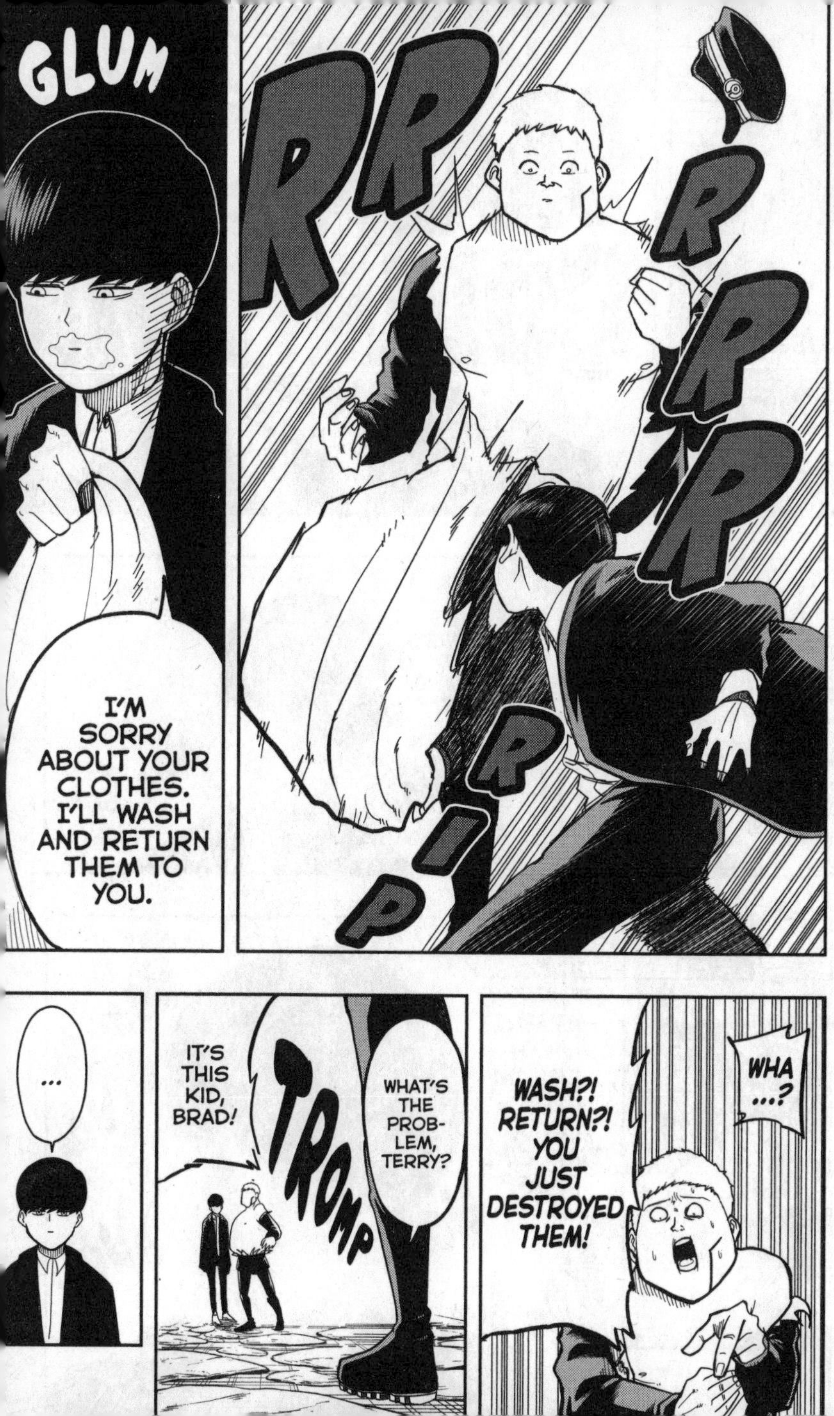
RRRRRRRIP
GLUM
I'M SORRY ABOUT YOUR CLOTHES. I'LL WASH AND RETURN THEM TO YOU.
WHA ...?
WASH?! RETURN?! YOU JUST DESTROYED THEM!
WHAT'S THE PROB-LEM, TERRY?
TROMP
IT'S THIS KID, BRAD!
...

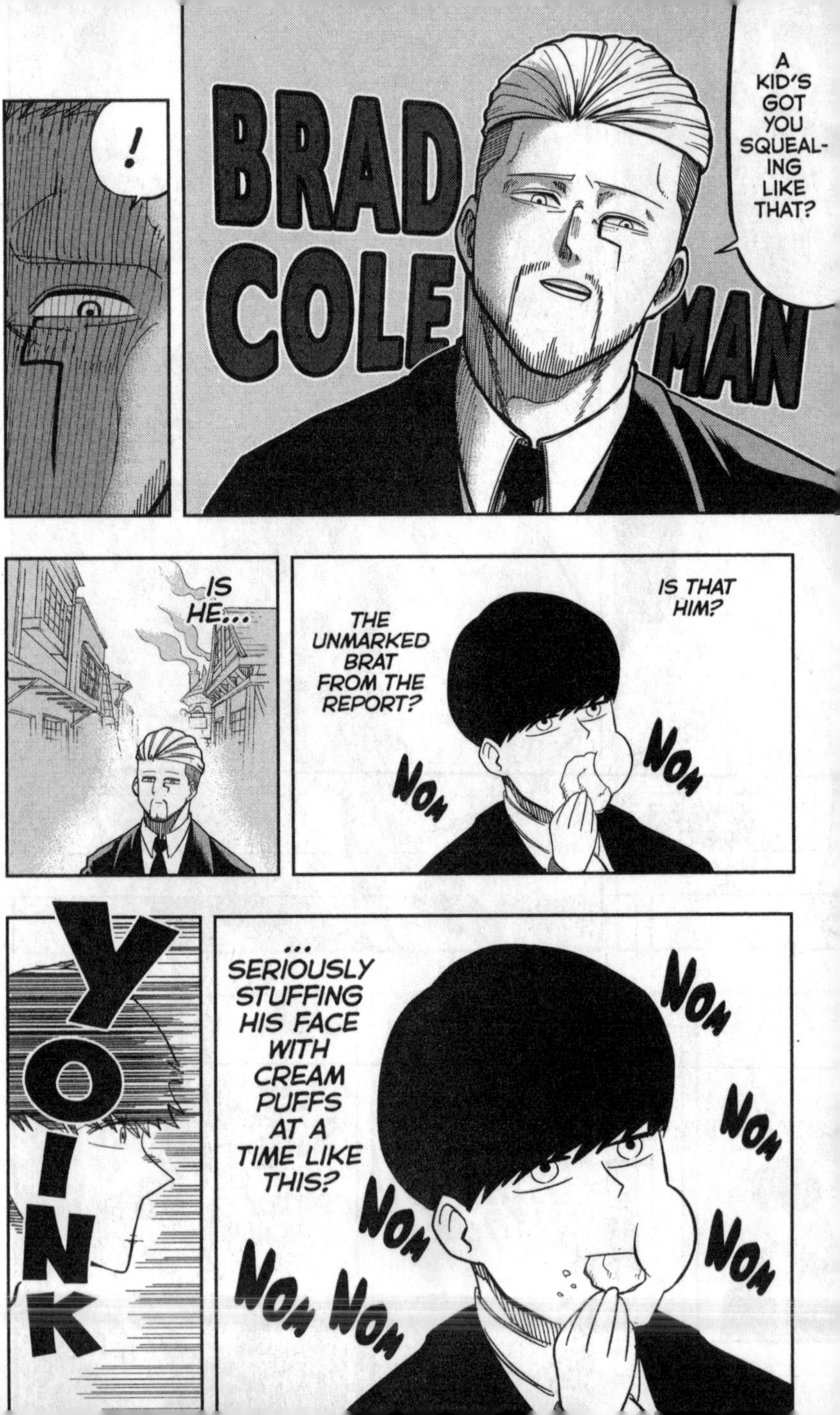
A KID'S GOT YOU SQUEALING LIKE THAT?
BRAD COLEMAN
!
IS THAT HIM?
THE UNMARKED BRAT FROM THE REPORT?
NOM
NOM
IS HE...
...SERIOUSLY STUFFING HIS FACE WITH CREAM PUFFS AT A TIME LIKE THIS?
NOM
NOM
NOM
NOM
NOM
NOM
YOINK

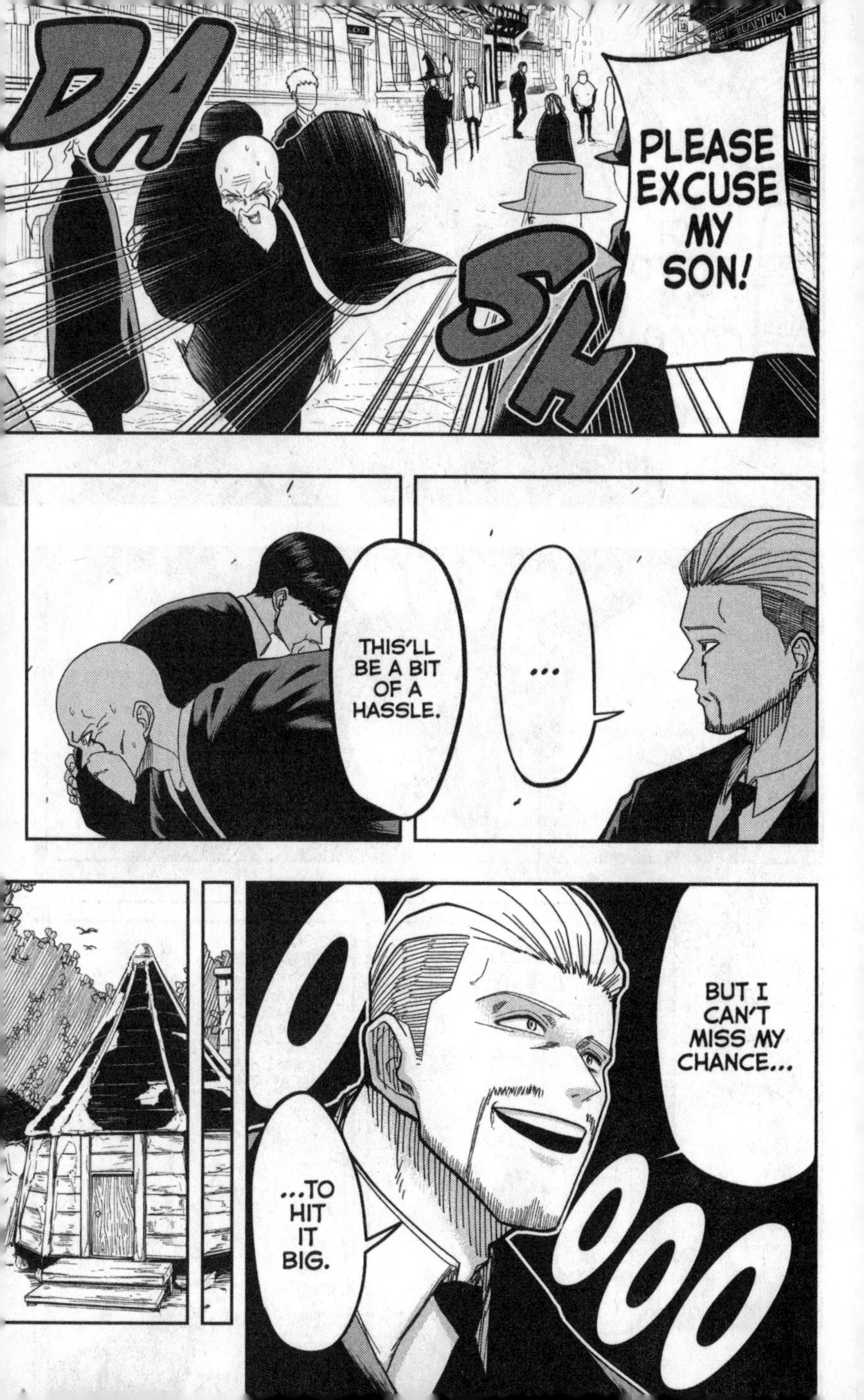

PLEASE EXCUSE MY SON!
DA
SH
...
THIS'LL BE A BIT OF A HASSLE.
BUT I CAN'T MISS MY CHANCE...
...TO HIT IT BIG.
O
OOO

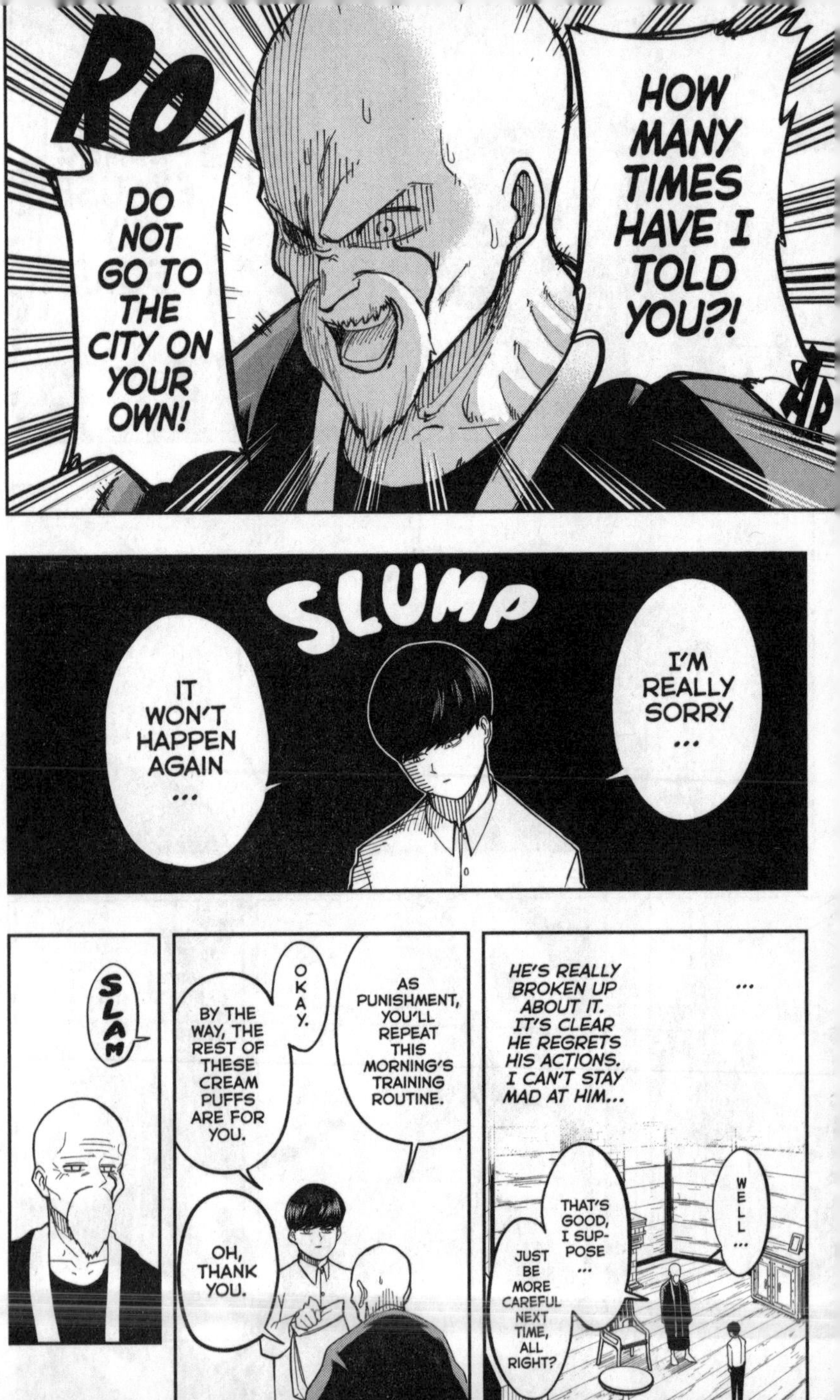
RO
HOW MANY TIMES HAVE I TOLD YOU?!
DO NOT GO TO THE CITY ON YOUR OWN!
AR
SLUMP
I'M REALLY SORRY...
IT WON'T HAPPEN AGAIN...
...
HE'S REALLY BROKEN UP ABOUT IT. IT'S CLEAR HE REGRETS HIS ACTIONS. I CAN'T STAY MAD AT HIM...
WELL...
THAT'S GOOD, I SUPPOSE...
JUST BE MORE CAREFUL NEXT TIME, ALL RIGHT?
AS PUNISHMENT, YOU'LL REPEAT THIS MORNING'S TRAINING ROUTINE.
OKAY.
BY THE WAY, THE REST OF THESE CREAM PUFFS ARE FOR YOU.
OH, THANK YOU.
SLAM

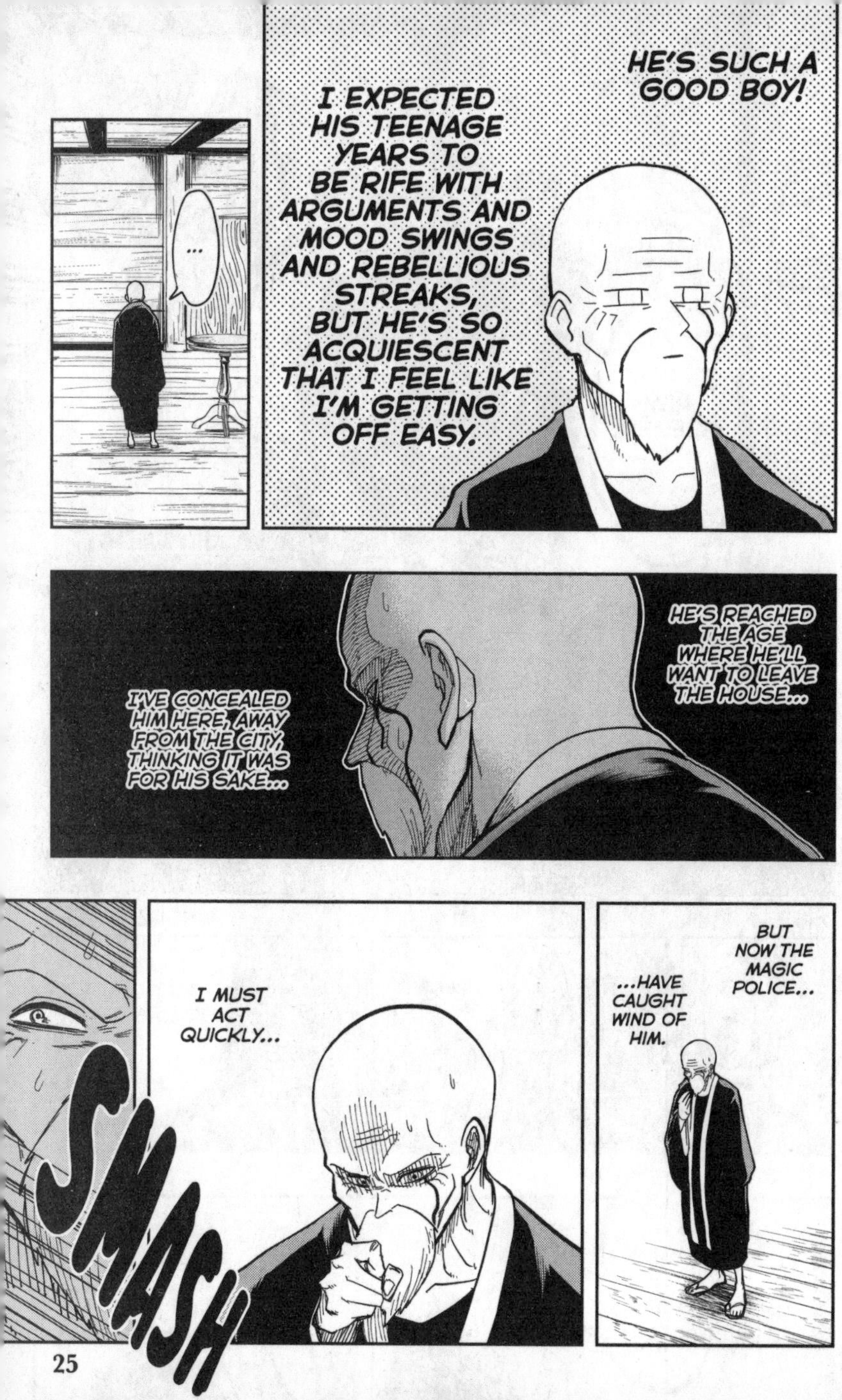
HE'S SUCH A GOOD BOY!
I EXPECTED HIS TEENAGE YEARS TO BE RIFE WITH ARGUMENTS AND MOOD SWINGS AND REBELLIOUS STREAKS, BUT HE'S SO ACQUIESCENT THAT I FEEL LIKE I'M GETTING OFF EASY.
...
HE'S REACHED THE AGE WHERE HE'LL WANT TO LEAVE THE HOUSE...
I'VE CONCEALED HIM HERE, AWAY FROM THE CITY, THINKING IT WAS FOR HIS SAKE...
BUT NOW THE MAGIC POLICE...
...HAVE CAUGHT WIND OF HIM.
I MUST ACT QUICKLY...
SMASH

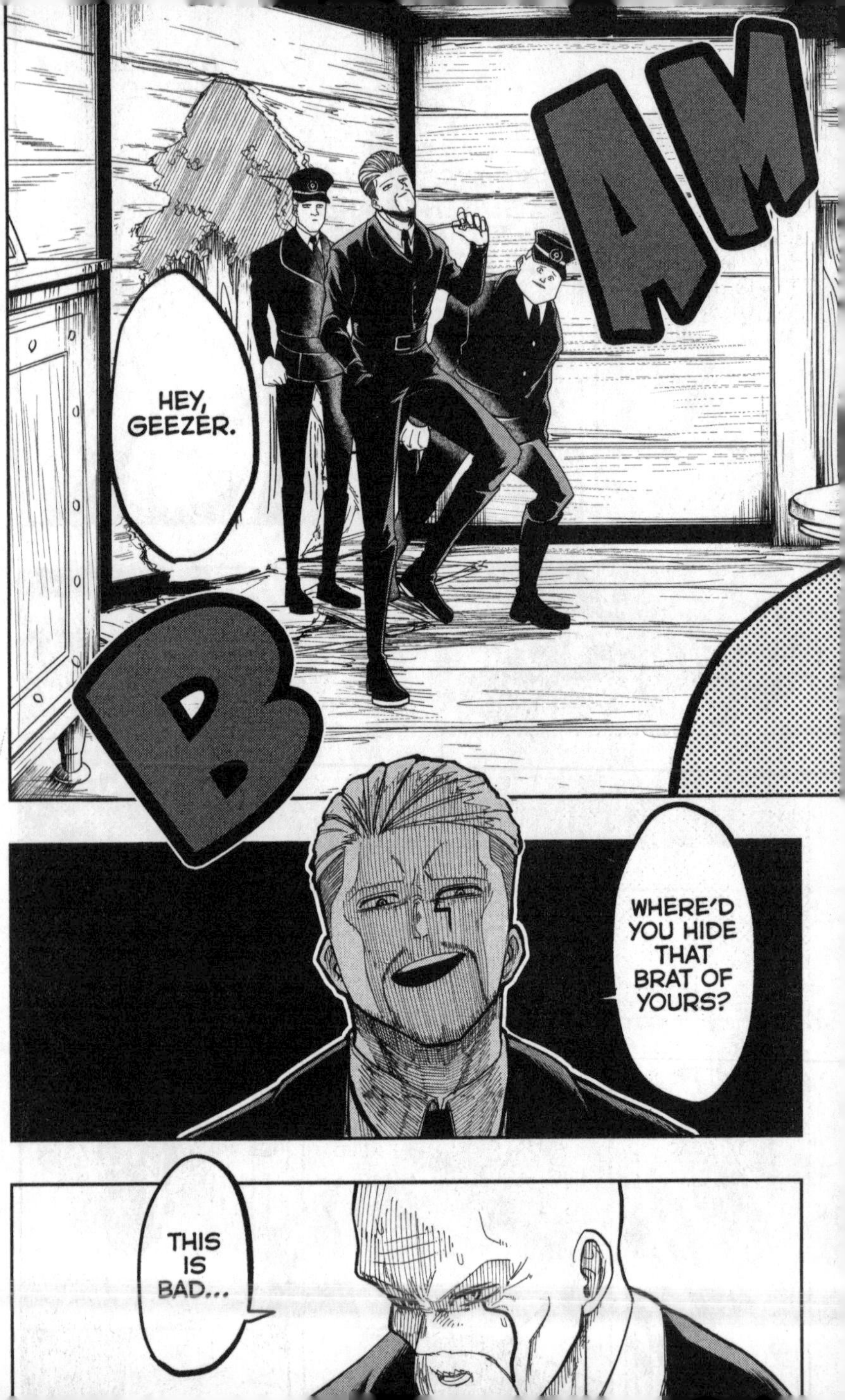
BAM
HEY, GEEZER.
WHERE'D YOU HIDE THAT BRAT OF YOURS?
THIS IS BAD...

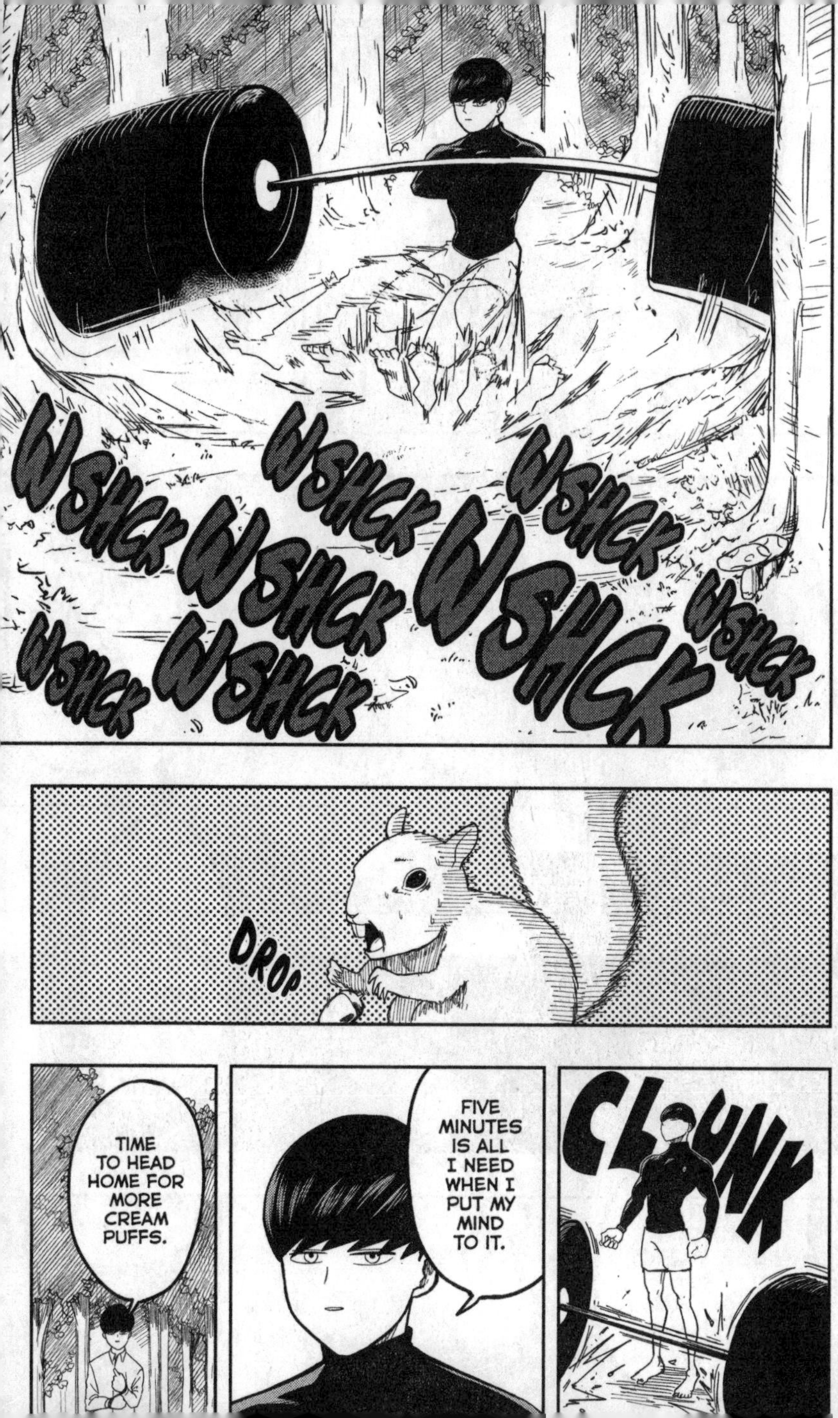
WSHCK WSHCK WSHCK WSHCK WSHCK WSHCK WSHCK WSHCK
DROP
CLUNK
FIVE MINUTES IS ALL I NEED WHEN I PUT MY MIND TO IT.
TIME TO HEAD HOME FOR MORE CREAM PUFFS.

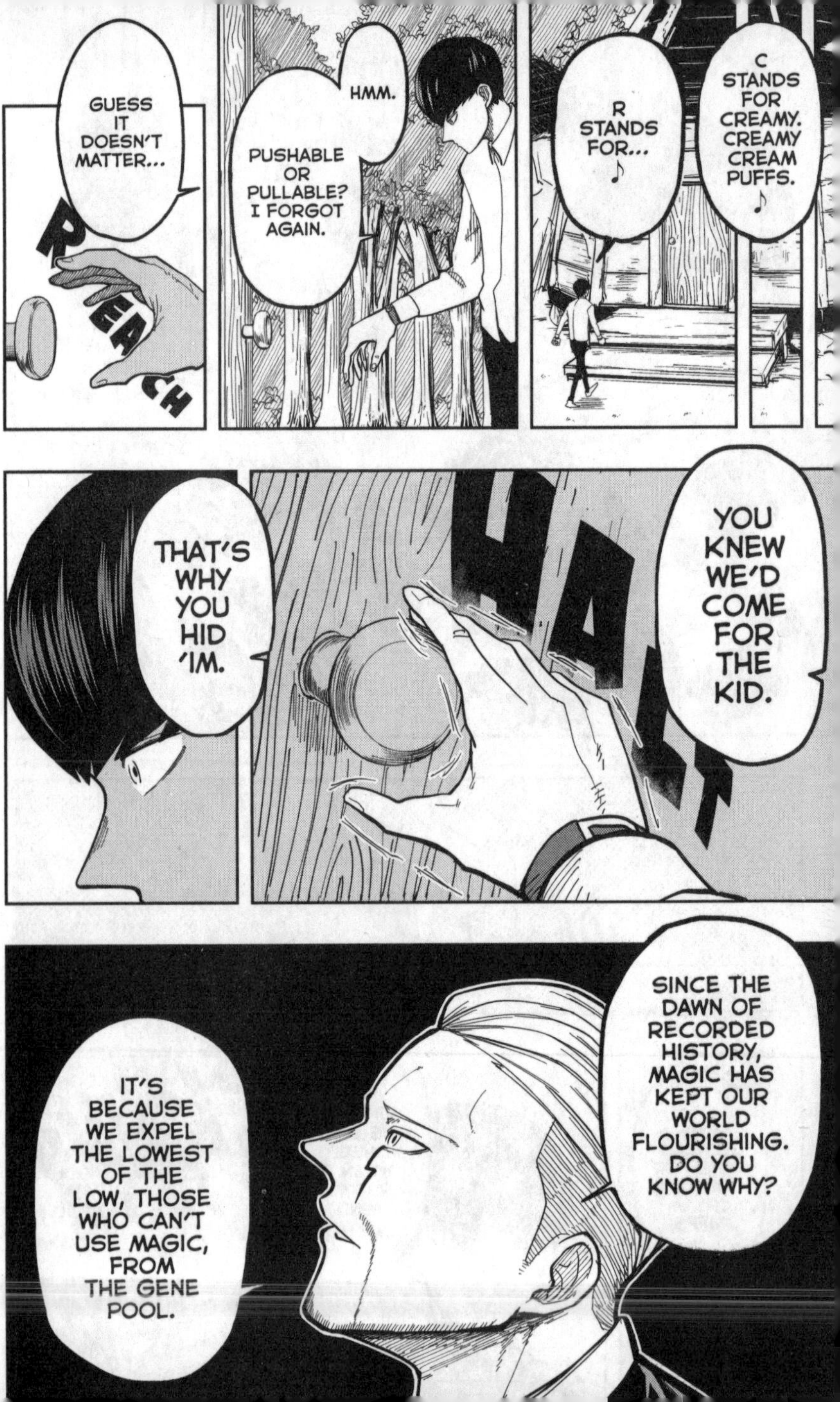
C STANDS FOR CREAMY. CREAMY CREAM PUFFS. ♪
R STANDS FOR... ♪
HMM.
PUSHABLE OR PULLABLE? I FORGOT AGAIN.
GUESS IT DOESN'T MATTER...
REACH
YOU KNEW WE'D COME FOR THE KID.
THAT'S WHY YOU HID 'IM.
SINCE THE DAWN OF RECORDED HISTORY, MAGIC HAS KEPT OUR WORLD FLOURISHING. DO YOU KNOW WHY?
IT'S BECAUSE WE EXPEL THE LOWEST OF THE LOW, THOSE WHO CAN'T USE MAGIC, FROM THE GENE POOL.

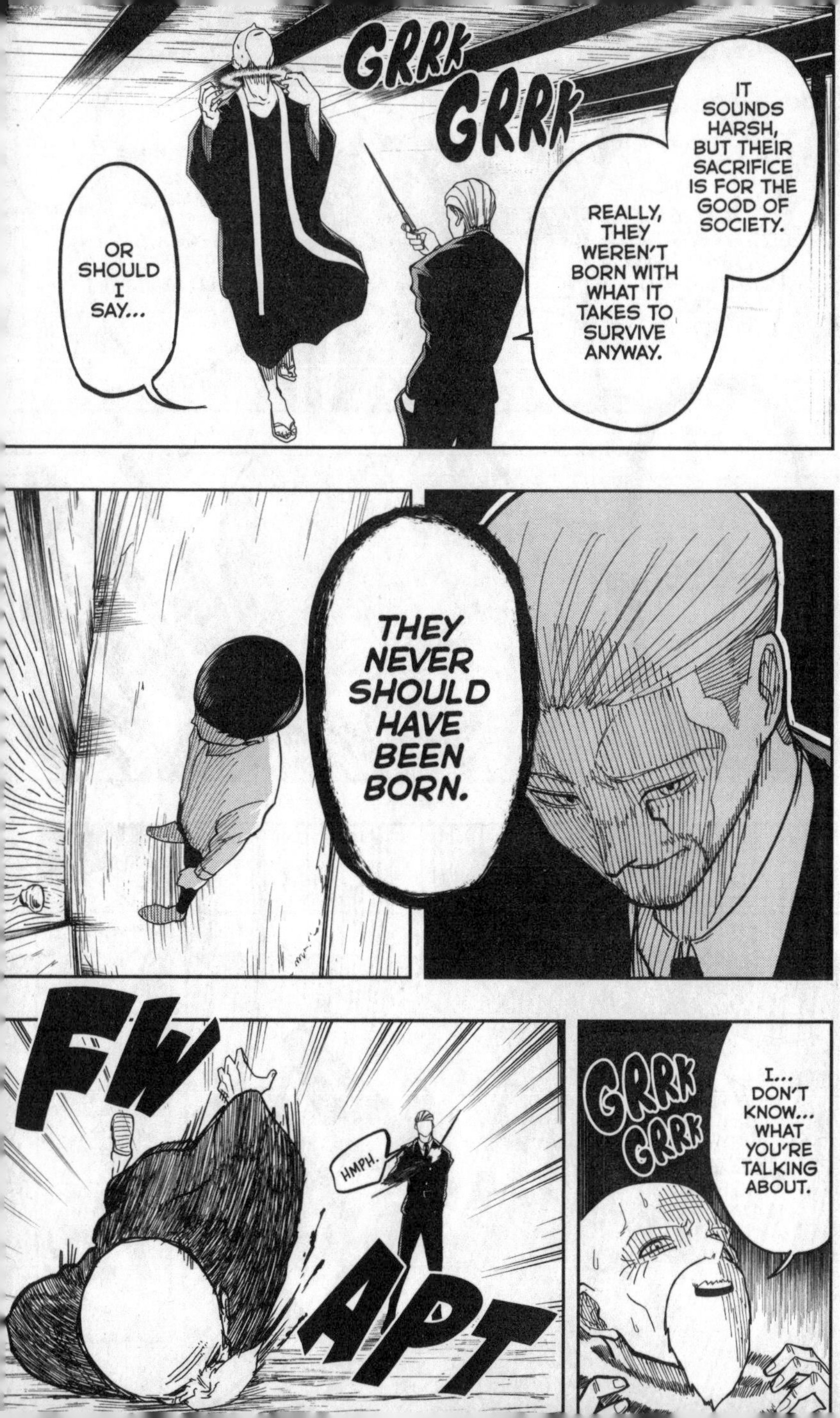
IT SOUNDS HARSH, BUT THEIR SACRIFICE IS FOR THE GOOD OF SOCIETY.
GRRK GRRK
REALLY, THEY WEREN'T BORN WITH WHAT IT TAKES TO SURVIVE ANYWAY.
OR SHOULD I SAY...
THEY NEVER SHOULD HAVE BEEN BORN.
I... DON'T KNOW... WHAT YOU'RE TALKING ABOUT.
GRRK GRRK
FW
HMPH.
APT

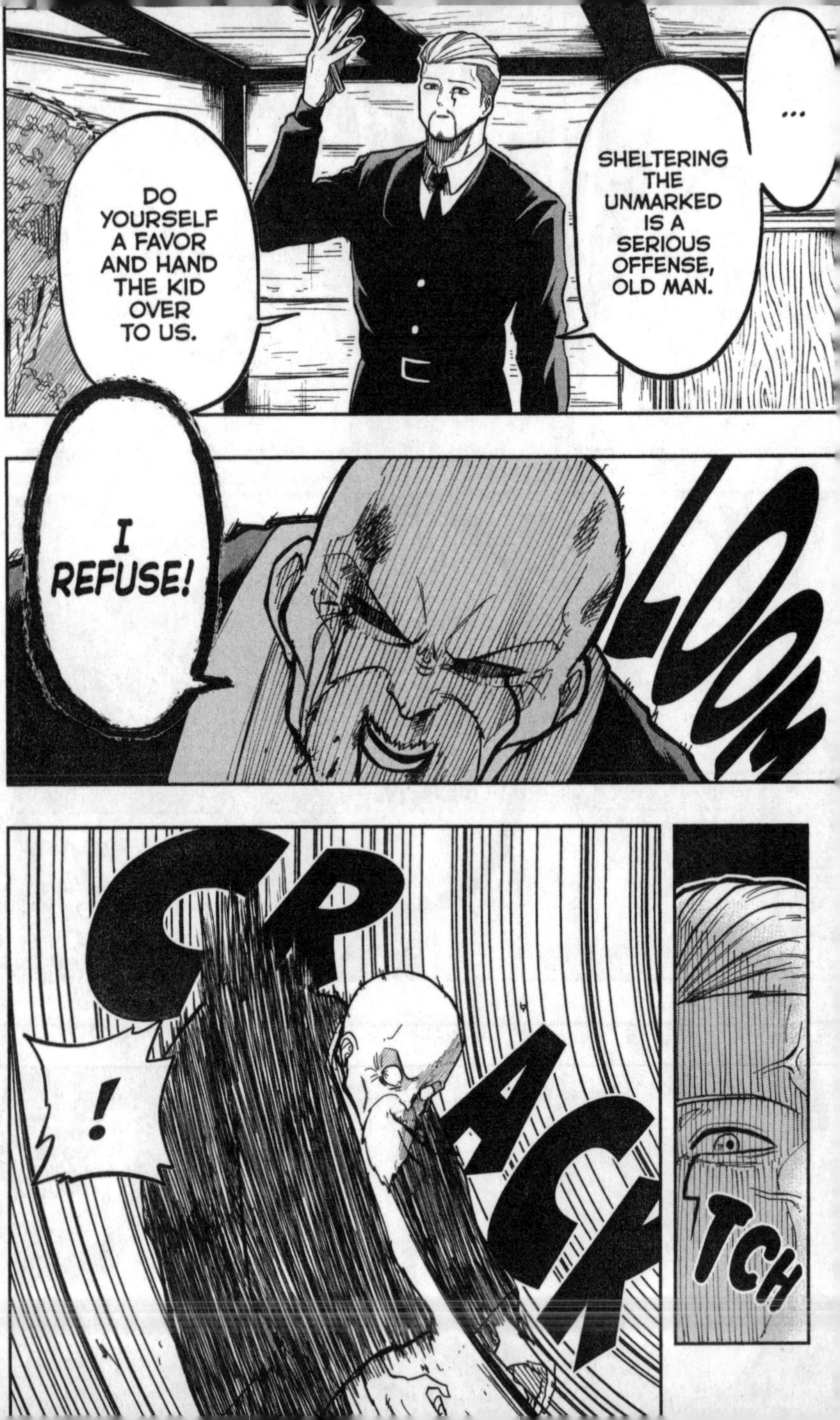
...
SHELTERING THE UNMARKED IS A SERIOUS OFFENSE, OLD MAN.
DO YOURSELF A FAVOR AND HAND THE KID OVER TO US.
LOOM
I REFUSE!
TCH
CRACK
!

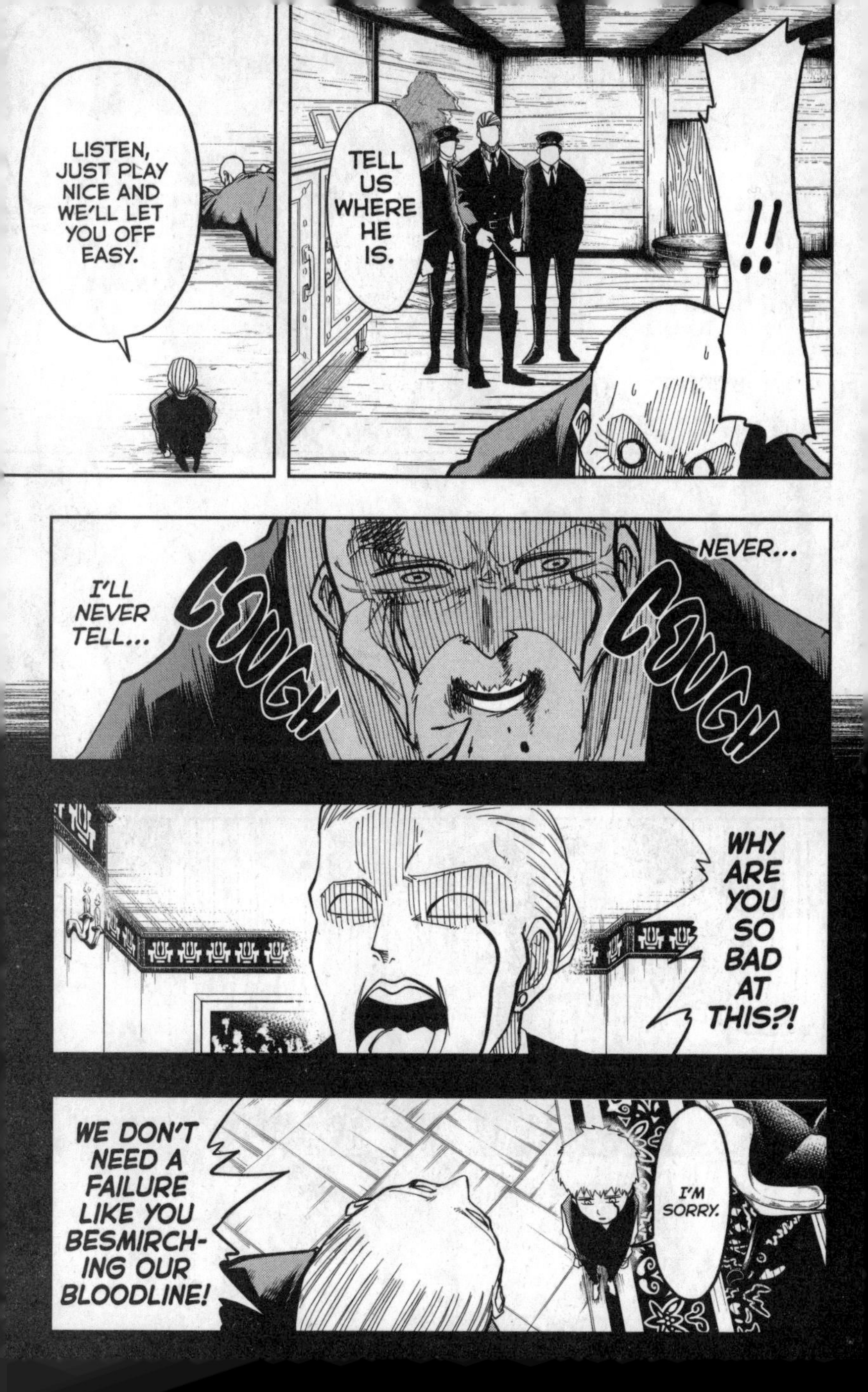
!!
TELL US WHERE HE IS.
LISTEN, JUST PLAY NICE AND WE'LL LET YOU OFF EASY.
NEVER...
COUGH
COUGH
I'LL NEVER TELL...
WHY ARE YOU SO BAD AT THIS?!
I'M SORRY.
WE DON'T NEED A FAILURE LIKE YOU BESMIRCH-ING OUR BLOODLINE!

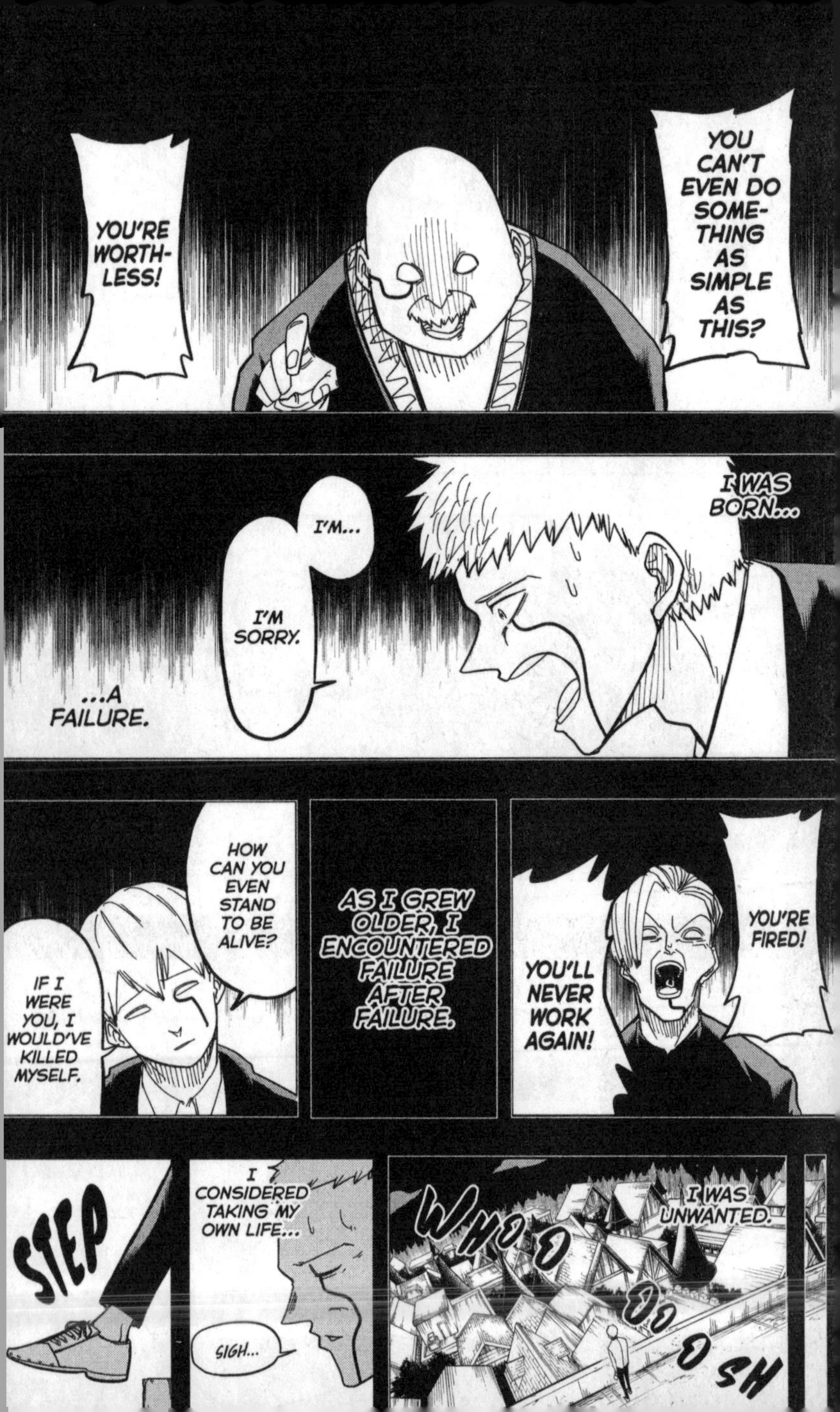
YOU CAN'T EVEN DO SOME-THING AS SIMPLE AS THIS?
YOU'RE WORTH-LESS!
I WAS BORN...
I'M...
I'M SORRY.
...A FAILURE.
YOU'RE FIRED!
YOU'LL NEVER WORK AGAIN!
AS I GREW OLDER, I ENCOUNTERED FAILURE AFTER FAILURE.
HOW CAN YOU EVEN STAND TO BE ALIVE?
IF I WERE YOU, I WOULD'VE KILLED MYSELF.
I WAS UNWANTED.
WHOOOOOOOSH
I CONSIDERED TAKING MY OWN LIFE...
SIGH...
STEP

WAAAAH!

WAAAAAAH!

FWP

THIS BABY...

WAAAAH!

WAAAAAH!

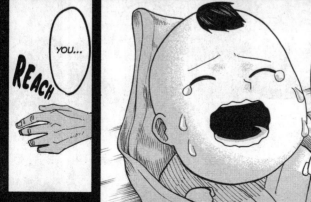

YOU...

REACH

...DOESN'T HAVE A MARK...

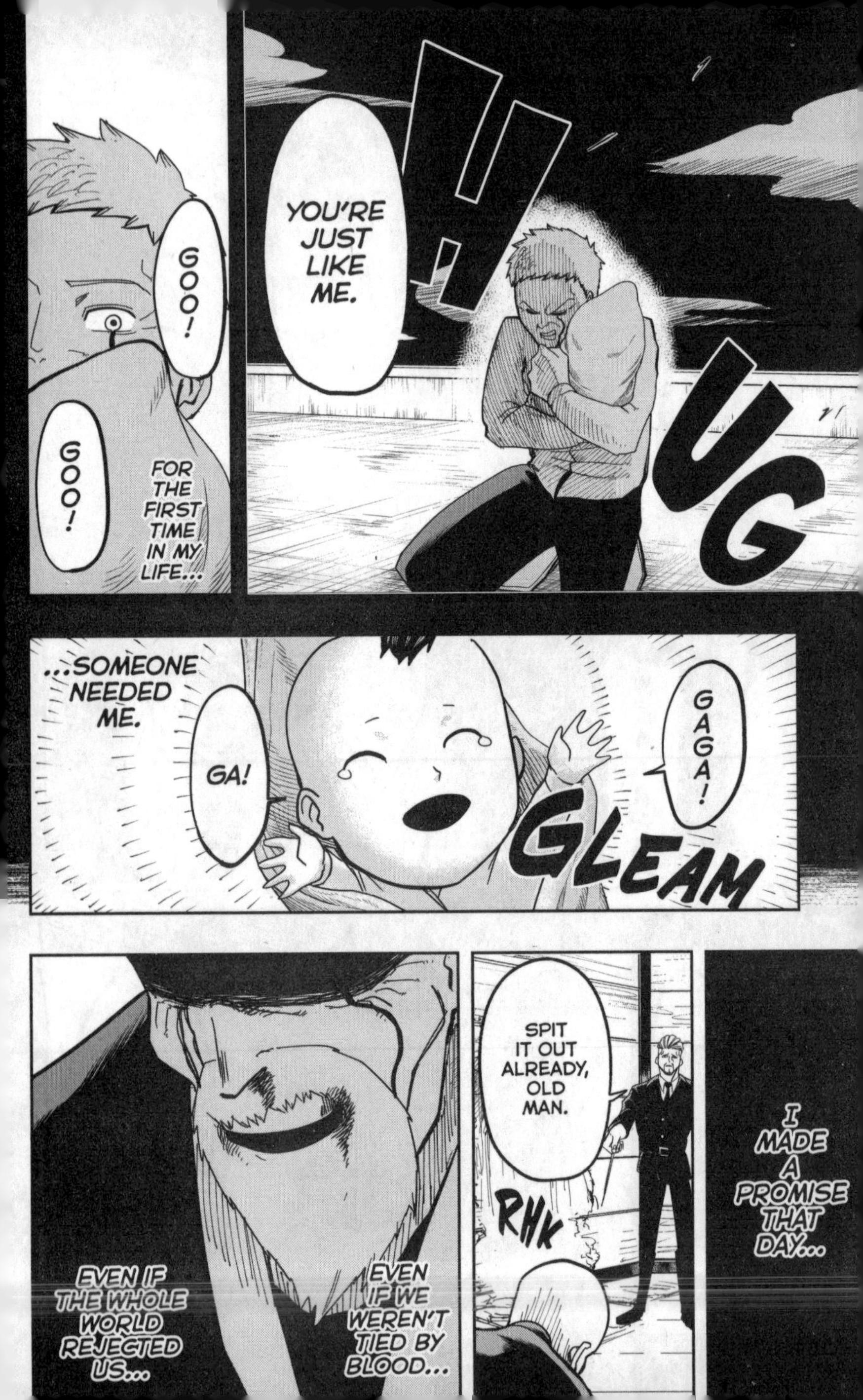
YOU'RE JUST LIKE ME.
UG
GOO!
GOO!
FOR THE FIRST TIME IN MY LIFE...
GAGA!
GLEAM
GA!
...SOMEONE NEEDED ME.
I MADE A PROMISE THAT DAY...
SPIT IT OUT ALREADY, OLD MAN.
RHK
EVEN IF WE WEREN'T TIED BY BLOOD...
EVEN IF THE WHOLE WORLD REJECTED US...

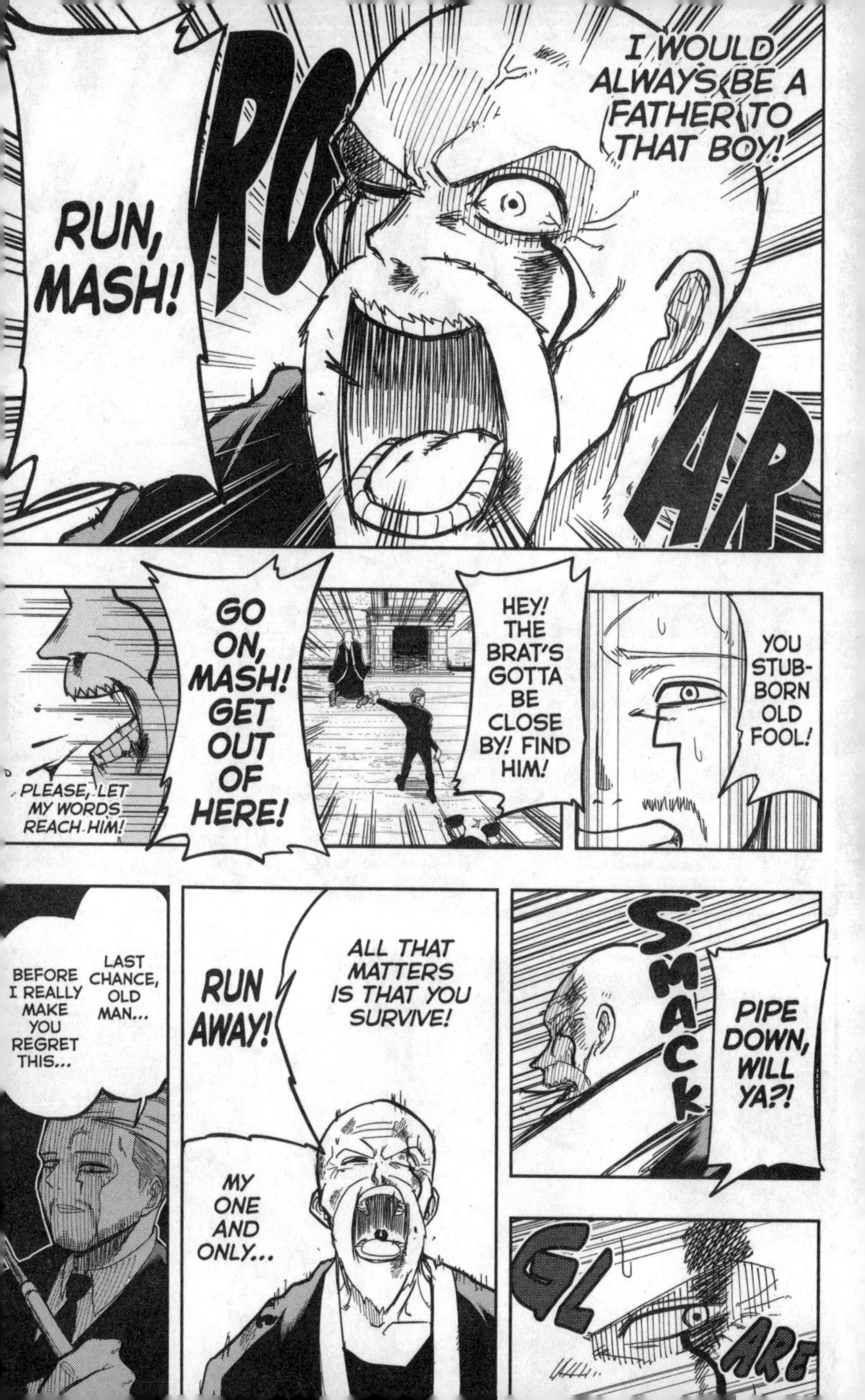
I WOULD ALWAYS BE A FATHER TO THAT BOY!
RO
AR
RUN, MASH!
YOU STUBBORN OLD FOOL!
HEY! THE BRAT'S GOTTA BE CLOSE BY! FIND HIM!
GO ON, MASH! GET OUT OF HERE!
PLEASE, LET MY WORDS REACH HIM!
SMACK
PIPE DOWN, WILL YA?!
GLARE
ALL THAT MATTERS IS THAT YOU SURVIVE!
RUN AWAY!
MY ONE AND ONLY...
LAST CHANCE, OLD MAN...
BEFORE I REALLY MAKE YOU REGRET THIS...

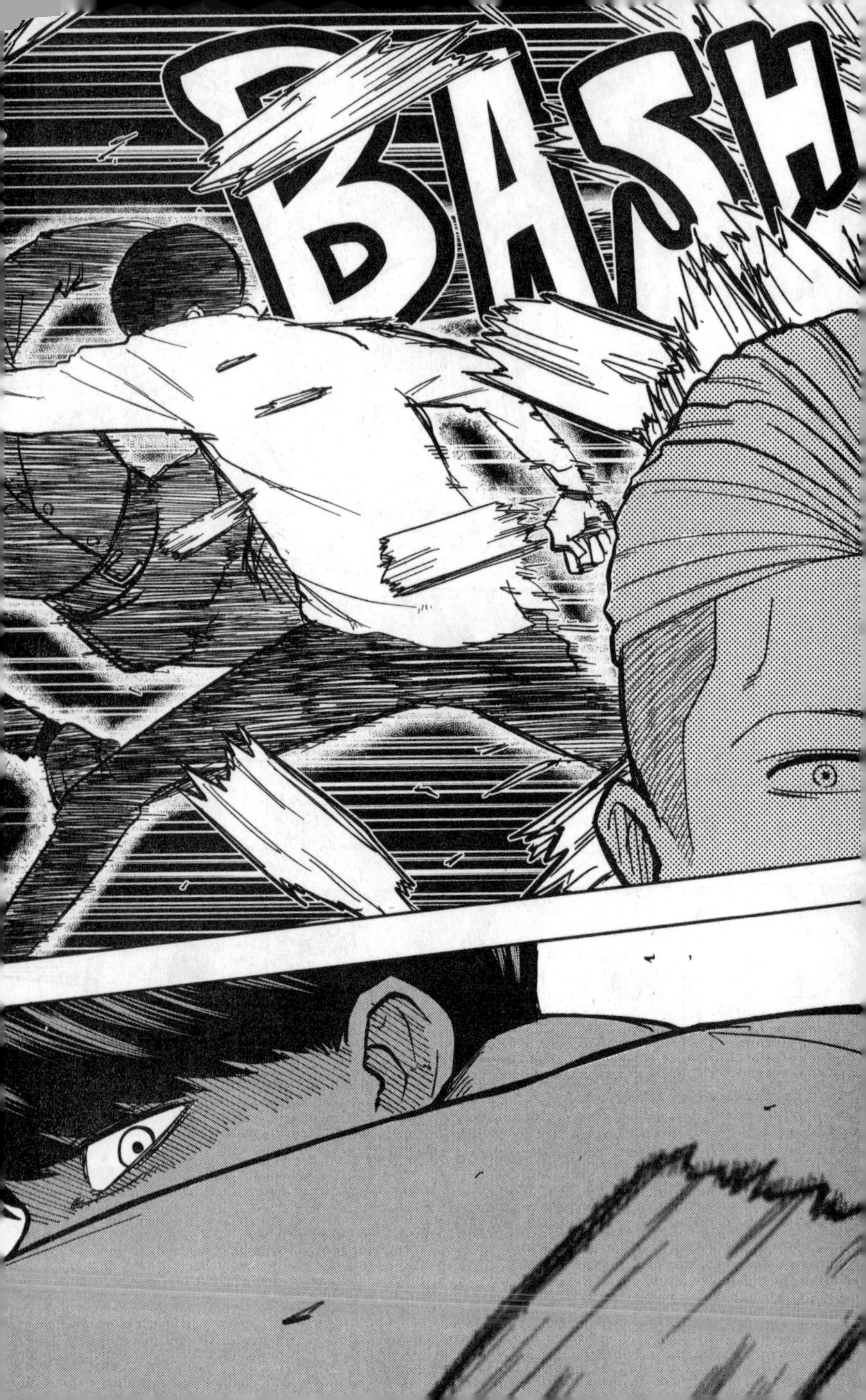
BASH

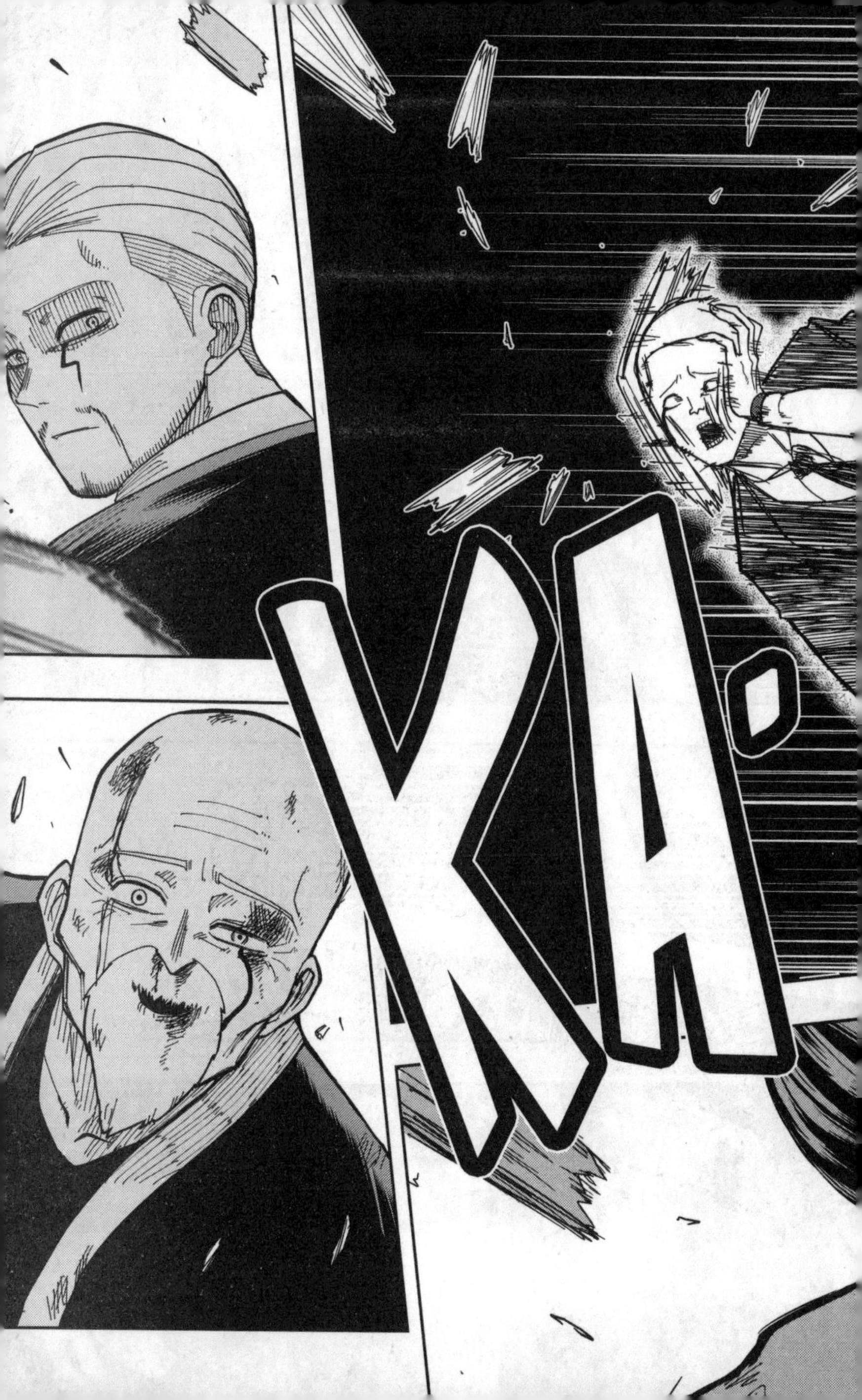
KA

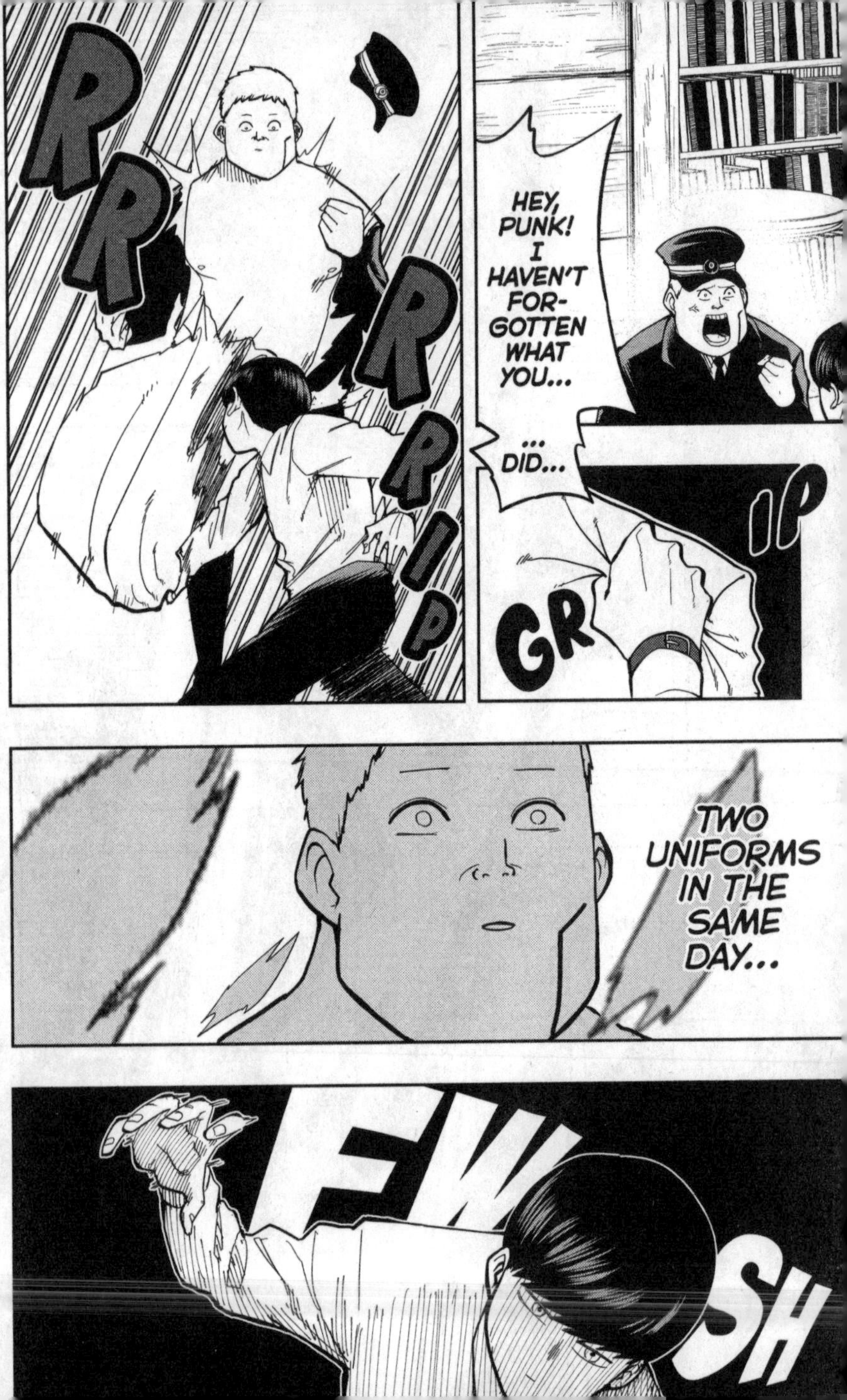
HEY, PUNK! I HAVEN'T FOR-GOTTEN WHAT YOU...
...DID...
GRIP
RRRRIP
TWO UNIFORMS IN THE SAME DAY...
FW
SH

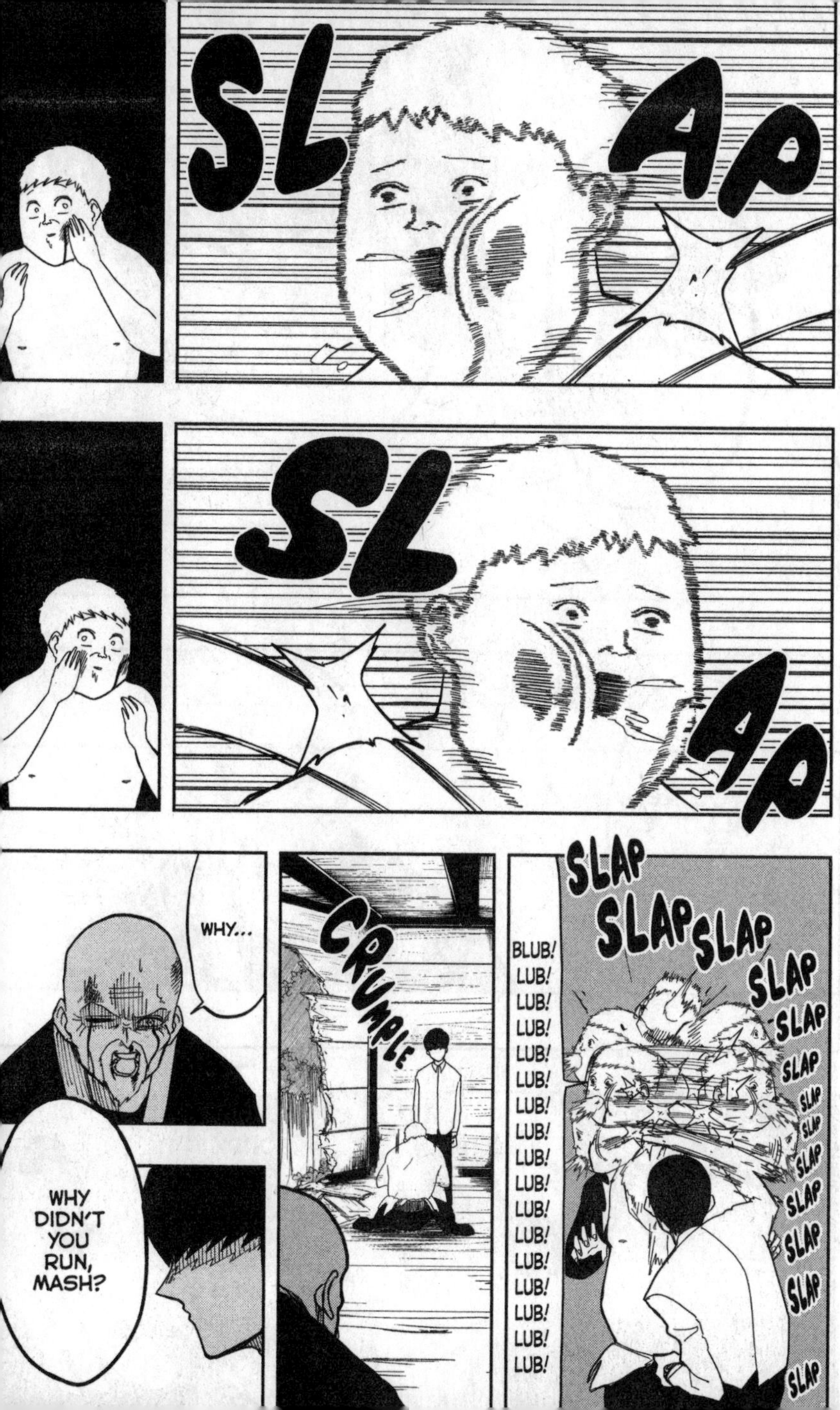
SLAP
SLAP
SLAP
SLAP
SLAP
SLAP
SLAP
SLAP
SLAP
SLAP
SLAP
SLAP
SLAP
SLAP
SLAP
SLAP
BLUB!
LUB!
LUB!
LUB!
LUB!
LUB!
LUB!
LUB!
LUB!
LUB!
LUB!
LUB!
LUB!
LUB!
LUB!
LUB!
LUB!
CRUMPLE
WHY...
WHY DIDN'T YOU RUN, MASH?

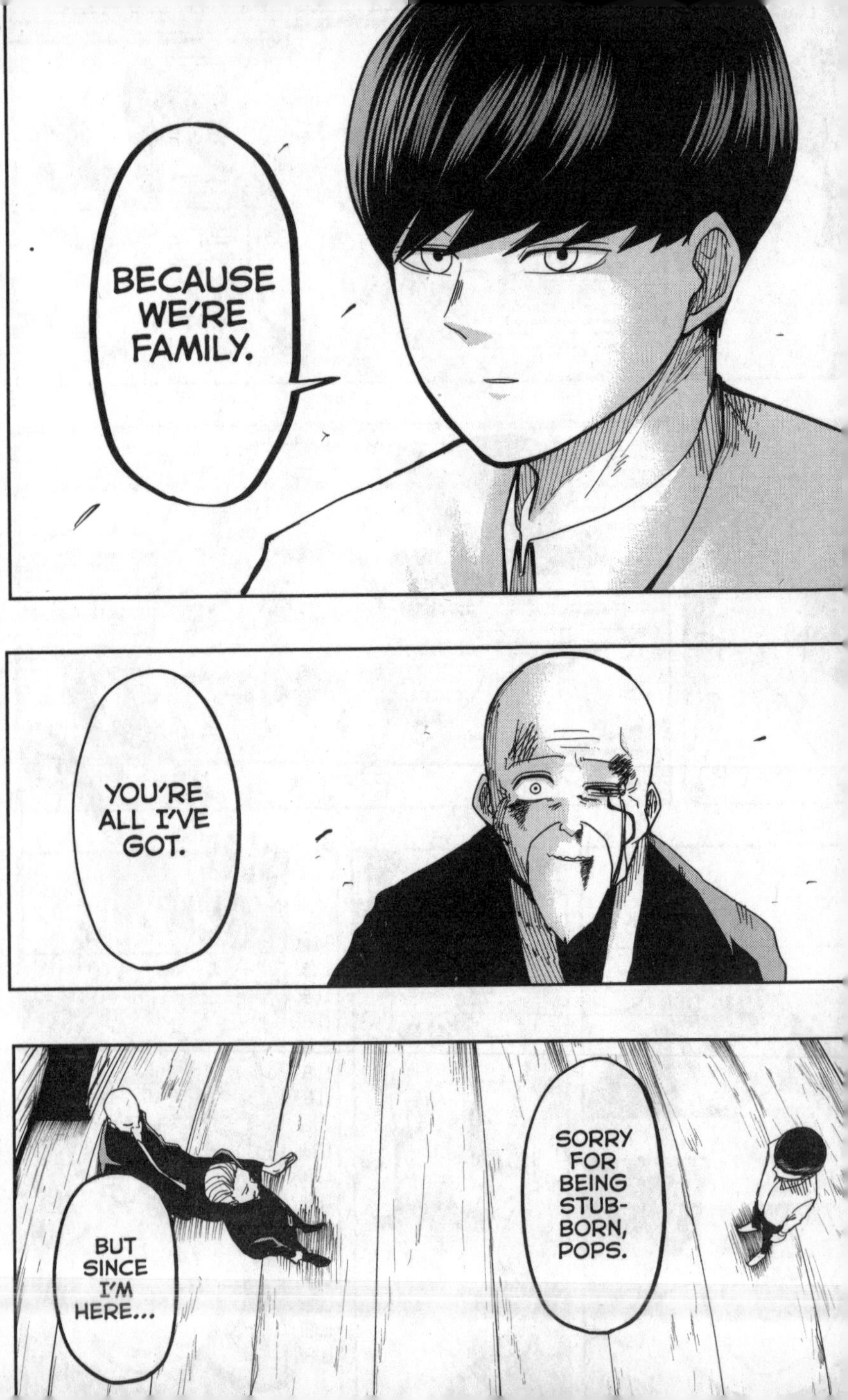
BECAUSE WE'RE FAMILY.
YOU'RE ALL I'VE GOT.
SORRY FOR BEING STUB-BORN, POPS.
BUT SINCE I'M HERE...

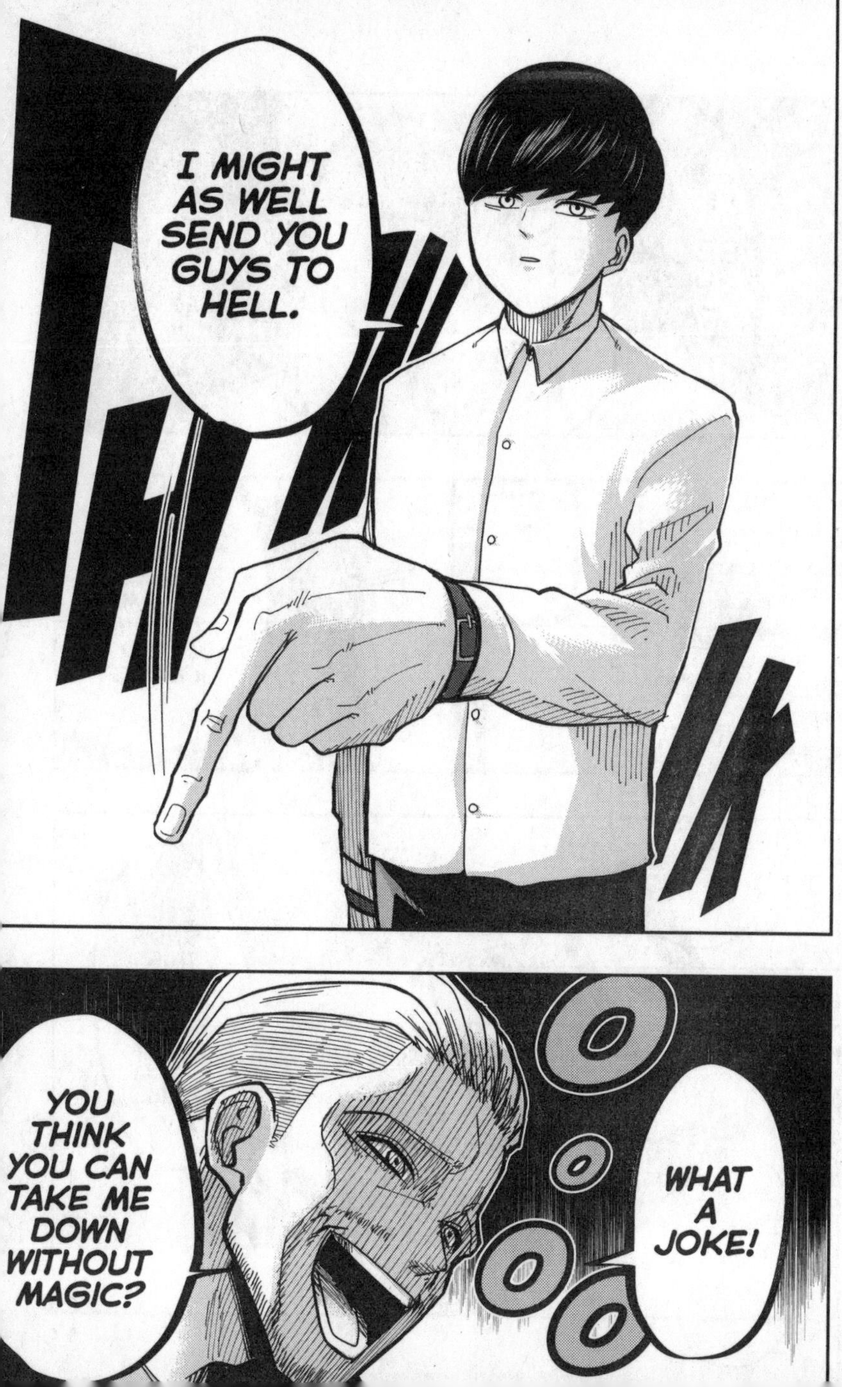
I MIGHT AS WELL SEND YOU GUYS TO HELL.
WHAT A JOKE!
YOU THINK YOU CAN TAKE ME DOWN WITHOUT MAGIC?

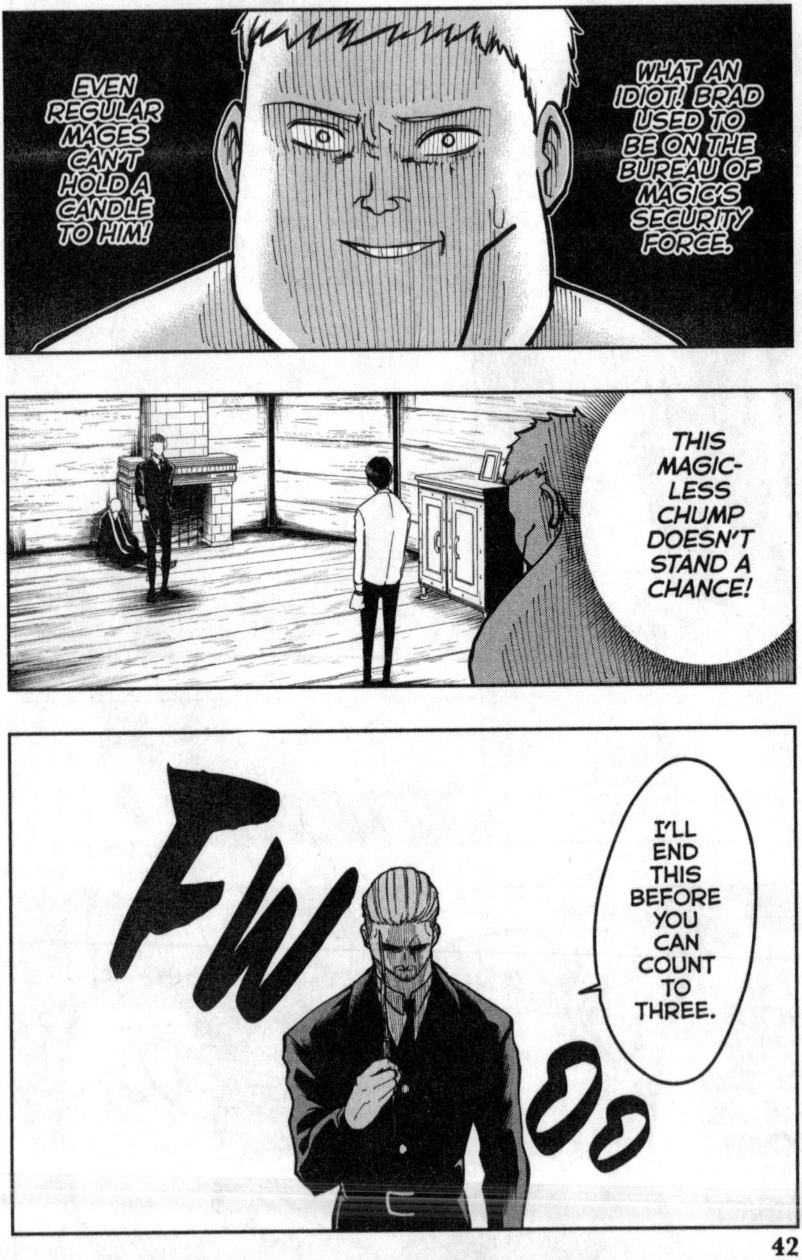
WHAT AN IDIOT! BRAD USED TO BE ON THE BUREAU OF MAGIC'S SECURITY FORCE.
EVEN REGULAR MAGES CAN'T HOLD A CANDLE TO HIM!
THIS MAGIC-LESS CHUMP DOESN'T STAND A CHANCE!
I'LL END THIS BEFORE YOU CAN COUNT TO THREE.
FWOO

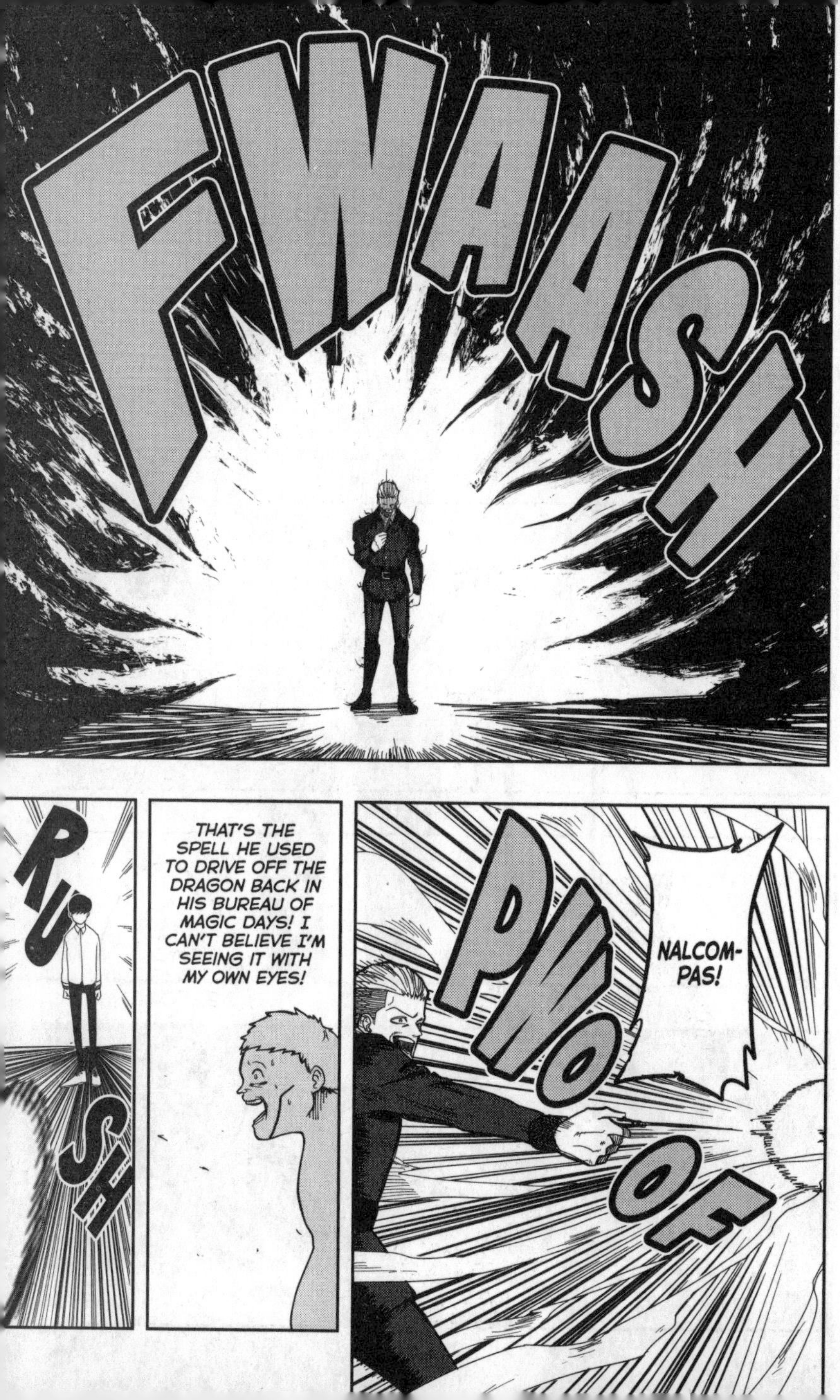
FWAASH
NALCOM-PAS!
PWOOF
THAT'S THE SPELL HE USED TO DRIVE OFF THE DRAGON BACK IN HIS BUREAU OF MAGIC DAYS! I CAN'T BELIEVE I'M SEEING IT WITH MY OWN EYES!
RUSH

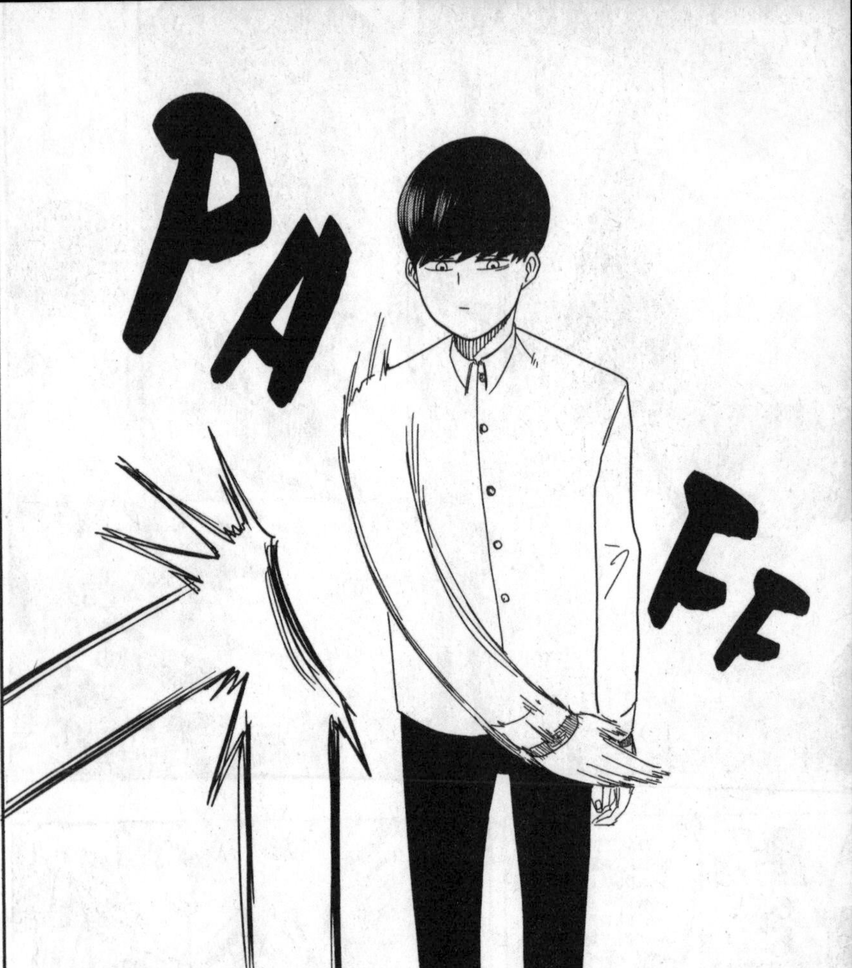
PAFF
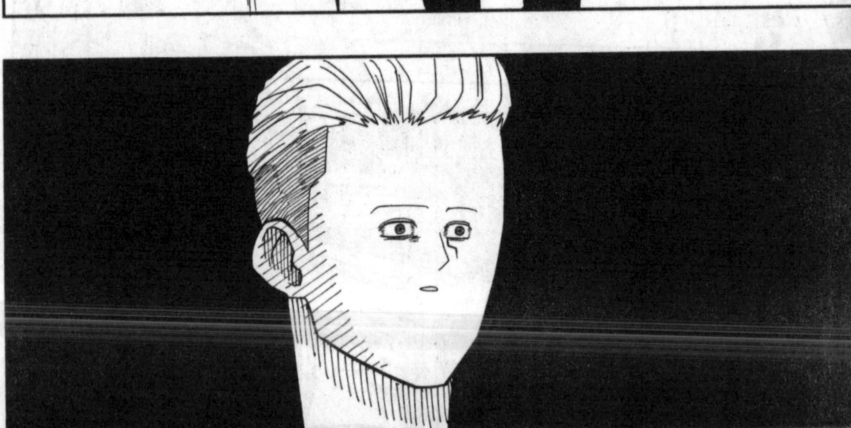

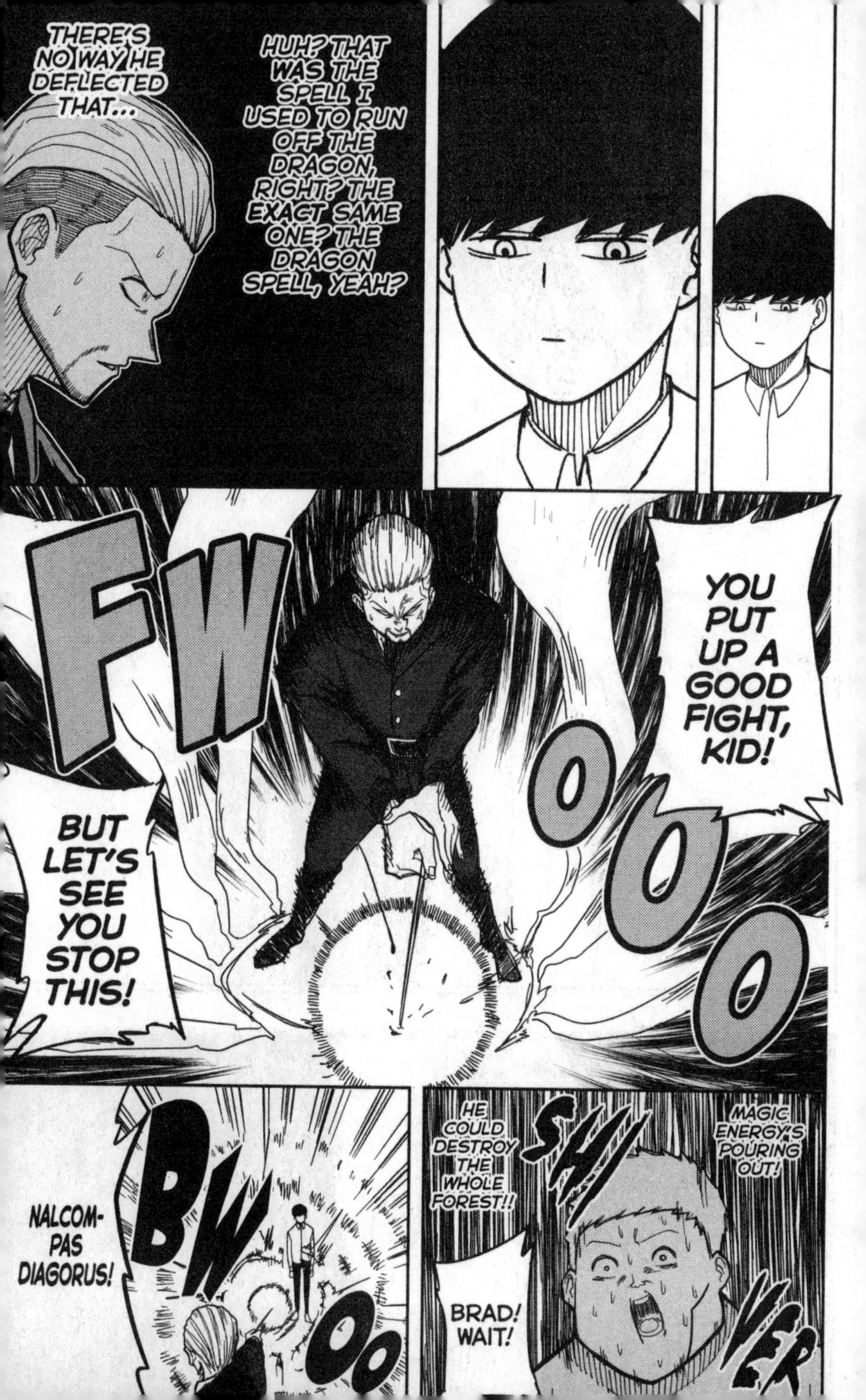
HUH? THAT WAS THE SPELL I USED TO RUN OFF THE DRAGON, RIGHT? THE EXACT SAME ONE? THE DRAGON SPELL, YEAH?
THERE'S NO WAY HE DEFLECTED THAT...
YOU PUT UP A GOOD FIGHT, KID!
FWOOOO
BUT LET'S SEE YOU STOP THIS!
MAGIC ENERGY'S POURING OUT!
SHIVER
HE COULD DESTROY THE WHOLE FOREST!!
BRAD! WAIT!
BWOO
NALCOM-PAS DIAGORUS!

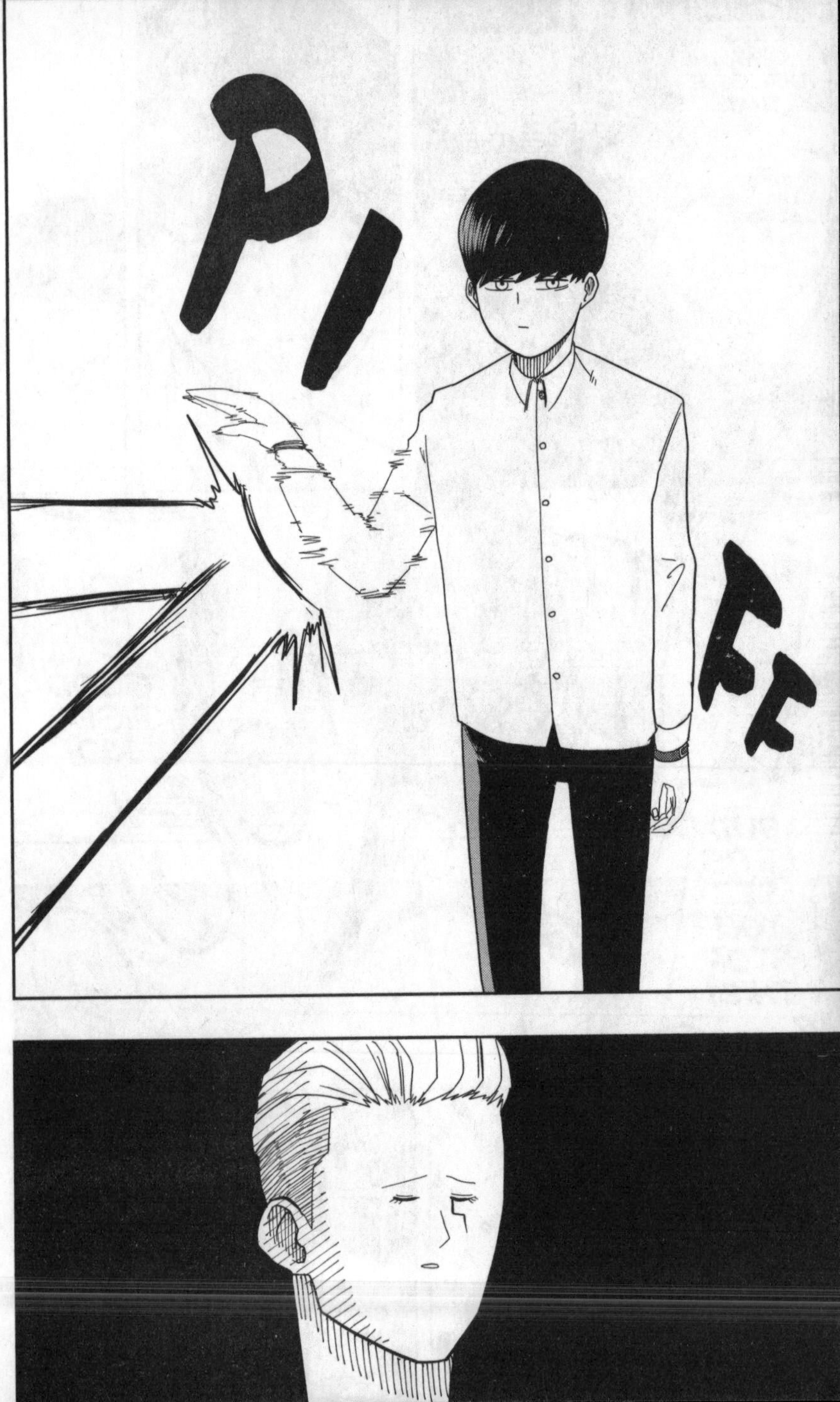
PI

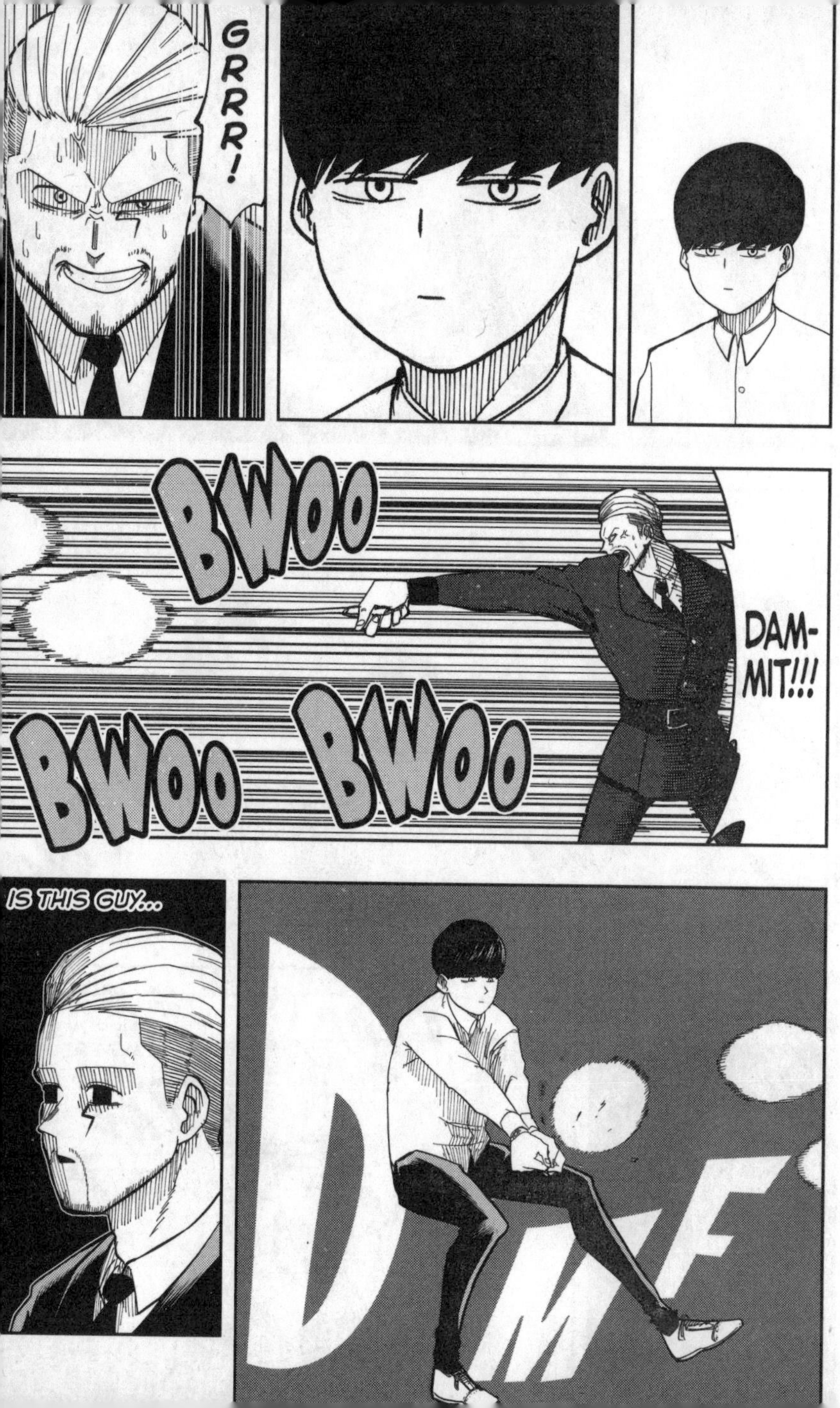
GRRR!
BWOO
BWOO
BWOO
DAM-MIT!!!
DMF
IS THIS GUY...

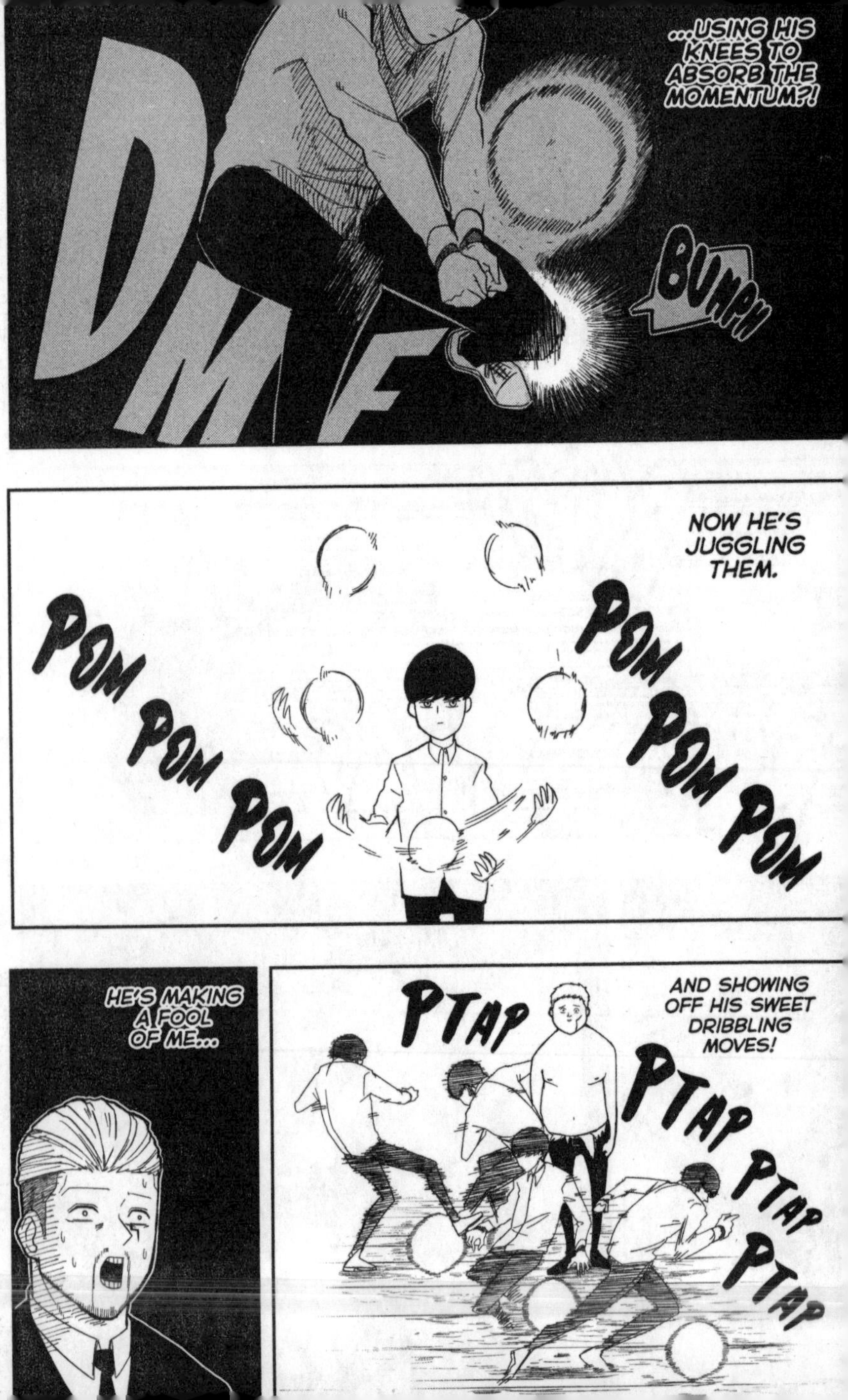
...USING HIS KNEES TO ABSORB THE MOMENTUM?!
BUMPH
DMF
NOW HE'S JUGGLING THEM.
POM POM POM
POM POM POM
AND SHOWING OFF HIS SWEET DRIBBLING MOVES!
PTAP
PTAP PTAP PTAP PTAP
HE'S MAKING A FOOL OF ME...

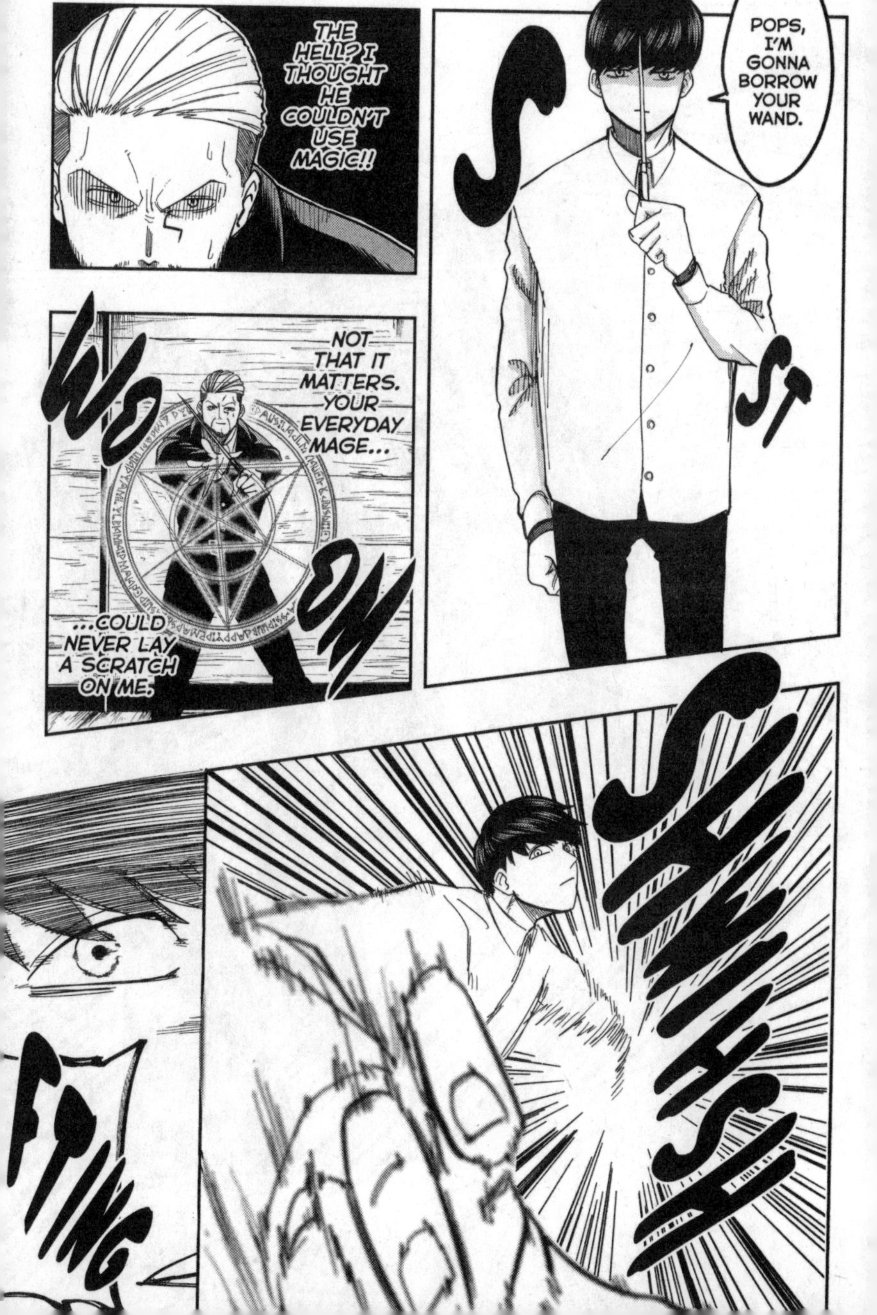
POPS, I'M GONNA BORROW YOUR WAND.
SST
THE HELL? I THOUGHT HE COULDN'T USE MAGIC!!
NOT THAT IT MATTERS. YOUR EVERYDAY MAGE...
...COULD NEVER LAY A SCRATCH ON ME.
SHWHSH
FFTING

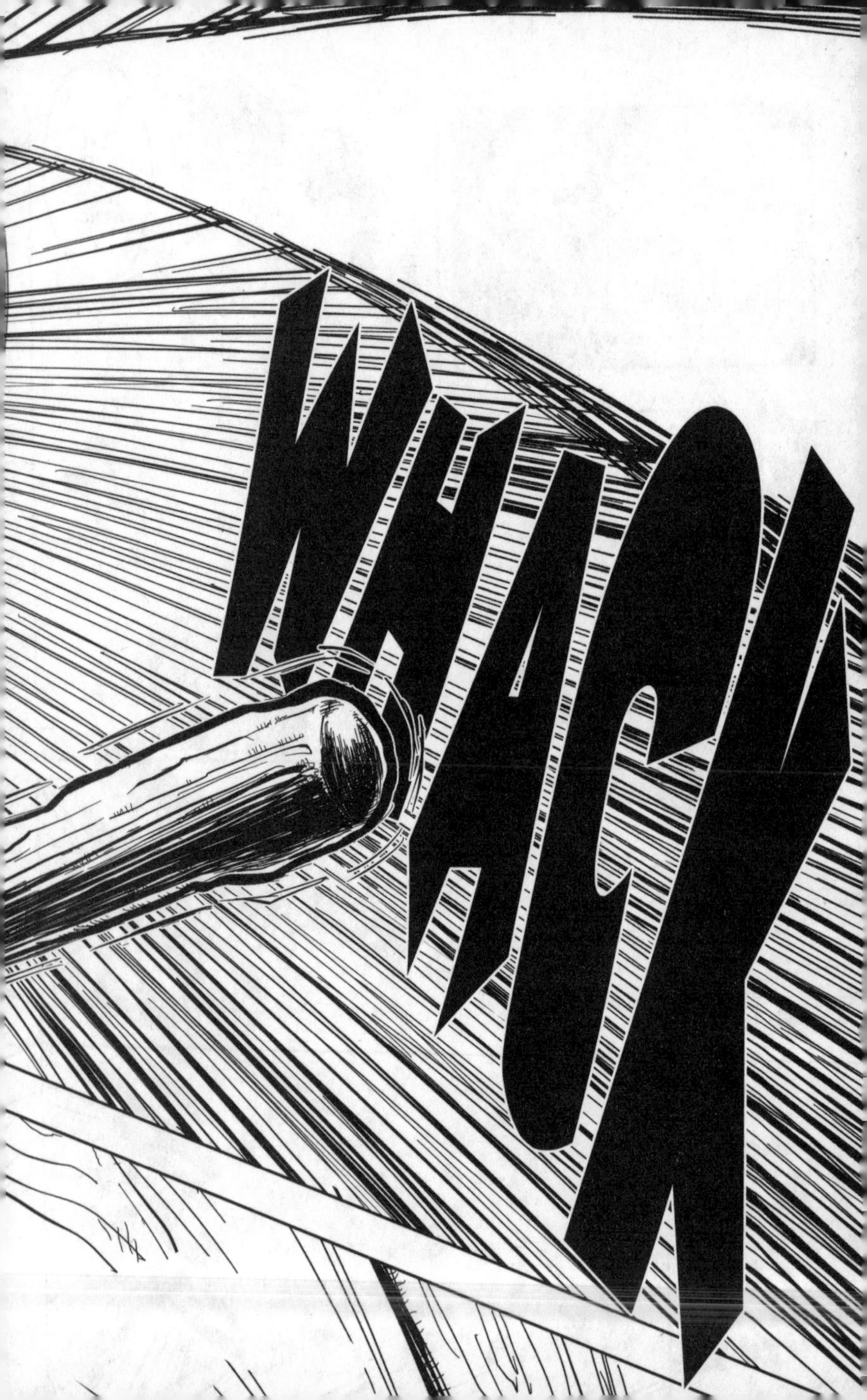
WHACK

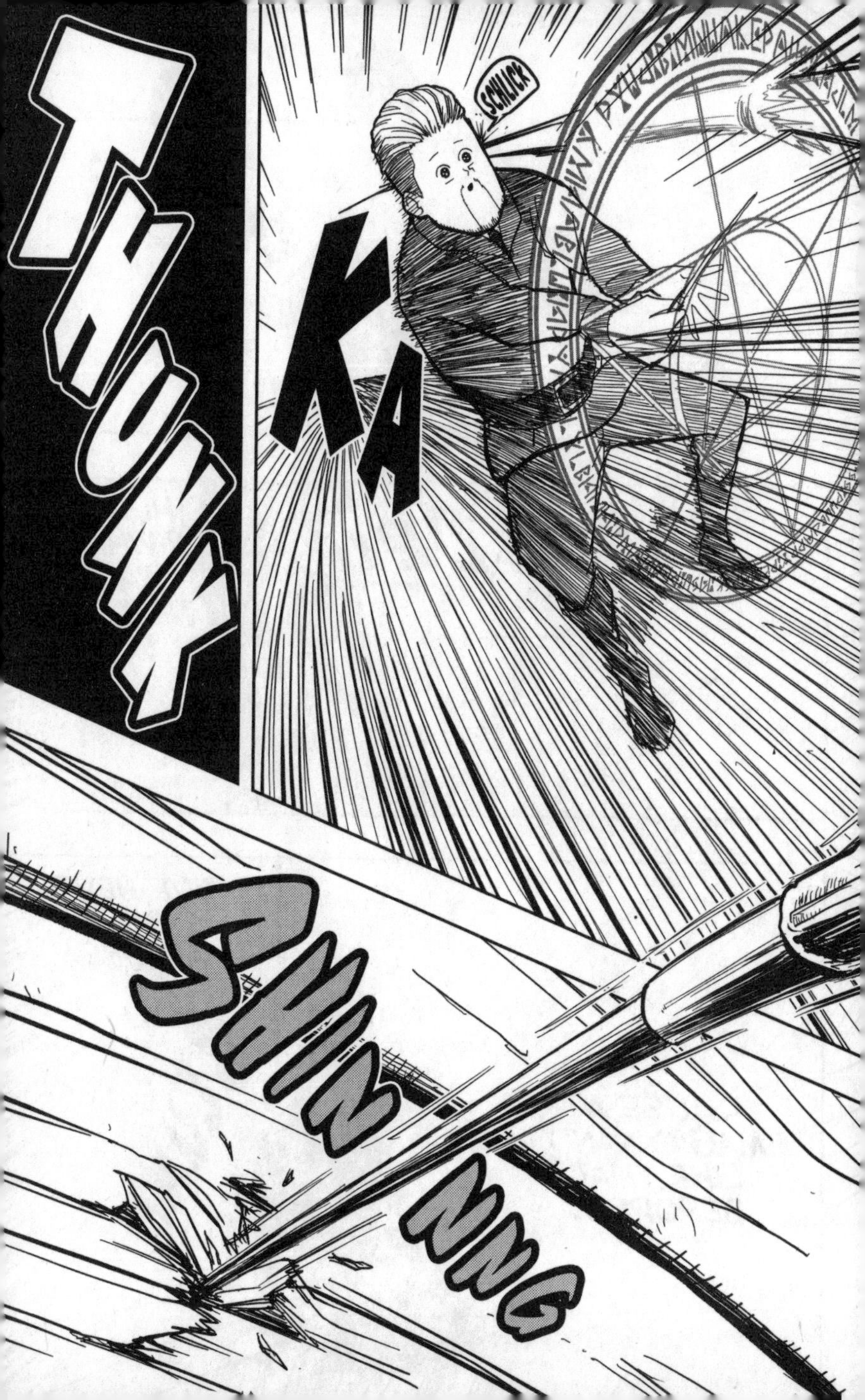
SCHLICK
KA
THUNK
SHINNNG

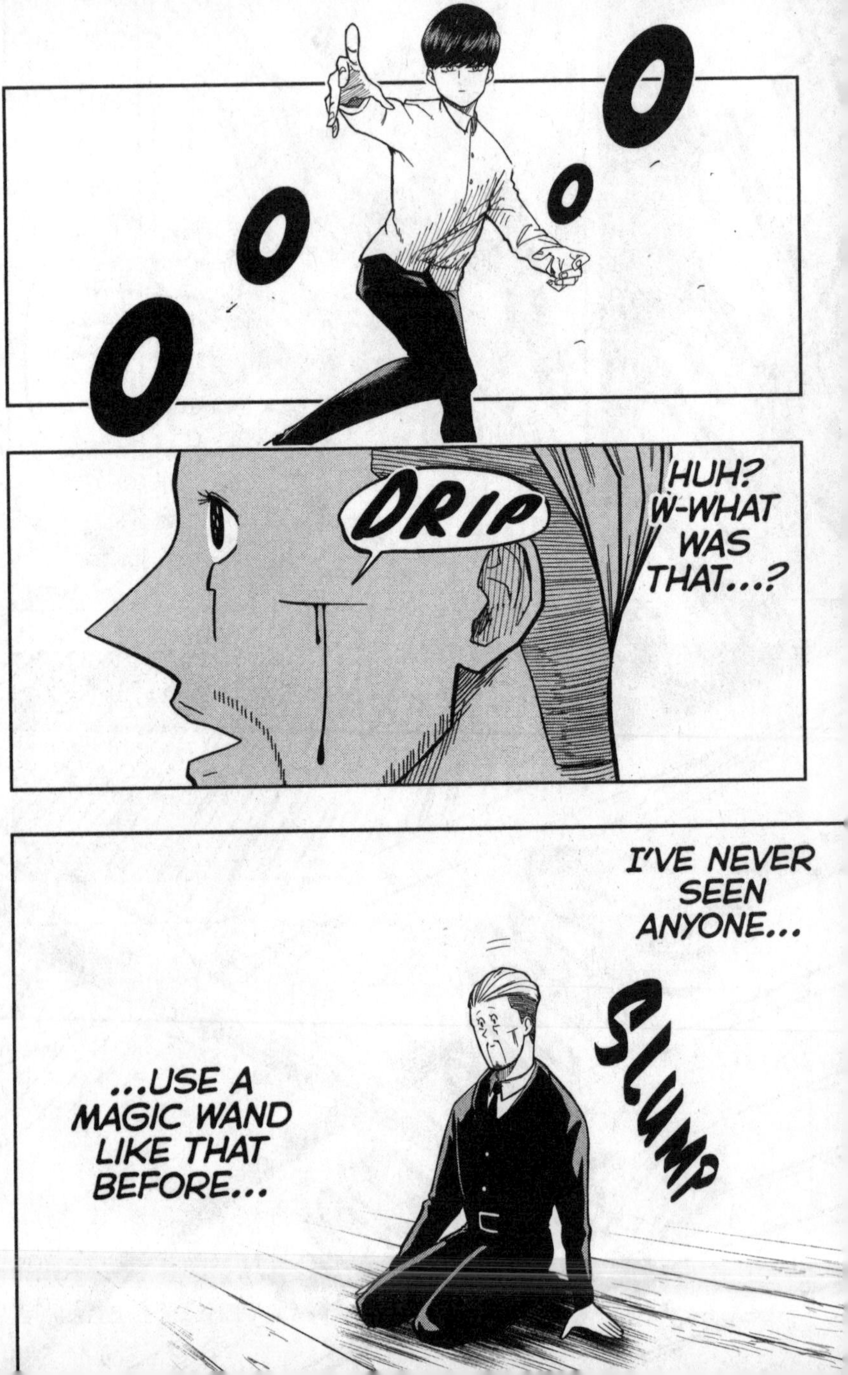
OOOOO
HUH? W-WHAT WAS THAT...?
DRIP
I'VE NEVER SEEN ANYONE...
SLUMP
...USE A MAGIC WAND LIKE THAT BEFORE...

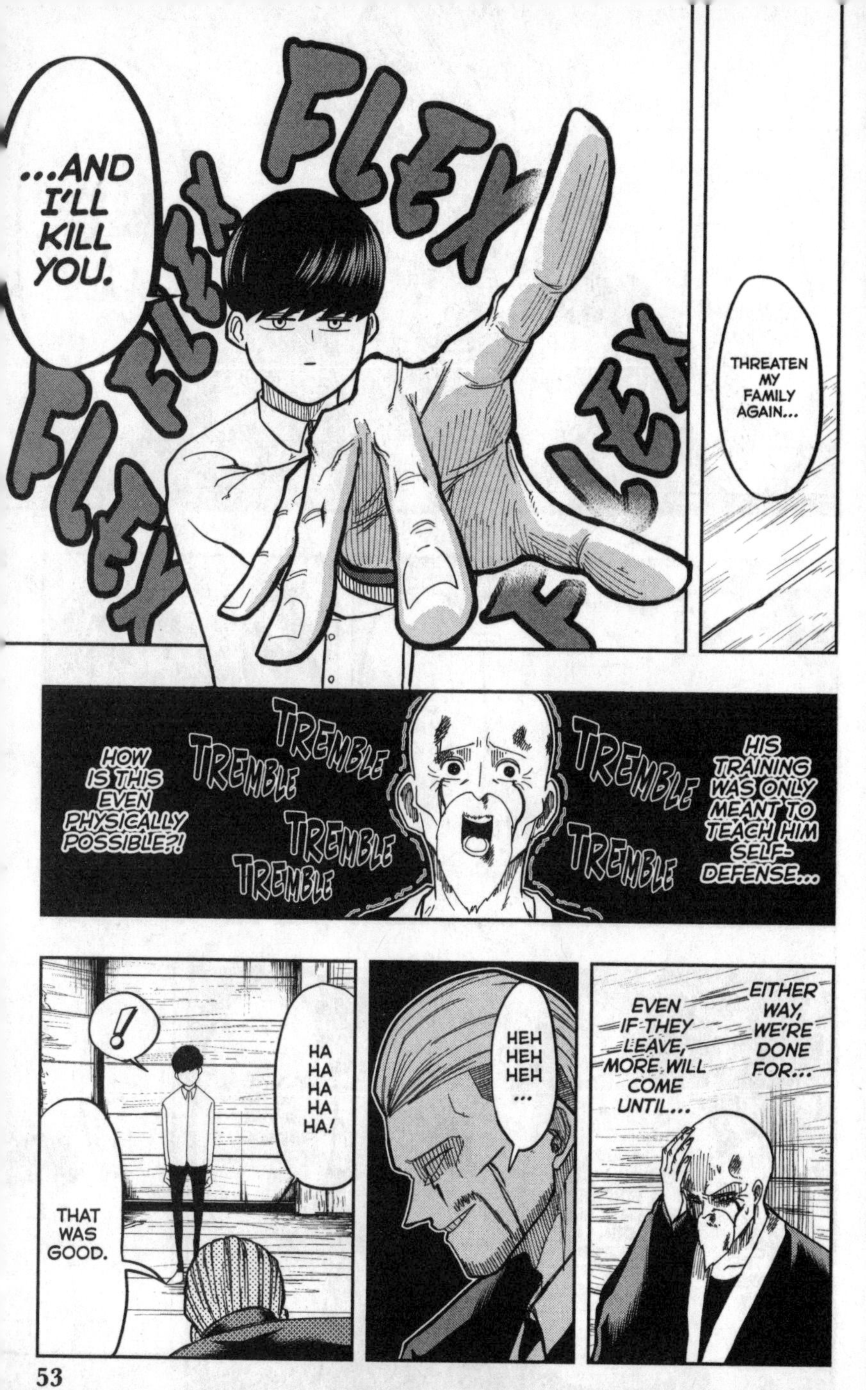
THREATEN MY FAMILY AGAIN...
FLEX
FLEX
FLEX
FLEX
...AND I'LL KILL YOU.
HIS TRAINING WAS ONLY MEANT TO TEACH HIM SELF-DEFENSE...
TREMBLE
TREMBLE
TREMBLE
TREMBLE
TREMBLE
TREMBLE
HOW IS THIS EVEN PHYSICALLY POSSIBLE?!
EITHER WAY, WE'RE DONE FOR...
EVEN IF THEY LEAVE, MORE WILL COME UNTIL...
HEH HEH HEH...
HA HA HA HA HA!
!
THAT WAS GOOD.

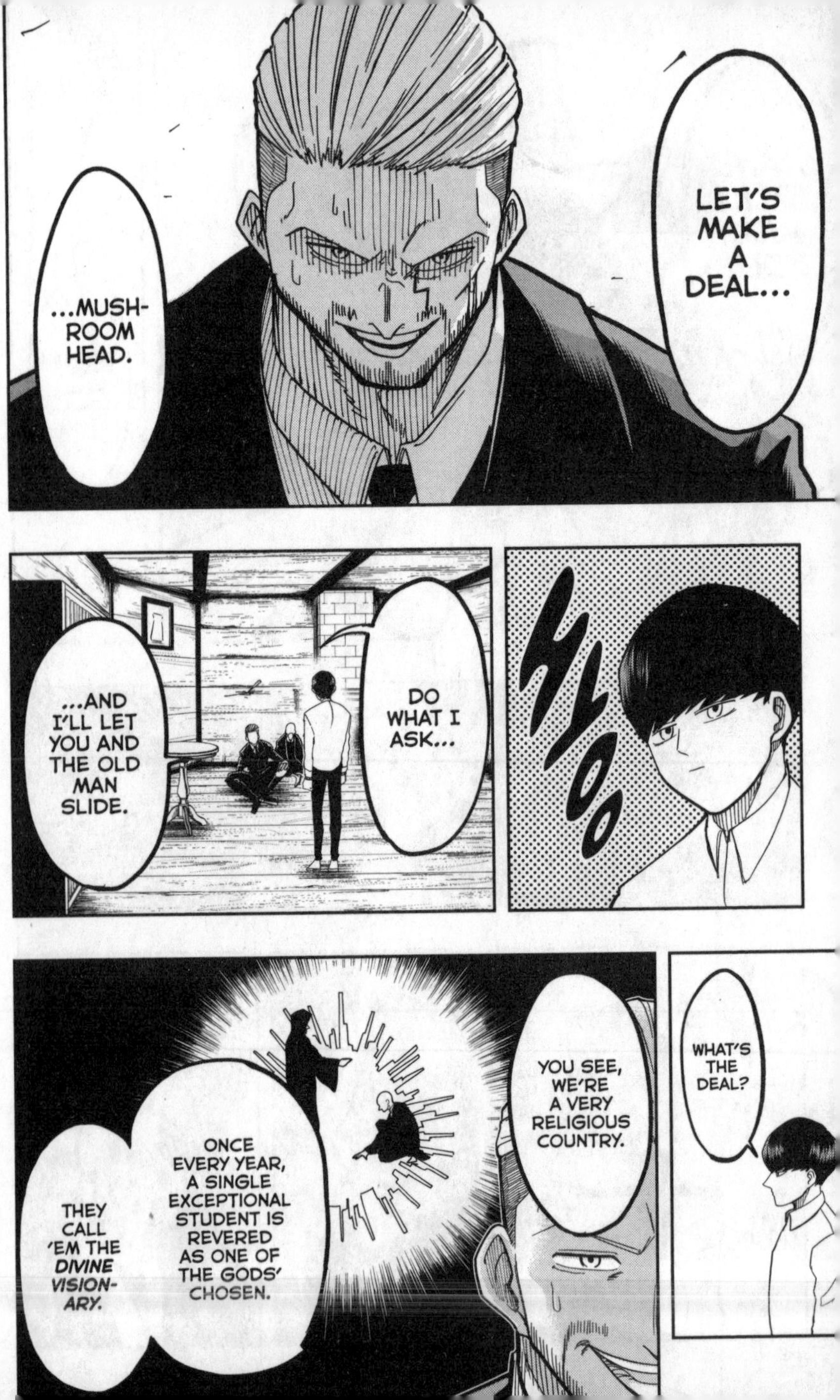
LET'S MAKE A DEAL...
...MUSH-ROOM HEAD.
DO WHAT I ASK...
...AND I'LL LET YOU AND THE OLD MAN SLIDE.
WHAT'S THE DEAL?
YOU SEE, WE'RE A VERY RELIGIOUS COUNTRY.
ONCE EVERY YEAR, A SINGLE EXCEPTIONAL STUDENT IS REVERED AS ONE OF THE GODS' CHOSEN.
THEY CALL 'EM THE *DIVINE VISIONARY.*

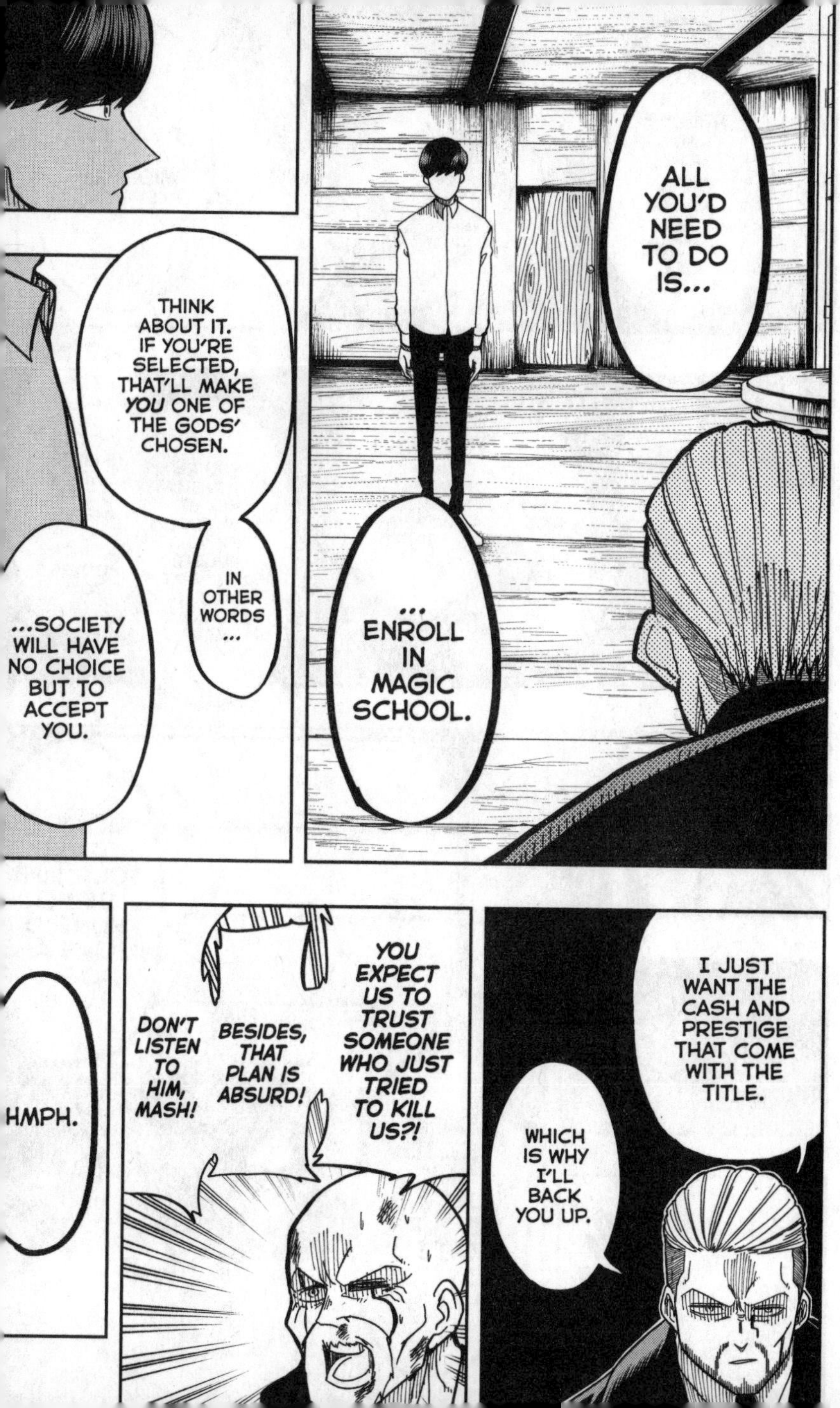
ALL YOU'D NEED TO DO IS...
...ENROLL IN MAGIC SCHOOL.
THINK ABOUT IT. IF YOU'RE SELECTED, THAT'LL MAKE *YOU* ONE OF THE GODS' CHOSEN.
IN OTHER WORDS...
...SOCIETY WILL HAVE NO CHOICE BUT TO ACCEPT YOU.
I JUST WANT THE CASH AND PRESTIGE THAT COME WITH THE TITLE.
WHICH IS WHY I'LL BACK YOU UP.
YOU EXPECT US TO TRUST SOMEONE WHO JUST TRIED TO KILL US?!
BESIDES, THAT PLAN IS ABSURD!
DON'T LISTEN TO HIM, MASH!
HMPH.

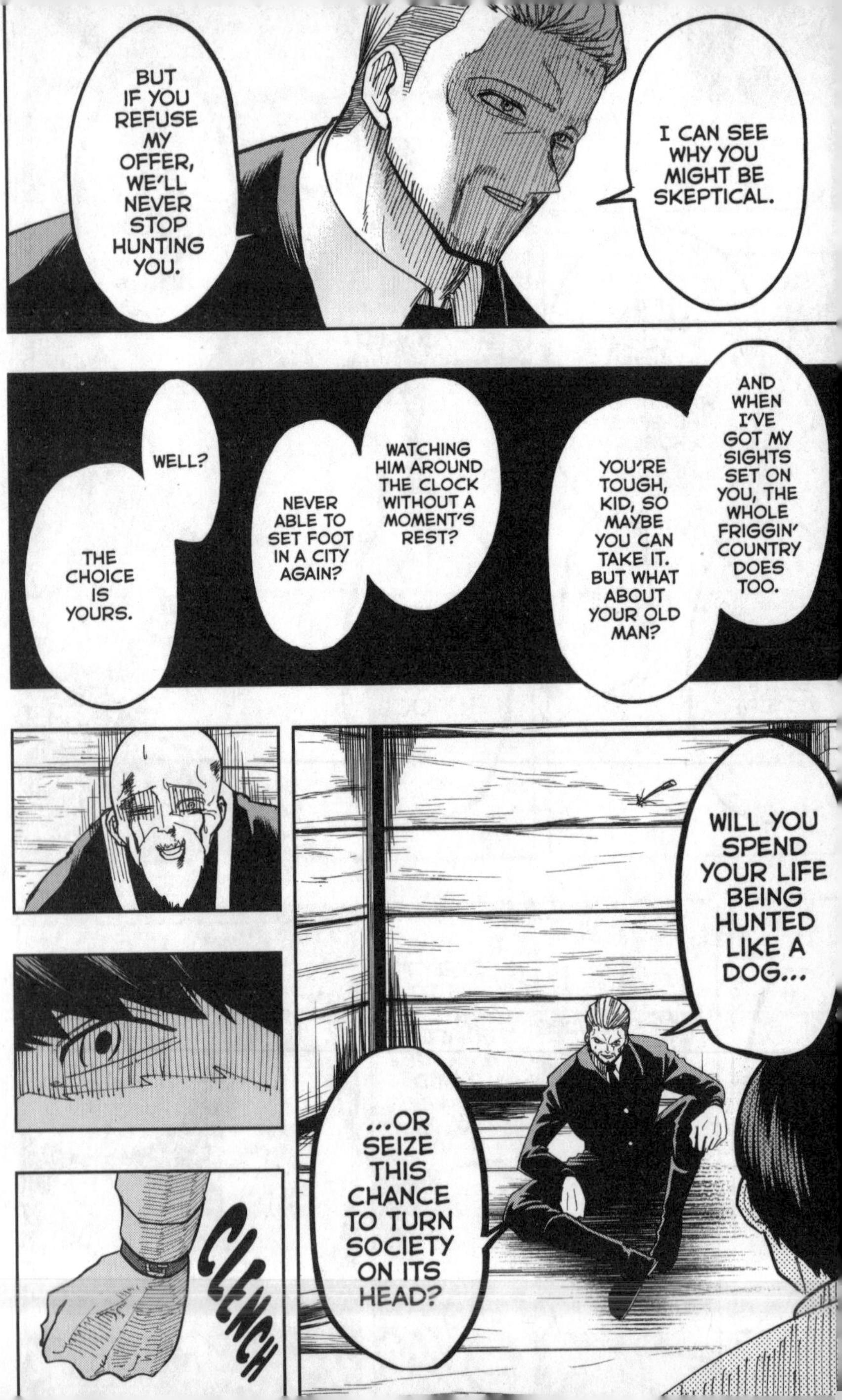
I CAN SEE WHY YOU MIGHT BE SKEPTICAL.
BUT IF YOU REFUSE MY OFFER, WE'LL NEVER STOP HUNTING YOU.
AND WHEN I'VE GOT MY SIGHTS SET ON YOU, THE WHOLE FRIGGIN' COUNTRY DOES TOO.
YOU'RE TOUGH, KID, SO MAYBE YOU CAN TAKE IT. BUT WHAT ABOUT YOUR OLD MAN?
WATCHING HIM AROUND THE CLOCK WITHOUT A MOMENT'S REST?
NEVER ABLE TO SET FOOT IN A CITY AGAIN?
WELL?
THE CHOICE IS YOURS.
WILL YOU SPEND YOUR LIFE BEING HUNTED LIKE A DOG...
...OR SEIZE THIS CHANCE TO TURN SOCIETY ON ITS HEAD?
CLENCH

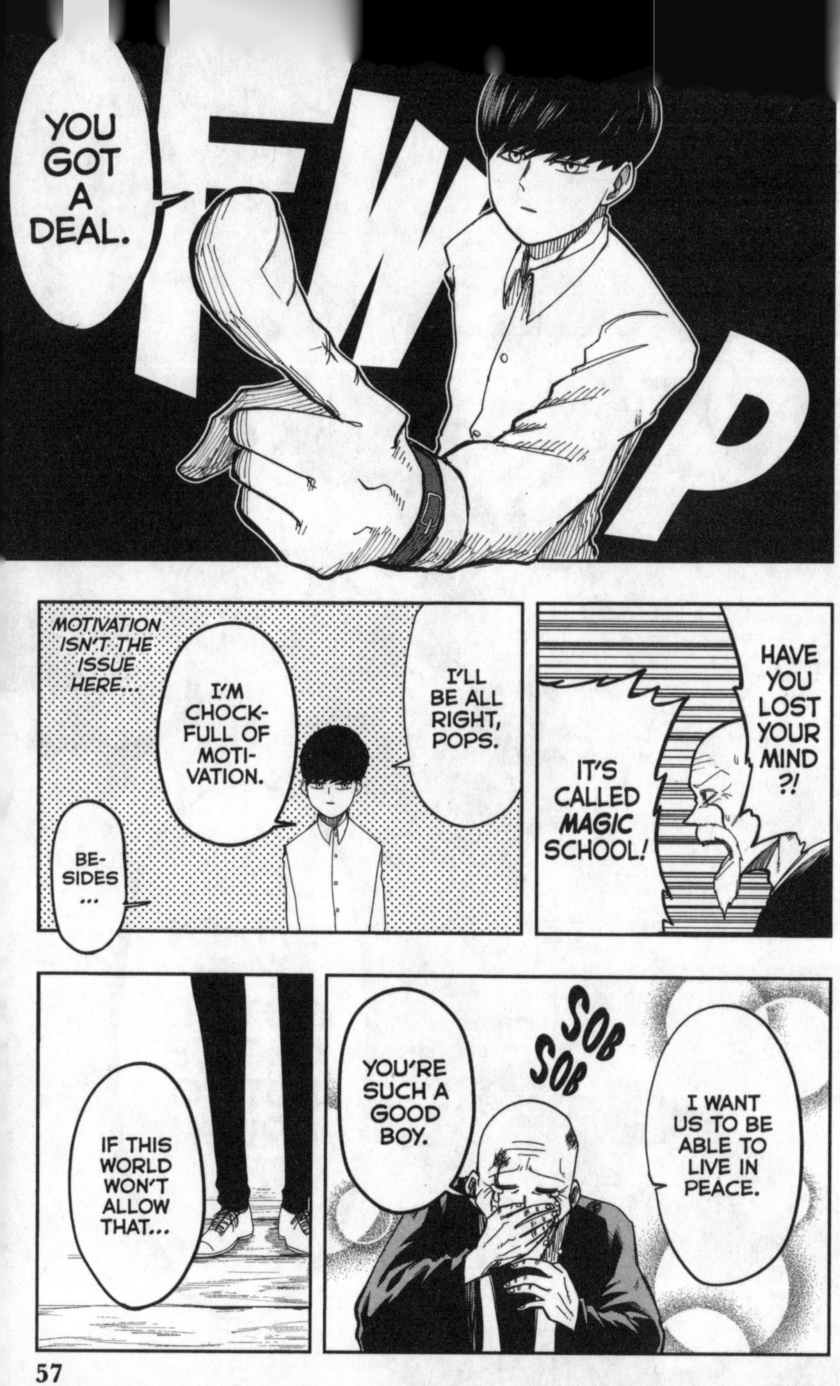
YOU GOT A DEAL.
HAVE YOU LOST YOUR MIND?!
IT'S CALLED *MAGIC* SCHOOL!
I'LL BE ALL RIGHT, POPS.
I'M CHOCK-FULL OF MOTIVATION.
MOTIVATION ISN'T THE ISSUE HERE...
BESIDES...
I WANT US TO BE ABLE TO LIVE IN PEACE.
SOB SOB
YOU'RE SUCH A GOOD BOY.
IF THIS WORLD WON'T ALLOW THAT...

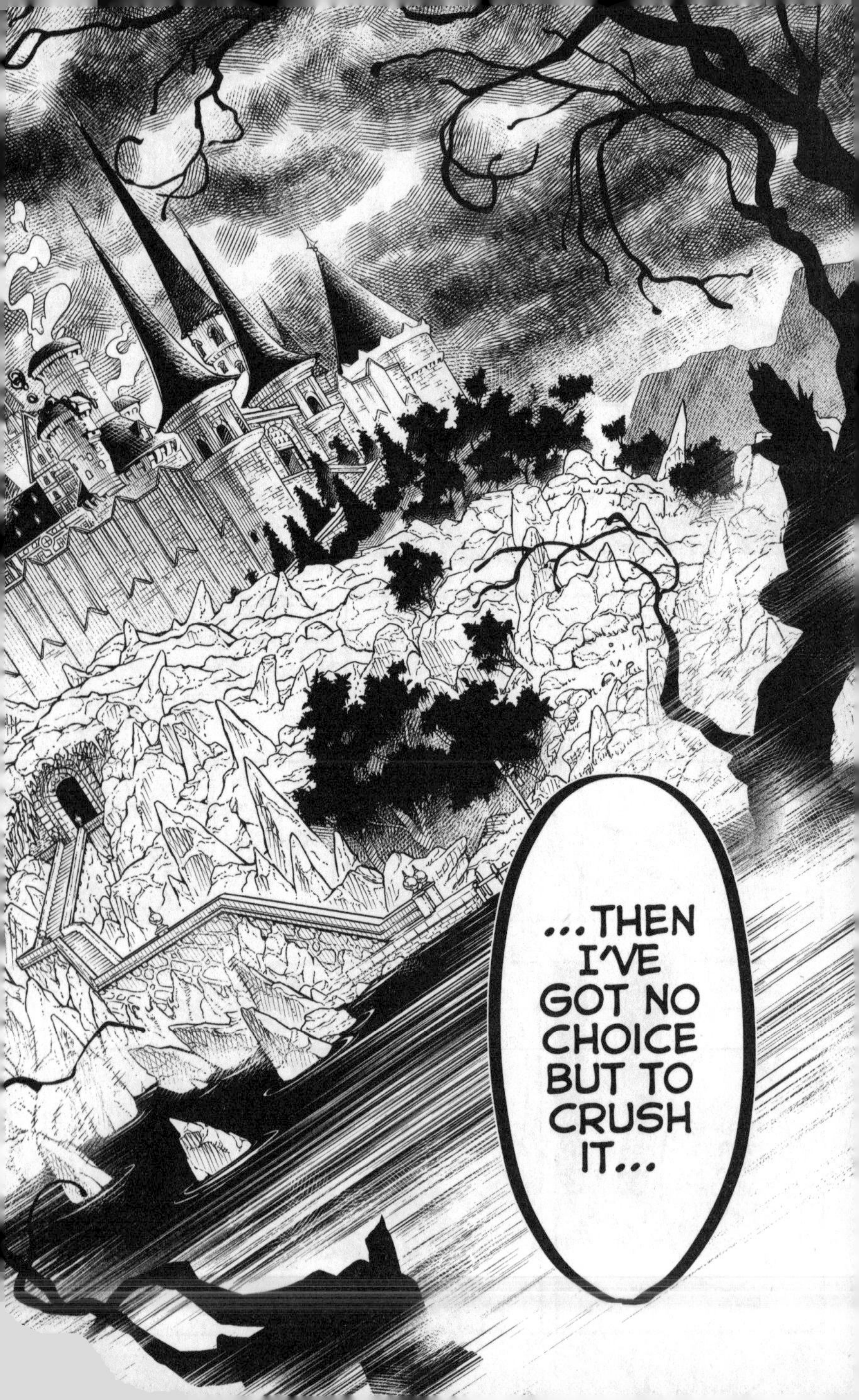
...THEN I'VE GOT NO CHOICE BUT TO CRUSH IT...

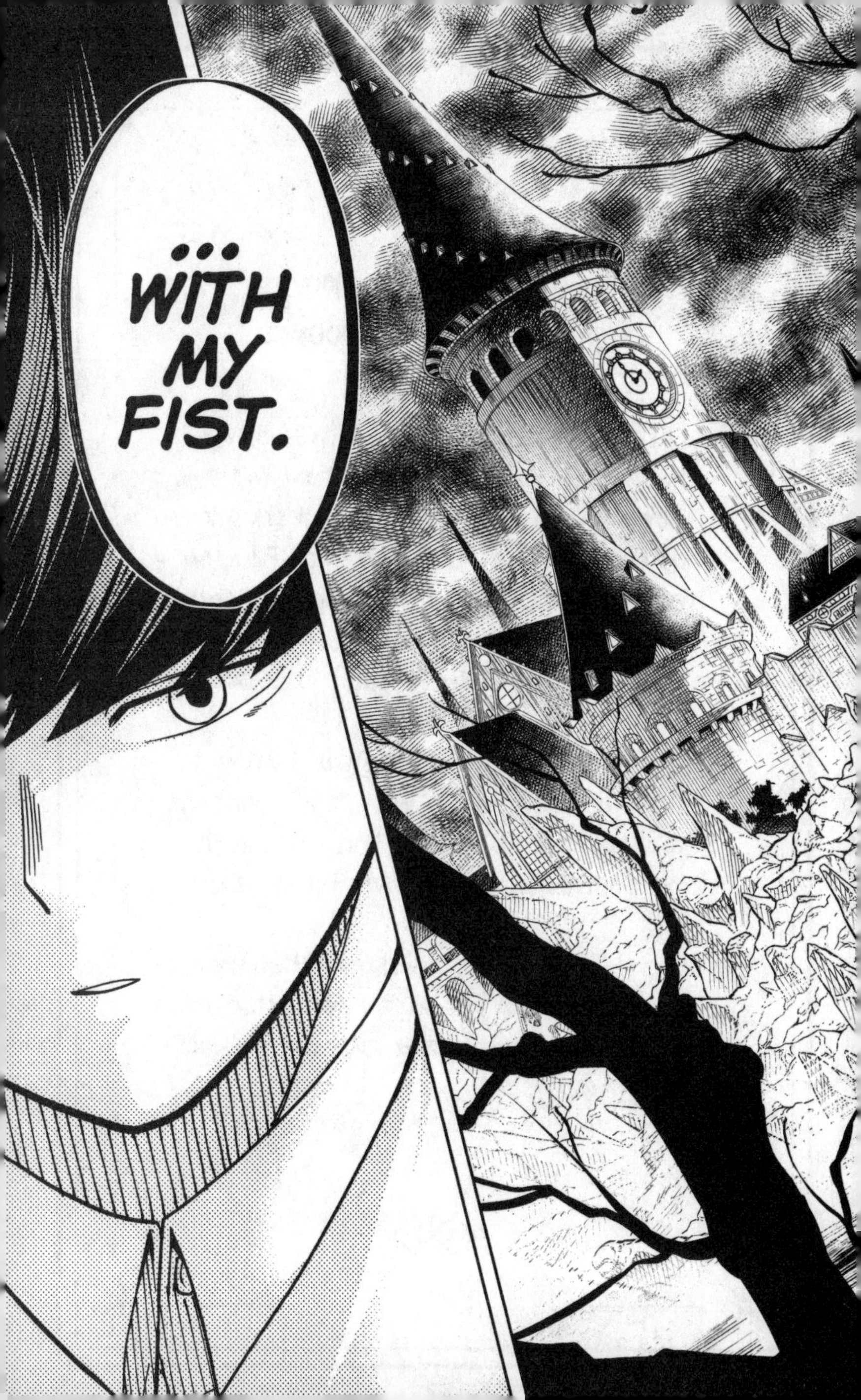
...WITH MY FIST.

To everyone who purchased this book...

Thank you for picking up this volume.
(My apologies if you bought it by mistake
somehow.) We live in an age where a lot
of entertainment is available for free, so
the importance of the fact that you spent
your money on this book is something
that can't be understated! It just...can't!

I'm truly filled with gratitude. I know I
still have much left to learn, so I'll continue
to push myself to keep this comic going
so that Mash can one day live in peace!

P.S. I've been unable to respond, but thank
you so much for all the fan letters,
candy, key holders and toilet paper! Woo!

CHAPTER 2:
MASH BURNEDEAD AND THE MYSTERIOUS MAZE

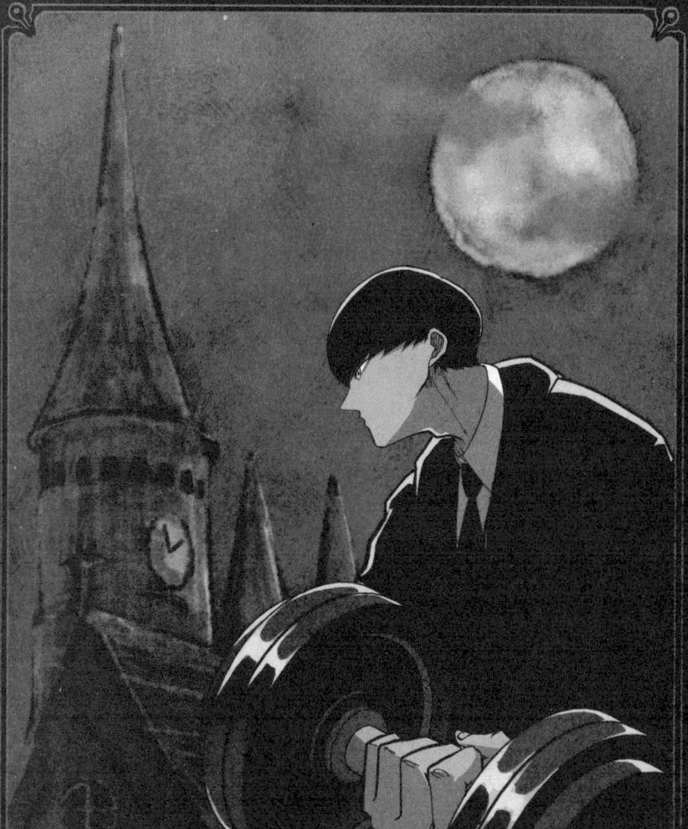

MAGIC PUBLISHING

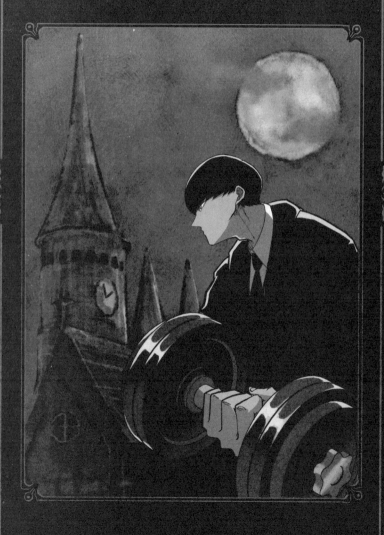

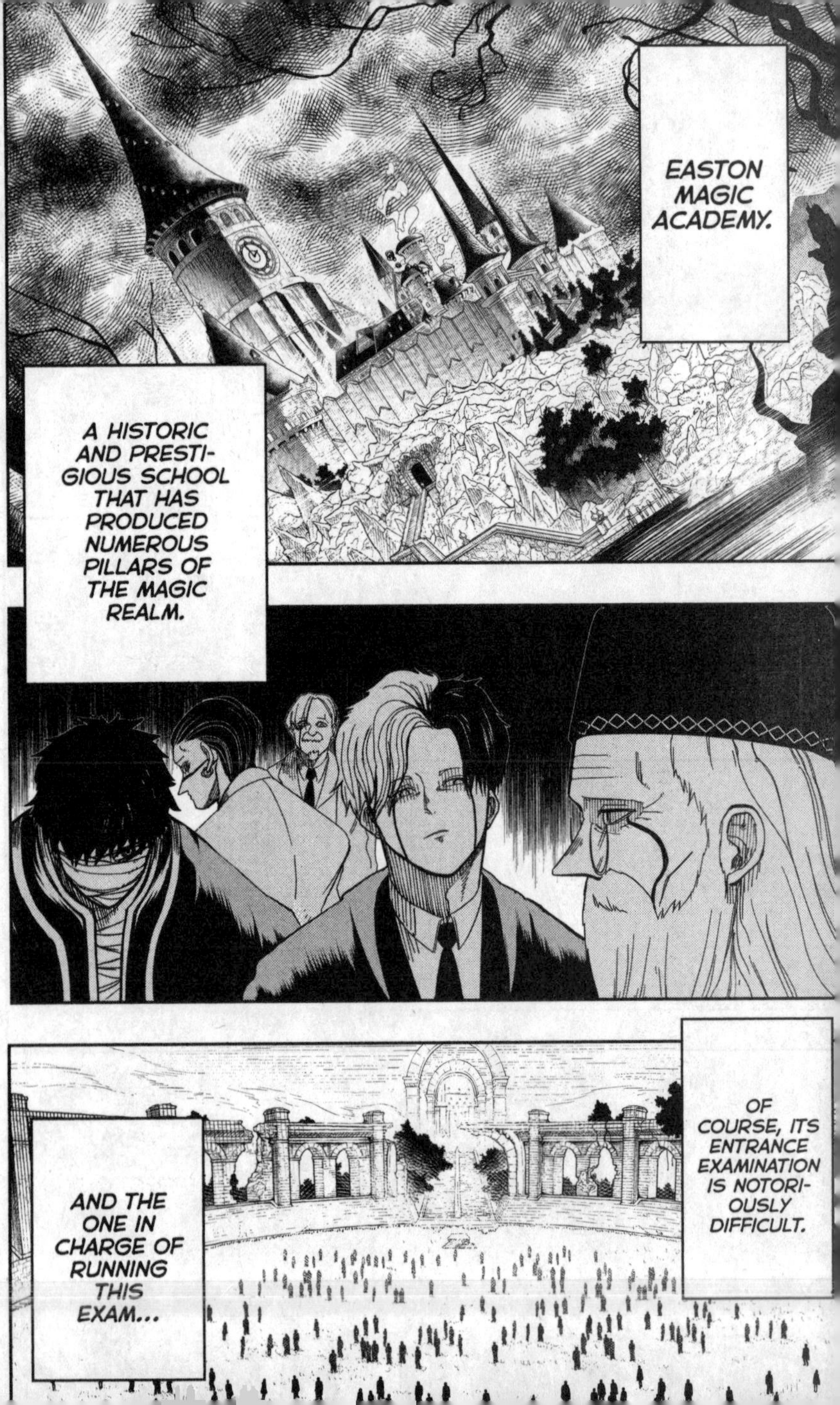
EASTON MAGIC ACADEMY.
A HISTORIC AND PRESTI-GIOUS SCHOOL THAT HAS PRODUCED NUMEROUS PILLARS OF THE MAGIC REALM.
OF COURSE, ITS ENTRANCE EXAMINATION IS NOTORI-OUSLY DIFFICULT.
AND THE ONE IN CHARGE OF RUNNING THIS EXAM...

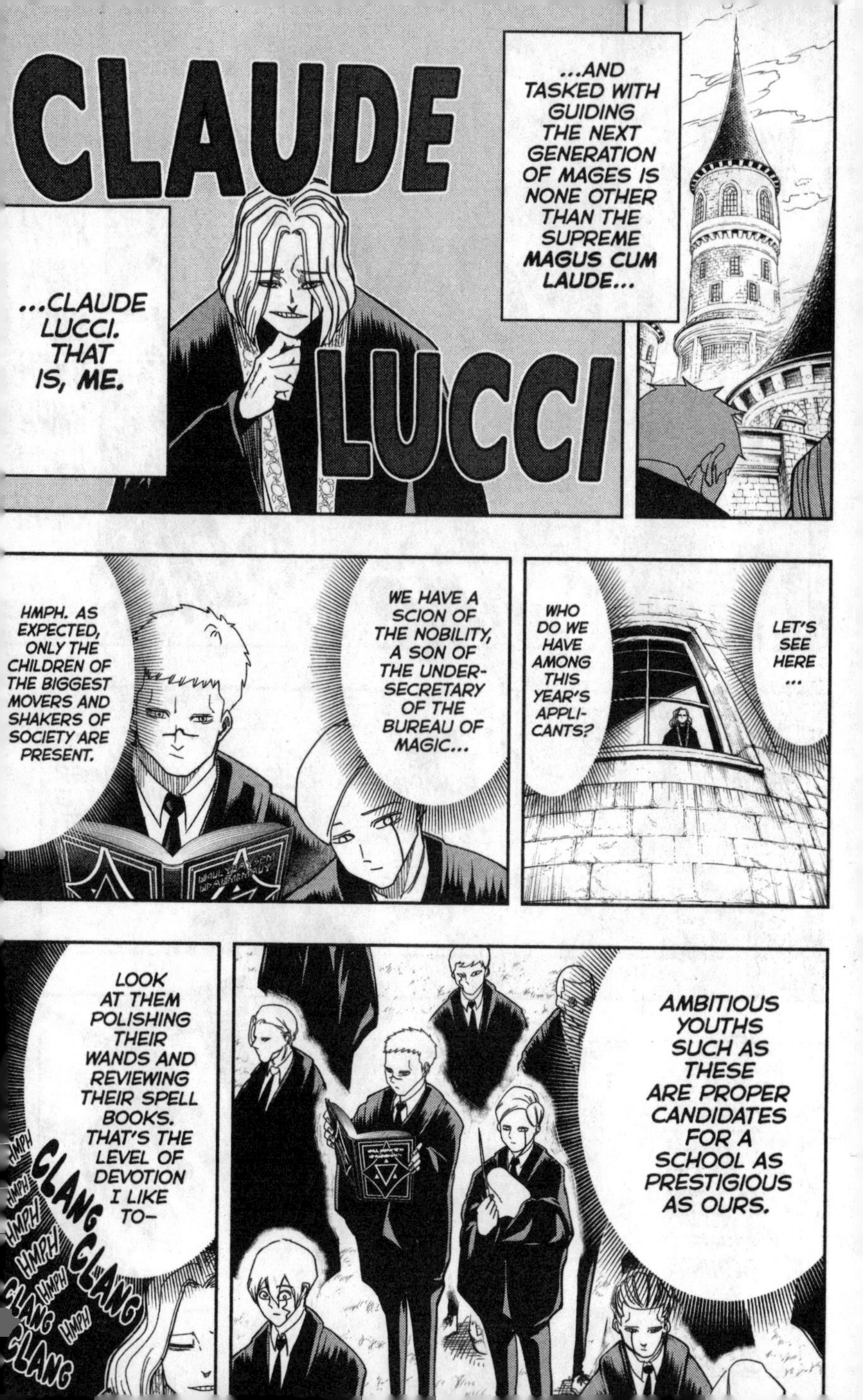
...AND TASKED WITH GUIDING THE NEXT GENERATION OF MAGES IS NONE OTHER THAN THE SUPREME MAGUS CUM LAUDE...
CLAUDE
LUCCI
...CLAUDE LUCCI. THAT IS, ME.
LET'S SEE HERE...
WHO DO WE HAVE AMONG THIS YEAR'S APPLICANTS?
WE HAVE A SCION OF THE NOBILITY, A SON OF THE UNDER-SECRETARY OF THE BUREAU OF MAGIC...
HMPH. AS EXPECTED, ONLY THE CHILDREN OF THE BIGGEST MOVERS AND SHAKERS OF SOCIETY ARE PRESENT.
AMBITIOUS YOUTHS SUCH AS THESE ARE PROPER CANDIDATES FOR A SCHOOL AS PRESTIGIOUS AS OURS.
LOOK AT THEM POLISHING THEIR WANDS AND REVIEWING THEIR SPELL BOOKS. THAT'S THE LEVEL OF DEVOTION I LIKE TO–
HMPH HMPH HMPH HMPH HMPH HMPH
CLANG CLANG CLANG CLANG CLANG

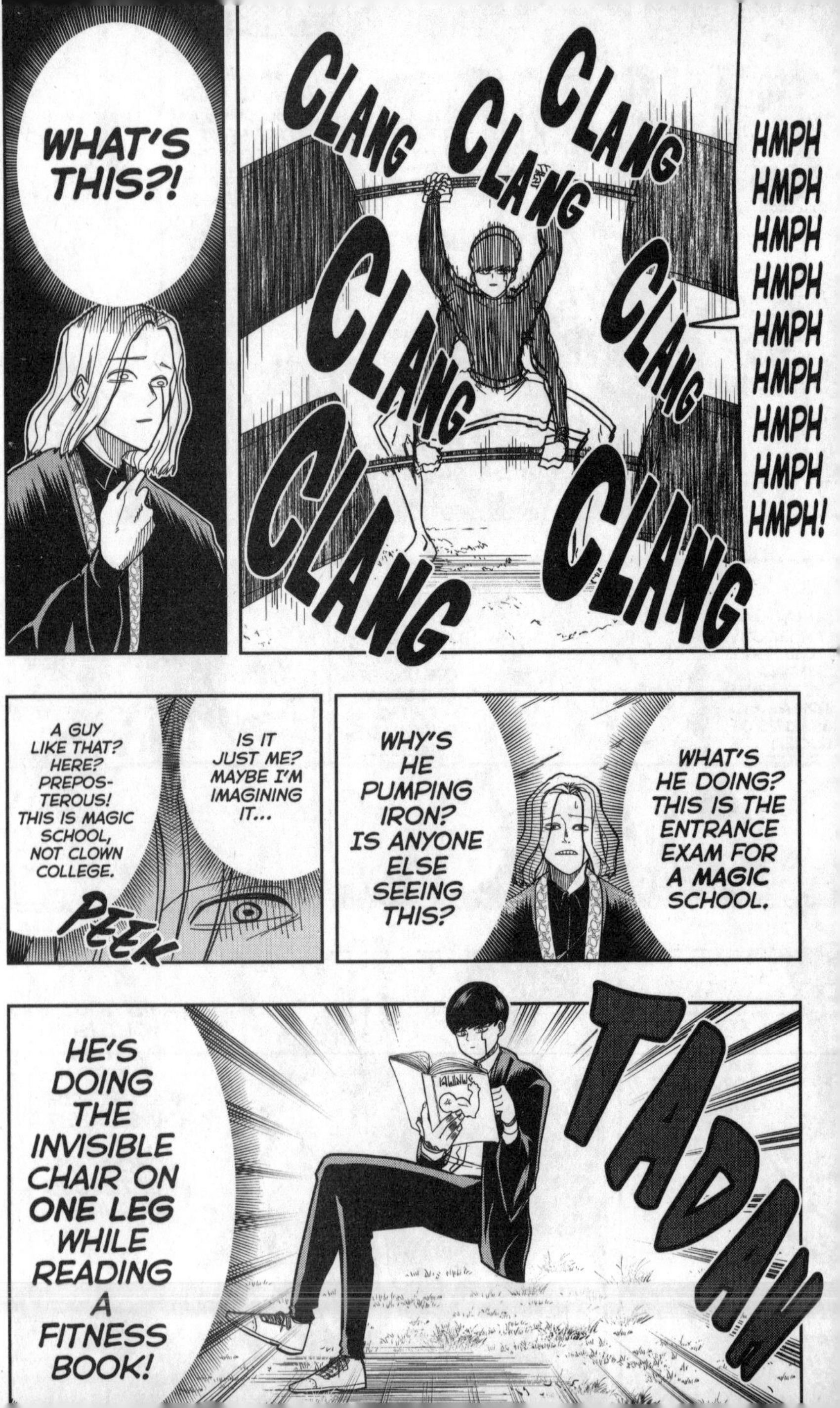
CLANG
CLANG
CLANG
CLANG
CLANG
CLANG
HMPH HMPH HMPH HMPH HMPH HMPH HMPH HMPH HMPH!
WHAT'S THIS?!
WHAT'S HE DOING? THIS IS THE ENTRANCE EXAM FOR A MAGIC SCHOOL.
WHY'S HE PUMPING IRON? IS ANYONE ELSE SEEING THIS?
IS IT JUST ME? MAYBE I'M IMAGINING IT...
A GUY LIKE THAT? HERE? PREPOS-TEROUS! THIS IS MAGIC SCHOOL, NOT CLOWN COLLEGE.
PEEK
TADAH
HE'S DOING THE INVISIBLE CHAIR ON ONE LEG WHILE READING A FITNESS BOOK!

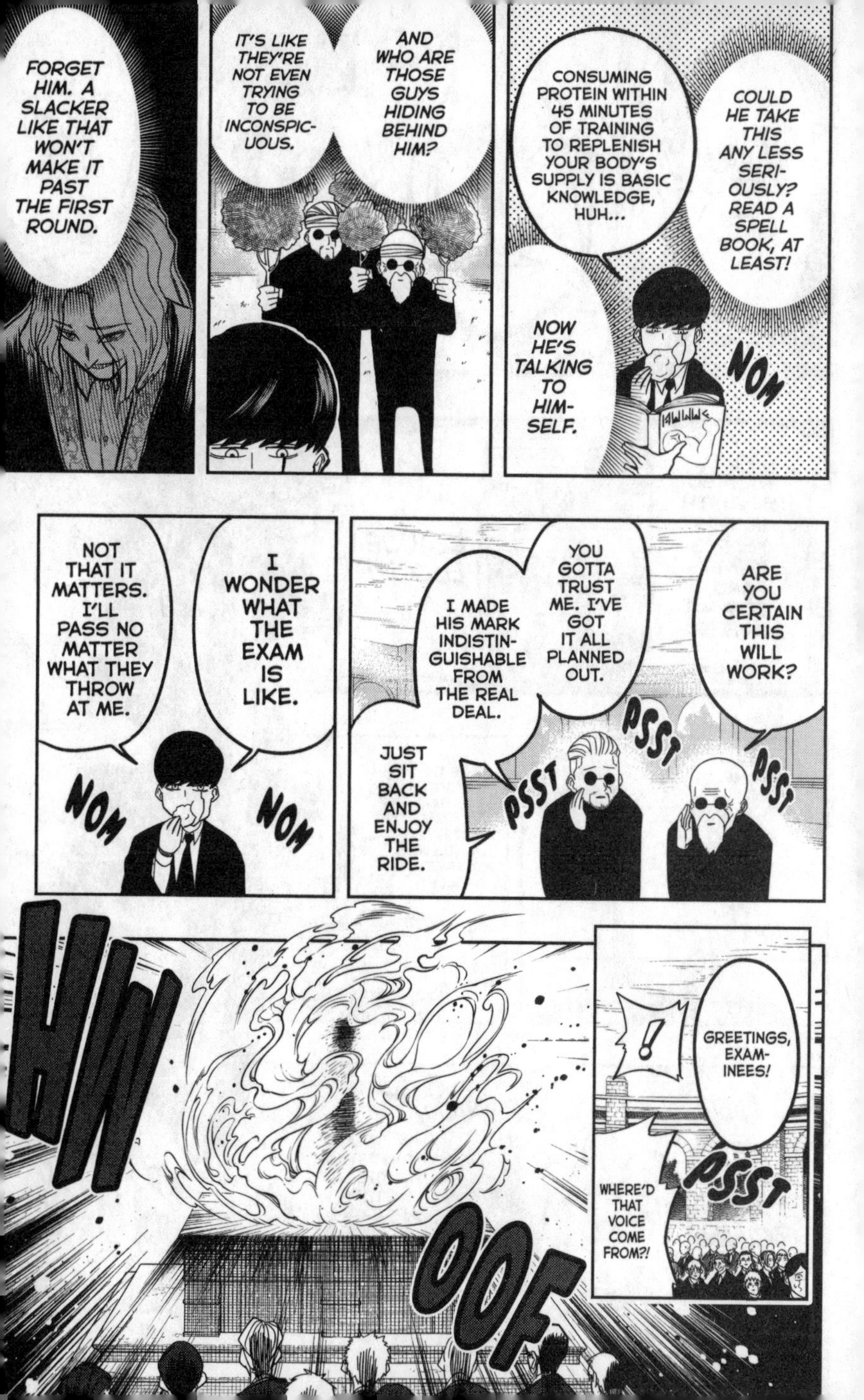
COULD HE TAKE THIS ANY LESS SERI-OUSLY? READ A SPELL BOOK, AT LEAST!
CONSUMING PROTEIN WITHIN 45 MINUTES OF TRAINING TO REPLENISH YOUR BODY'S SUPPLY IS BASIC KNOWLEDGE, HUH...
NOM
NOW HE'S TALKING TO HIM-SELF.
AND WHO ARE THOSE GUYS HIDING BEHIND HIM?
IT'S LIKE THEY'RE NOT EVEN TRYING TO BE INCONSPIC-UOUS.
FORGET HIM. A SLACKER LIKE THAT WON'T MAKE IT PAST THE FIRST ROUND.
ARE YOU CERTAIN THIS WILL WORK?
PSST
YOU GOTTA TRUST ME. I'VE GOT IT ALL PLANNED OUT.
PSST
I MADE HIS MARK INDISTIN-GUISHABLE FROM THE REAL DEAL.
PSST
JUST SIT BACK AND ENJOY THE RIDE.
I WONDER WHAT THE EXAM IS LIKE.
NOT THAT IT MATTERS. I'LL PASS NO MATTER WHAT THEY THROW AT ME.
NOM
NOM
GREETINGS, EXAM-INEES!
!
PSST
WHERE'D THAT VOICE COME FROM?!
OOF

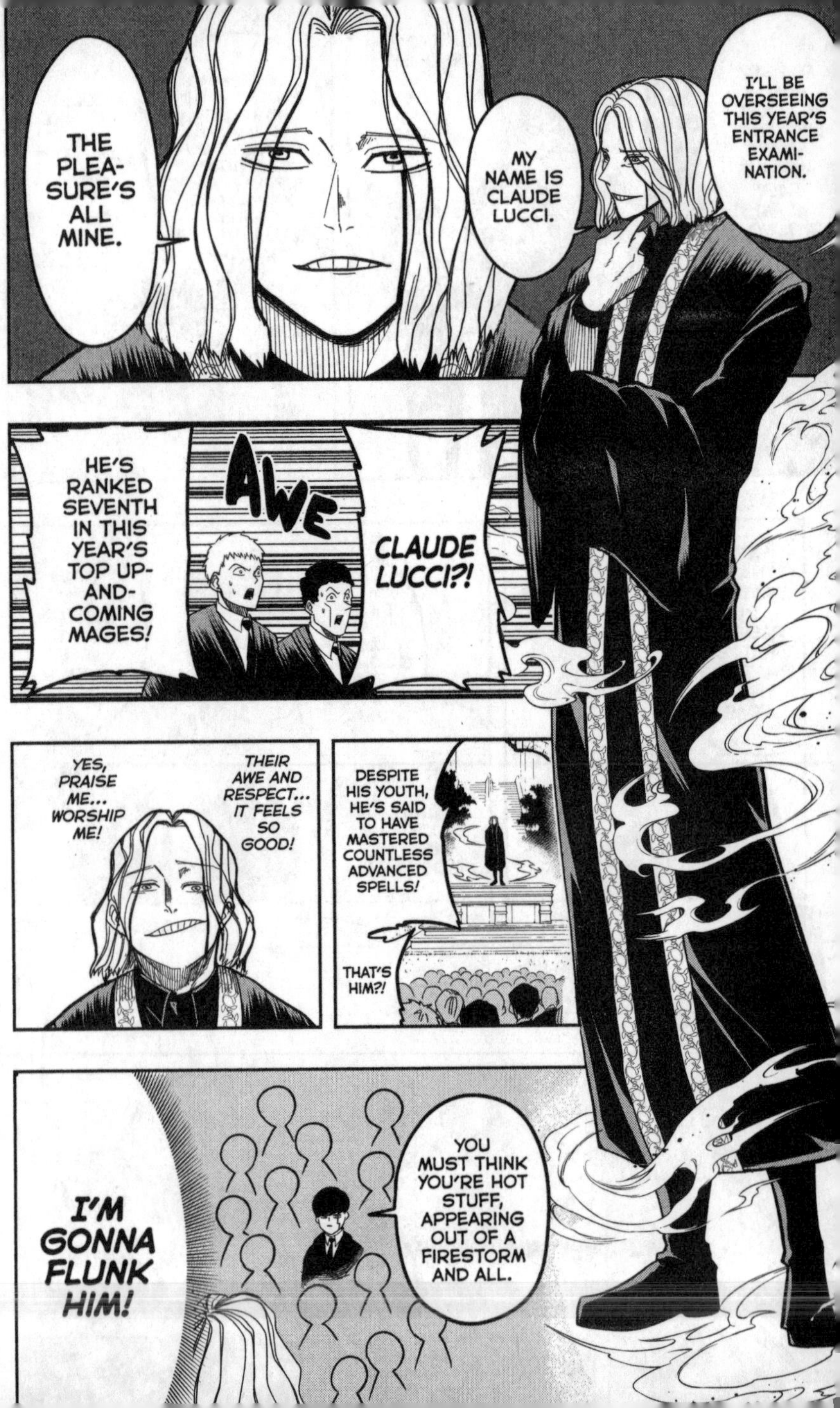
I'LL BE OVERSEEING THIS YEAR'S ENTRANCE EXAMI-NATION.
MY NAME IS CLAUDE LUCCI.
THE PLEA-SURE'S ALL MINE.
CLAUDE LUCCI?!
AWE
HE'S RANKED SEVENTH IN THIS YEAR'S TOP UP-AND-COMING MAGES!
DESPITE HIS YOUTH, HE'S SAID TO HAVE MASTERED COUNTLESS ADVANCED SPELLS!
THAT'S HIM?!
THEIR AWE AND RESPECT... IT FEELS SO GOOD!
YES, PRAISE ME... WORSHIP ME!
YOU MUST THINK YOU'RE HOT STUFF, APPEARING OUT OF A FIRESTORM AND ALL.
I'M GONNA FLUNK HIM!

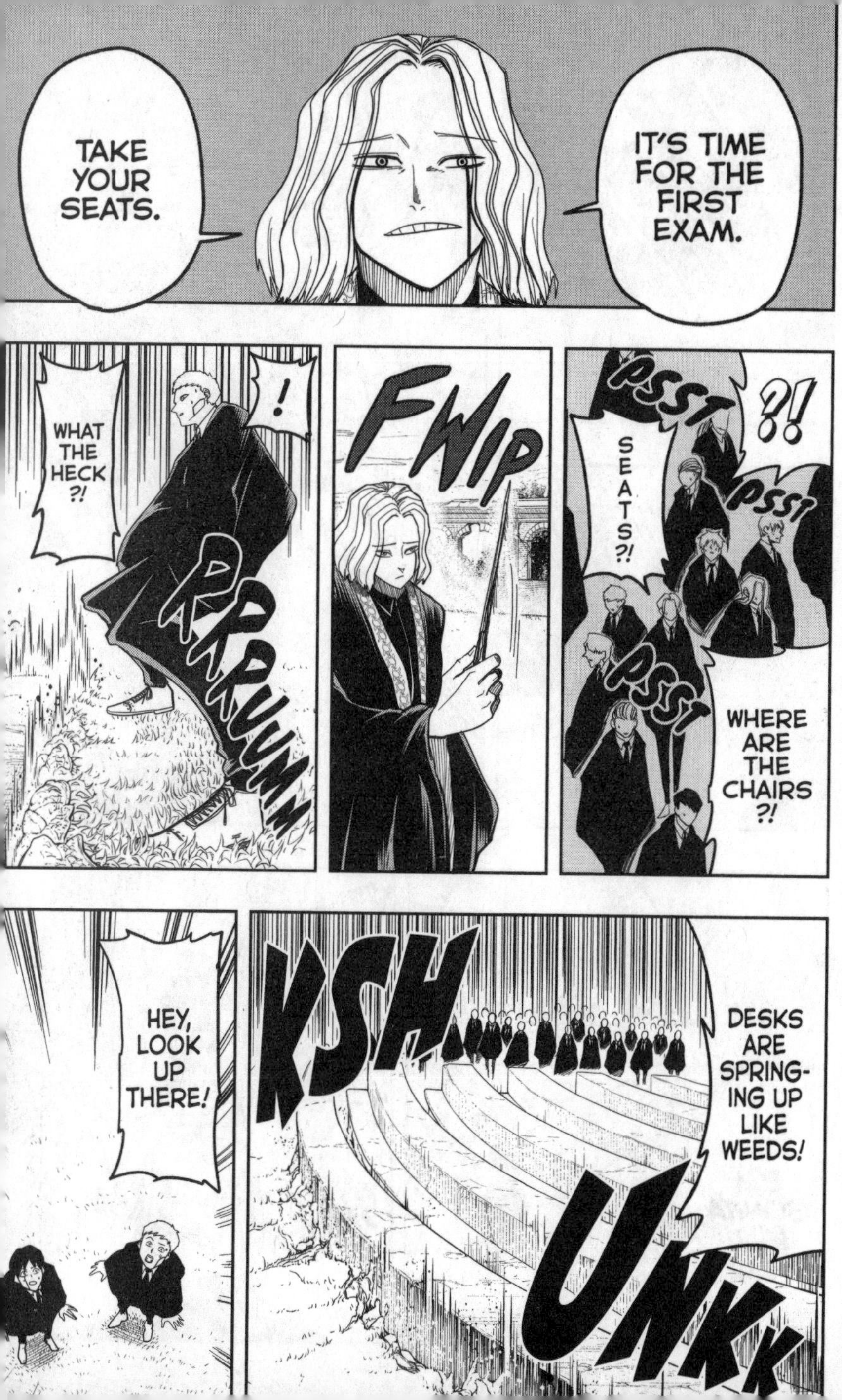
IT'S TIME FOR THE FIRST EXAM.
TAKE YOUR SEATS.
?!
PSST
PSST
SEATS?!
PSST
WHERE ARE THE CHAIRS?!
FWIP
!
WHAT THE HECK?!
RRRUMMM
KSH
DESKS ARE SPRING-ING UP LIKE WEEDS!
UNKK
HEY, LOOK UP THERE!

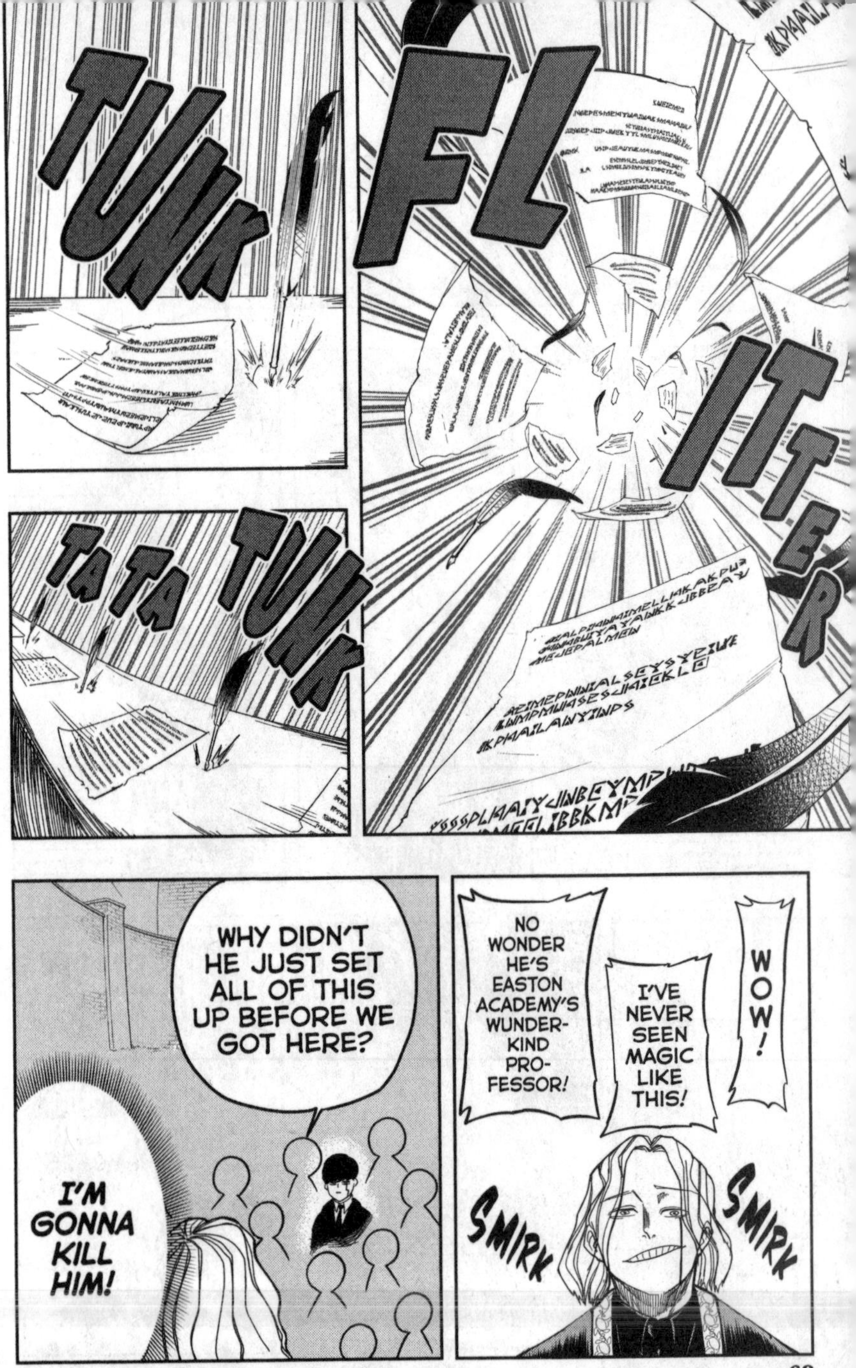
FLITTER
TUNK
TA TA TUNK
WOW!
I'VE NEVER SEEN MAGIC LIKE THIS!
NO WONDER HE'S EASTON ACADEMY'S WUNDER-KIND PRO-FESSOR!
SMIRK SMIRK
WHY DIDN'T HE JUST SET ALL OF THIS UP BEFORE WE GOT HERE?
I'M GONNA KILL HIM!

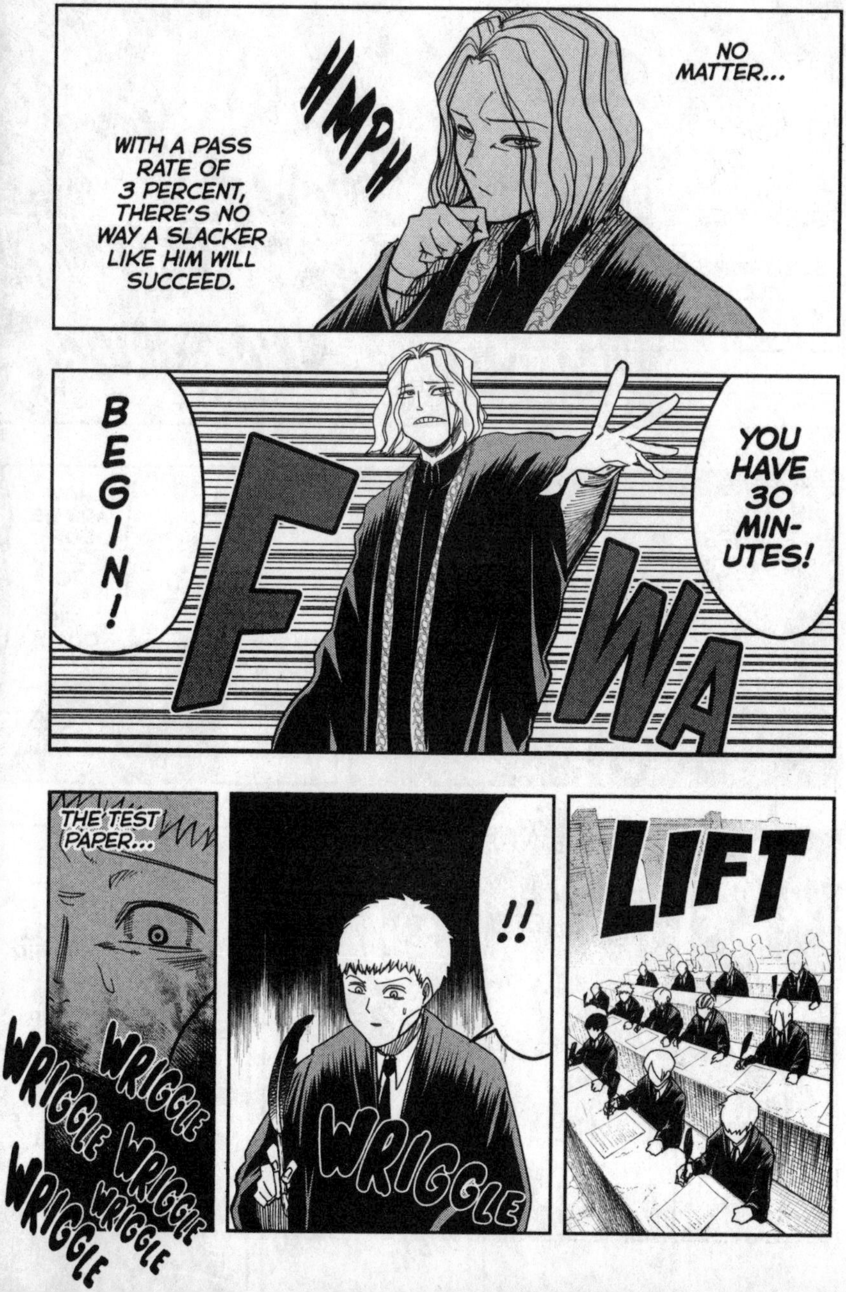
NO MATTER...
HMPH
WITH A PASS RATE OF 3 PERCENT, THERE'S NO WAY A SLACKER LIKE HIM WILL SUCCEED.
YOU HAVE 30 MIN-UTES!
FWA
BEGIN!
LIFT
!!
WRIGGLE
THE TEST PAPER...
WRIGGLE
WRIGGLE WRIGGLE
WRIGGLE
WRIGGLE

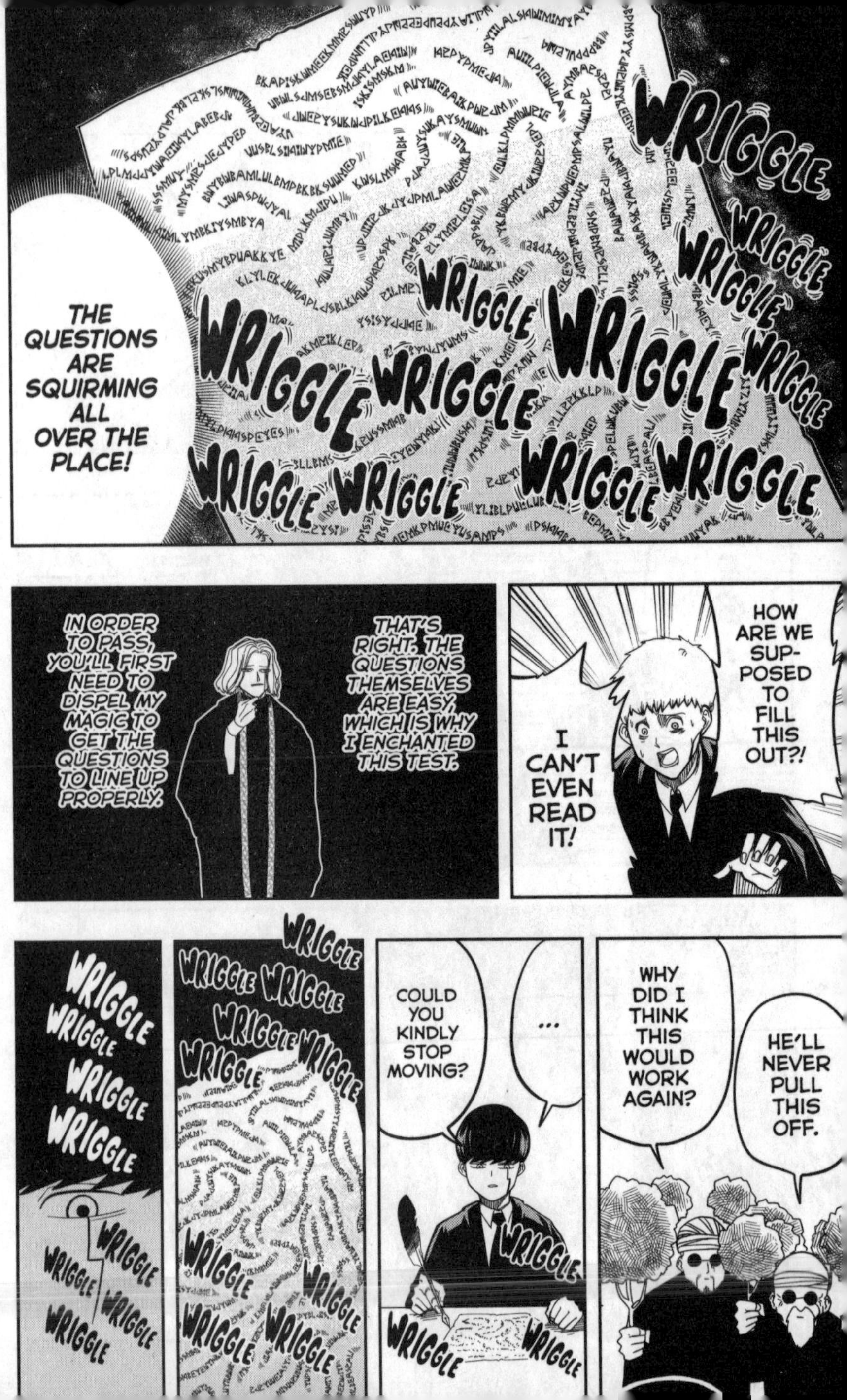
WRIGGLE
WRIGGLE
WRIGGLE
WRIGGLE
WRIGGLE
WRIGGLE
WRIGGLE
WRIGGLE
WRIGGLE
WRIGGLE
WRIGGLE
THE QUESTIONS ARE SQUIRMING ALL OVER THE PLACE!
HOW ARE WE SUP-POSED TO FILL THIS OUT?!
I CAN'T EVEN READ IT!
THAT'S RIGHT. THE QUESTIONS THEMSELVES ARE EASY, WHICH IS WHY I ENCHANTED THIS TEST.
IN ORDER TO PASS, YOU'LL FIRST NEED TO DISPEL MY MAGIC TO GET THE QUESTIONS TO LINE UP PROPERLY.
HE'LL NEVER PULL THIS OFF.
WHY DID I THINK THIS WOULD WORK AGAIN?
...
COULD YOU KINDLY STOP MOVING?
WRIGGLE
WRIGGLE
WRIGGLE
WRIGGLE
WRIGGLE
WRIGGLE
WRIGGLE
WRIGGLE
WRIGGLE
WRIGGLE
WRIGGLE
WRIGGLE
WRIGGLE
WRIGGLE
WRIGGLE
WRIGGLE
WRIGGLE
WRIGGLE
WRIGGLE

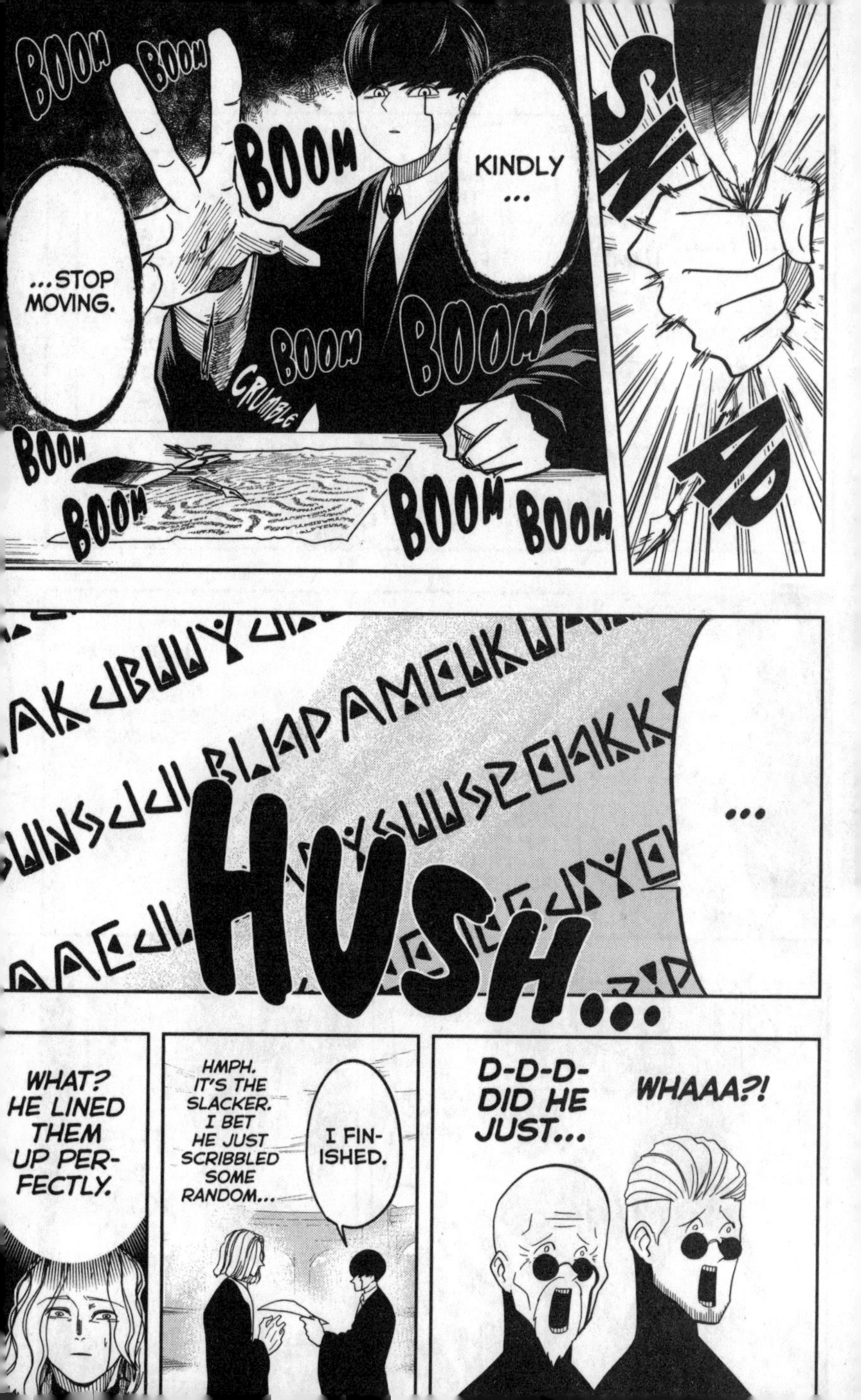
SNAP
KINDLY ...
...STOP MOVING.
BOOM BOOM
BOOM
BOOM
BOOM
CRUMBLE
BOOM
BOOM
BOOM BOOM
...
HUSH...
WHAAA?!
D-D-D-DID HE JUST...
I FIN-ISHED.
HMPH. IT'S THE SLACKER. I BET HE JUST SCRIBBLED SOME RANDOM...
WHAT? HE LINED THEM UP PER-FECTLY.

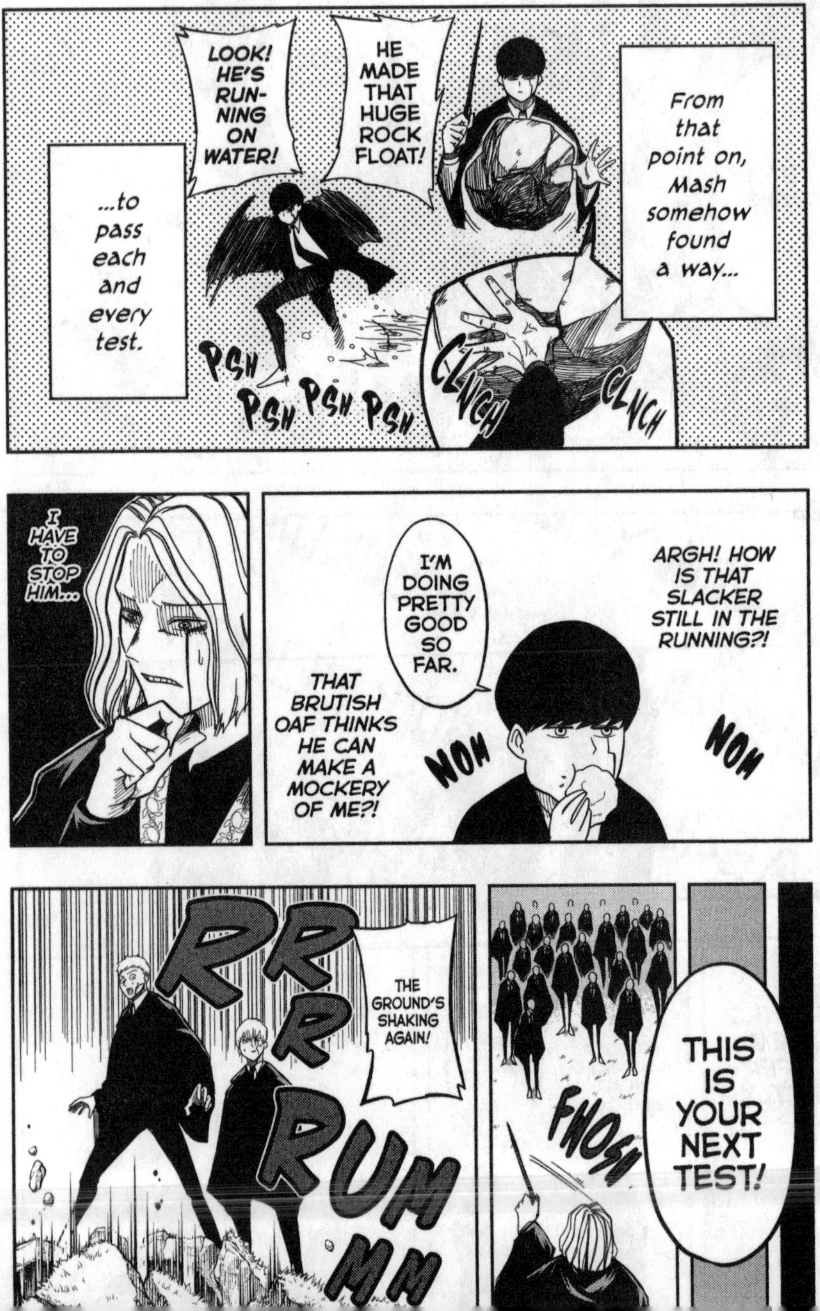
From that point on, Mash somehow found a way...
HE MADE THAT HUGE ROCK FLOAT!
LOOK! HE'S RUN-NING ON WATER!
CLNCH
CLNCH
...to pass each and every test.
PSH PSH PSH PSH
ARGH! HOW IS THAT SLACKER STILL IN THE RUNNING?!
I'M DOING PRETTY GOOD SO FAR.
NOM
THAT BRUTISH OAF THINKS HE CAN MAKE A MOCKERY OF ME?!
NOM
I HAVE TO STOP HIM...
THIS IS YOUR NEXT TEST!
FWOSH
THE GROUND'S SHAKING AGAIN!
RRRRUMMMN

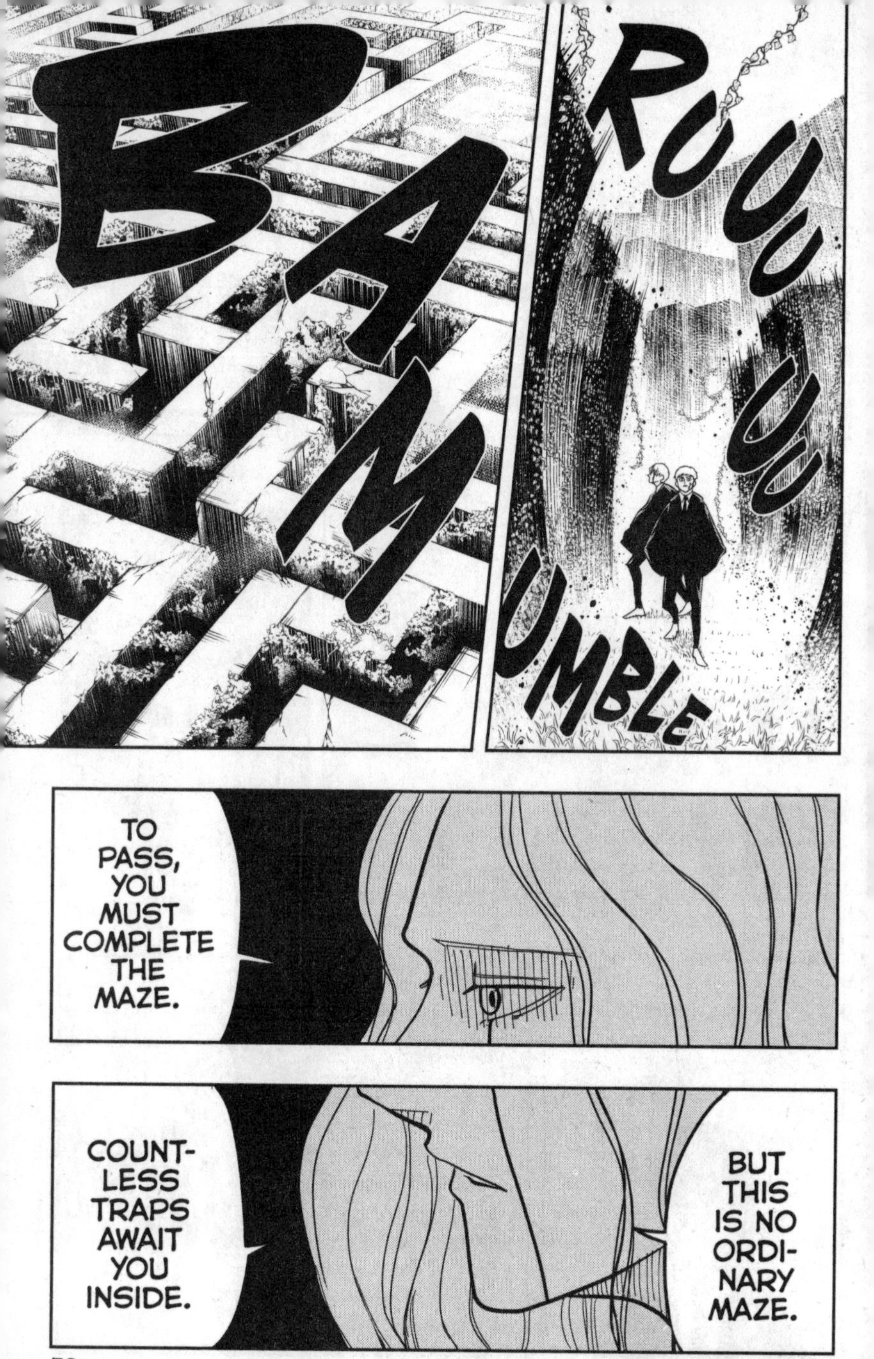
RUUUUUMBLE
BAM
TO PASS, YOU MUST COMPLETE THE MAZE.
BUT THIS IS NO ORDINARY MAZE.
COUNTLESS TRAPS AWAIT YOU INSIDE.

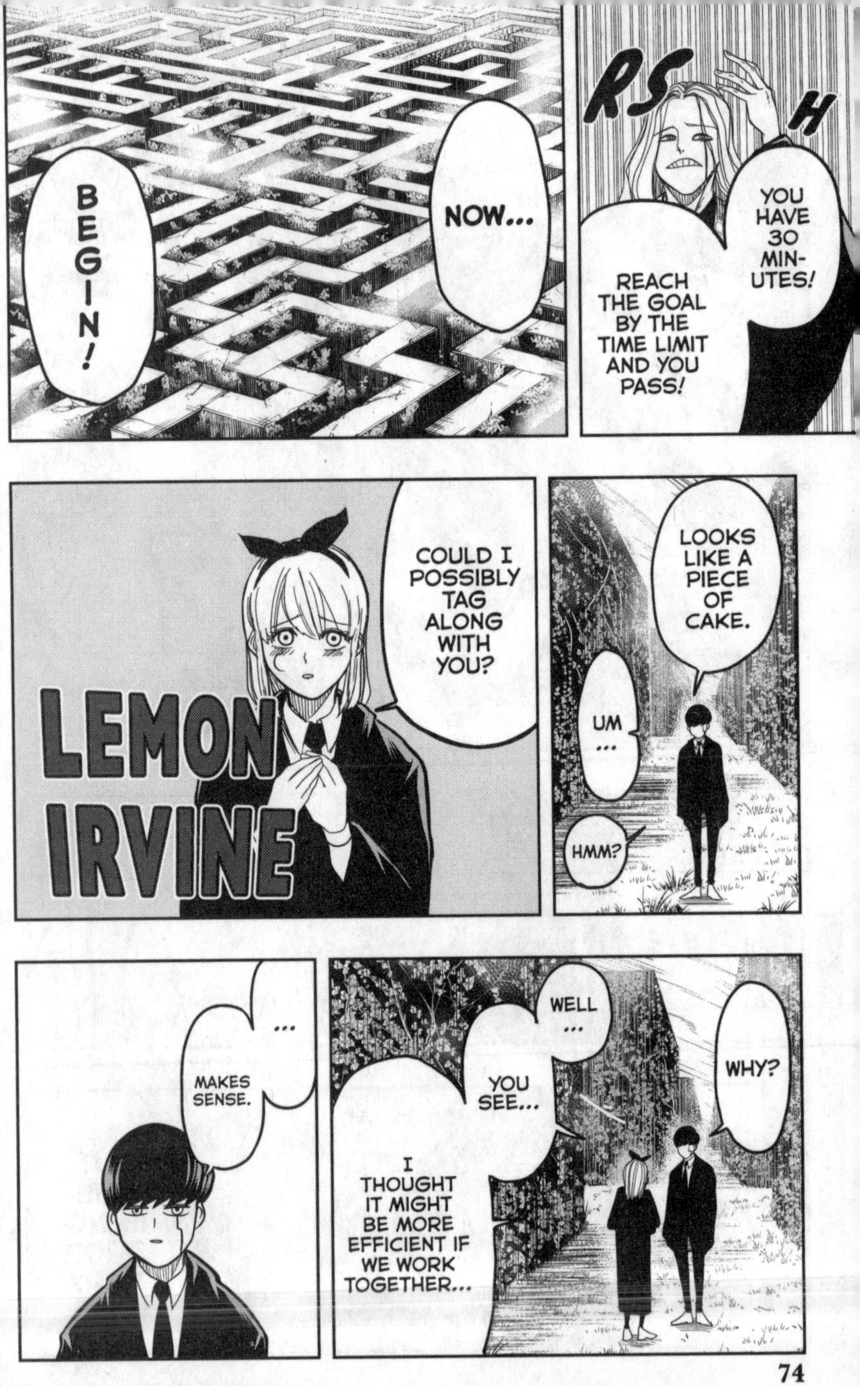
RSH
YOU HAVE 30 MIN-UTES!
REACH THE GOAL BY THE TIME LIMIT AND YOU PASS!
NOW...
BEGIN!
LOOKS LIKE A PIECE OF CAKE.
UM...
HMM?
COULD I POSSIBLY TAG ALONG WITH YOU?
LEMON IRVINE
WHY?
WELL...
YOU SEE...
I THOUGHT IT MIGHT BE MORE EFFICIENT IF WE WORK TOGETHER...
...
MAKES SENSE.

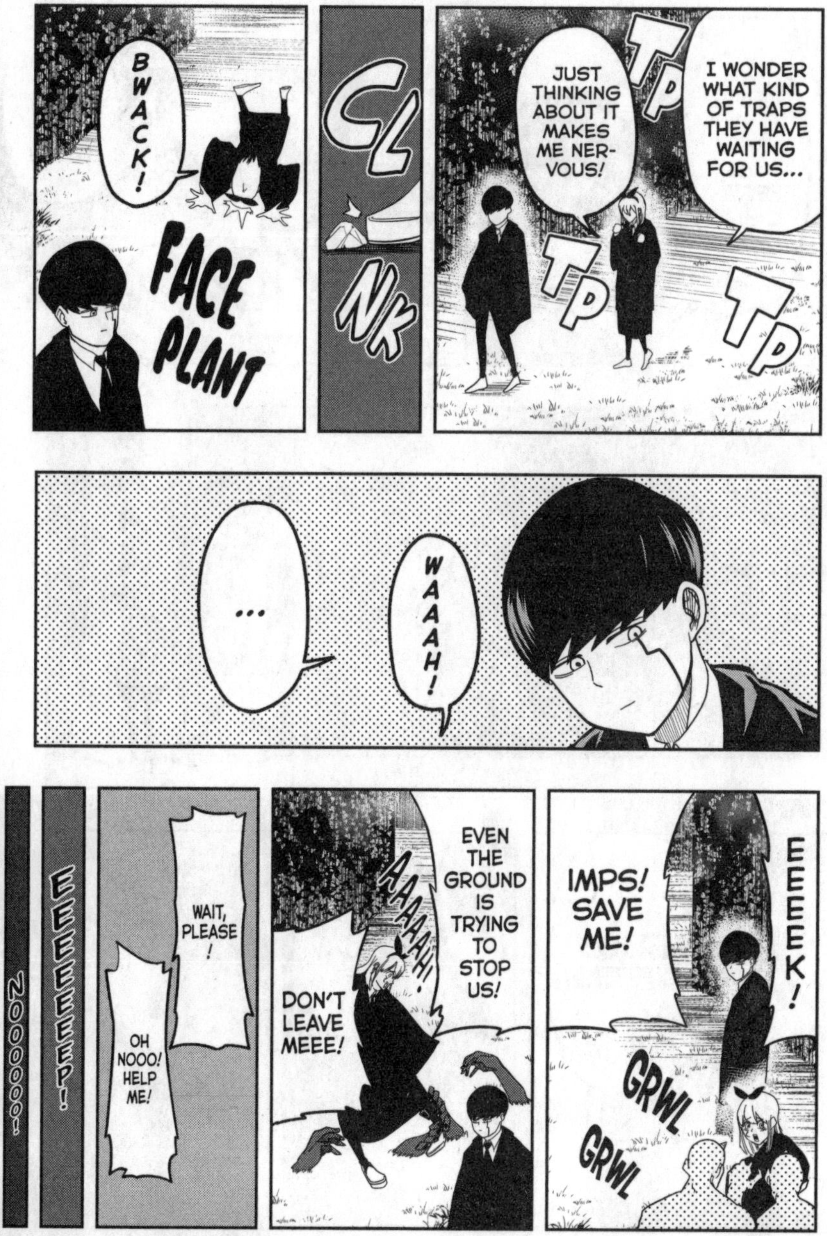
I WONDER WHAT KIND OF TRAPS THEY HAVE WAITING FOR US...
TP
JUST THINKING ABOUT IT MAKES ME NER-VOUS!
TP
TP
TP
CLNK
BWACK!
FACE PLANT
WAAAAH!
...
EEEEEK!
IMPS! SAVE ME!
GRWL
GRWL
EVEN THE GROUND IS TRYING TO STOP US!
AAAAAH!
DON'T LEAVE MEEE!
WAIT, PLEASE!
OH NOOO! HELP ME!
EEEEEEEP!
NOOOOOO!

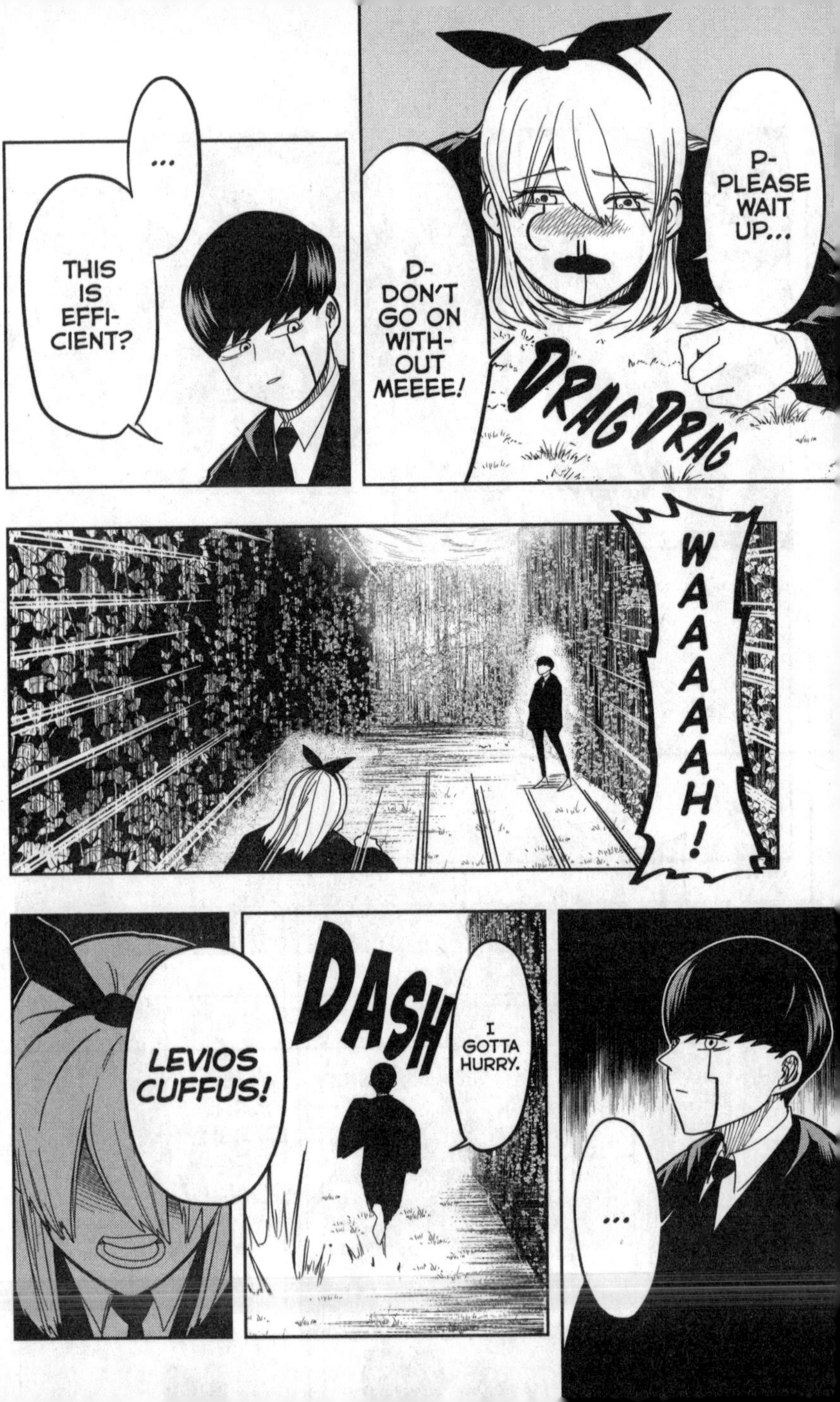
P- PLEASE WAIT UP...
D- DON'T GO ON WITH-OUT MEEEE!
DRAG DRAG
...
THIS IS EFFI-CIENT?
WAAAAAAH!
...
DASH
I GOTTA HURRY.
LEVIOS CUFFUS!

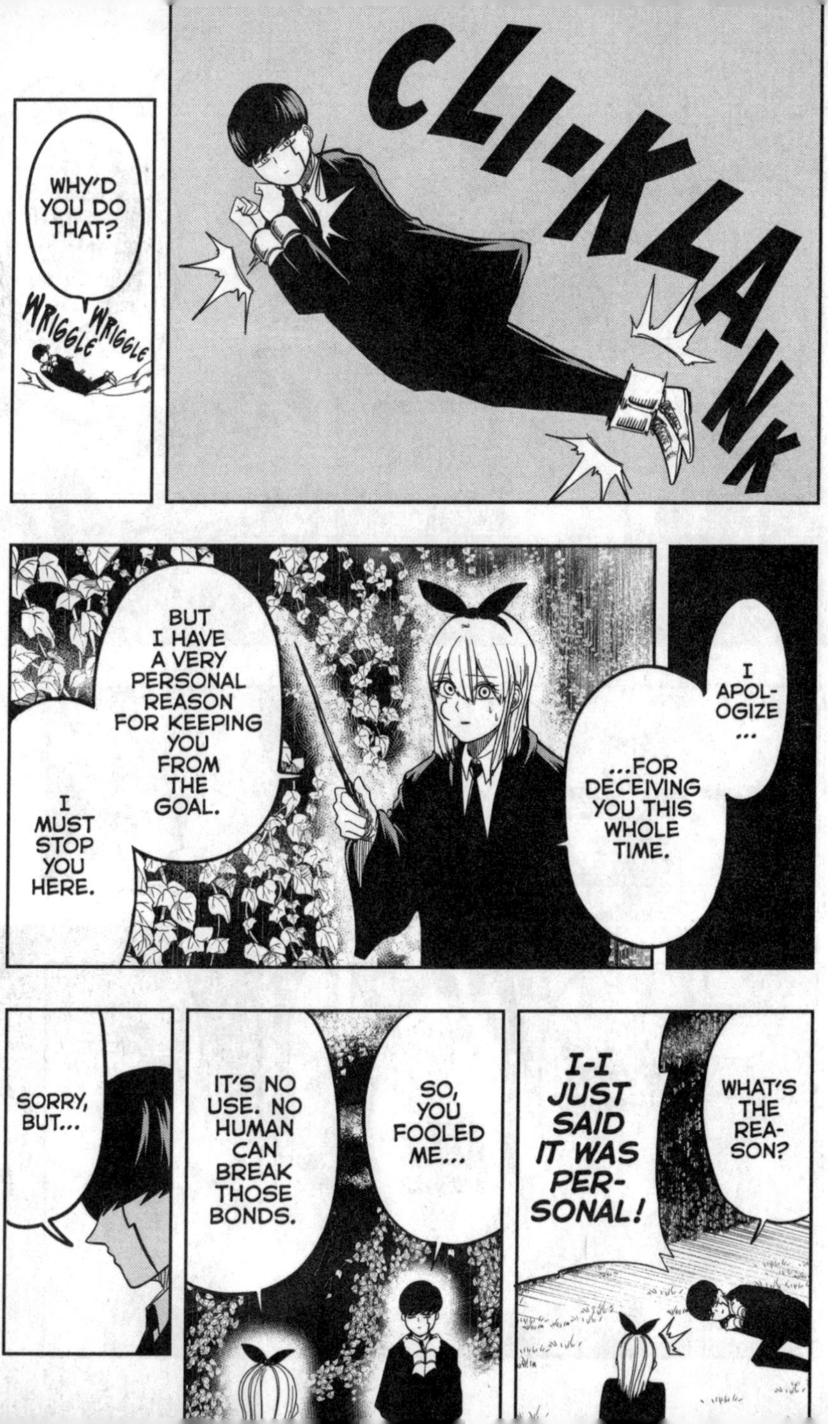
CLI-KLANK
WHY'D YOU DO THAT?
WRIGGLE WRIGGLE
I APOLOGIZE...
...FOR DECEIVING YOU THIS WHOLE TIME.
BUT I HAVE A VERY PERSONAL REASON FOR KEEPING YOU FROM THE GOAL.
I MUST STOP YOU HERE.
WHAT'S THE REA-SON?
I-I JUST SAID IT WAS PER-SONAL!
SO, YOU FOOLED ME...
IT'S NO USE. NO HUMAN CAN BREAK THOSE BONDS.
SORRY, BUT...

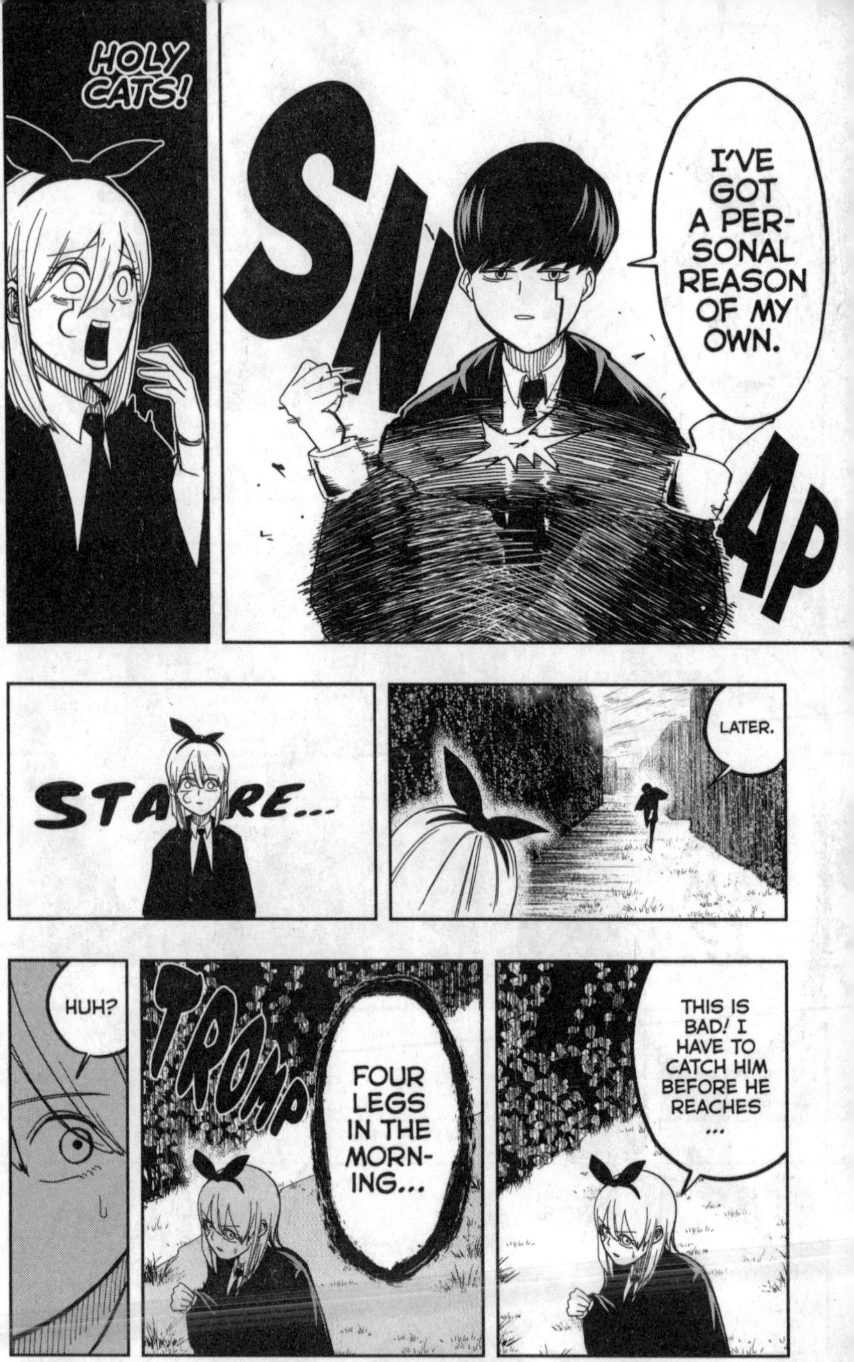
SNAP
I'VE GOT A PERSONAL REASON OF MY OWN.
HOLY CATS!
LATER.
STARE...
THIS IS BAD! I HAVE TO CATCH HIM BEFORE HE REACHES ...
FOUR LEGS IN THE MORNING...
TROMP
HUH?

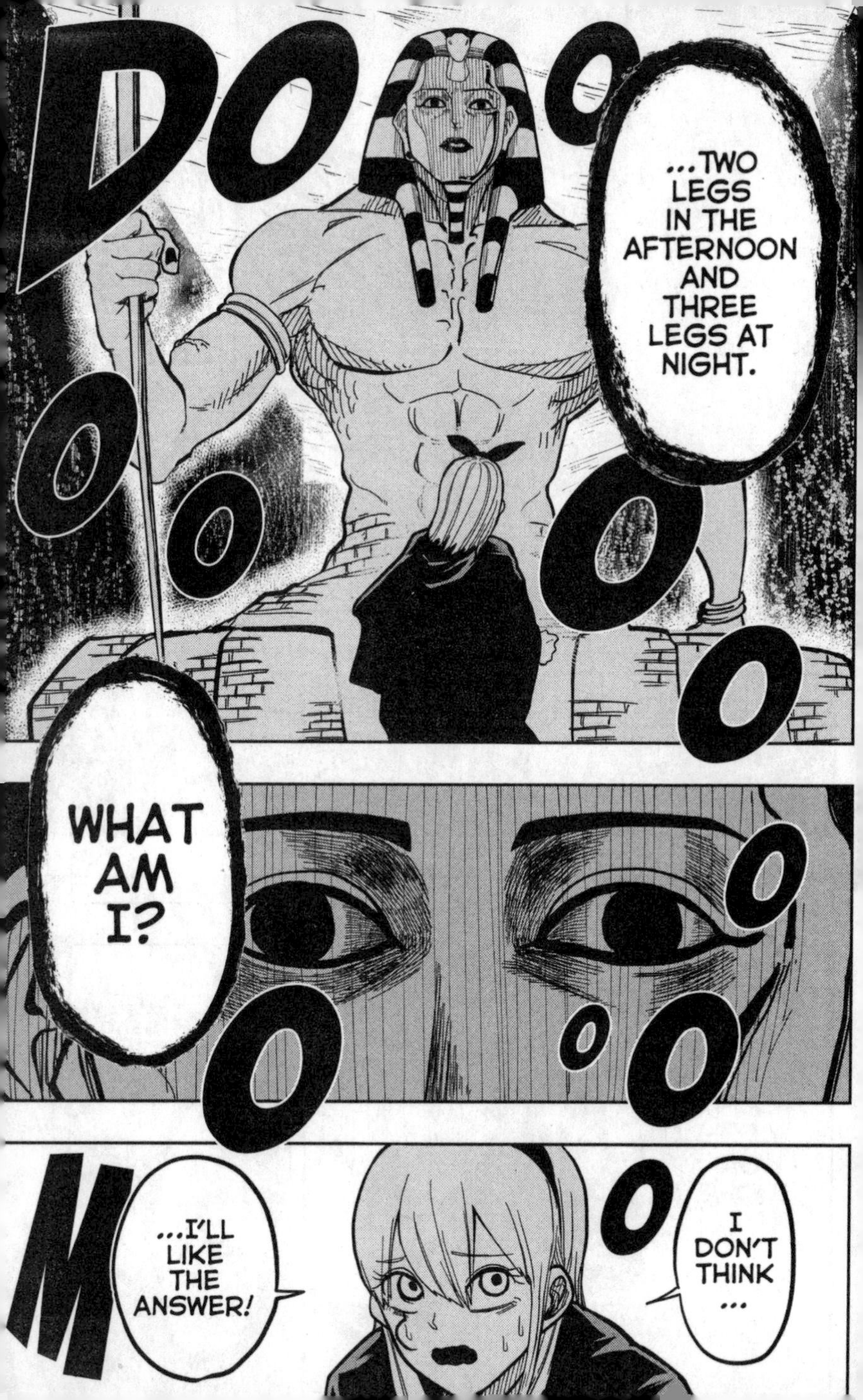
DOOOOOOOOOOOOM
...TWO LEGS IN THE AFTERNOON AND THREE LEGS AT NIGHT.
WHAT AM I?
I DON'T THINK...
...I'LL LIKE THE ANSWER!

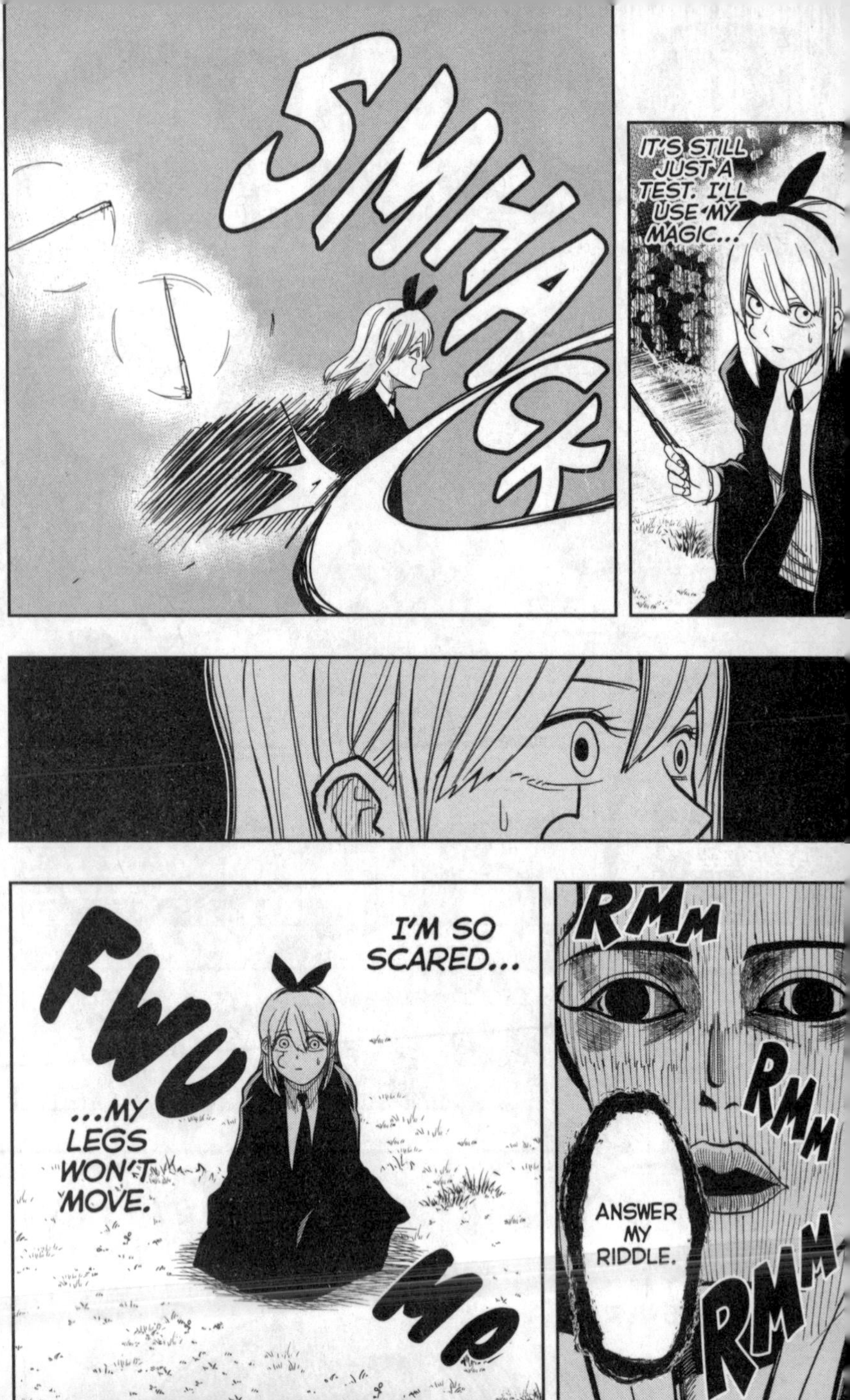
IT'S STILL JUST A TEST. I'LL USE MY MAGIC...
SMHACK
RMM RMM RMM
RMM
ANSWER MY RIDDLE.
FWUMP
I'M SO SCARED...
...MY LEGS WON'T MOVE.

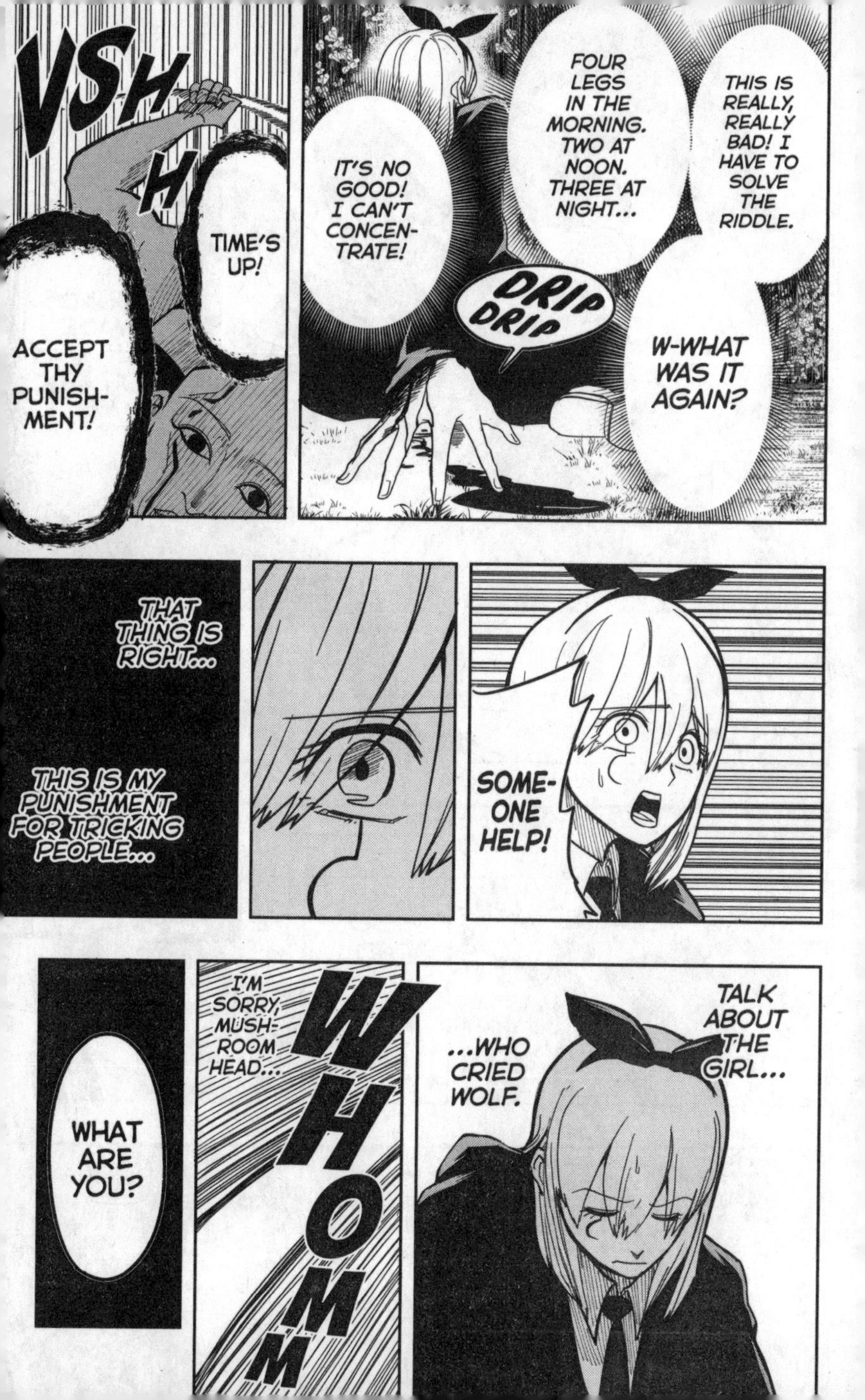
THIS IS REALLY, REALLY BAD! I HAVE TO SOLVE THE RIDDLE.
FOUR LEGS IN THE MORNING. TWO AT NOON. THREE AT NIGHT...
W-WHAT WAS IT AGAIN?
IT'S NO GOOD! I CAN'T CONCEN-TRATE!
DRIP DRIP
VSHH
TIME'S UP!
ACCEPT THY PUNISH-MENT!
SOME-ONE HELP!
THAT THING IS RIGHT...
THIS IS MY PUNISHMENT FOR TRICKING PEOPLE...
TALK ABOUT THE GIRL...
...WHO CRIED WOLF.
WHOOMMM
I'M SORRY, MUSH-ROOM HEAD...
WHAT ARE YOU?

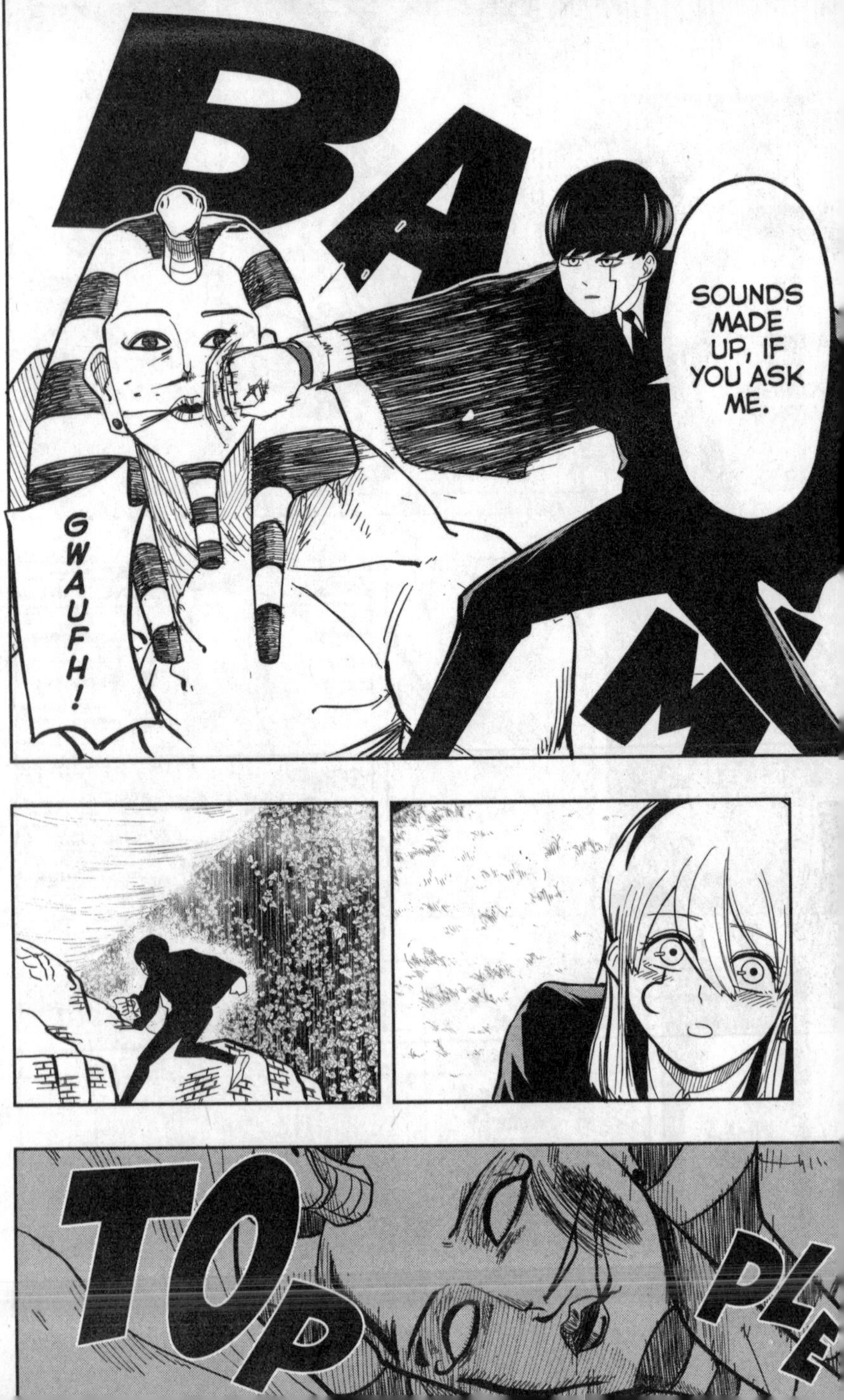
BAM
SOUNDS MADE UP, IF YOU ASK ME.
GWAUFH!
TOPPLE

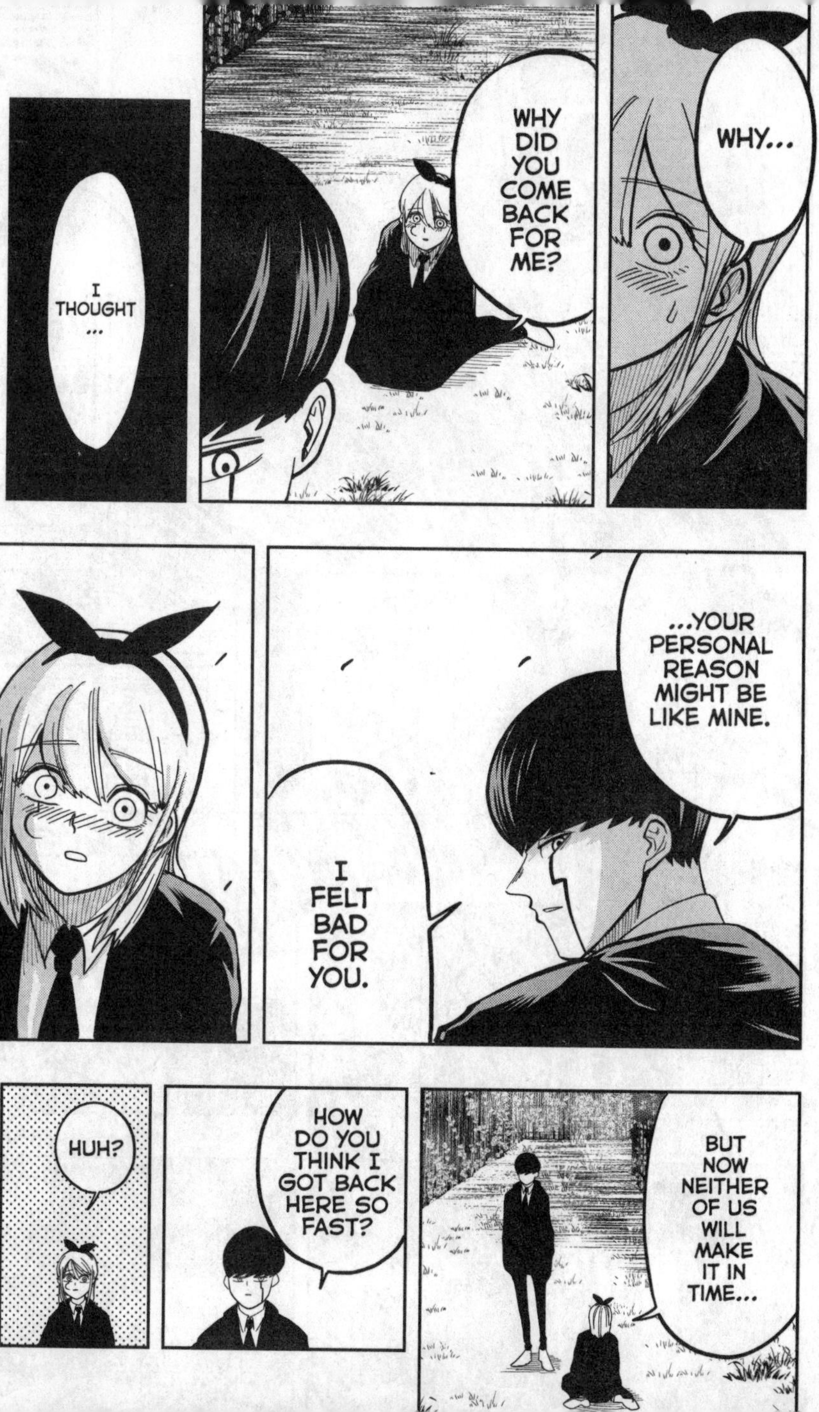
WHY...
WHY DID YOU COME BACK FOR ME?
I THOUGHT ...
...YOUR PERSONAL REASON MIGHT BE LIKE MINE.
I FELT BAD FOR YOU.
BUT NOW NEITHER OF US WILL MAKE IT IN TIME...
HOW DO YOU THINK I GOT BACK HERE SO FAST?
HUH?

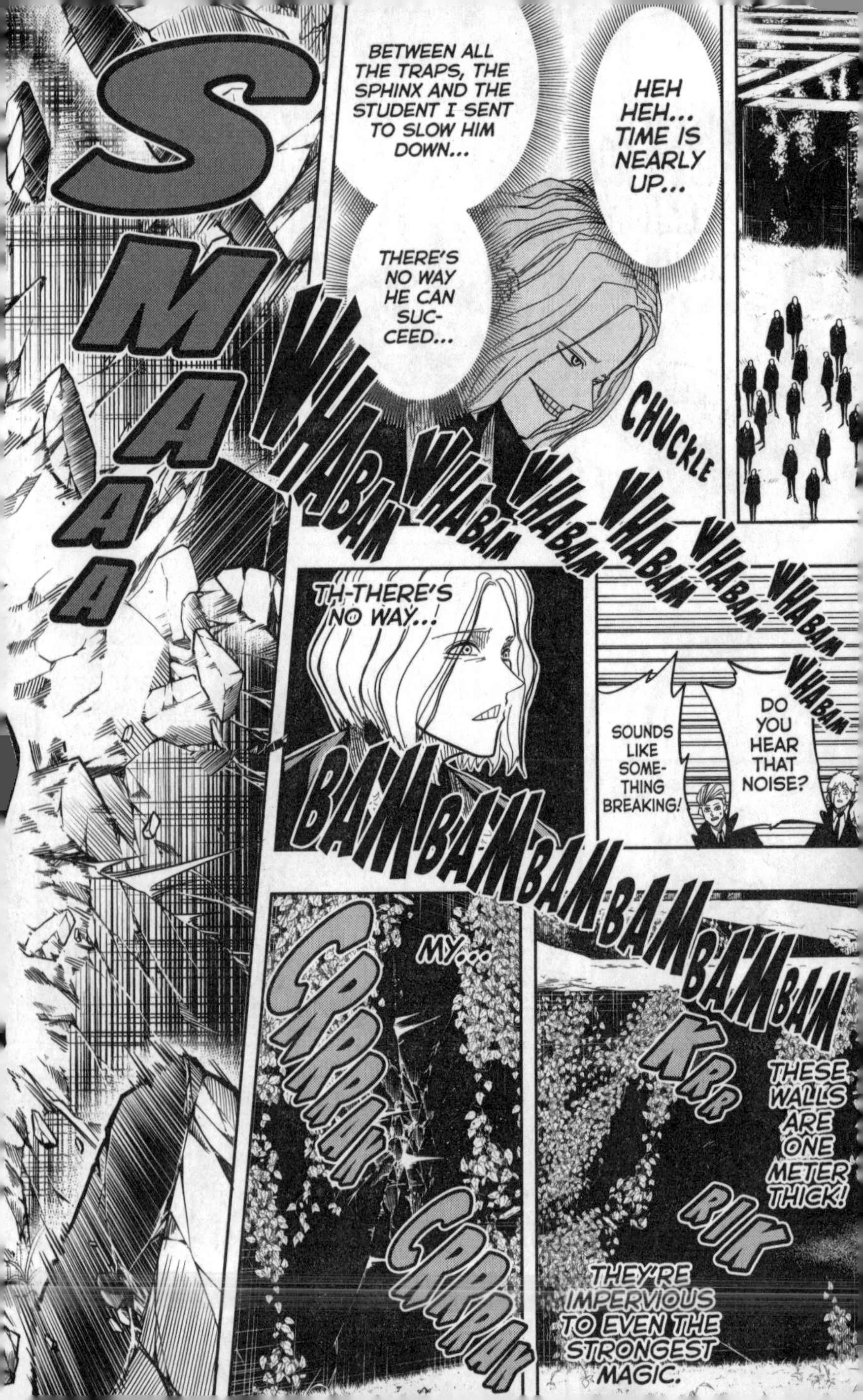
HEH HEH... TIME IS NEARLY UP...
BETWEEN ALL THE TRAPS, THE SPHINX AND THE STUDENT I SENT TO SLOW HIM DOWN...
THERE'S NO WAY HE CAN SUC- CEED...
CHUCKLE
WHABAM WHABAM WHABAM WHABAM WHABAM WHABAM WHABAM
DO YOU HEAR THAT NOISE?
SOUNDS LIKE SOME- THING BREAKING!
TH-THERE'S NO WAY...!
BAM BAM BAM BAM BAM BAM BAM BAM
THESE WALLS ARE ONE METER THICK!
KRRRIK
THEY'RE IMPERVIOUS TO EVEN THE STRONGEST MAGIC.
MY...
CRRRAK CRRRAK
SMAAAA

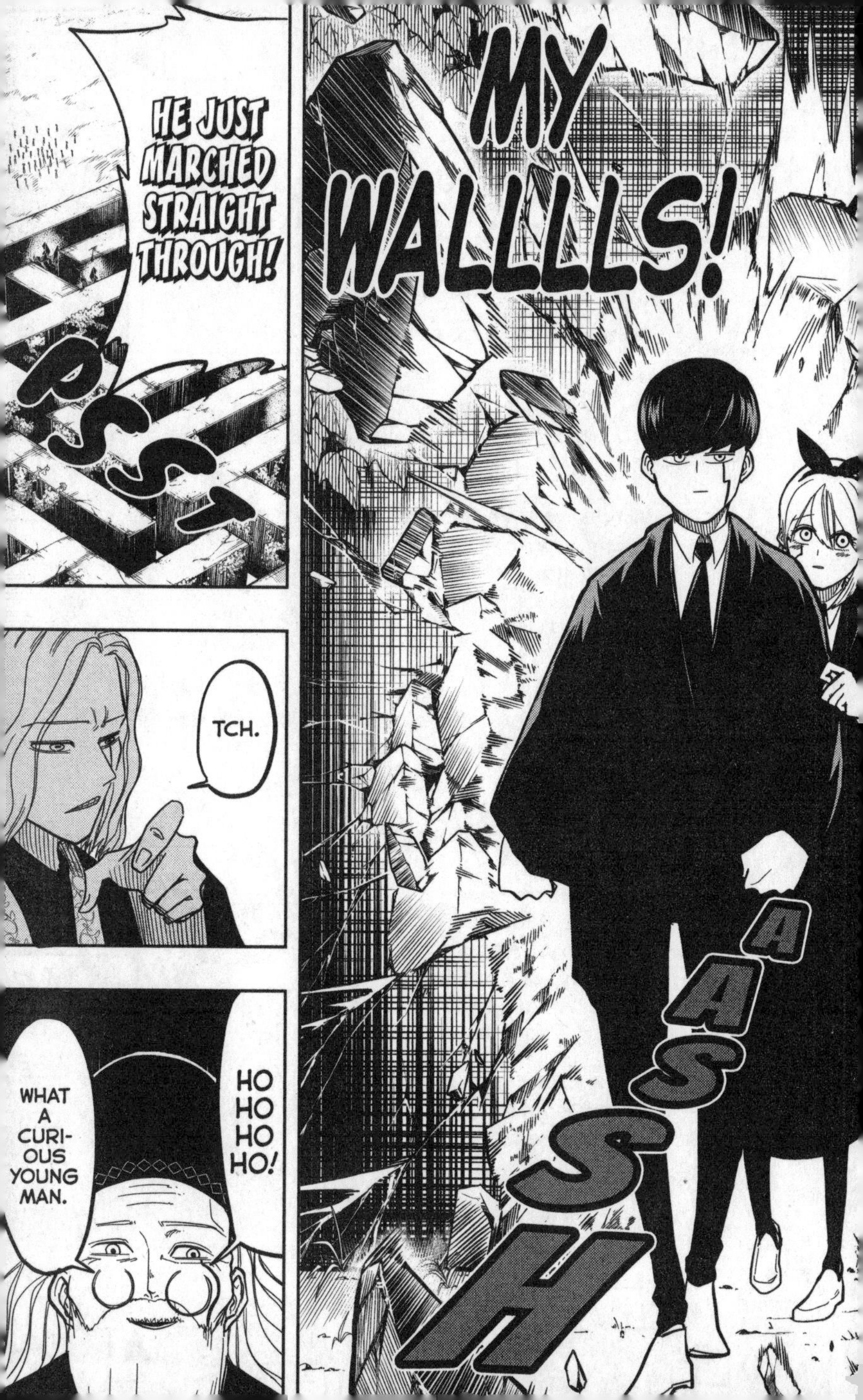
MY WALLLLS!
AASSH
HE JUST MARCHED STRAIGHT THROUGH!
PSST
TCH.
HO HO HO HO!
WHAT A CURIOUS YOUNG MAN.

The path to Weekly Jump serialization... (1)

Grade school
Be huge into Bobobo and Gintama.

↓

9th–10th grade
Aim for comedy writer and attempt the newcomer's prize multiple times. → See no results.

↓

Witness the rise of a megatalented newcomer who happens to be my age.
Fall into despair and give up.

↓ Proceed to study and enjoy clubs in the typical fashion.

4 years of college
Apply for jobs at and fail to get hired by some 40 different companies. Watch contemporaries get offers with big-name companies. Fall into a depression and go clamming.

↓

Somehow get an offer with a company.

↓

Office worker
Go to the office, ready to work.
Notice it's different than how they described in the seminar...
Realize that this is true office life...

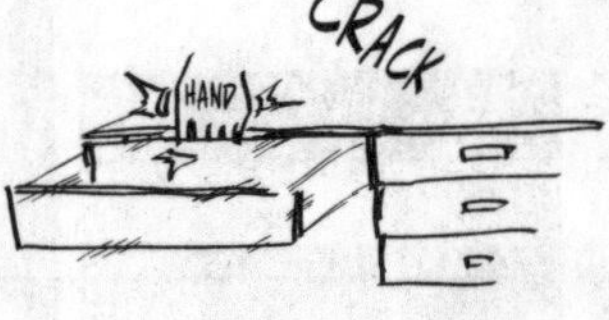
CRACK
HAND

↓

Go out to lunch with a senior employee.
Get told if you make too many mistakes, they'll use the desk as a finger guillotine on you.
Realize the dangers of office life. Decide to quit.

↓

Start searching for a future without finger guillotines...
To be continued.

CHAPTER 3: MASH BURNEDEAD AND THE DEADLY DOLL

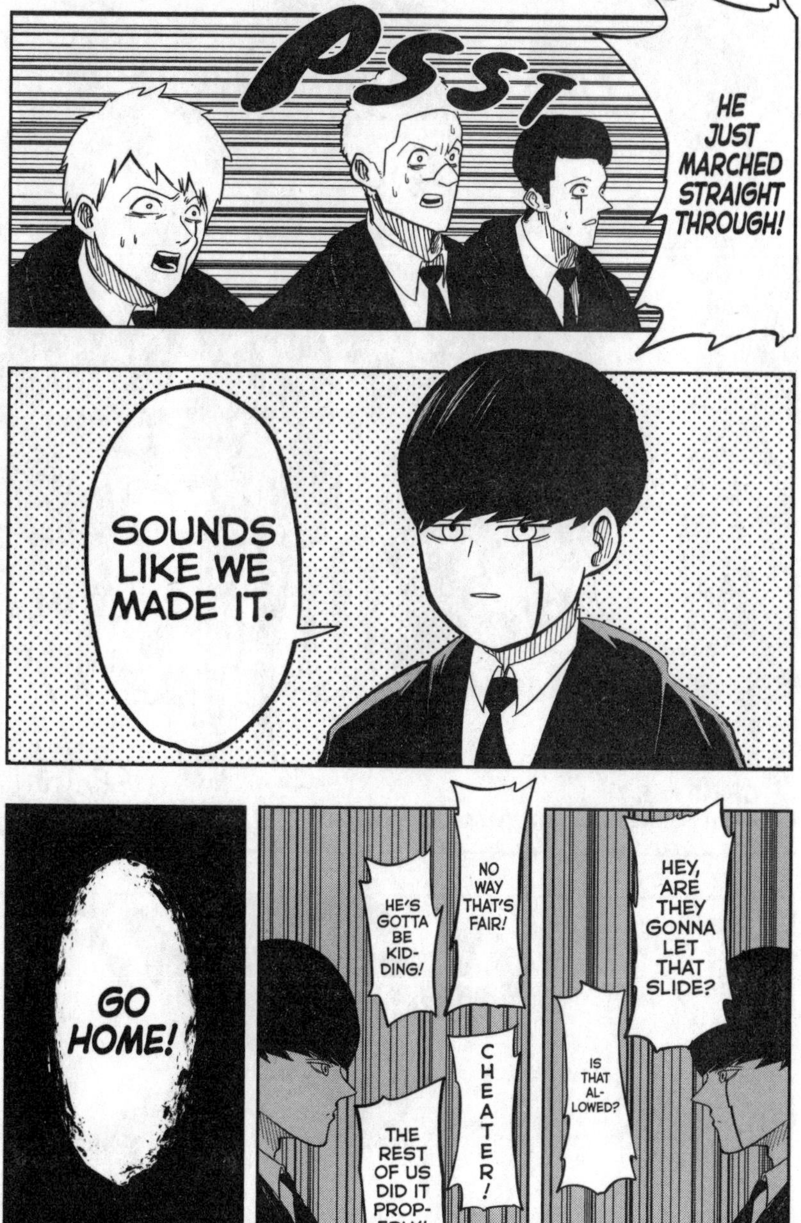
PSST
HE JUST MARCHED STRAIGHT THROUGH!
SOUNDS LIKE WE MADE IT.
HEY, ARE THEY GONNA LET THAT SLIDE?
IS THAT AL-LOWED?
NO WAY THAT'S FAIR!
HE'S GOTTA BE KID-DING!
CHEATER!
THE REST OF US DID IT PROP-ERLY!
GO HOME!

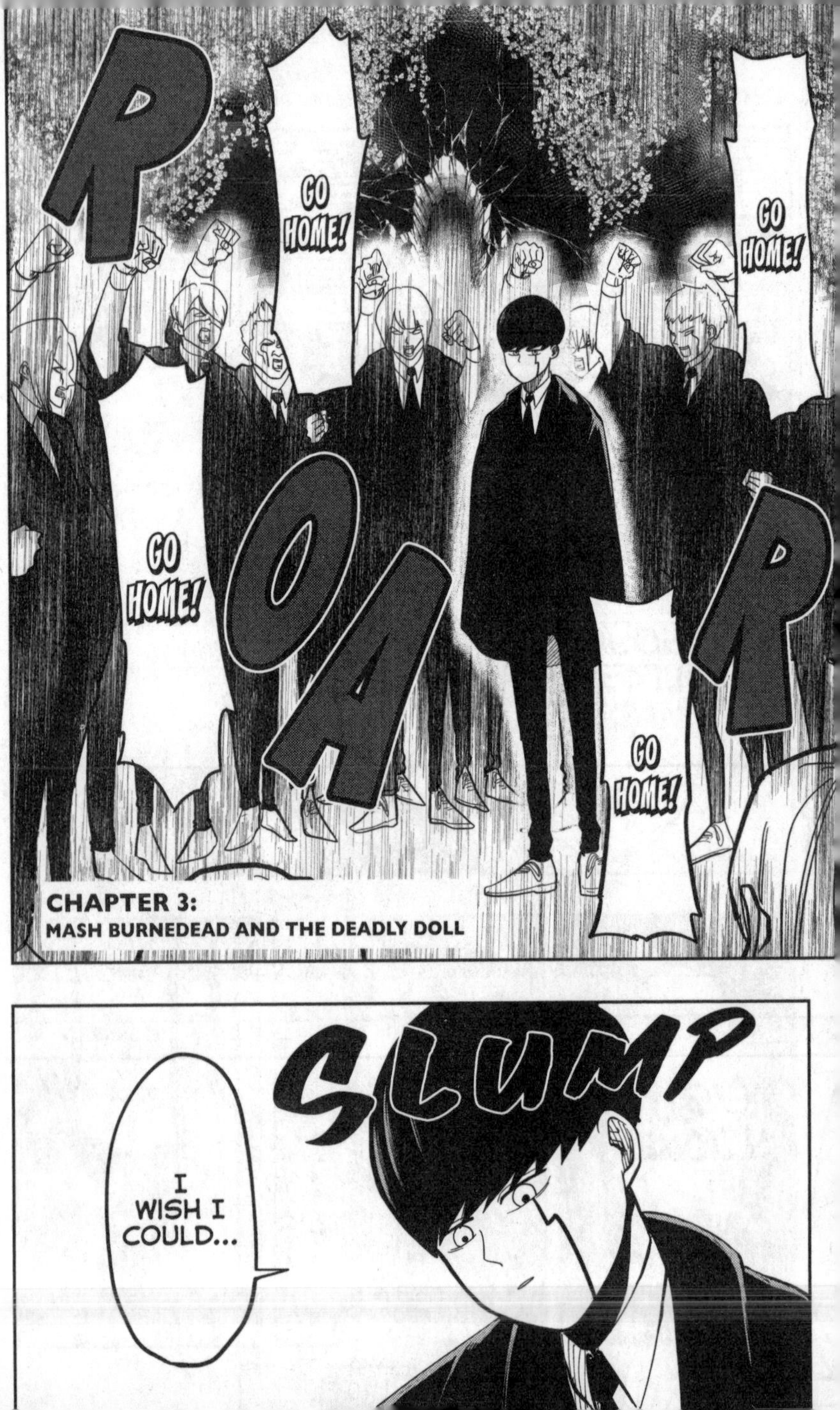
GO HOME!
GO HOME!
GO HOME!
GO HOME!
ROAR
CHAPTER 3:
MASH BURNEDEAD AND THE DEADLY DOLL
SLUMP
I WISH I COULD...

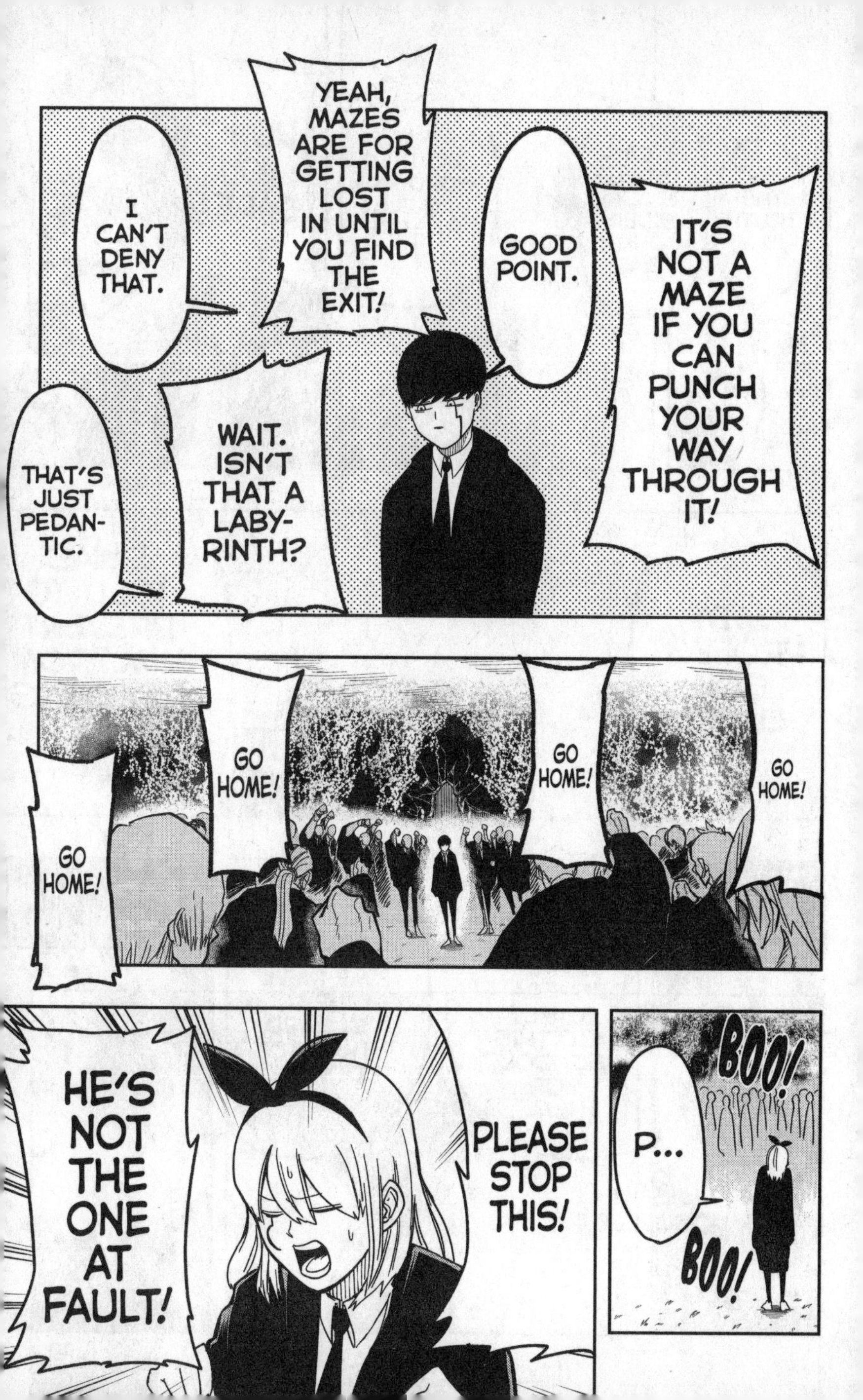
IT'S NOT A MAZE IF YOU CAN PUNCH YOUR WAY THROUGH IT!
GOOD POINT.
YEAH, MAZES ARE FOR GETTING LOST IN UNTIL YOU FIND THE EXIT!
I CAN'T DENY THAT.
WAIT. ISN'T THAT A LABY-RINTH?
THAT'S JUST PEDAN-TIC.
GO HOME!
GO HOME!
GO HOME!
GO HOME!
BOO!
P...
BOO!
PLEASE STOP THIS!
HE'S NOT THE ONE AT FAULT!

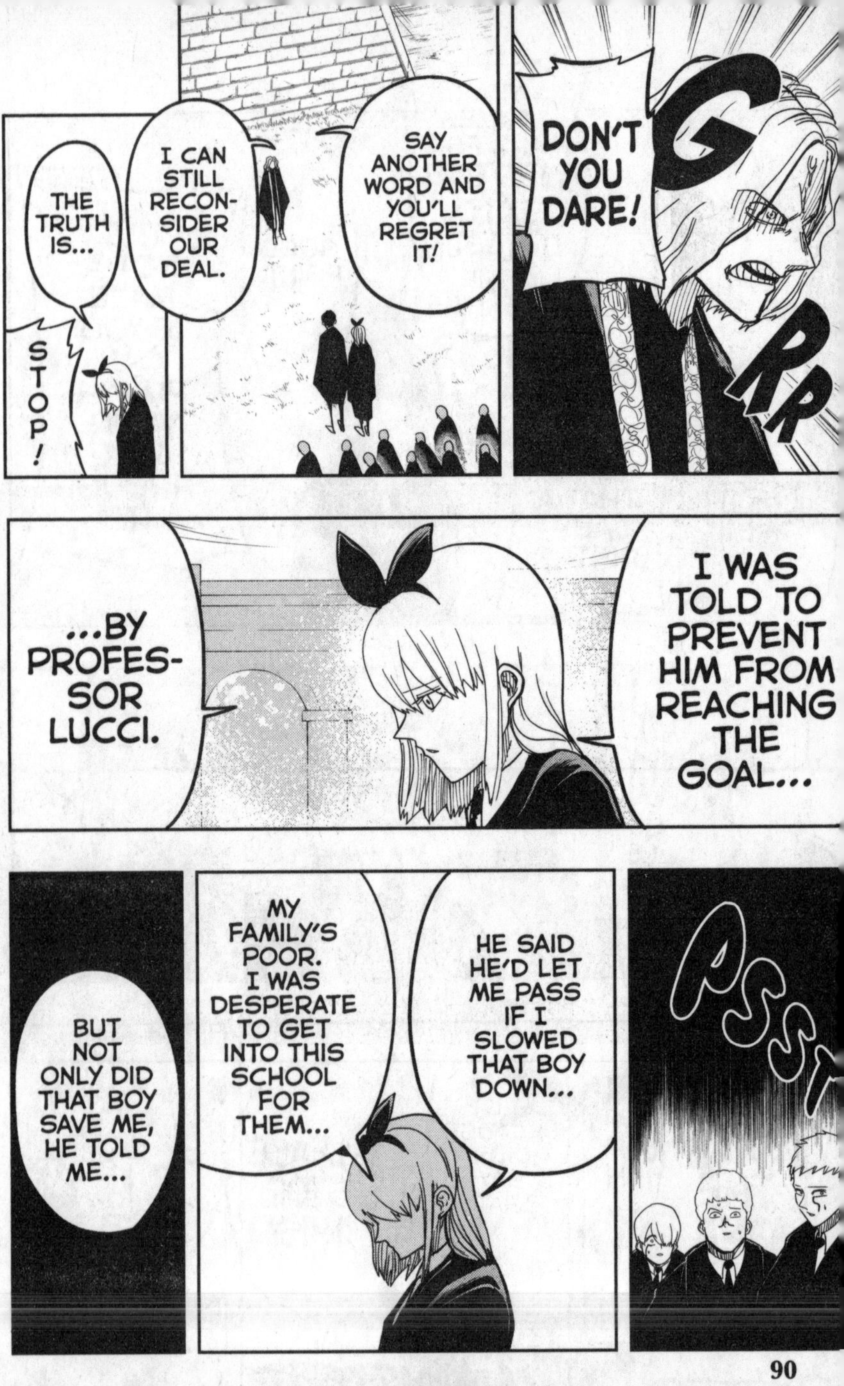
GRR
DON'T YOU DARE!
SAY ANOTHER WORD AND YOU'LL REGRET IT!
I CAN STILL RECONSIDER OUR DEAL.
THE TRUTH IS...
STOP!
I WAS TOLD TO PREVENT HIM FROM REACHING THE GOAL...
...BY PROFESSOR LUCCI.
PSST
HE SAID HE'D LET ME PASS IF I SLOWED THAT BOY DOWN...
MY FAMILY'S POOR. I WAS DESPERATE TO GET INTO THIS SCHOOL FOR THEM...
BUT NOT ONLY DID THAT BOY SAVE ME, HE TOLD ME...

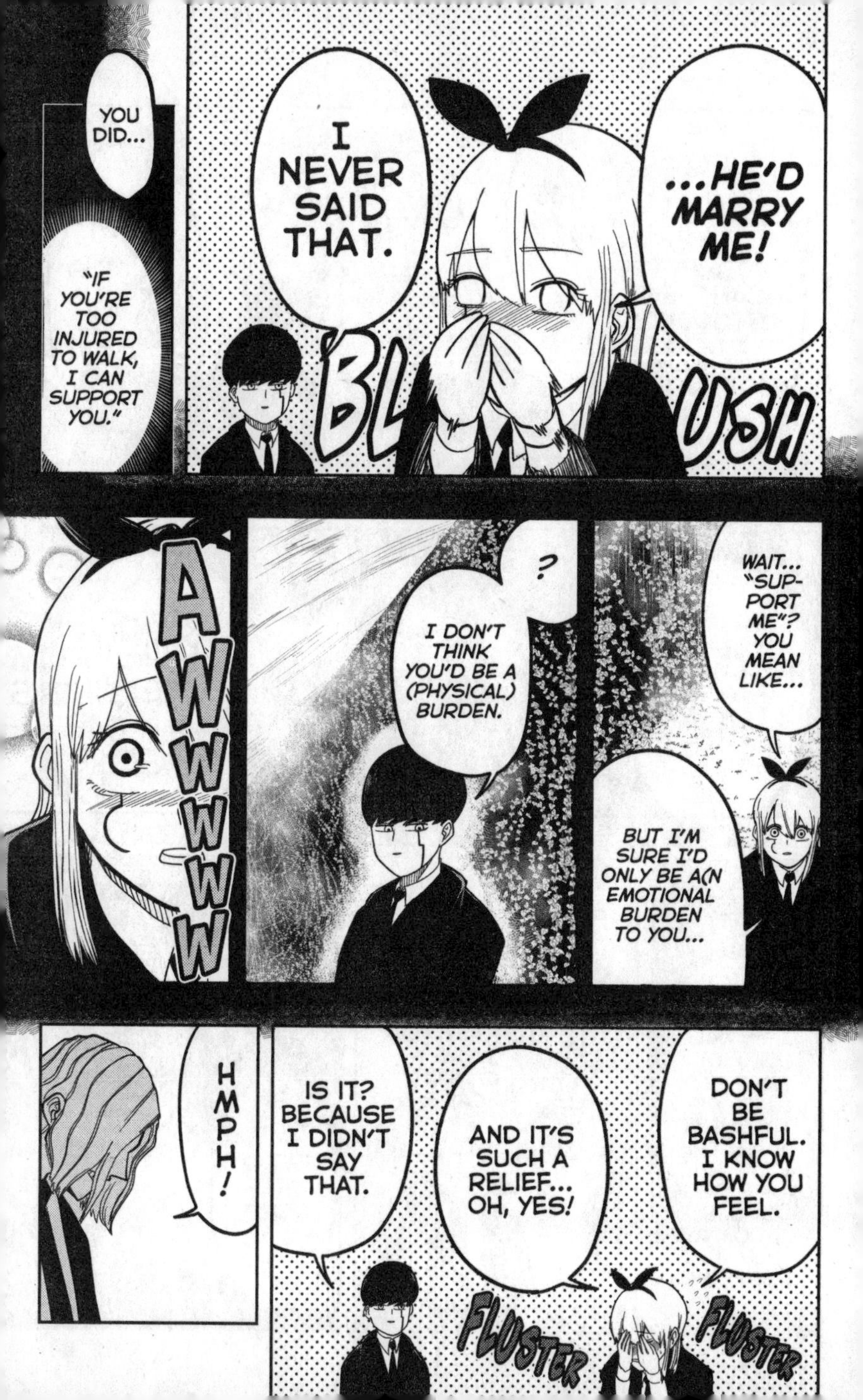
...HE'D MARRY ME!
BLUSH
I NEVER SAID THAT.
YOU DID...
“IF YOU'RE TOO INJURED TO WALK, I CAN SUPPORT YOU.”
WAIT... “SUP-PORT ME”? YOU MEAN LIKE...
BUT I'M SURE I'D ONLY BE A(N EMOTIONAL BURDEN TO YOU...
?
I DON'T THINK YOU'D BE A (PHYSICAL) BURDEN.
AWWWWWW
DON'T BE BASHFUL. I KNOW HOW YOU FEEL.
AND IT'S SUCH A RELIEF... OH, YES!
FLUSTER
FLUSTER
IS IT? BECAUSE I DIDN'T SAY THAT.
HMPH!

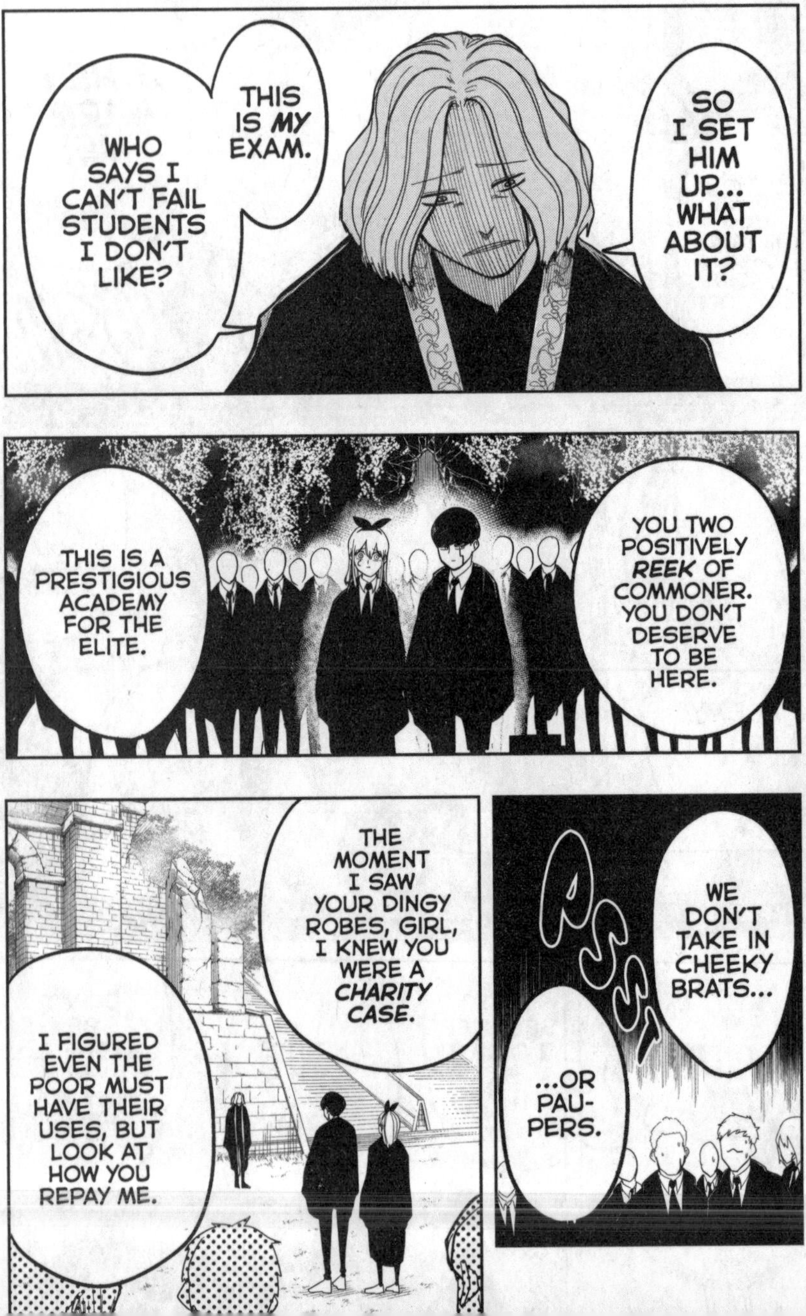
SO I SET HIM UP... WHAT ABOUT IT?
THIS IS *MY* EXAM.
WHO SAYS I CAN'T FAIL STUDENTS I DON'T LIKE?
YOU TWO POSITIVELY *REEK* OF COMMONER. YOU DON'T DESERVE TO BE HERE.
THIS IS A PRESTIGIOUS ACADEMY FOR THE ELITE.
PSSST
WE DON'T TAKE IN CHEEKY BRATS...
...OR PAU-PERS.
THE MOMENT I SAW YOUR DINGY ROBES, GIRL, I KNEW YOU WERE A *CHARITY CASE.*
I FIGURED EVEN THE POOR MUST HAVE THEIR USES, BUT LOOK AT HOW YOU REPAY ME.

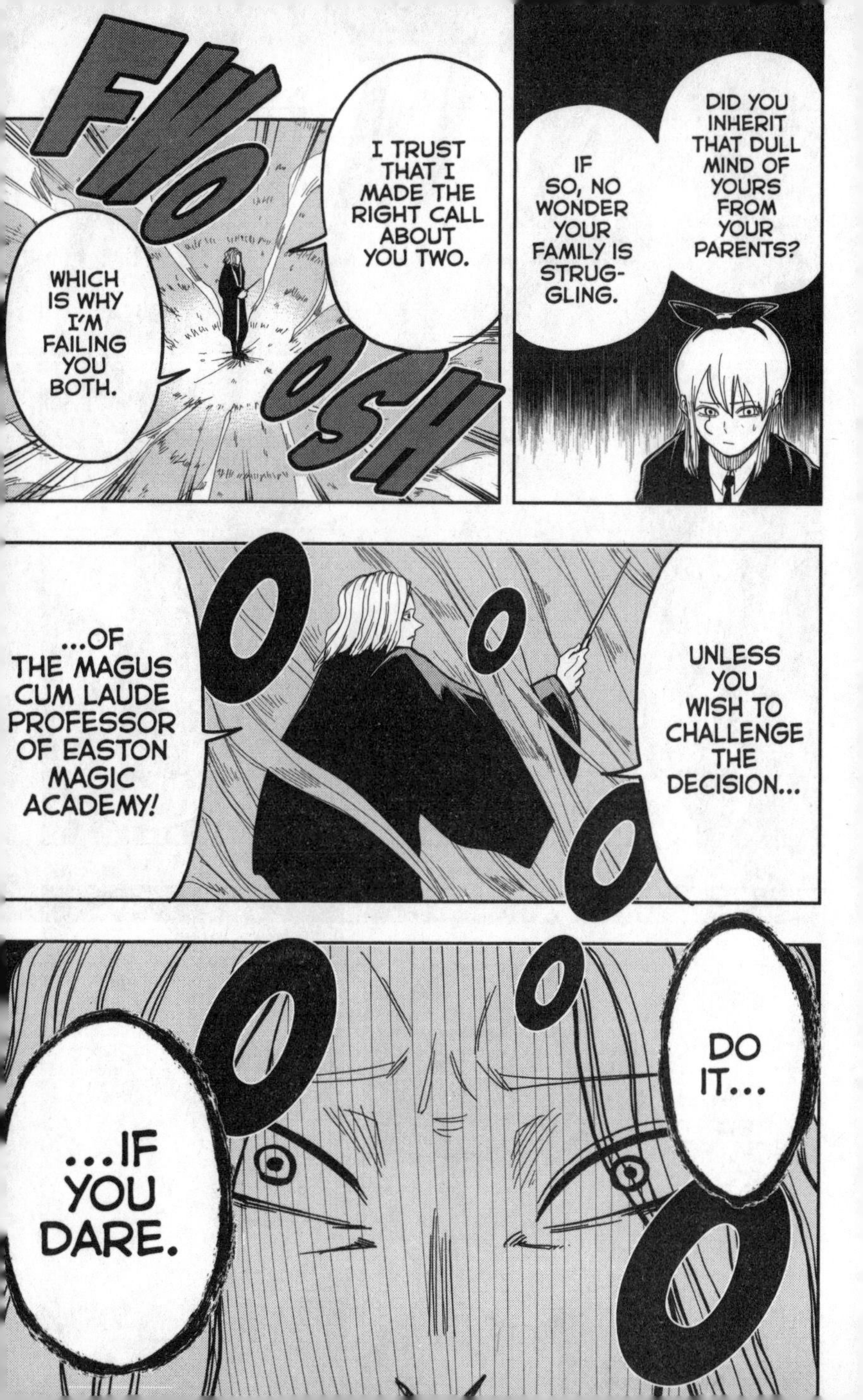
DID YOU INHERIT THAT DULL MIND OF YOURS FROM YOUR PARENTS?
IF SO, NO WONDER YOUR FAMILY IS STRUG-GLING.
I TRUST THAT I MADE THE RIGHT CALL ABOUT YOU TWO.
FWOOSH
WHICH IS WHY I'M FAILING YOU BOTH.
UNLESS YOU WISH TO CHALLENGE THE DECISION...
...OF THE MAGUS CUM LAUDE PROFESSOR OF EASTON MAGIC ACADEMY!
DO IT...
...IF YOU DARE.

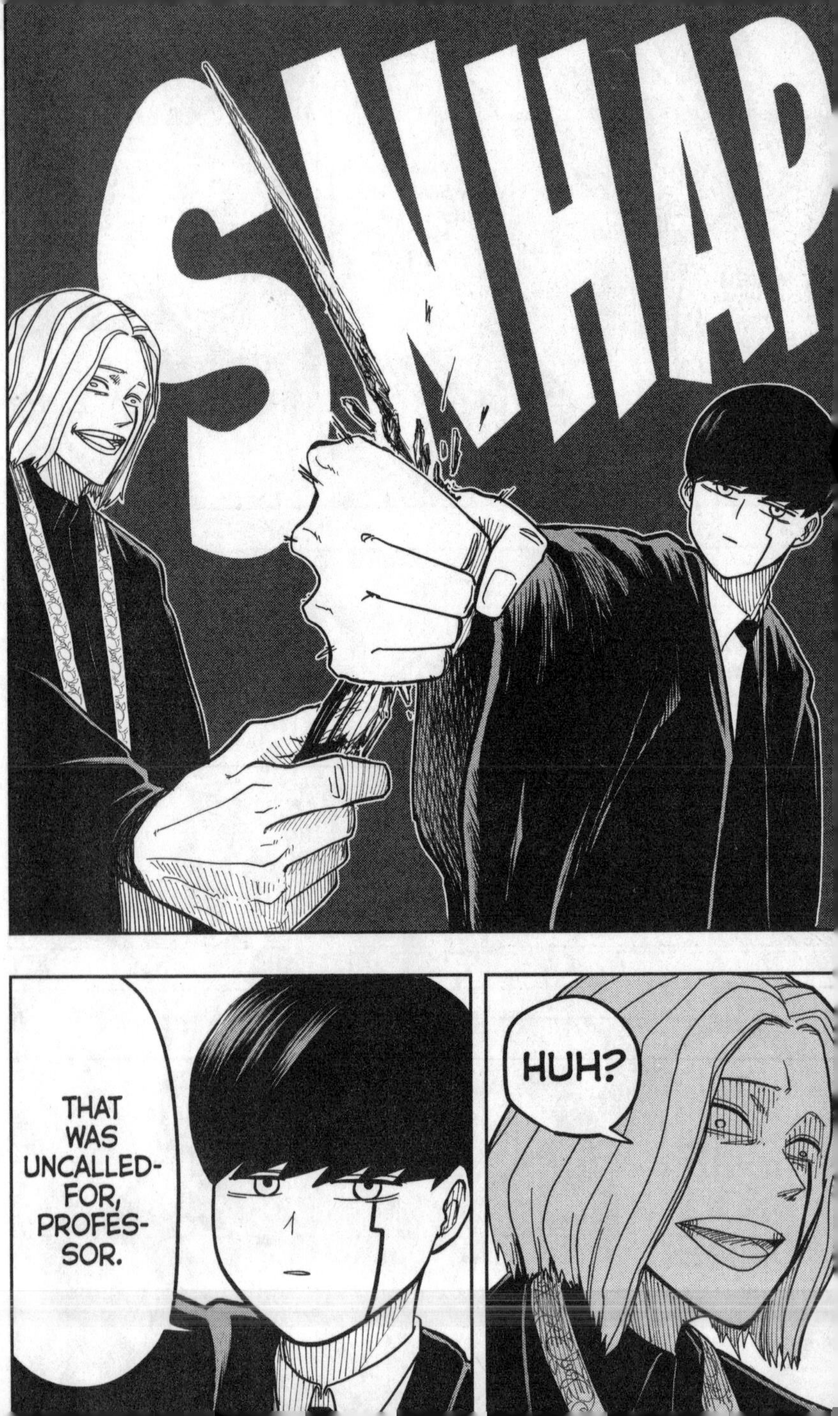
SNAP
HUH?
THAT WAS UNCALLED-FOR, PROFES-SOR.

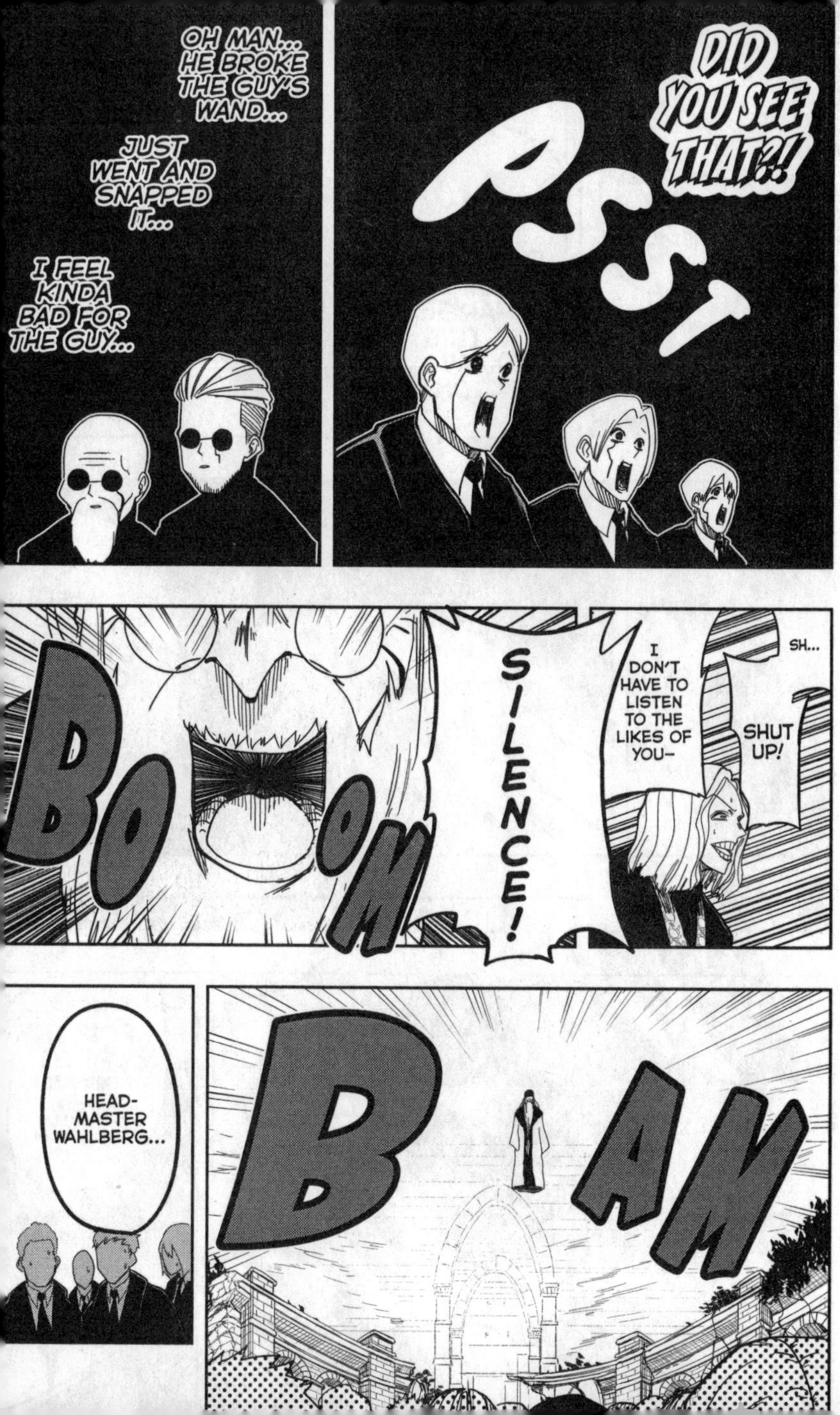
DID YOU SEE THAT?!
PSST
OH MAN... HE BROKE THE GUY'S WAND...
JUST WENT AND SNAPPED IT...
I FEEL KINDA BAD FOR THE GUY...
SH...
SHUT UP!
I DON'T HAVE TO LISTEN TO THE LIKES OF YOU–
SILENCE!
BOOOM
BAM
HEAD-MASTER WAHLBERG...

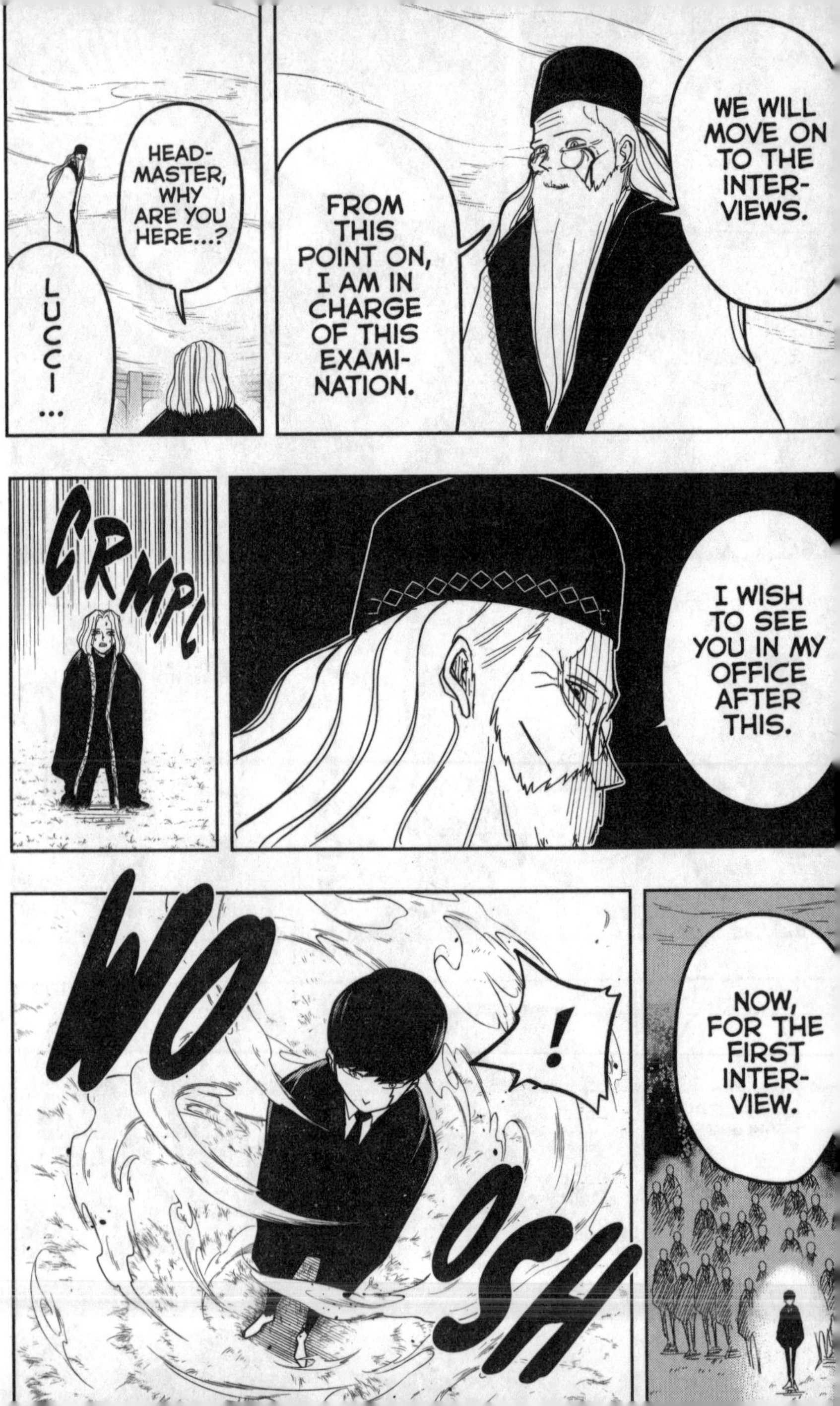
WE WILL MOVE ON TO THE INTERVIEWS.
FROM THIS POINT ON, I AM IN CHARGE OF THIS EXAMINATION.
HEADMASTER, WHY ARE YOU HERE...?
LUCCI...
I WISH TO SEE YOU IN MY OFFICE AFTER THIS.
CRMPL
NOW, FOR THE FIRST INTERVIEW.
!
WOOSH

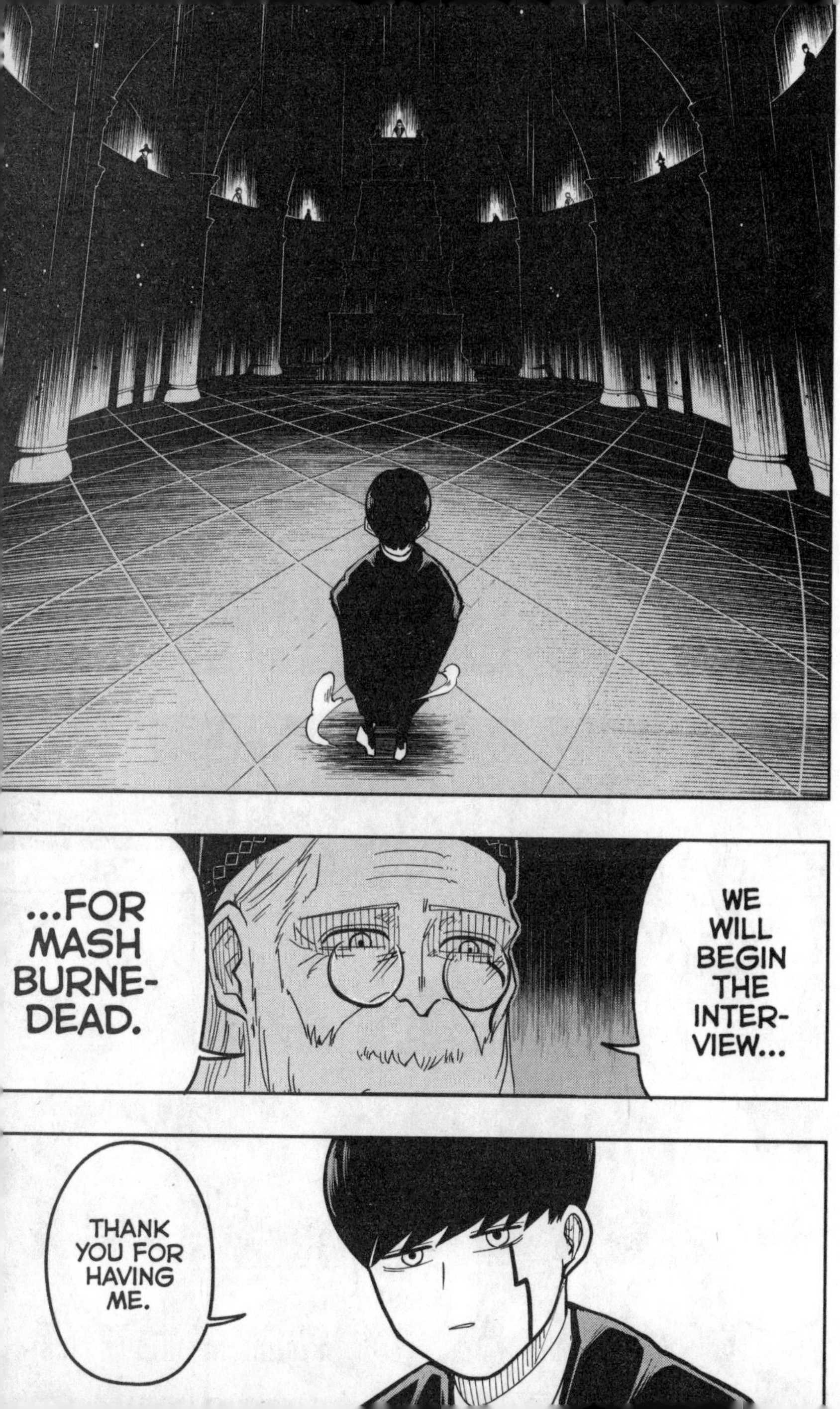
WE WILL BEGIN THE INTERVIEW...
...FOR MASH BURNEDEAD.
THANK YOU FOR HAVING ME.

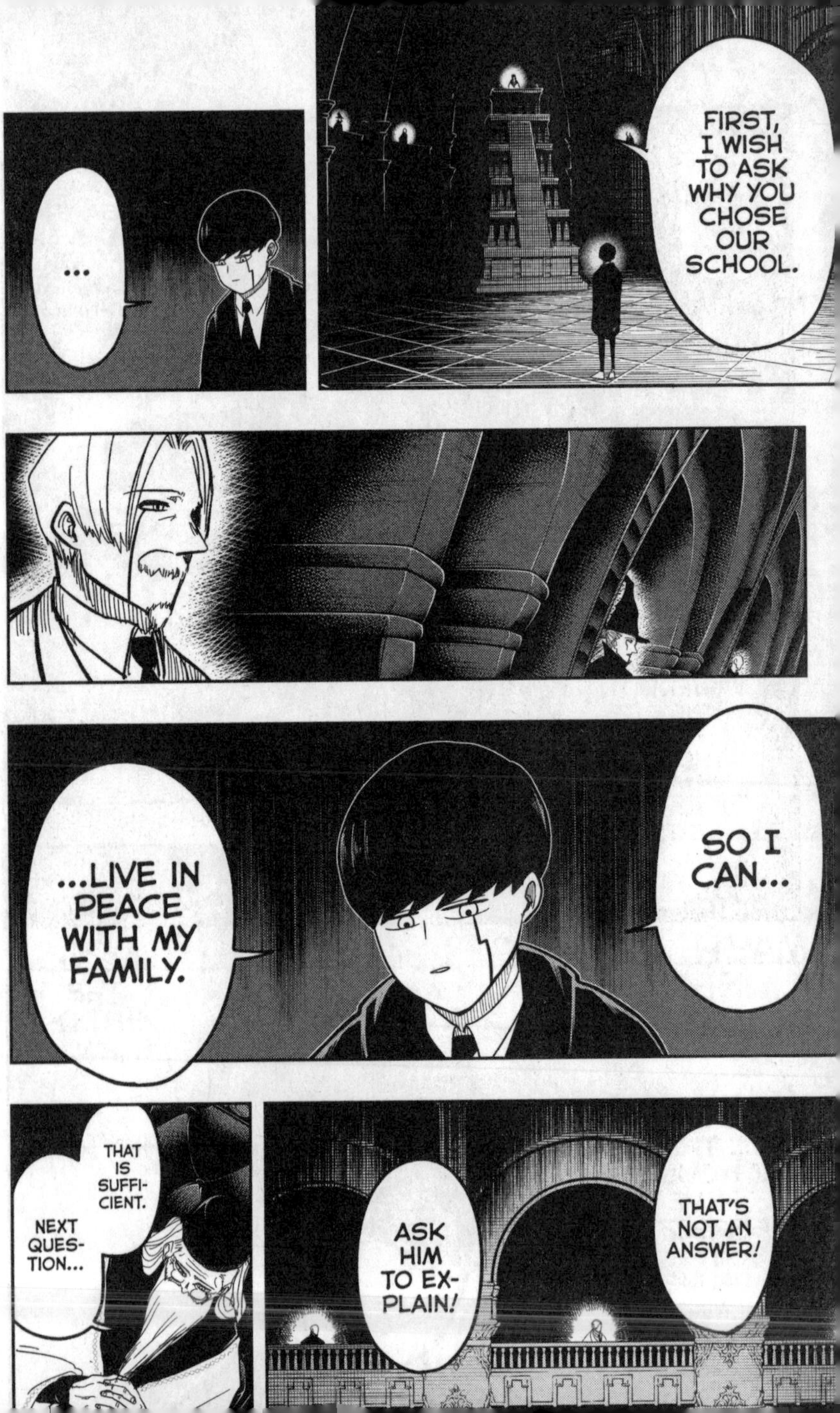
FIRST, I WISH TO ASK WHY YOU CHOSE OUR SCHOOL.
...
SO I CAN...
...LIVE IN PEACE WITH MY FAMILY.
THAT'S NOT AN ANSWER!
ASK HIM TO EX-PLAIN!
THAT IS SUFFI-CIENT.
NEXT QUES-TION...

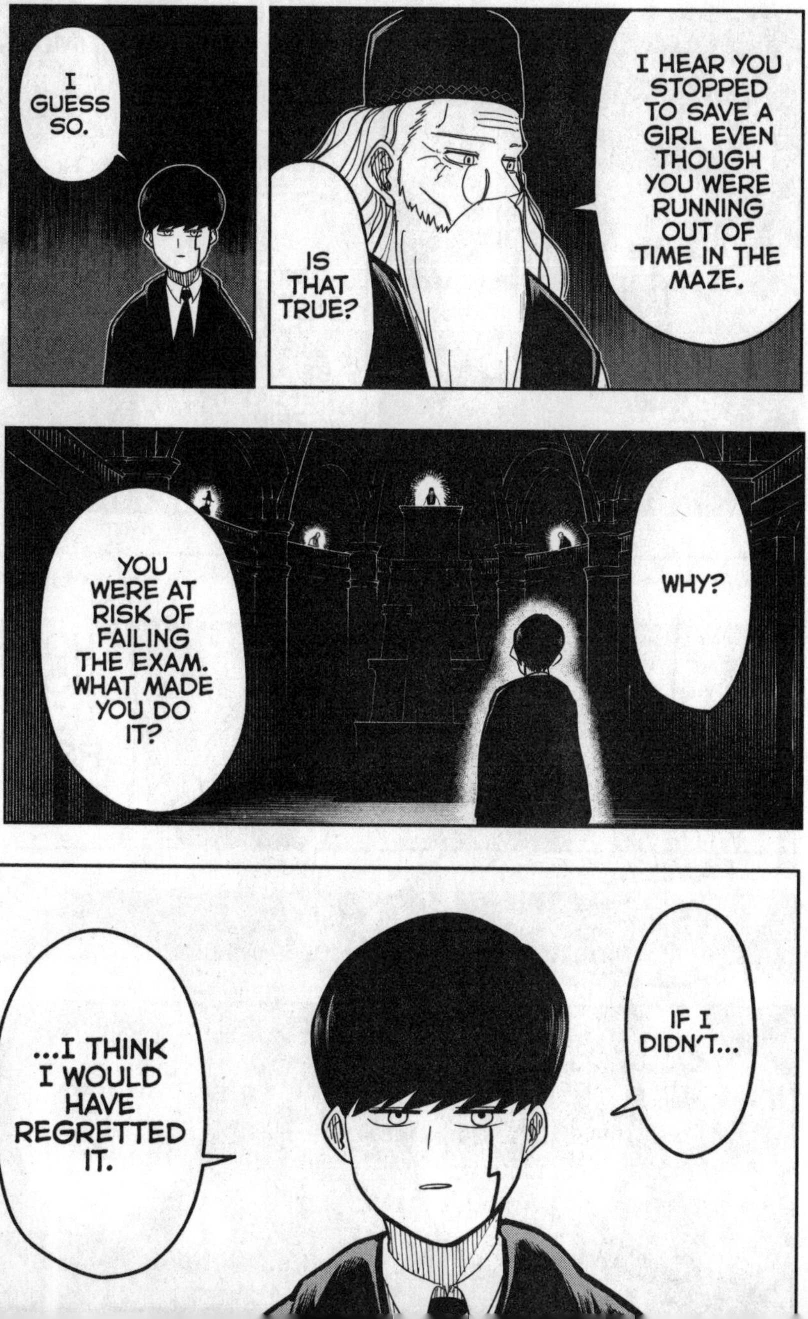
I HEAR YOU STOPPED TO SAVE A GIRL EVEN THOUGH YOU WERE RUNNING OUT OF TIME IN THE MAZE.
IS THAT TRUE?
I GUESS SO.
WHY?
YOU WERE AT RISK OF FAILING THE EXAM. WHAT MADE YOU DO IT?
IF I DIDN'T...
...I THINK I WOULD HAVE REGRETTED IT.

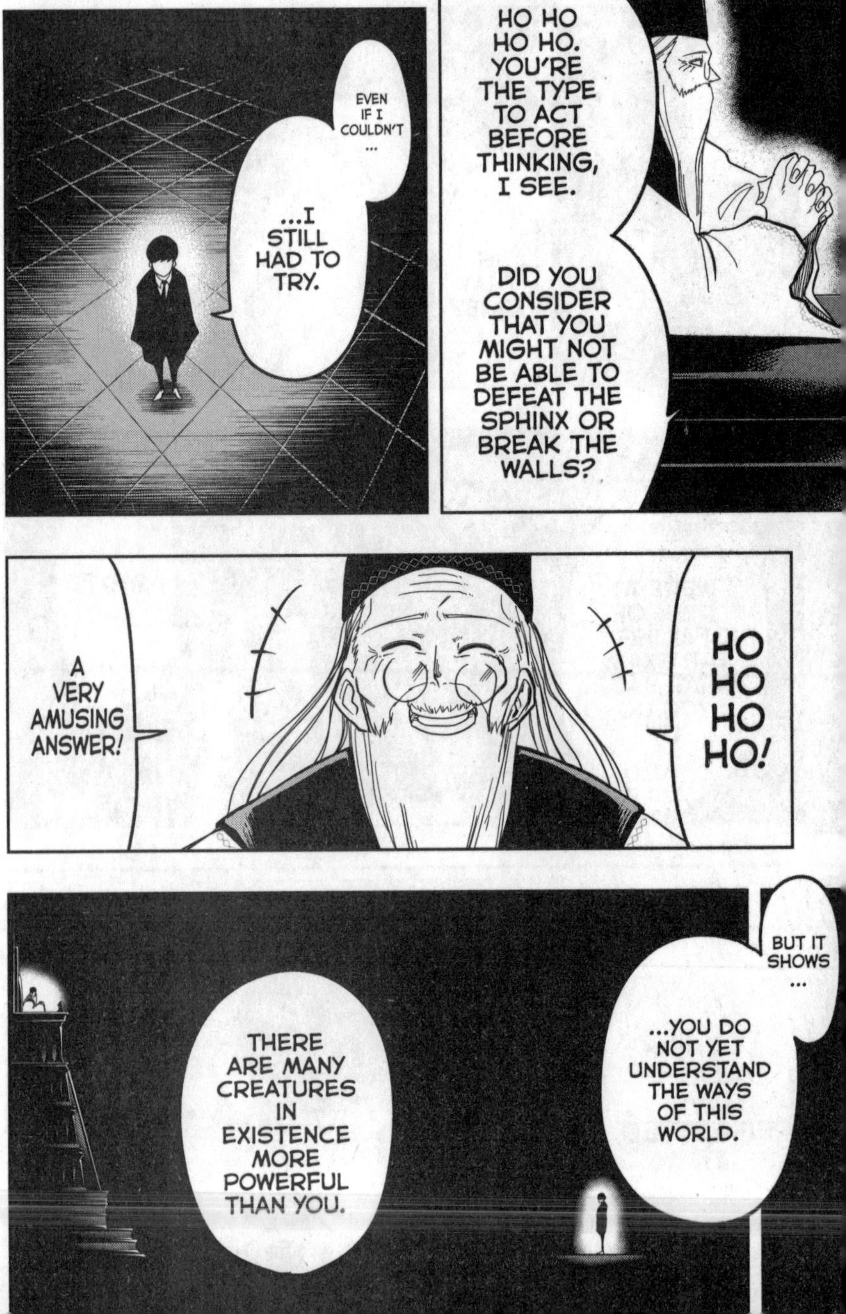
HO HO HO HO. YOU'RE THE TYPE TO ACT BEFORE THINKING, I SEE.
DID YOU CONSIDER THAT YOU MIGHT NOT BE ABLE TO DEFEAT THE SPHINX OR BREAK THE WALLS?
EVEN IF I COULDN'T ...
...I STILL HAD TO TRY.
HO HO HO HO!
A VERY AMUSING ANSWER!
BUT IT SHOWS ...
...YOU DO NOT YET UNDERSTAND THE WAYS OF THIS WORLD.
THERE ARE MANY CREATURES IN EXISTENCE MORE POWERFUL THAN YOU.

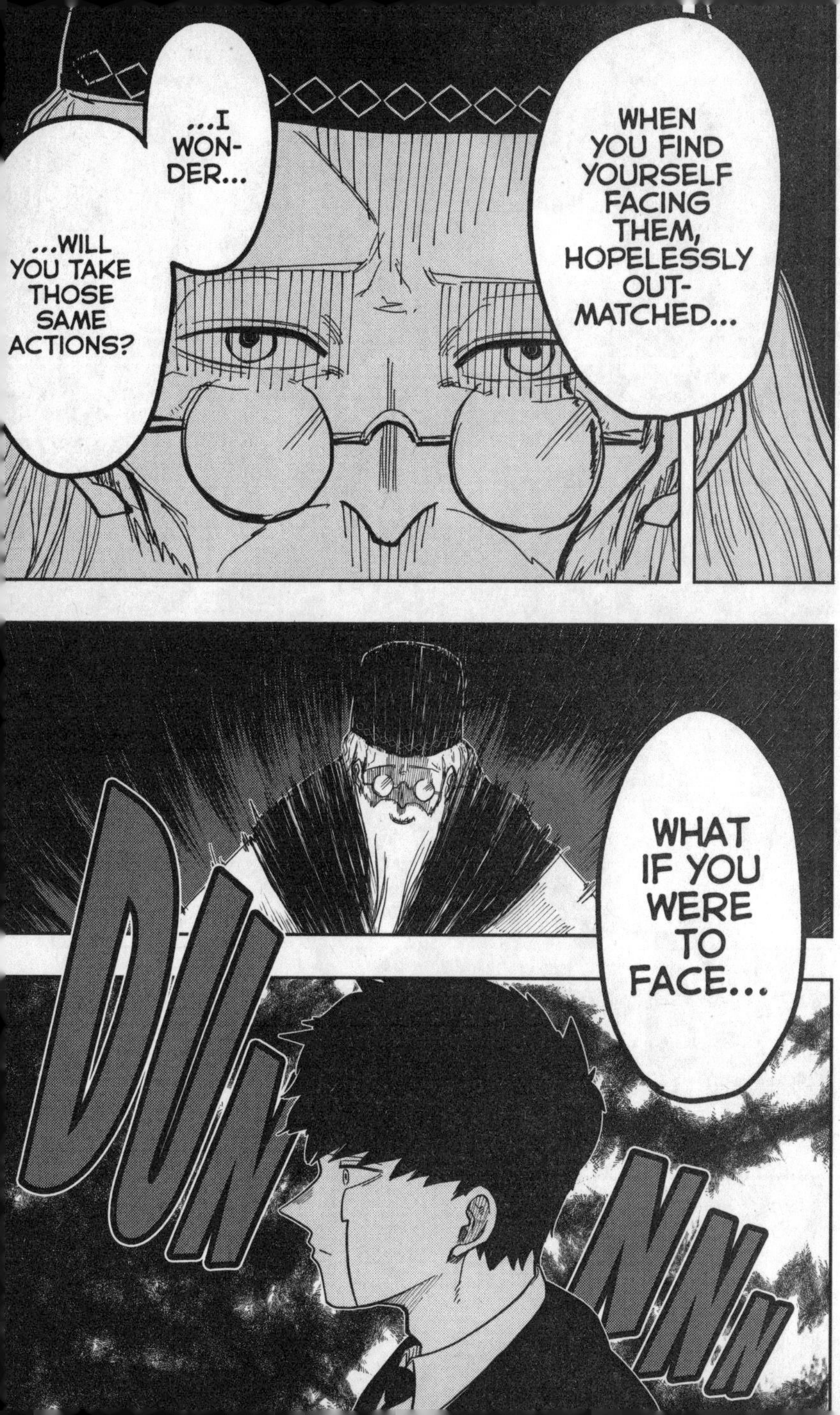
WHEN YOU FIND YOURSELF FACING THEM, HOPELESSLY OUT-MATCHED...
...I WONDER...
...WILL YOU TAKE THOSE SAME ACTIONS?
WHAT IF YOU WERE TO FACE...
DUNNNNN

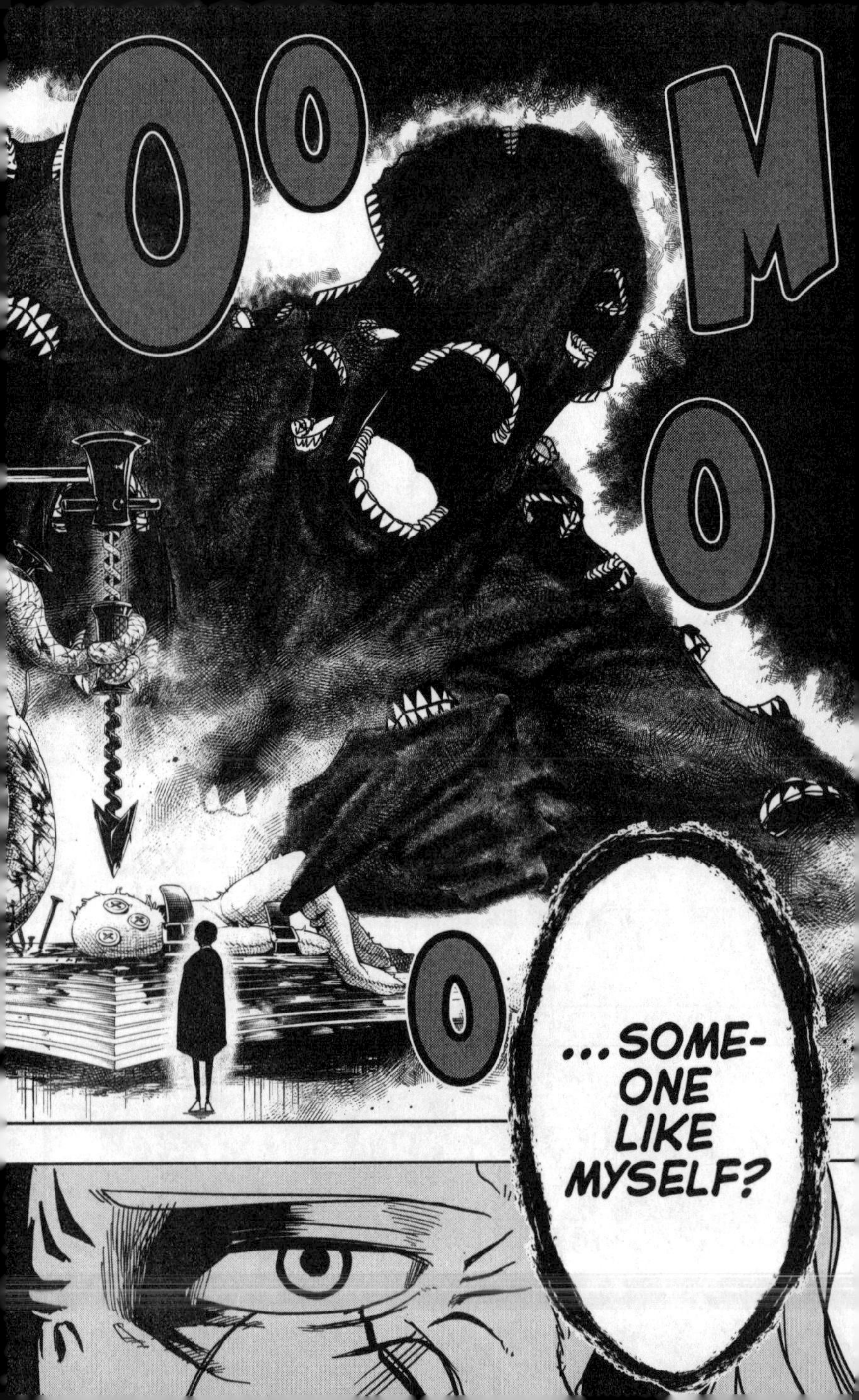
OOOMOO
...SOME-ONE LIKE MYSELF?

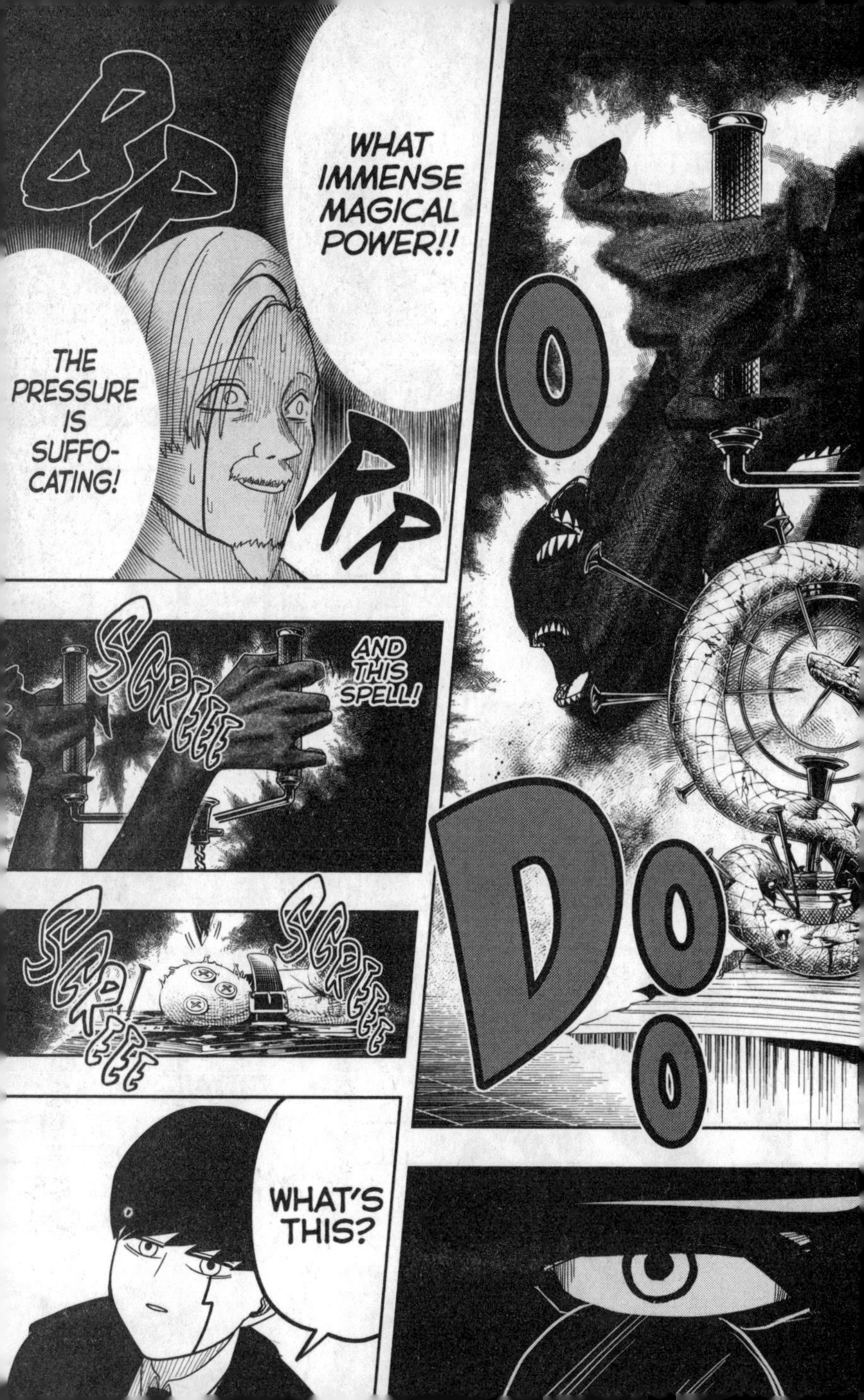
DOOOO
WHAT IMMENSE MAGICAL POWER!!
BRRR
THE PRESSURE IS SUFFOCATING!
AND THIS SPELL!
SCREEE
SCREEE
SCREEE
WHAT'S THIS?

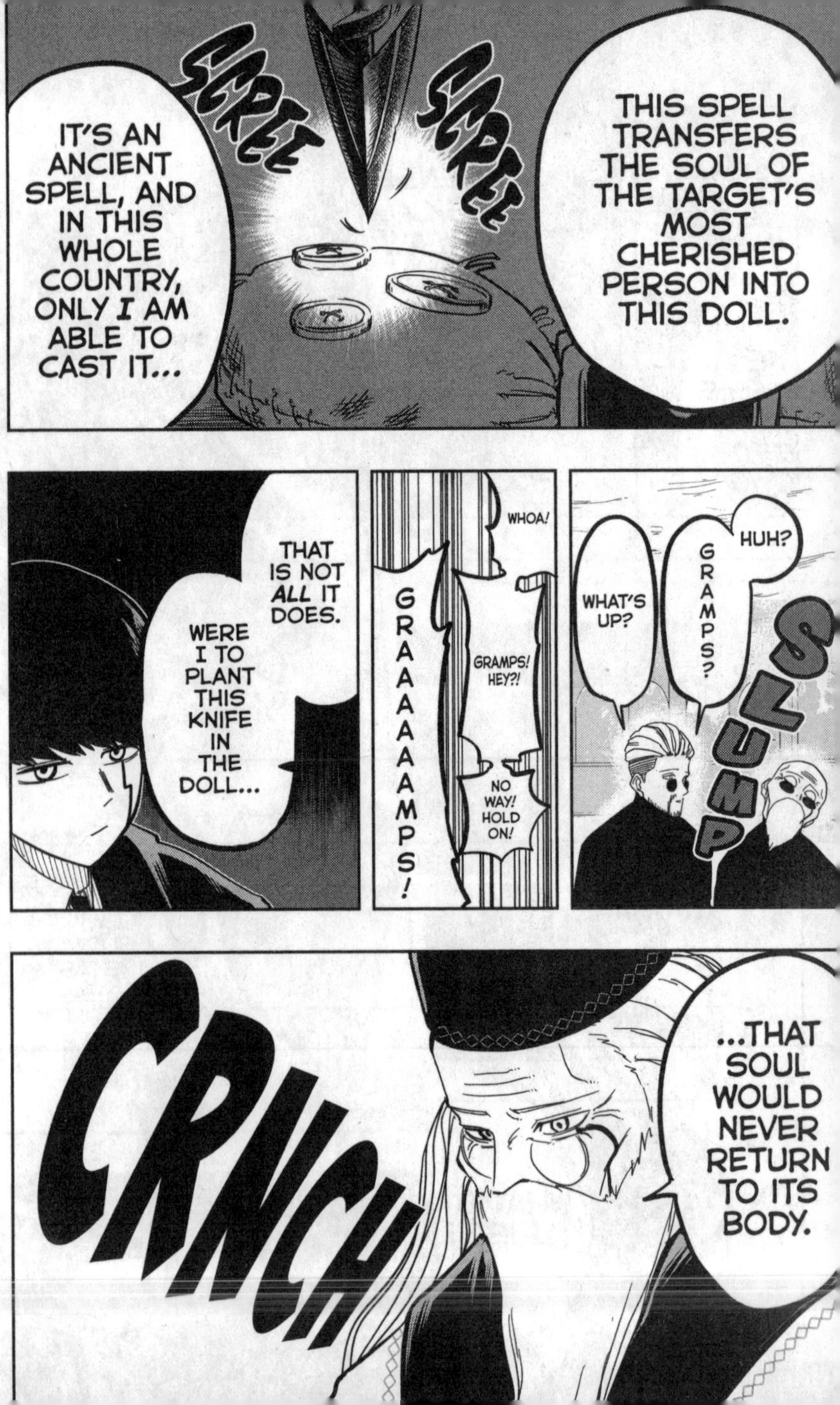
THIS SPELL TRANSFERS THE SOUL OF THE TARGET'S MOST CHERISHED PERSON INTO THIS DOLL.
SCREE
SCREE
IT'S AN ANCIENT SPELL, AND IN THIS WHOLE COUNTRY, ONLY *I* AM ABLE TO CAST IT...
HUH?
GRAMPS?
WHAT'S UP?
SLUMP
WHOA!
GRAMPS! HEY?!
NO WAY! HOLD ON!
GRAAAAAAAMPS!
THAT IS NOT *ALL* IT DOES.
WERE I TO PLANT THIS KNIFE IN THE DOLL...
...THAT SOUL WOULD NEVER RETURN TO ITS BODY.
CRNCH

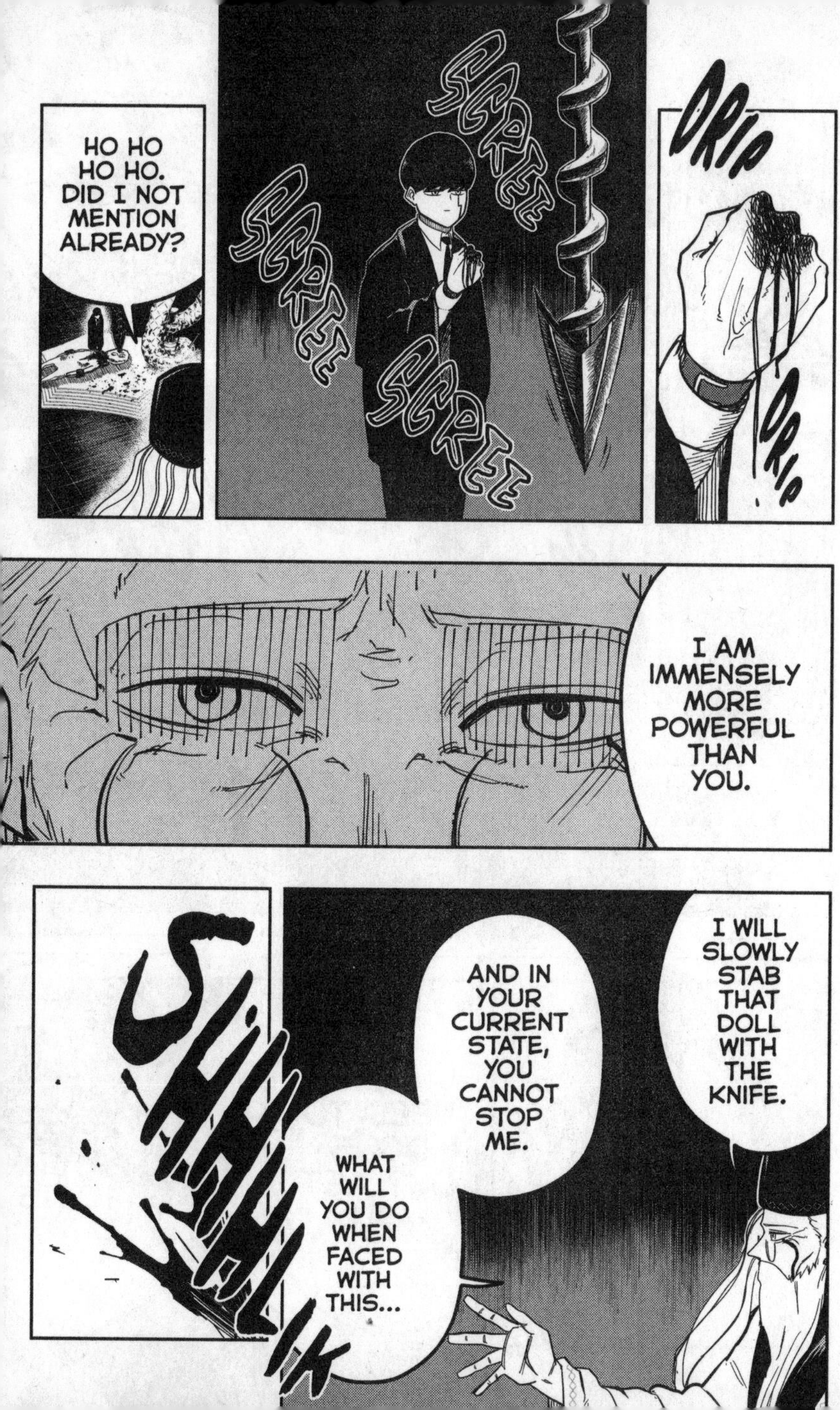
DRIP
DRIP
SCREE
SCREE
SCREE
SCREE
HO HO HO HO. DID I NOT MENTION ALREADY?
I AM IMMENSELY MORE POWERFUL THAN YOU.
I WILL SLOWLY STAB THAT DOLL WITH THE KNIFE.
AND IN YOUR CURRENT STATE, YOU CANNOT STOP ME.
WHAT WILL YOU DO WHEN FACED WITH THIS...
SHHHLIK

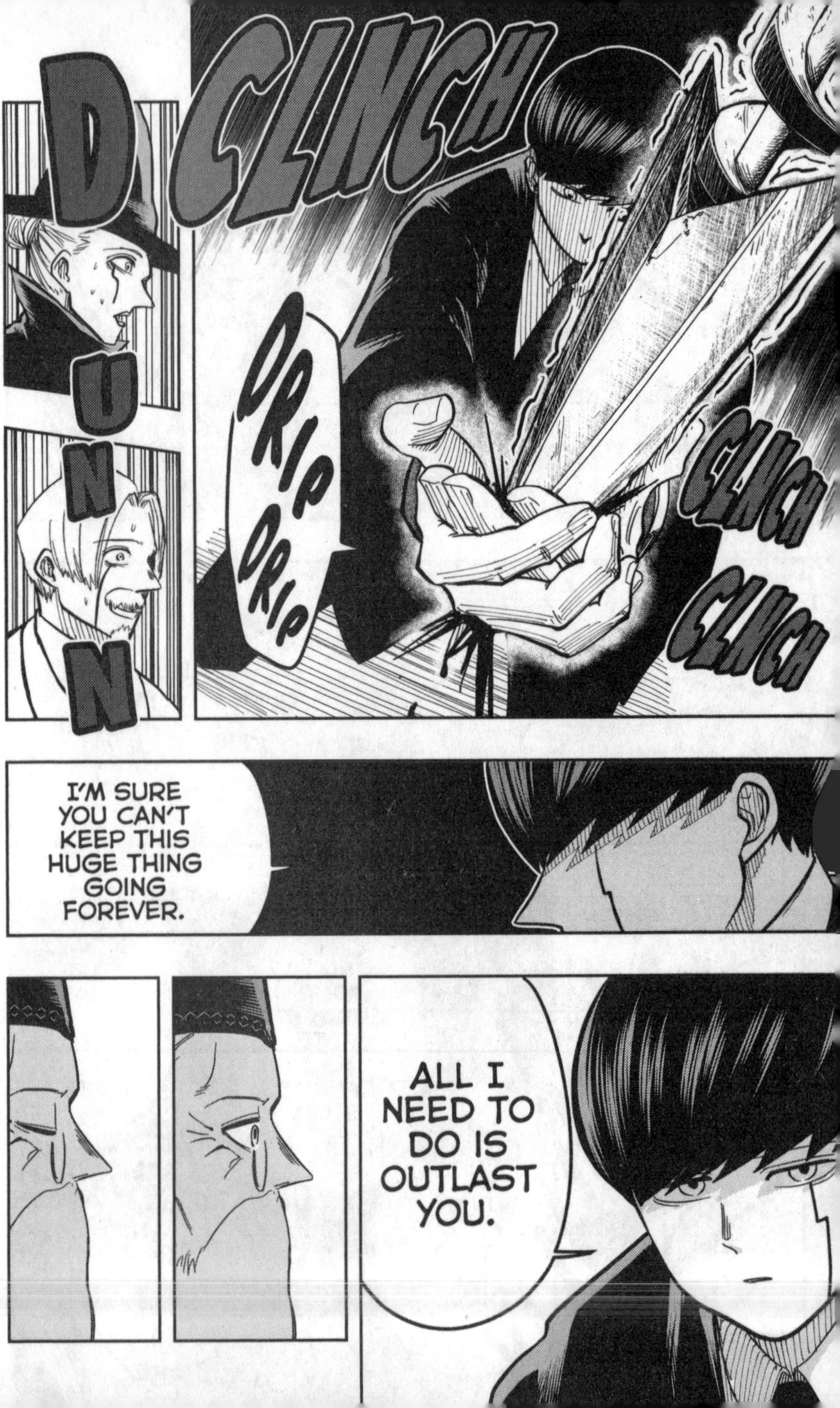
CLINCH
DRIP DRIP
CLINCH CLINCH
DUNN
I'M SURE YOU CAN'T KEEP THIS HUGE THING GOING FOREVER.
ALL I NEED TO DO IS OUTLAST YOU.

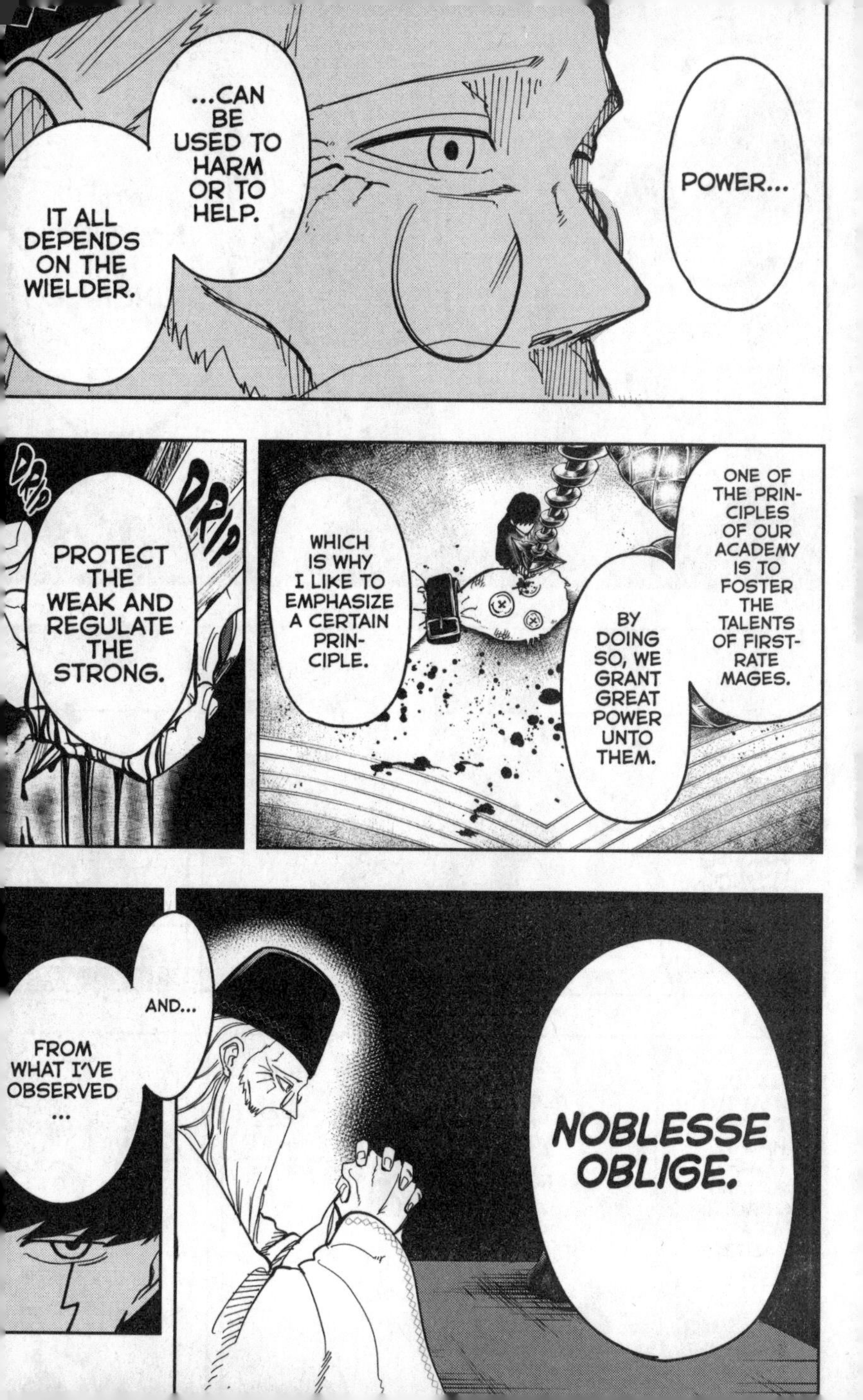
POWER...
...CAN BE USED TO HARM OR TO HELP.
IT ALL DEPENDS ON THE WIELDER.
ONE OF THE PRINCIPLES OF OUR ACADEMY IS TO FOSTER THE TALENTS OF FIRST-RATE MAGES.
BY DOING SO, WE GRANT GREAT POWER UNTO THEM.
WHICH IS WHY I LIKE TO EMPHASIZE A CERTAIN PRINCIPLE.
DRIP
DRIP
PROTECT THE WEAK AND REGULATE THE STRONG.
NOBLESSE OBLIGE.
AND...
FROM WHAT I'VE OBSERVED ...

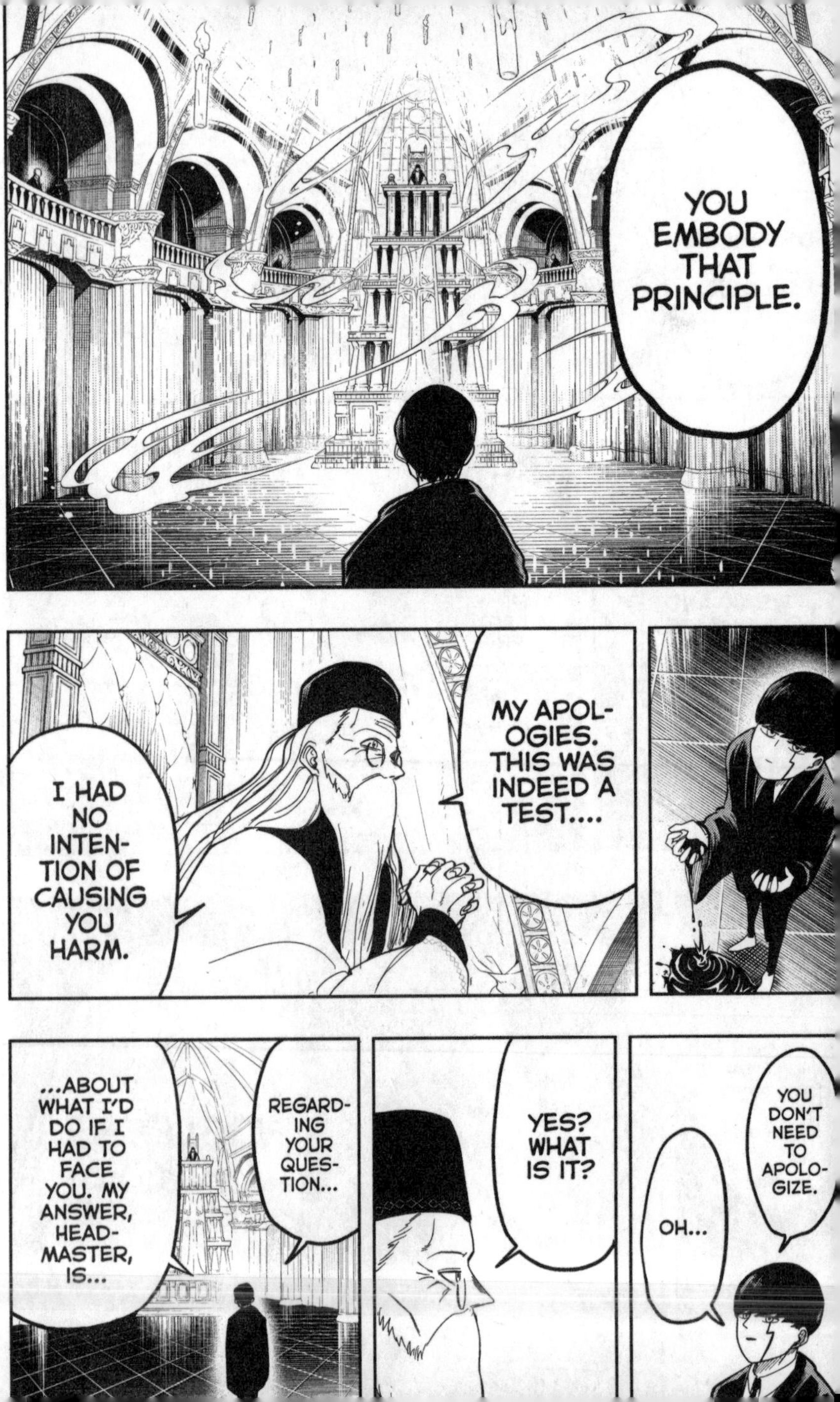
YOU EMBODY THAT PRINCIPLE.
MY APOLOGIES. THIS WAS INDEED A TEST....
I HAD NO INTENTION OF CAUSING YOU HARM.
YOU DON'T NEED TO APOLOGIZE.
OH...
YES? WHAT IS IT?
REGARDING YOUR QUESTION...
...ABOUT WHAT I'D DO IF I HAD TO FACE YOU. MY ANSWER, HEADMASTER, IS...

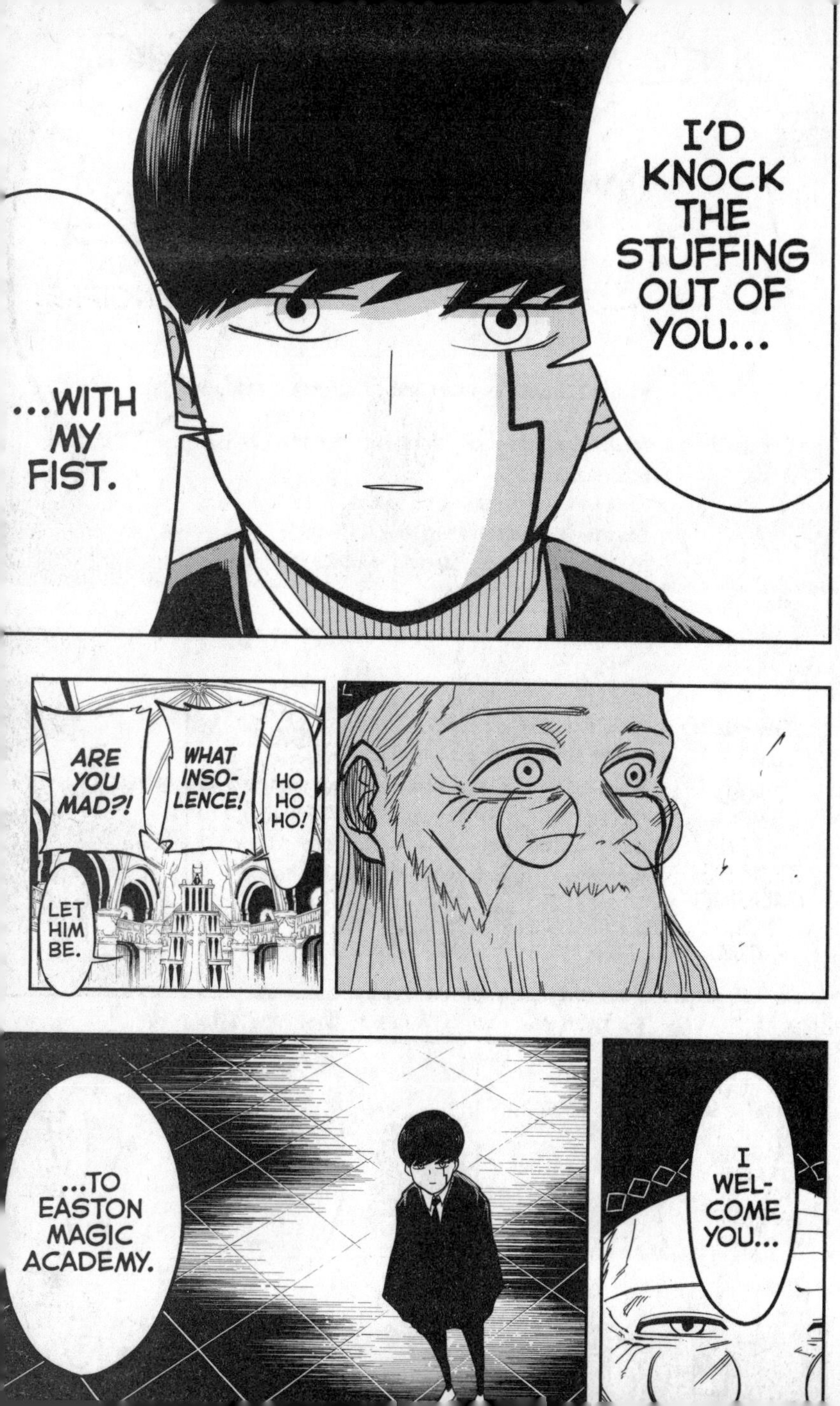
I'D KNOCK THE STUFFING OUT OF YOU...
...WITH MY FIST.
HO HO HO!
WHAT INSO-LENCE!
ARE YOU MAD?!
LET HIM BE.
I WEL-COME YOU...
...TO EASTON MAGIC ACADEMY.

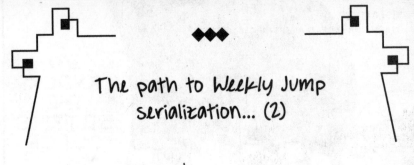

The path to Weekly Jump serialization... (2)

↓

Realize I've got no choice but to become a manga artist.

The doubt phase

Accept that it's risky to become a manga artist postcollege.
Know my parents will be against it. Have doubts.
Descend into desperation and tell myself, "You only live once" while secretly quitting my job.
(Sorry, Dad. Sorry, Mom.)

↓

The freeter phase

Allay my parents' fears by promising to give up if I can't get a serial in two years.
Work part-time as a security guard while drawing manga.
Struggle with making good storyboards for a serial.
Get sad when everyone else talks about their bonuses.
Remember the threat of finger guillotines and keep at it.

↓

Miraculously, I'm given a serial.
My editor and I are both new to this. Panic sets in.

To be continued...

CHAPTER 4:
MASH BURNEDEAD AND THE CLEAN SWEEP

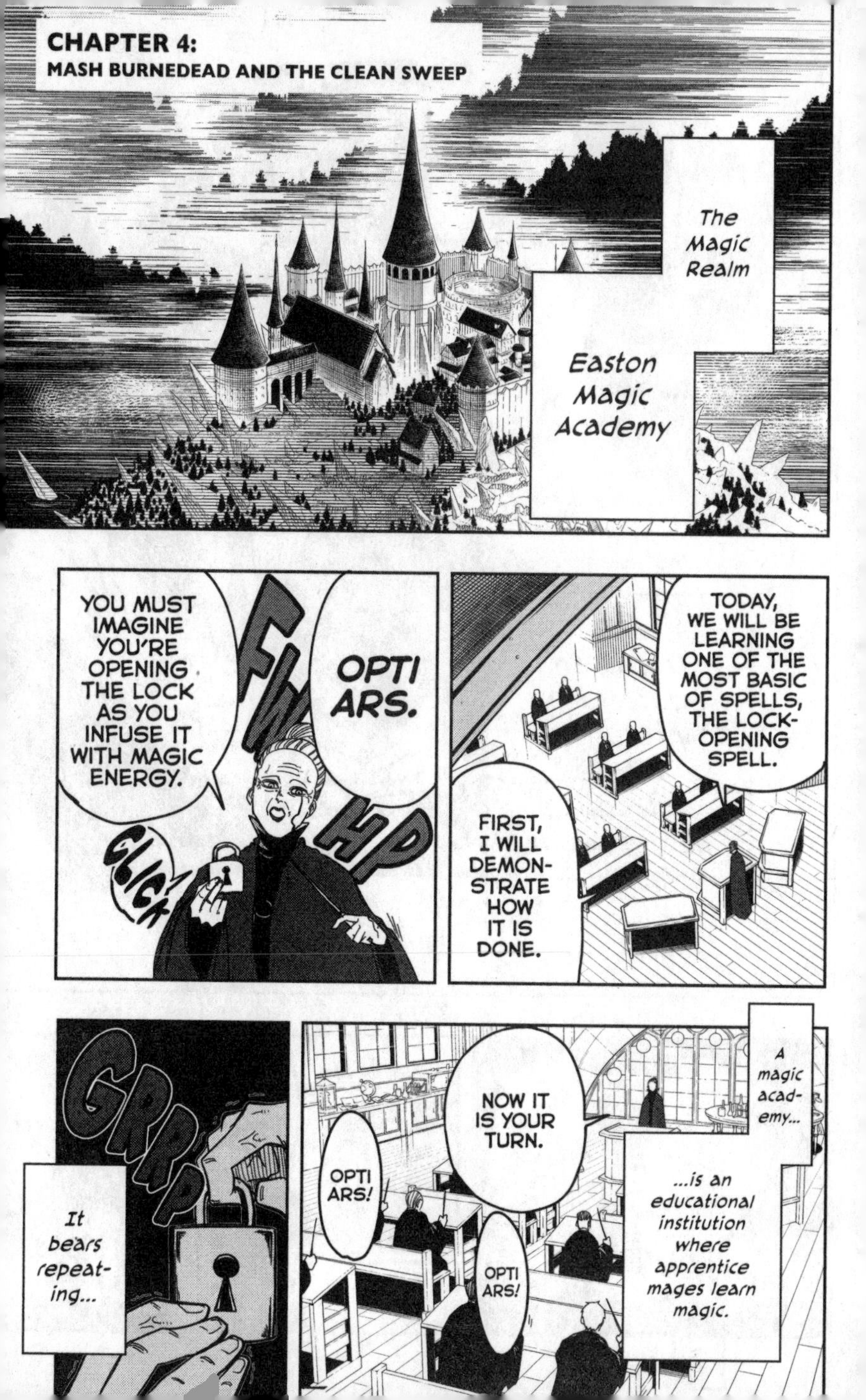
The Magic Realm
Easton Magic Academy
TODAY, WE WILL BE LEARNING ONE OF THE MOST BASIC OF SPELLS, THE LOCK-OPENING SPELL.
FIRST, I WILL DEMON-STRATE HOW IT IS DONE.
OPTI ARS.
FWHP
CLICK
YOU MUST IMAGINE YOU'RE OPENING THE LOCK AS YOU INFUSE IT WITH MAGIC ENERGY.
A magic acad-emy...
...is an educational institution where apprentice mages learn magic.
NOW IT IS YOUR TURN.
OPTI ARS!
OPTI ARS!
GRIP
It bears repeat-ing...

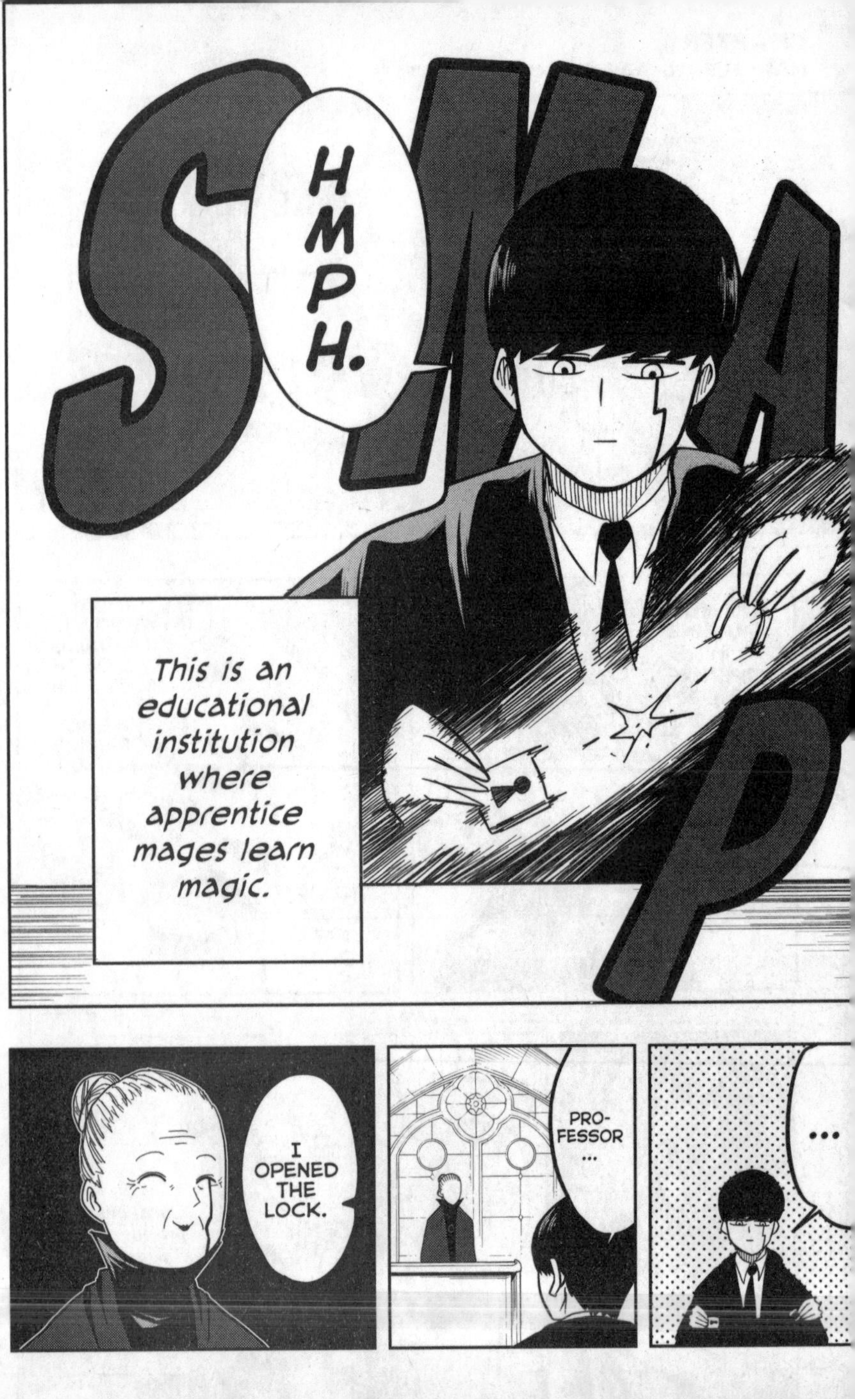

SNAP
HMPH.
This is an educational institution where apprentice mages learn magic.
...
PROFESSOR...
I OPENED THE LOCK.

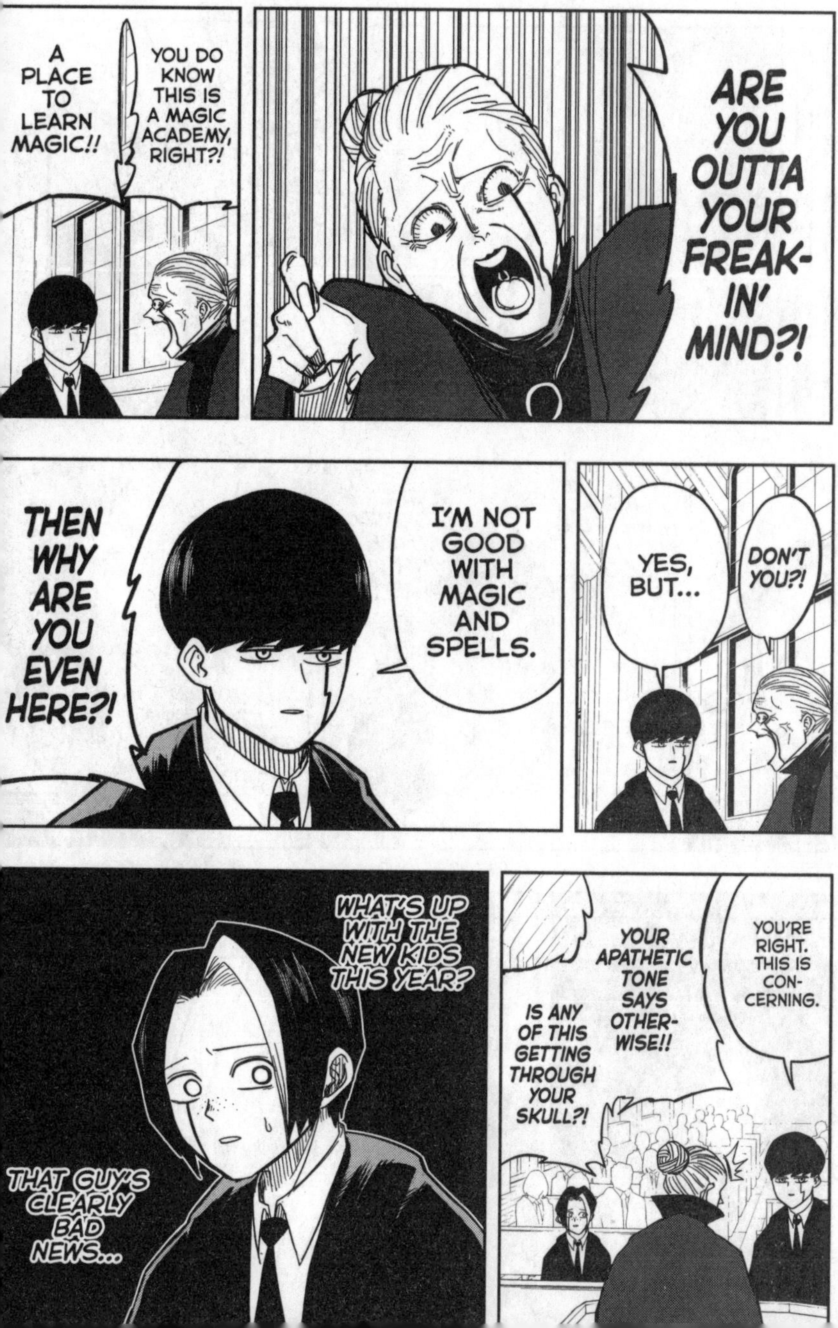
ARE YOU OUTTA YOUR FREAKIN' MIND?!
YOU DO KNOW THIS IS A MAGIC ACADEMY, RIGHT?!
A PLACE TO LEARN MAGIC!!
DON'T YOU?!
YES, BUT...
I'M NOT GOOD WITH MAGIC AND SPELLS.
THEN WHY ARE YOU EVEN HERE?!
YOU'RE RIGHT. THIS IS CONCERNING.
YOUR APATHETIC TONE SAYS OTHERWISE!!
IS ANY OF THIS GETTING THROUGH YOUR SKULL?!
WHAT'S UP WITH THE NEW KIDS THIS YEAR?
THAT GUY'S CLEARLY BAD NEWS...

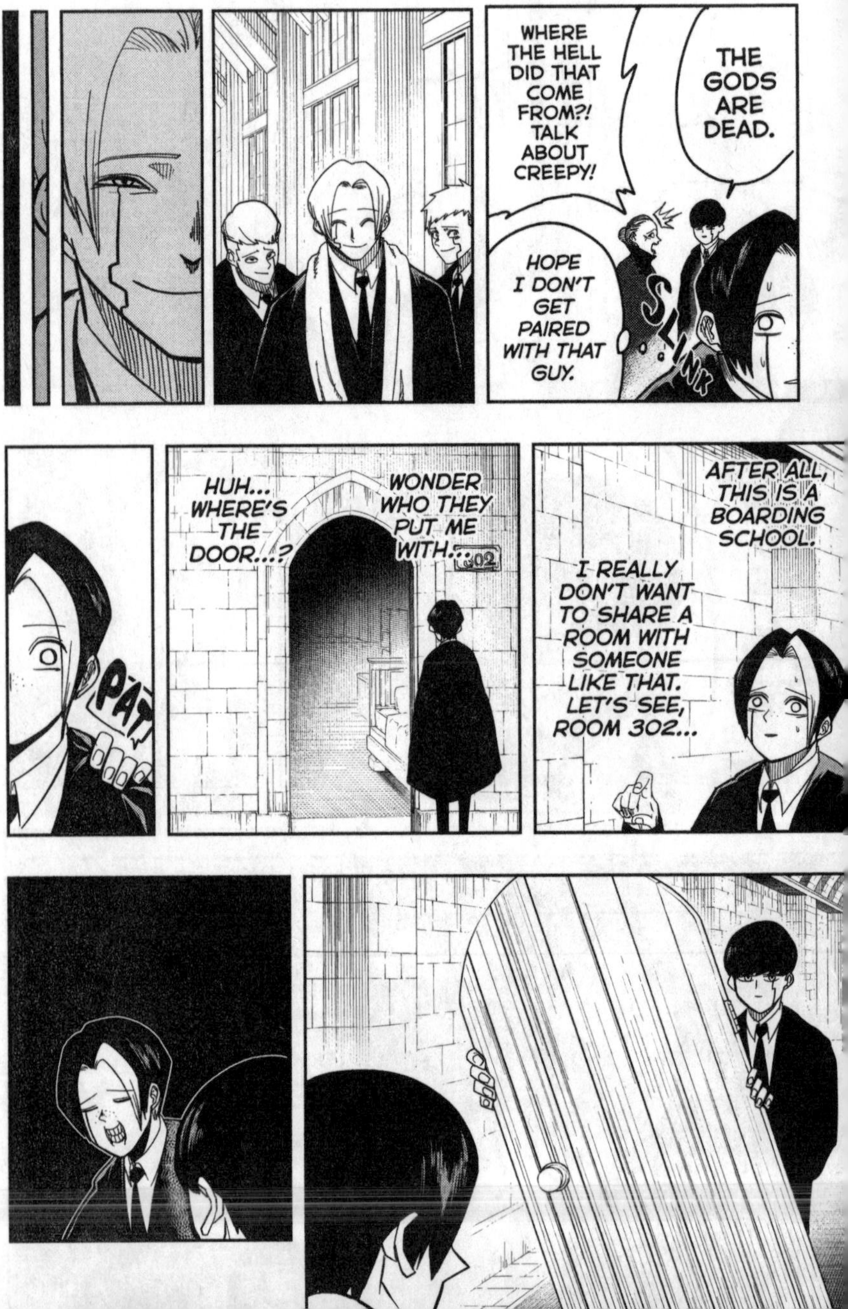
THE GODS ARE DEAD.
WHERE THE HELL DID THAT COME FROM?! TALK ABOUT CREEPY!
HOPE I DON'T GET PAIRED WITH THAT GUY.
SLINK
AFTER ALL, THIS IS A BOARDING SCHOOL.
I REALLY DON'T WANT TO SHARE A ROOM WITH SOMEONE LIKE THAT. LET'S SEE, ROOM 302...
WONDER WHO THEY PUT ME WITH...
302
HUH... WHERE'S THE DOOR...?
PAT

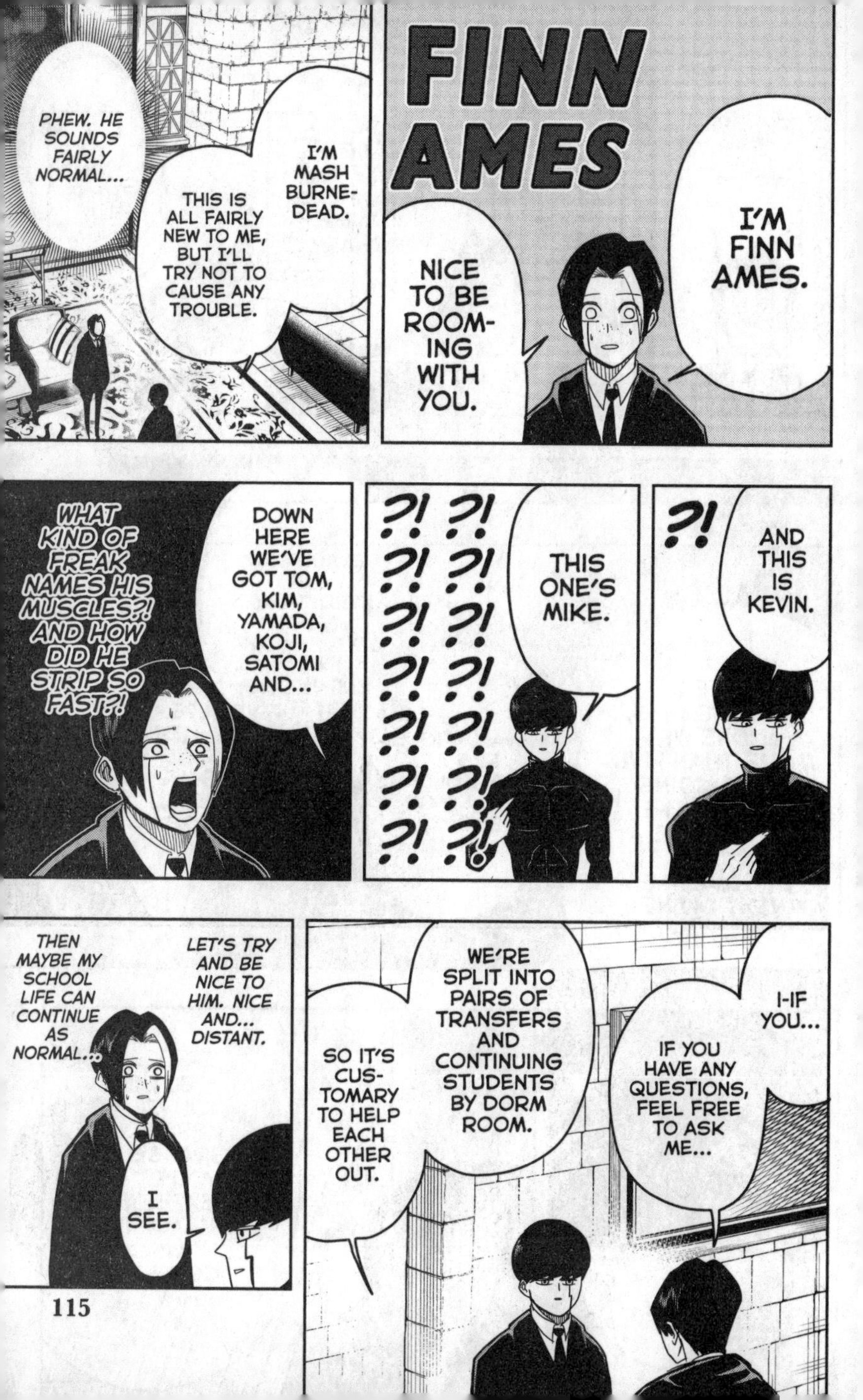
FINN AMES
I'M FINN AMES.
NICE TO BE ROOMING WITH YOU.
I'M MASH BURNE-DEAD.
THIS IS ALL FAIRLY NEW TO ME, BUT I'LL TRY NOT TO CAUSE ANY TROUBLE.
PHEW. HE SOUNDS FAIRLY NORMAL...
?!
AND THIS IS KEVIN.
?! ?! ?! ?! ?! ?! ?! ?! ?! ?! ?! ?! ?! ?!
THIS ONE'S MIKE.
DOWN HERE WE'VE GOT TOM, KIM, YAMADA, KOJI, SATOMI AND...
WHAT KIND OF FREAK NAMES HIS MUSCLES?! AND HOW DID HE STRIP SO FAST?!
I-IF YOU...
IF YOU HAVE ANY QUESTIONS, FEEL FREE TO ASK ME...
WE'RE SPLIT INTO PAIRS OF TRANSFERS AND CONTINUING STUDENTS BY DORM ROOM.
SO IT'S CUSTOMARY TO HELP EACH OTHER OUT.
LET'S TRY AND BE NICE TO HIM. NICE AND... DISTANT.
THEN MAYBE MY SCHOOL LIFE CAN CONTINUE AS NORMAL...
I SEE.

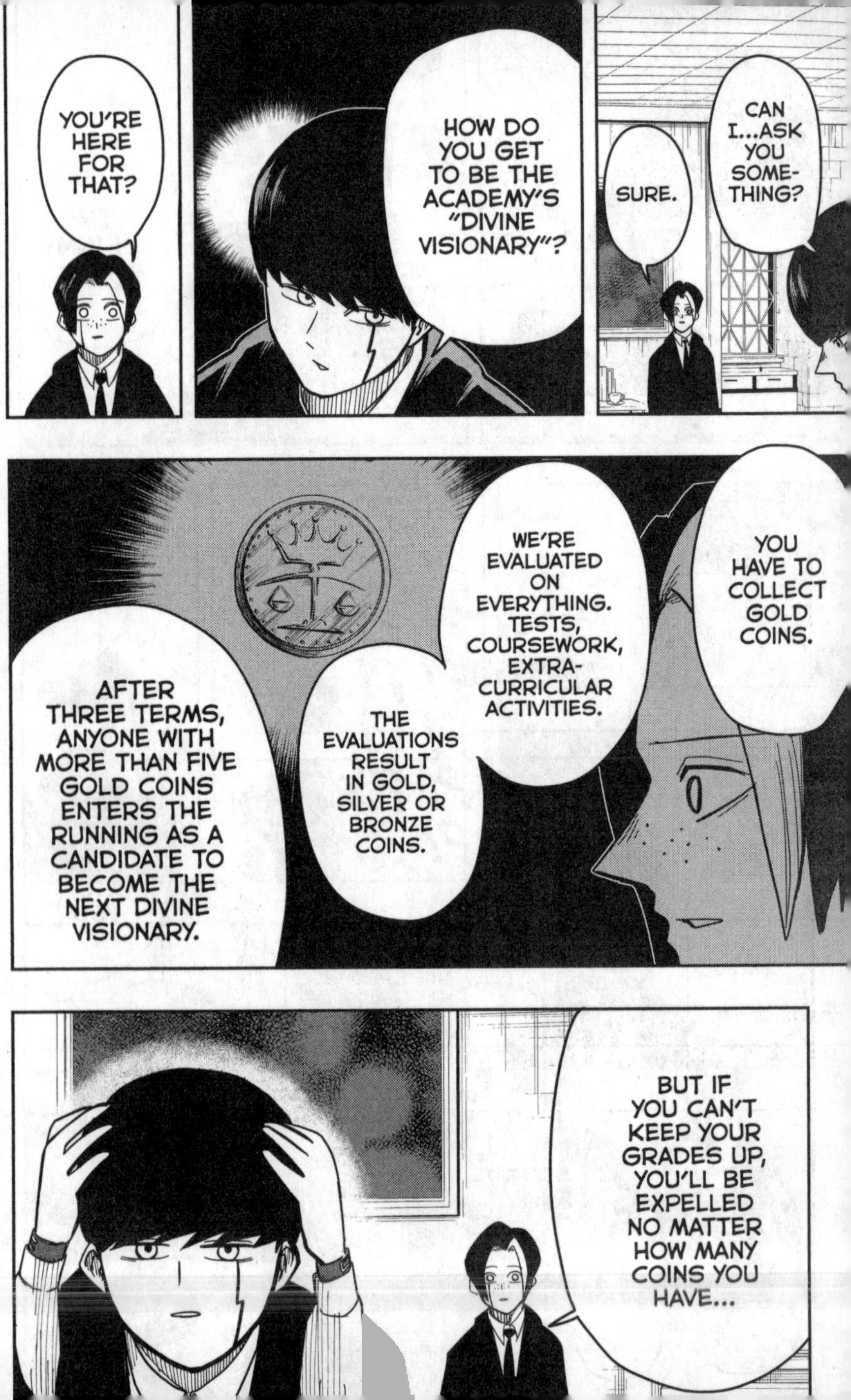
CAN I...ASK YOU SOME-THING?
SURE.
HOW DO YOU GET TO BE THE ACADEMY'S "DIVINE VISIONARY"?
YOU'RE HERE FOR THAT?
YOU HAVE TO COLLECT GOLD COINS.
WE'RE EVALUATED ON EVERYTHING. TESTS, COURSEWORK, EXTRA-CURRICULAR ACTIVITIES.
THE EVALUATIONS RESULT IN GOLD, SILVER OR BRONZE COINS.
AFTER THREE TERMS, ANYONE WITH MORE THAN FIVE GOLD COINS ENTERS THE RUNNING AS A CANDIDATE TO BECOME THE NEXT DIVINE VISIONARY.
BUT IF YOU CAN'T KEEP YOUR GRADES UP, YOU'LL BE EXPELLED NO MATTER HOW MANY COINS YOU HAVE...

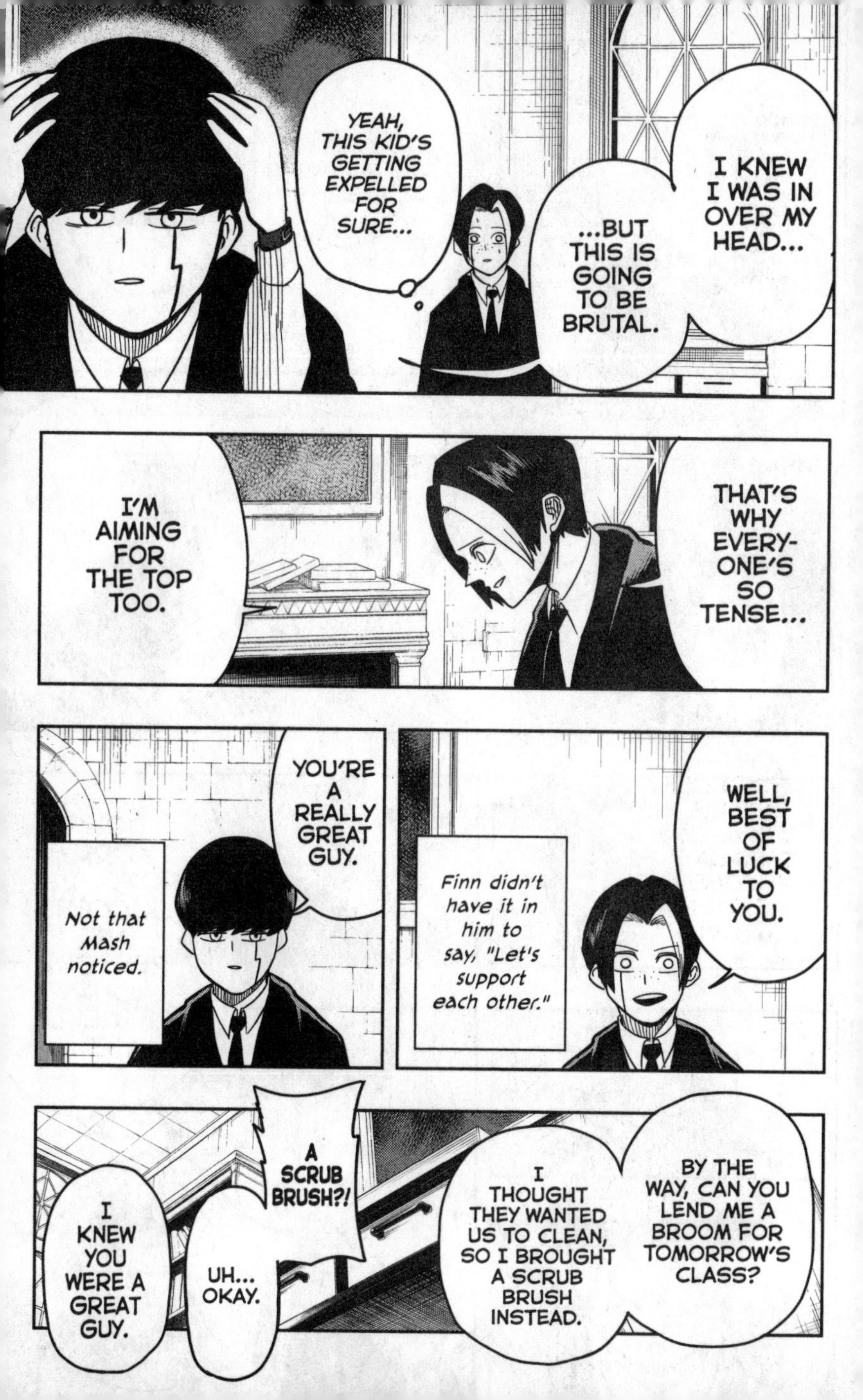
I KNEW I WAS IN OVER MY HEAD...
...BUT THIS IS GOING TO BE BRUTAL.
YEAH, THIS KID'S GETTING EXPELLED FOR SURE...
THAT'S WHY EVERYONE'S SO TENSE...
I'M AIMING FOR THE TOP TOO.
WELL, BEST OF LUCK TO YOU.
Finn didn't have it in him to say, "Let's support each other."
YOU'RE A REALLY GREAT GUY.
Not that Mash noticed.
BY THE WAY, CAN YOU LEND ME A BROOM FOR TOMORROW'S CLASS?
I THOUGHT THEY WANTED US TO CLEAN, SO I BROUGHT A SCRUB BRUSH INSTEAD.
A SCRUB BRUSH?!
UH... OKAY.
I KNEW YOU WERE A GREAT GUY.

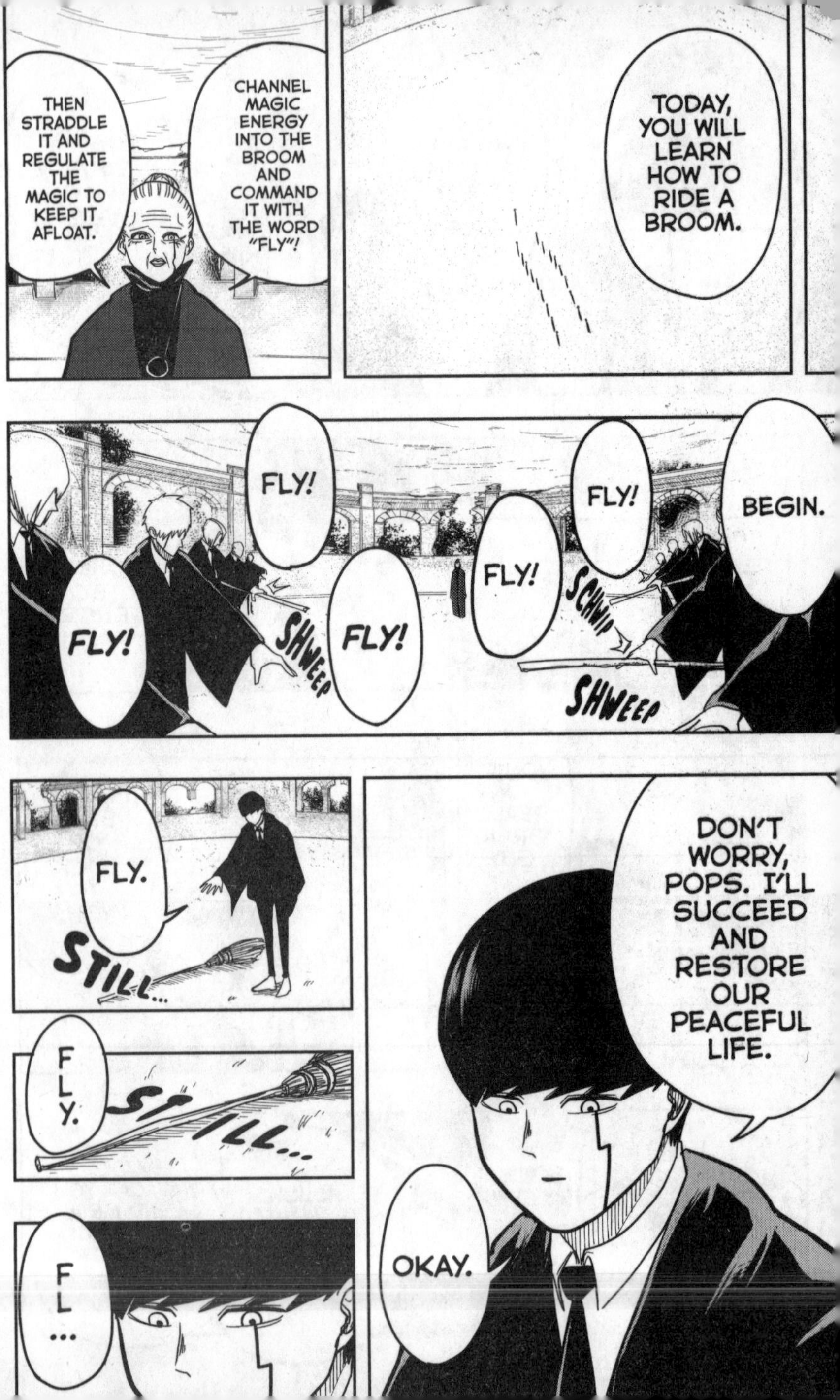
TODAY, YOU WILL LEARN HOW TO RIDE A BROOM.
CHANNEL MAGIC ENERGY INTO THE BROOM AND COMMAND IT WITH THE WORD "FLY"!
THEN STRADDLE IT AND REGULATE THE MAGIC TO KEEP IT AFLOAT.
BEGIN.
FLY!
SCHWIP
SHWEEP
FLY!
FLY!
FLY!
SHWEEP
FLY!
DON'T WORRY, POPS. I'LL SUCCEED AND RESTORE OUR PEACEFUL LIFE.
OKAY.
FLY.
STILL...
FLY.
STILL...
FL...

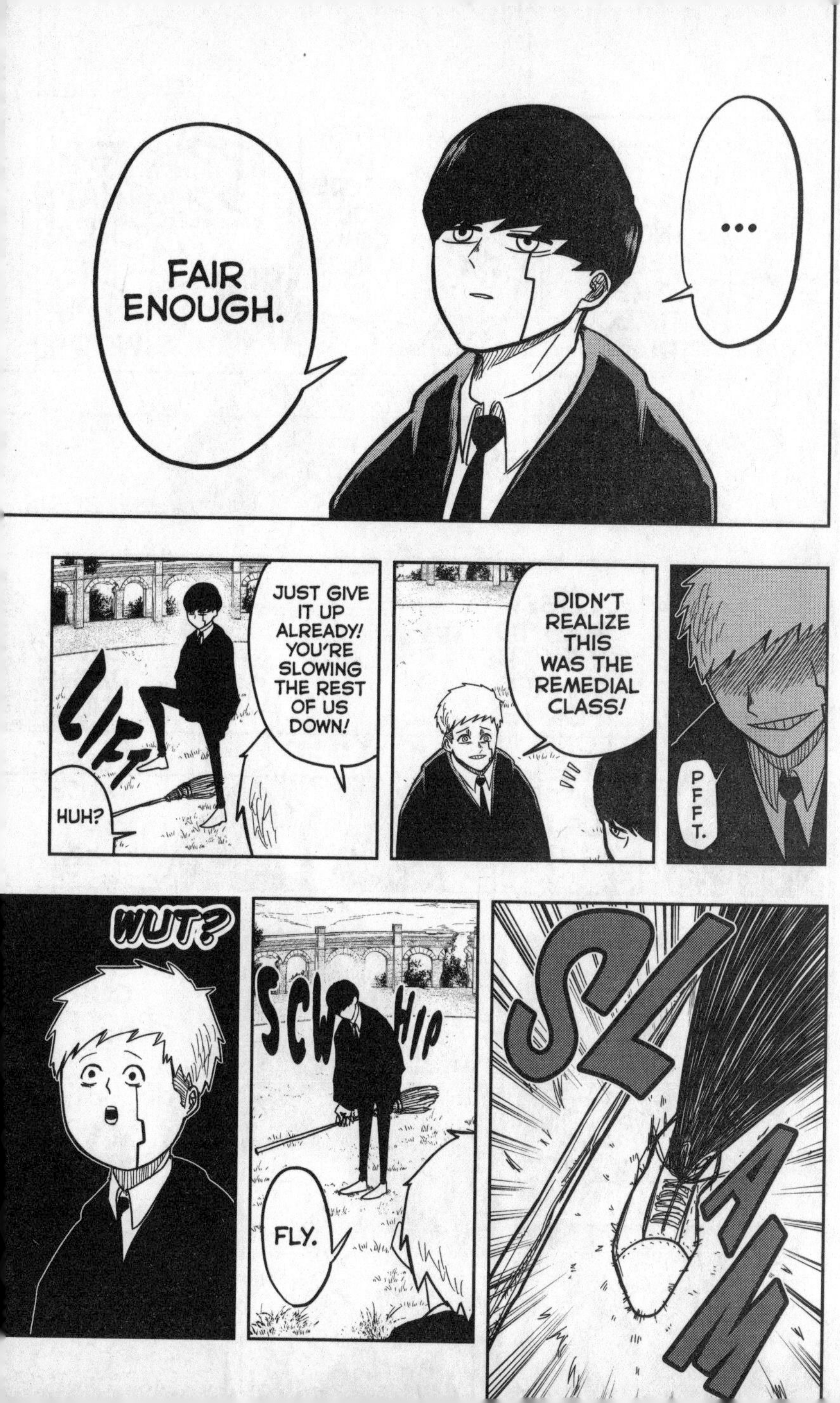
...
FAIR ENOUGH.
PFFT.
DIDN'T REALIZE THIS WAS THE REMEDIAL CLASS!
JUST GIVE IT UP ALREADY! YOU'RE SLOWING THE REST OF US DOWN!
LIFT
HUH?
SLAM
SCWHIP
FLY.
WUT?

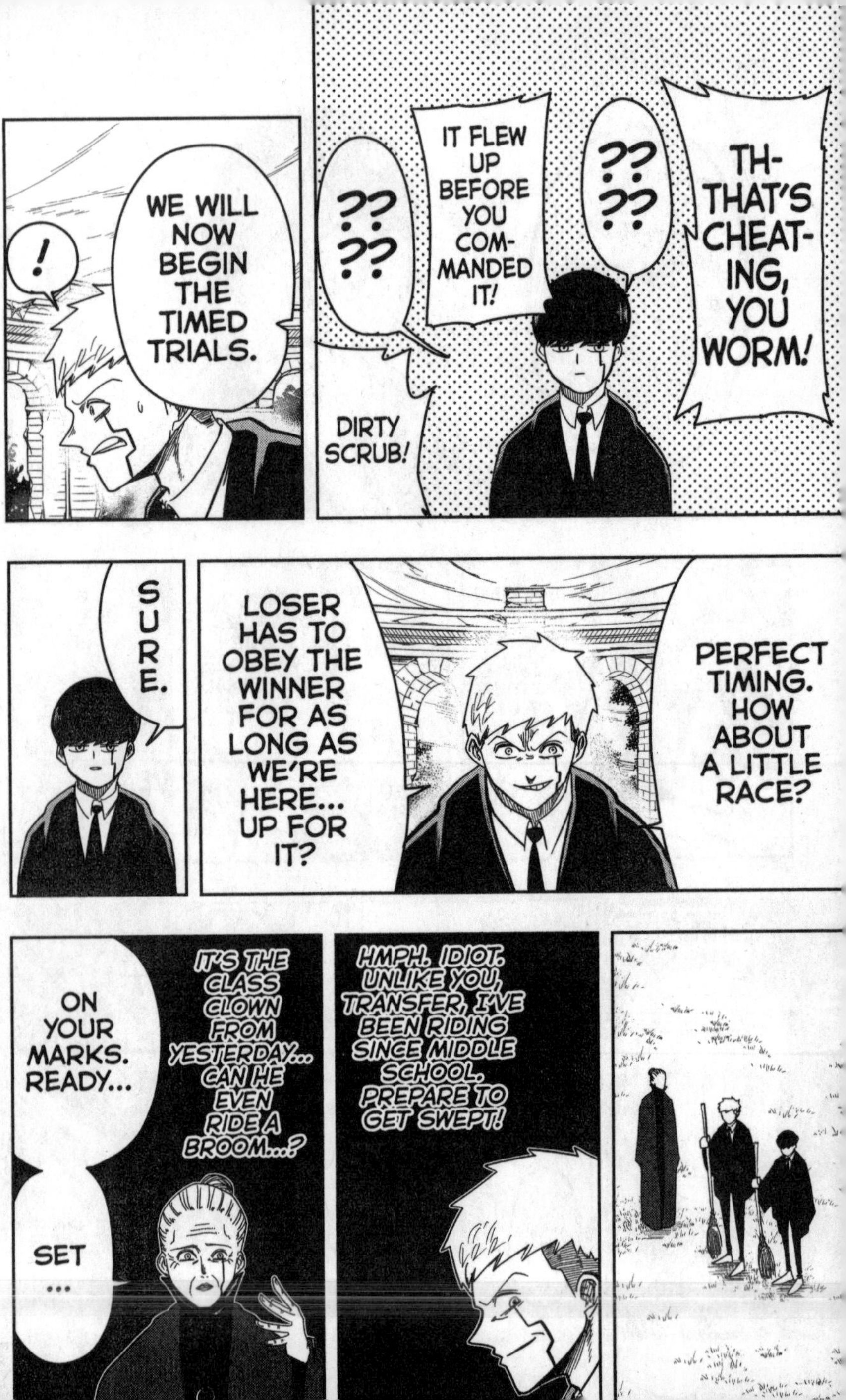
TH-THAT'S CHEAT-ING, YOU WORM!
????
IT FLEW UP BEFORE YOU COM-MANDED IT!
????
DIRTY SCRUB!
WE WILL NOW BEGIN THE TIMED TRIALS.
!
PERFECT TIMING. HOW ABOUT A LITTLE RACE?
LOSER HAS TO OBEY THE WINNER FOR AS LONG AS WE'RE HERE... UP FOR IT?
SURE.
HMPH. IDIOT. UNLIKE YOU, TRANSFER, I'VE BEEN RIDING SINCE MIDDLE SCHOOL. PREPARE TO GET SWEPT!
IT'S THE CLASS CLOWN FROM YESTERDAY... CAN HE EVEN RIDE A BROOM...?
ON YOUR MARKS. READY...
SET...

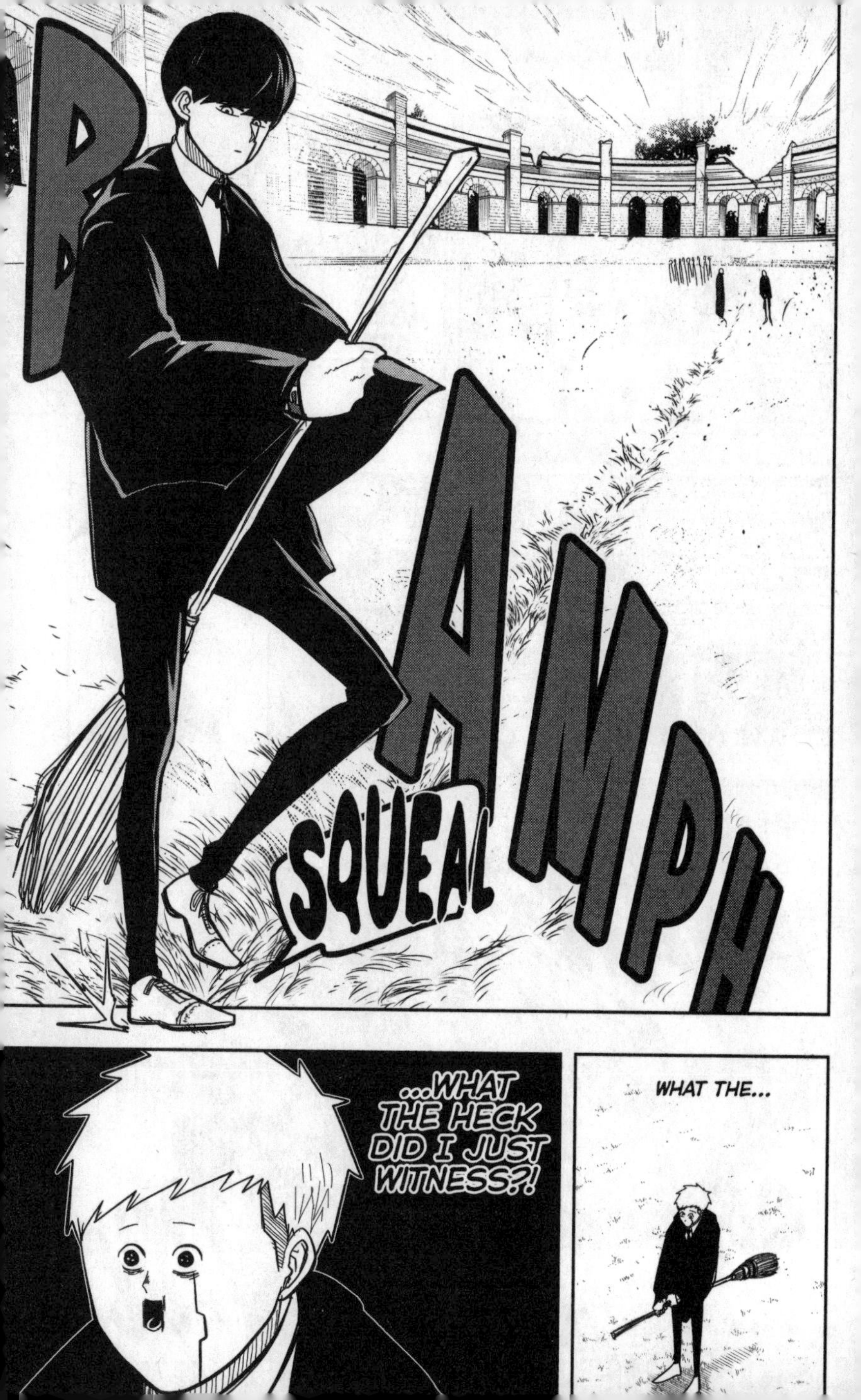
BAMPH
SQUEAL
WHAT THE...
...WHAT THE HECK DID I JUST WITNESS?!

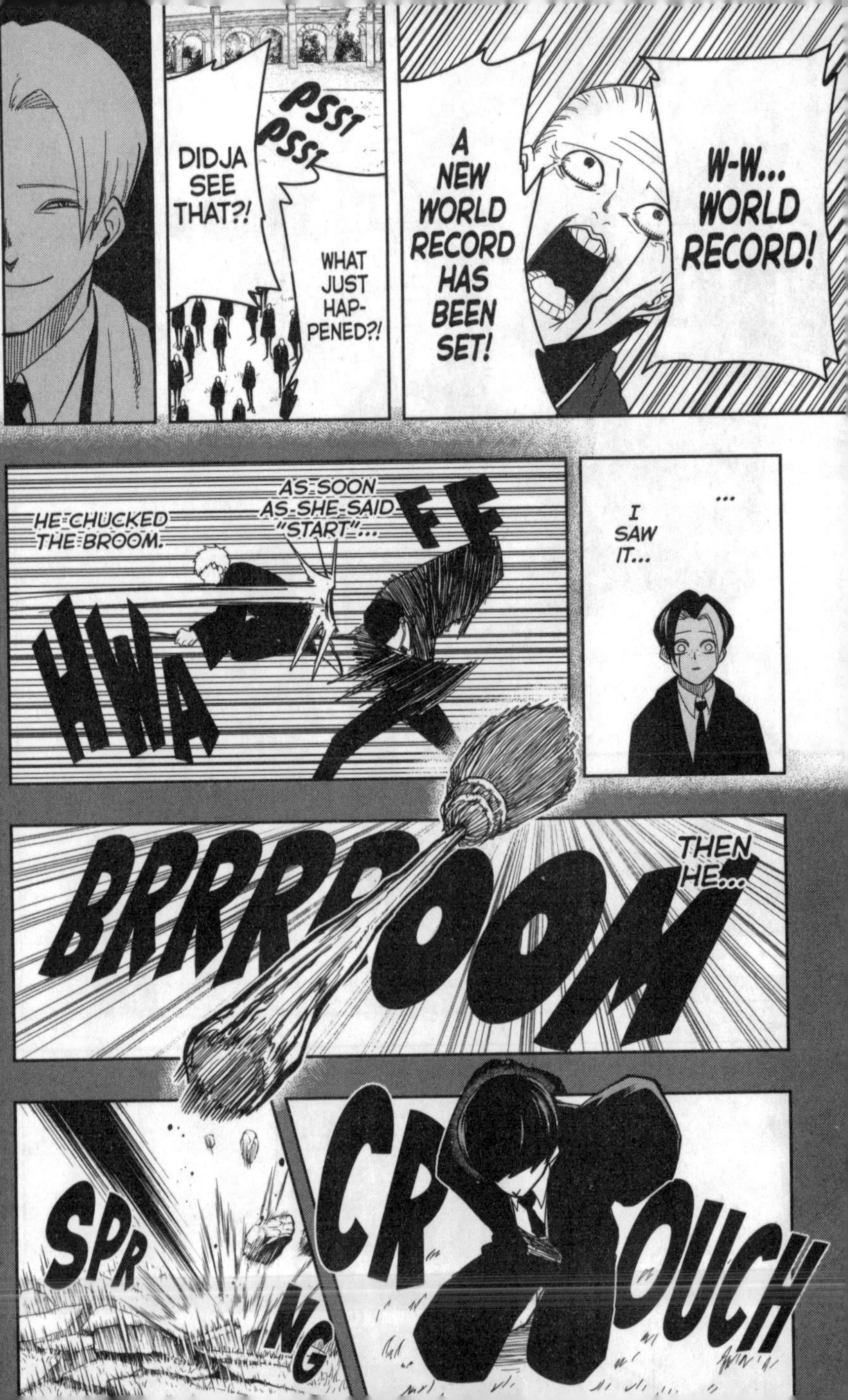
W-W... WORLD RECORD!
A NEW WORLD RECORD HAS BEEN SET!
PSST PSST
DIDJA SEE THAT?!
WHAT JUST HAP-PENED?!
...
I SAW IT...
AS SOON AS SHE SAID "START"...
FF
HE CHUCKED THE BROOM.
HWA
THEN HE...
BRRRROOM
CR OUCH
SPR
NG

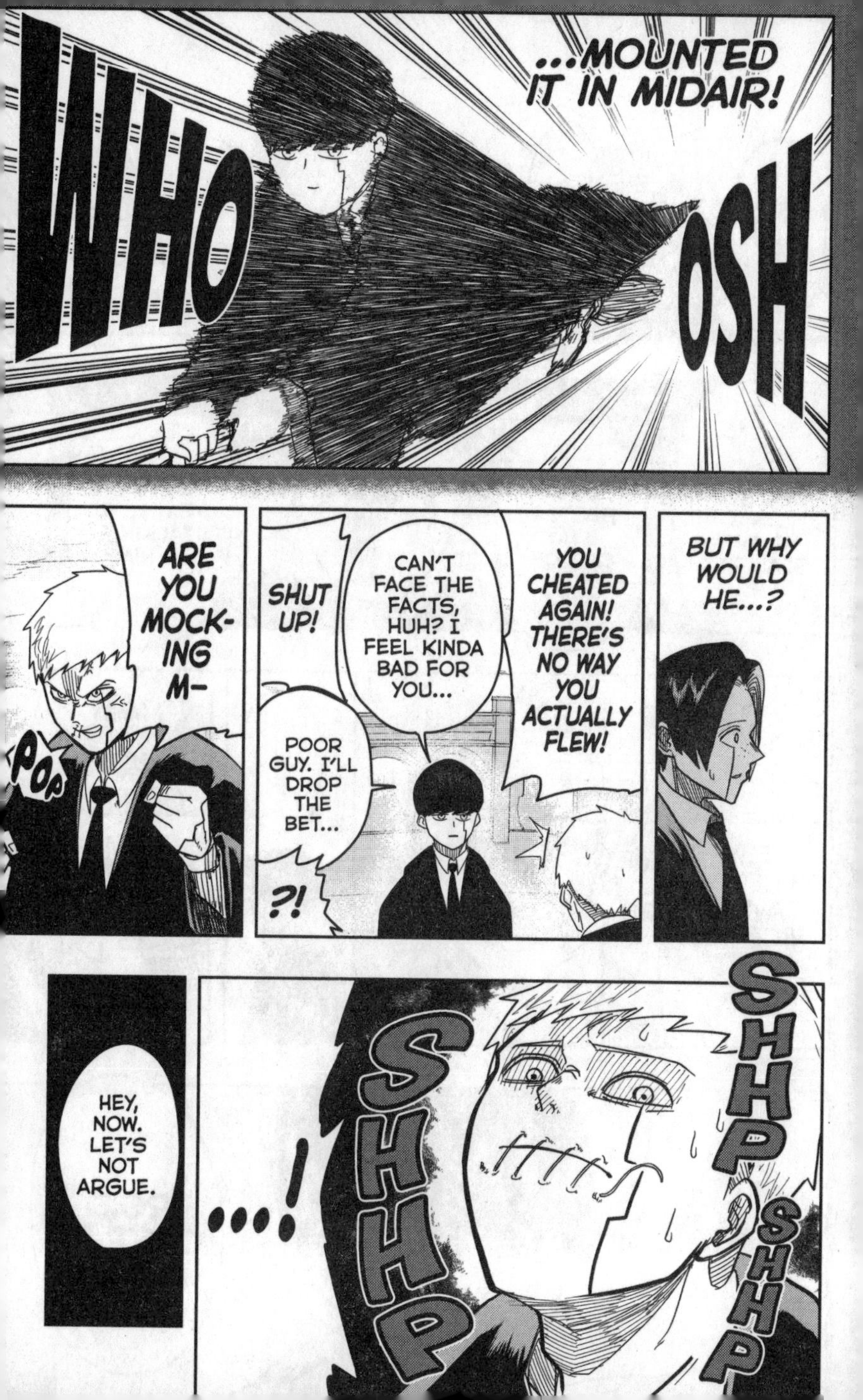
...MOUNTED IT IN MIDAIR!
WHOOSH
BUT WHY WOULD HE...?
YOU CHEATED AGAIN! THERE'S NO WAY YOU ACTUALLY FLEW!
CAN'T FACE THE FACTS, HUH? I FEEL KINDA BAD FOR YOU...
SHUT UP!
POOR GUY. I'LL DROP THE BET...
?!
ARE YOU MOCK-ING M-
POP
SHHP
SHHP
SHHP
...!
HEY, NOW. LET'S NOT ARGUE.

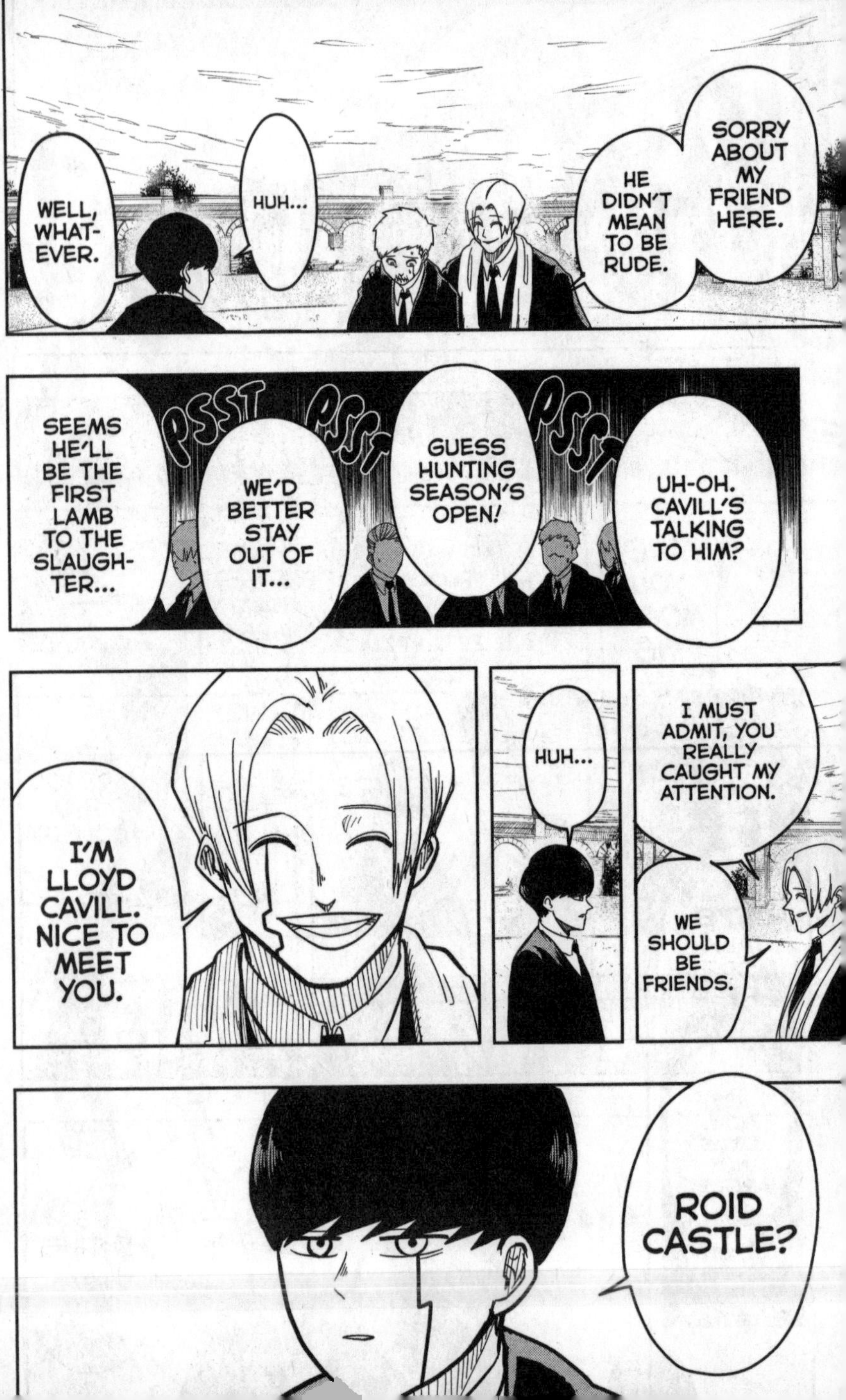
SORRY ABOUT MY FRIEND HERE.
HE DIDN'T MEAN TO BE RUDE.
HUH...
WELL, WHAT-EVER.
UH-OH. CAVILL'S TALKING TO HIM?
PSSST
GUESS HUNTING SEASON'S OPEN!
PSSST
WE'D BETTER STAY OUT OF IT...
PSSST
SEEMS HE'LL BE THE FIRST LAMB TO THE SLAUGH-TER...
I MUST ADMIT, YOU REALLY CAUGHT MY ATTENTION.
WE SHOULD BE FRIENDS.
HUH...
I'M LLOYD CAVILL. NICE TO MEET YOU.
ROID CASTLE?

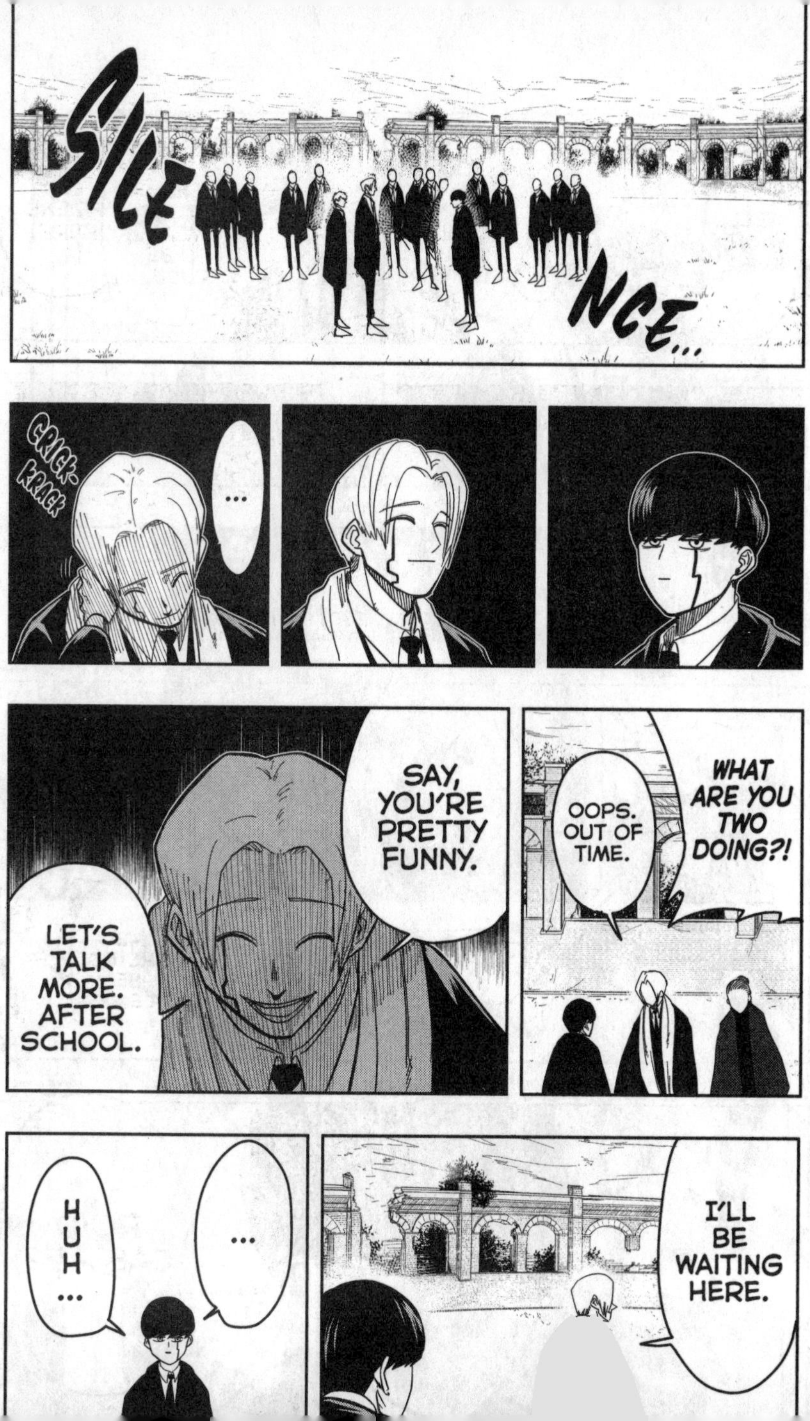
SILENCE...
CRICK-KRACK
...
WHAT ARE YOU TWO DOING?!
OOPS. OUT OF TIME.
SAY, YOU'RE PRETTY FUNNY.
LET'S TALK MORE. AFTER SCHOOL.
I'LL BE WAITING HERE.
...
HUH...

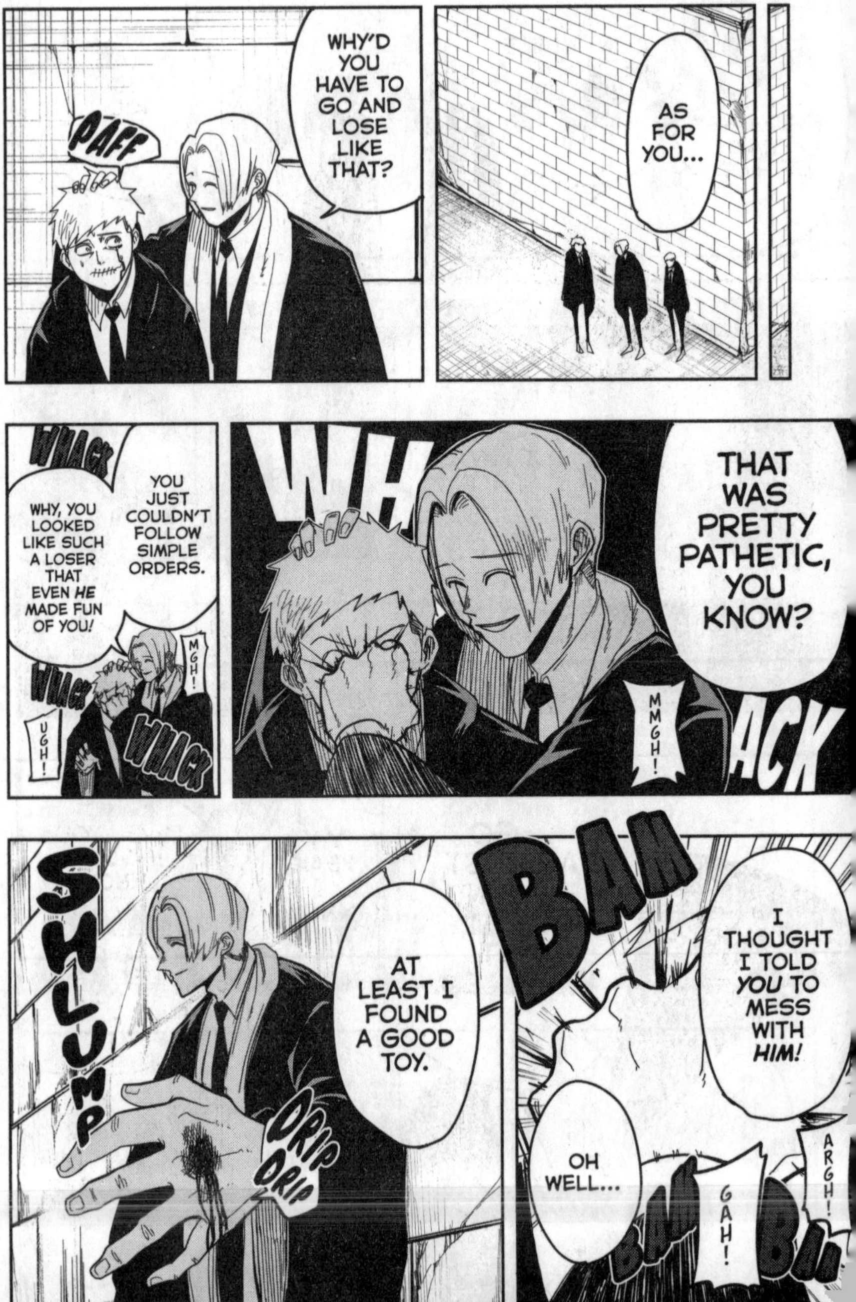
AS FOR YOU...
PAFF
WHY'D YOU HAVE TO GO AND LOSE LIKE THAT?
THAT WAS PRETTY PATHETIC, YOU KNOW?
WH
ACK
MMGH!
WHACK
YOU JUST COULDN'T FOLLOW SIMPLE ORDERS.
WHY, YOU LOOKED LIKE SUCH A LOSER THAT EVEN *HE* MADE FUN OF YOU!
MGH!
WHACK
UGH!
WHACK
BAM
I THOUGHT I TOLD *YOU* TO MESS WITH *HIM!*
ARGH!
GAH!
OH WELL...
AT LEAST I FOUND A GOOD TOY.
SHLUMP
DRIP DRIP

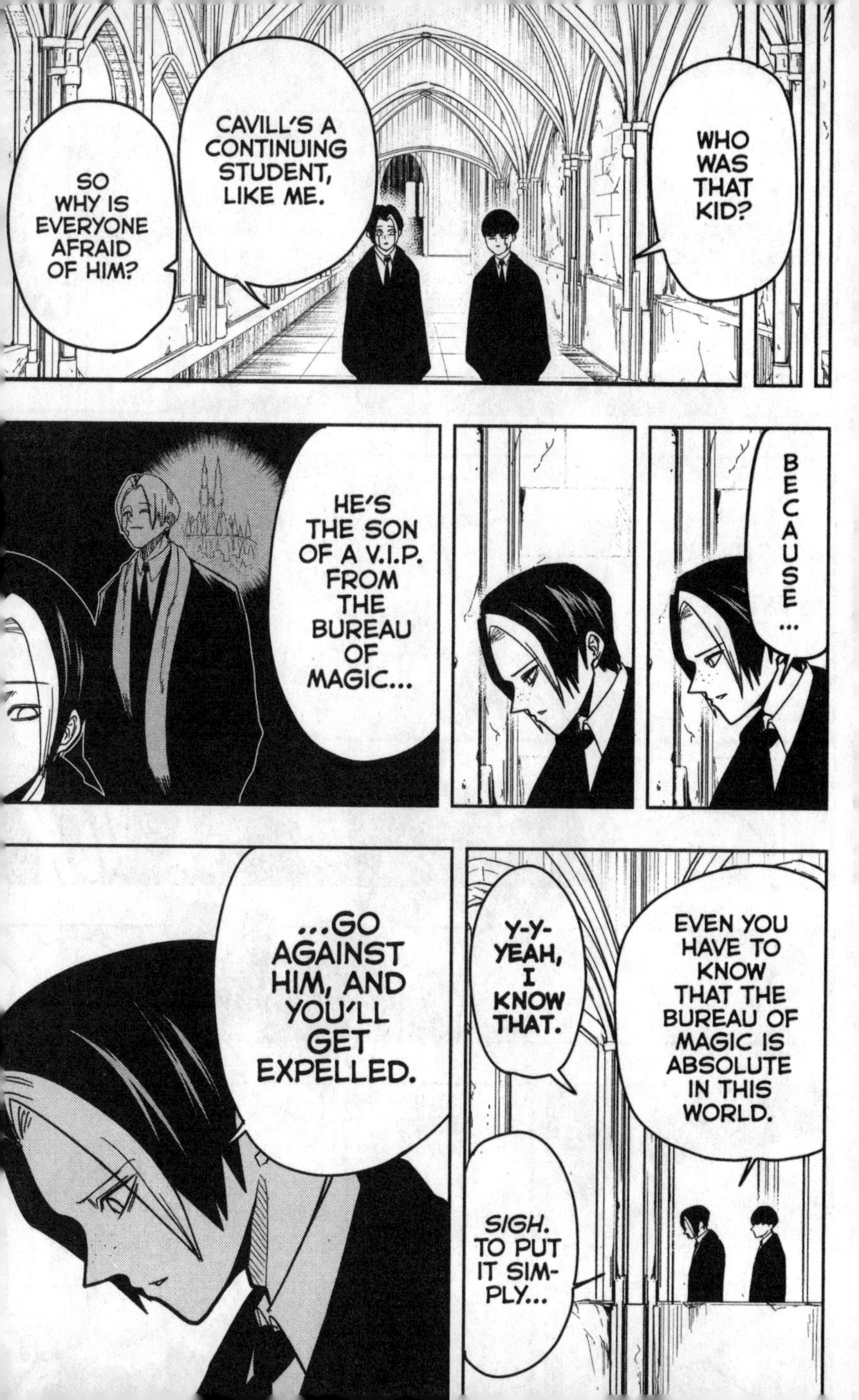
WHO WAS THAT KID?
CAVILL'S A CONTINUING STUDENT, LIKE ME.
SO WHY IS EVERYONE AFRAID OF HIM?
BECAUSE...
HE'S THE SON OF A V.I.P. FROM THE BUREAU OF MAGIC...
EVEN YOU HAVE TO KNOW THAT THE BUREAU OF MAGIC IS ABSOLUTE IN THIS WORLD.
Y-Y-YEAH, I KNOW THAT.
SIGH. TO PUT IT SIMPLY...
...GO AGAINST HIM, AND YOU'LL GET EXPELLED.

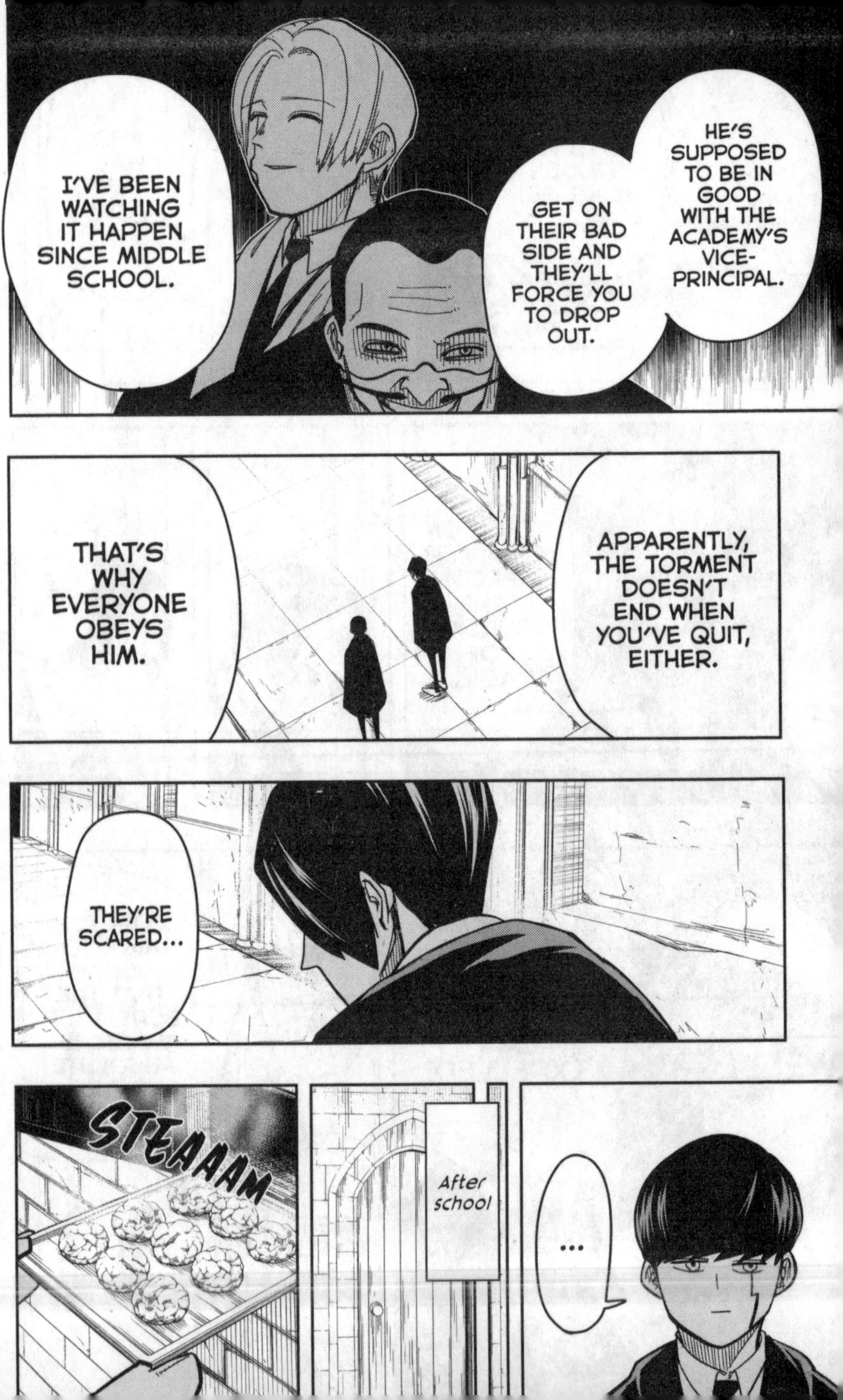
HE'S SUPPOSED TO BE IN GOOD WITH THE ACADEMY'S VICE-PRINCIPAL.
GET ON THEIR BAD SIDE AND THEY'LL FORCE YOU TO DROP OUT.
I'VE BEEN WATCHING IT HAPPEN SINCE MIDDLE SCHOOL.
APPARENTLY, THE TORMENT DOESN'T END WHEN YOU'VE QUIT, EITHER.
THAT'S WHY EVERYONE OBEYS HIM.
THEY'RE SCARED...
...
After school
STEAAAM

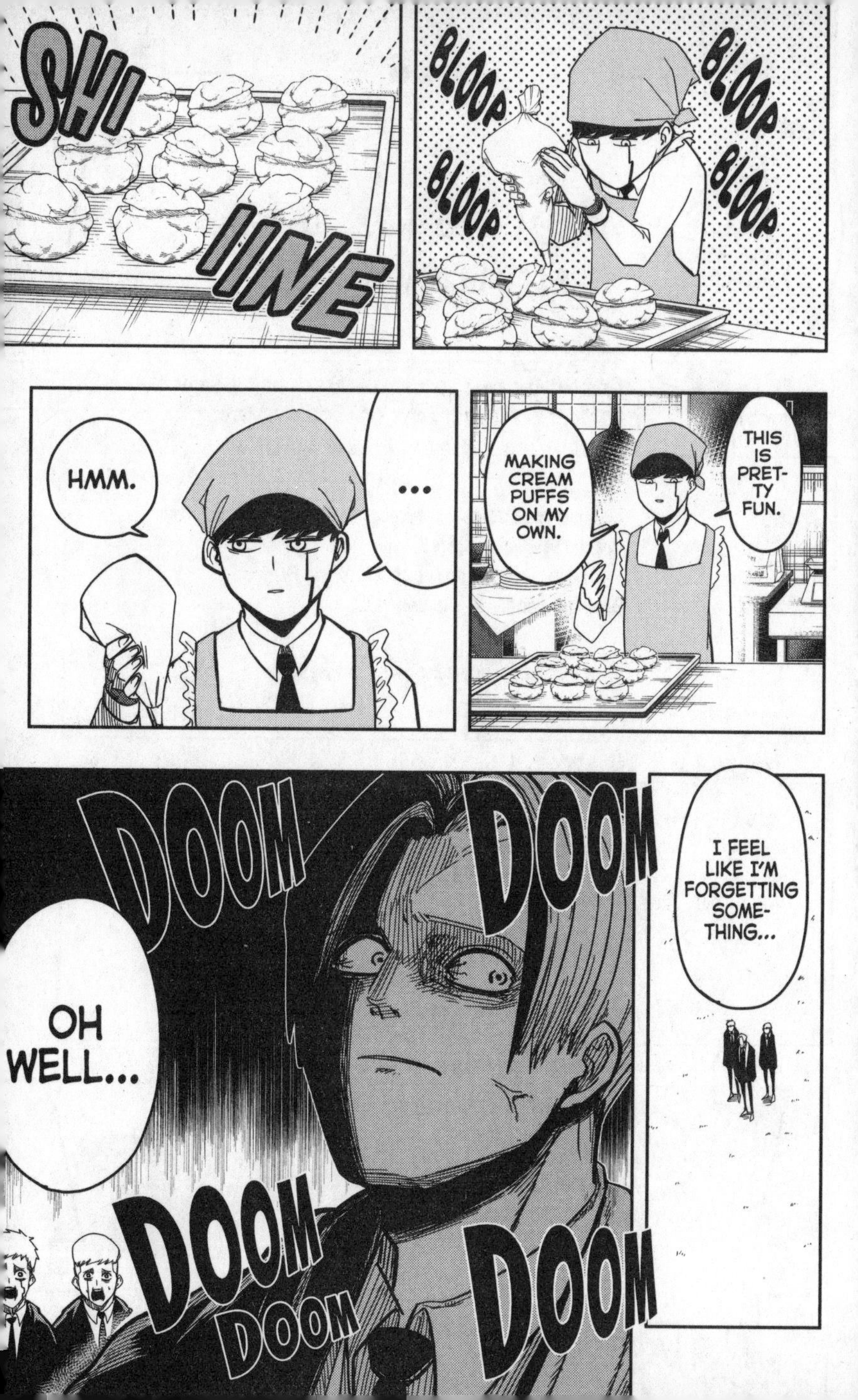
BLOOP
BLOOP
BLOOP
BLOOP
SHIIINE
THIS IS PRET-TY FUN.
MAKING CREAM PUFFS ON MY OWN.
...
HMM.
I FEEL LIKE I'M FORGETTING SOME-THING...
DOOM
DOOM
OH WELL...
DOOM
DOOM
DOOM

The path to Weekly Jump serialization... (3)

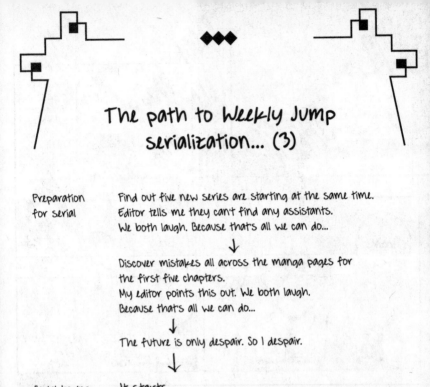

Preparation for serial

Find out five new series are starting at the same time.
Editor tells me they can't find any assistants.
We both laugh. Because that's all we can do...

↓

Discover mistakes all across the manga pages for the first five chapters.
My editor points this out. We both laugh.
Because that's all we can do...

↓

The future is only despair. So I despair.

↓

Serial begins

It starts.

↓

I get fan mail.
I'm thrilled about the fan mail!! I did it!!

The present.

Every time I get even a single piece of fan mail, it inspires me to give it my all!!

Thanks for sticking with me!!

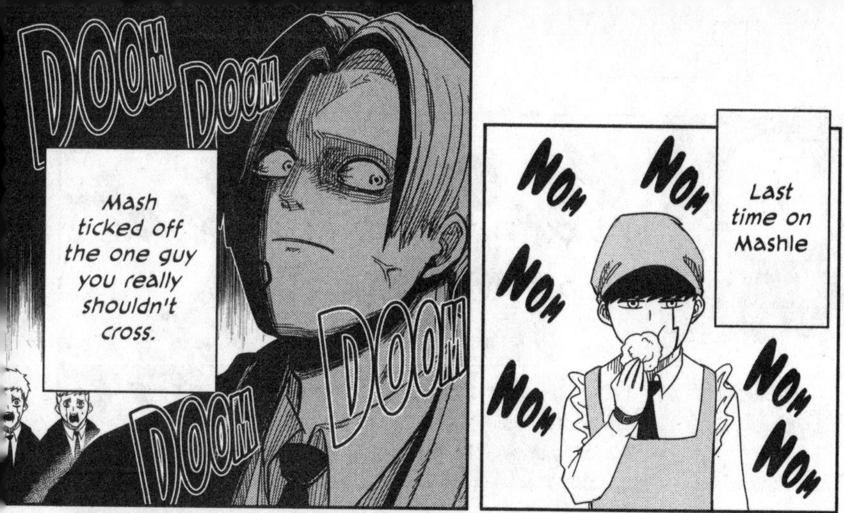
Last time on Mashle
NOM NOM
NOM NOM
NOM NOM
NOM NOM
DOOM DOOM
Mash ticked off the one guy you really shouldn't cross.
DOOM DOOM

CHAPTER 5: MASH BURNEDEAD AND THE BALEFUL BULLY

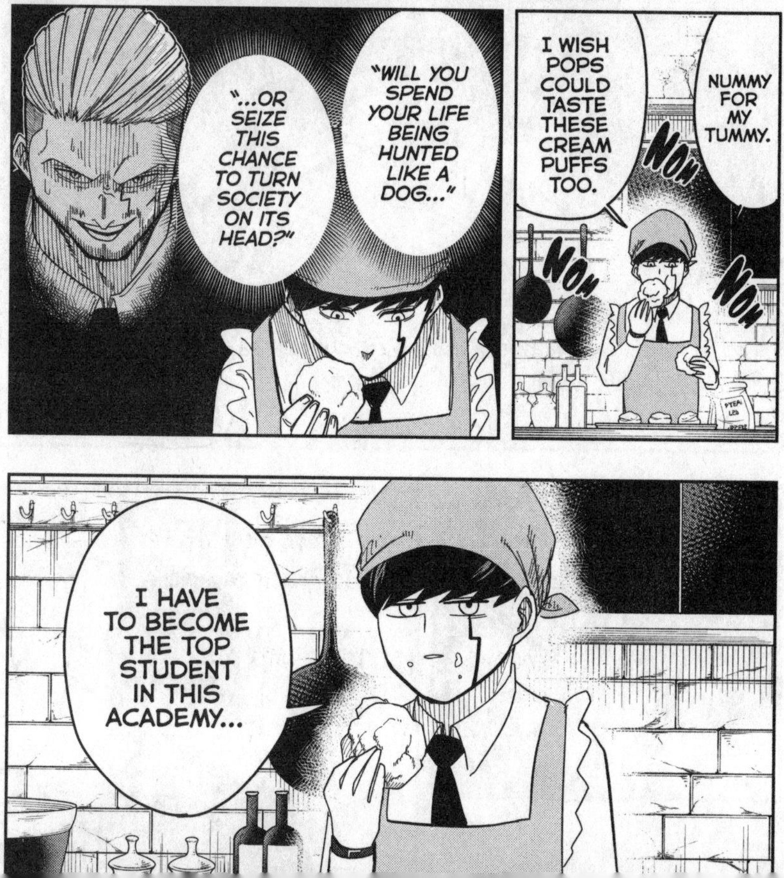
NUMMY FOR MY TUMMY.
I WISH POPS COULD TASTE THESE CREAM PUFFS TOO.
NOM NOM NOM
"WILL YOU SPEND YOUR LIFE BEING HUNTED LIKE A DOG..."
"...OR SEIZE THIS CHANCE TO TURN SOCIETY ON ITS HEAD?"
I HAVE TO BECOME THE TOP STUDENT IN THIS ACADEMY...

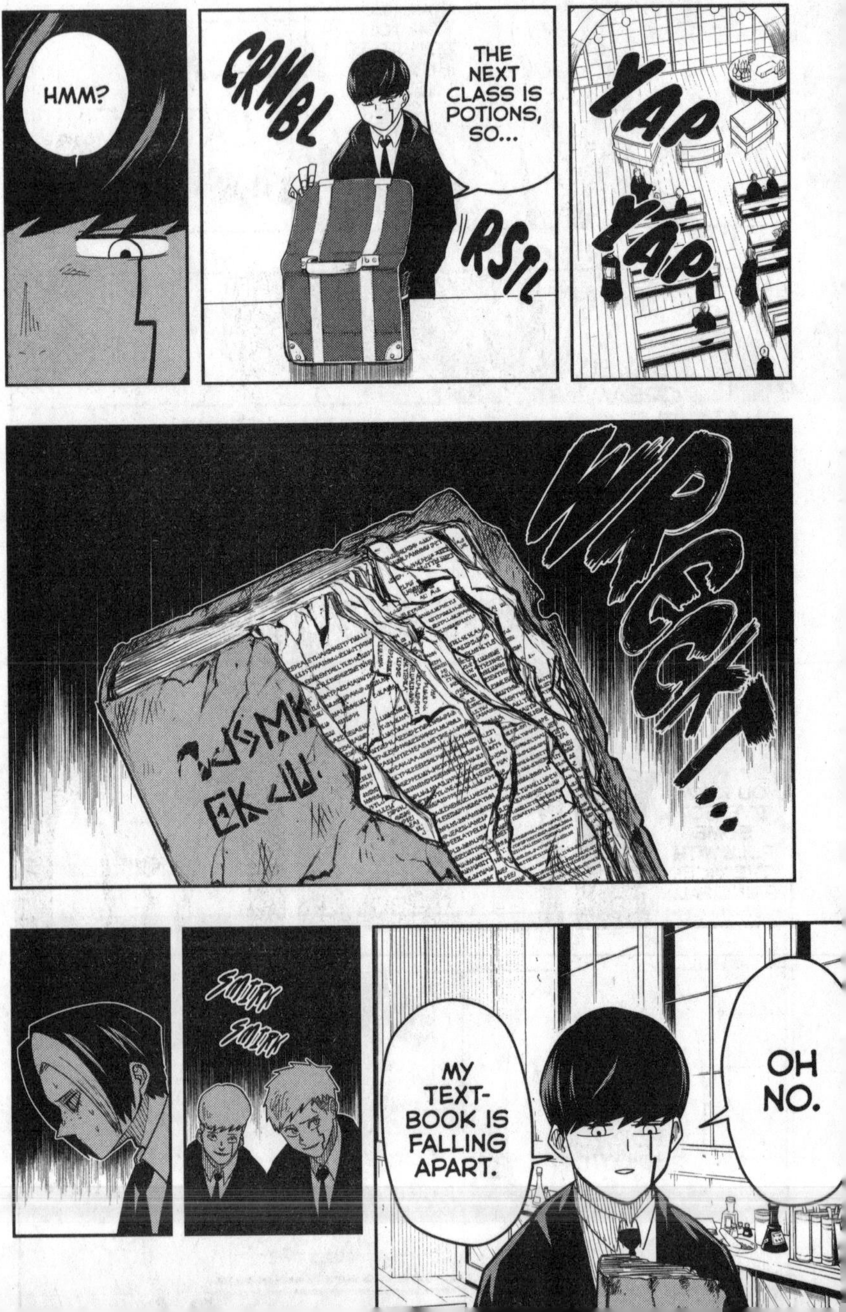
YAP
YAP
CRMBL
THE NEXT CLASS IS POTIONS, SO...
RSTL
HMM?
WRECK...
OH NO.
MY TEXTBOOK IS FALLING APART.

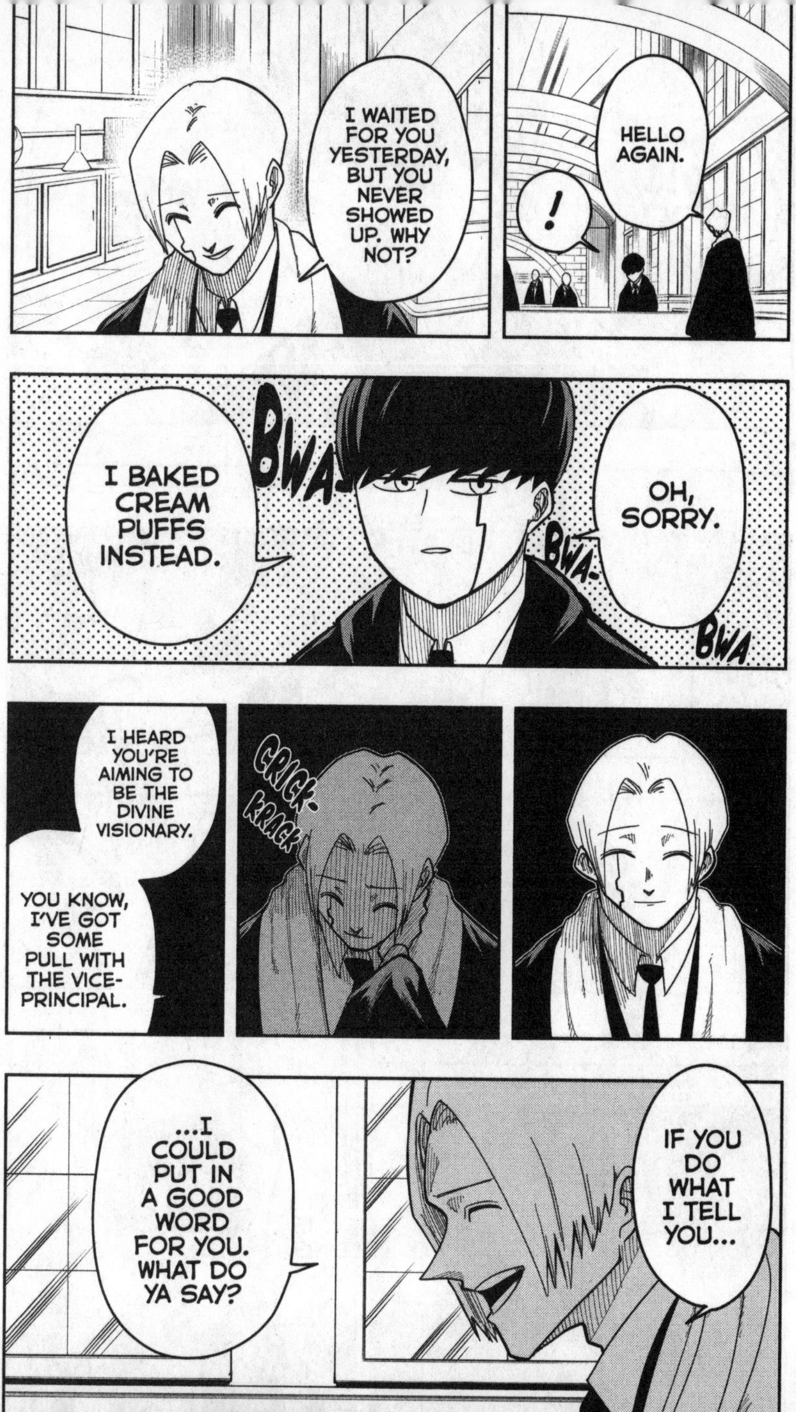
HELLO AGAIN.
!
I WAITED FOR YOU YESTERDAY, BUT YOU NEVER SHOWED UP. WHY NOT?
OH, SORRY.
BWA-
BWA-
BWA
I BAKED CREAM PUFFS INSTEAD.
CRICK-KRACK
I HEARD YOU'RE AIMING TO BE THE DIVINE VISIONARY.
YOU KNOW, I'VE GOT SOME PULL WITH THE VICE-PRINCIPAL.
IF YOU DO WHAT I TELL YOU...
...I COULD PUT IN A GOOD WORD FOR YOU. WHAT DO YA SAY?

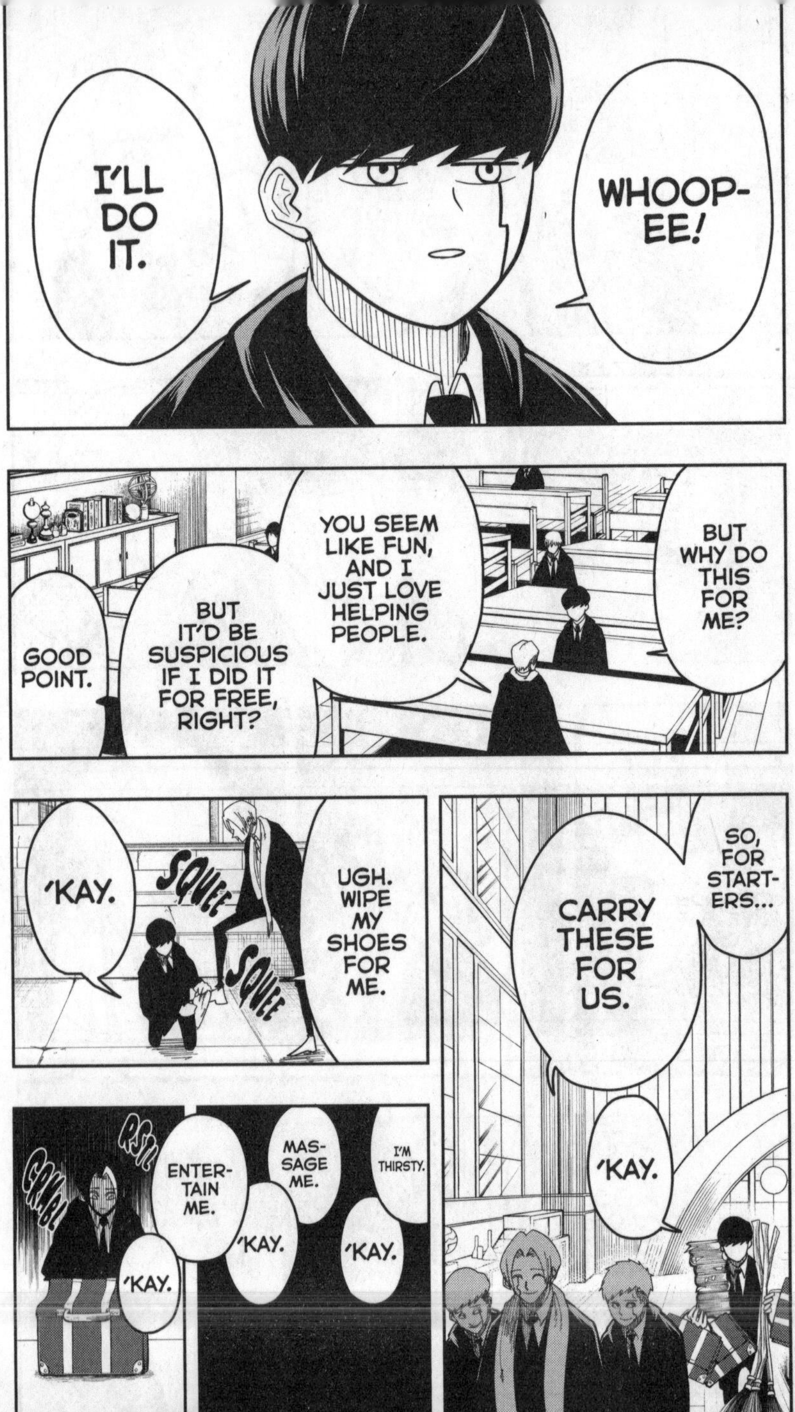
WHOOP-EE!
I'LL DO IT.
BUT WHY DO THIS FOR ME?
YOU SEEM LIKE FUN, AND I JUST LOVE HELPING PEOPLE.
BUT IT'D BE SUSPICIOUS IF I DID IT FOR FREE, RIGHT?
GOOD POINT.
SO, FOR STARTERS...
CARRY THESE FOR US.
'KAY.
UGH. WIPE MY SHOES FOR ME.
SQUEE
SQUEE
'KAY.
I'M THIRSTY.
'KAY.
MAS-SAGE ME.
'KAY.
ENTER-TAIN ME.
RSTL
CRMB!
'KAY.

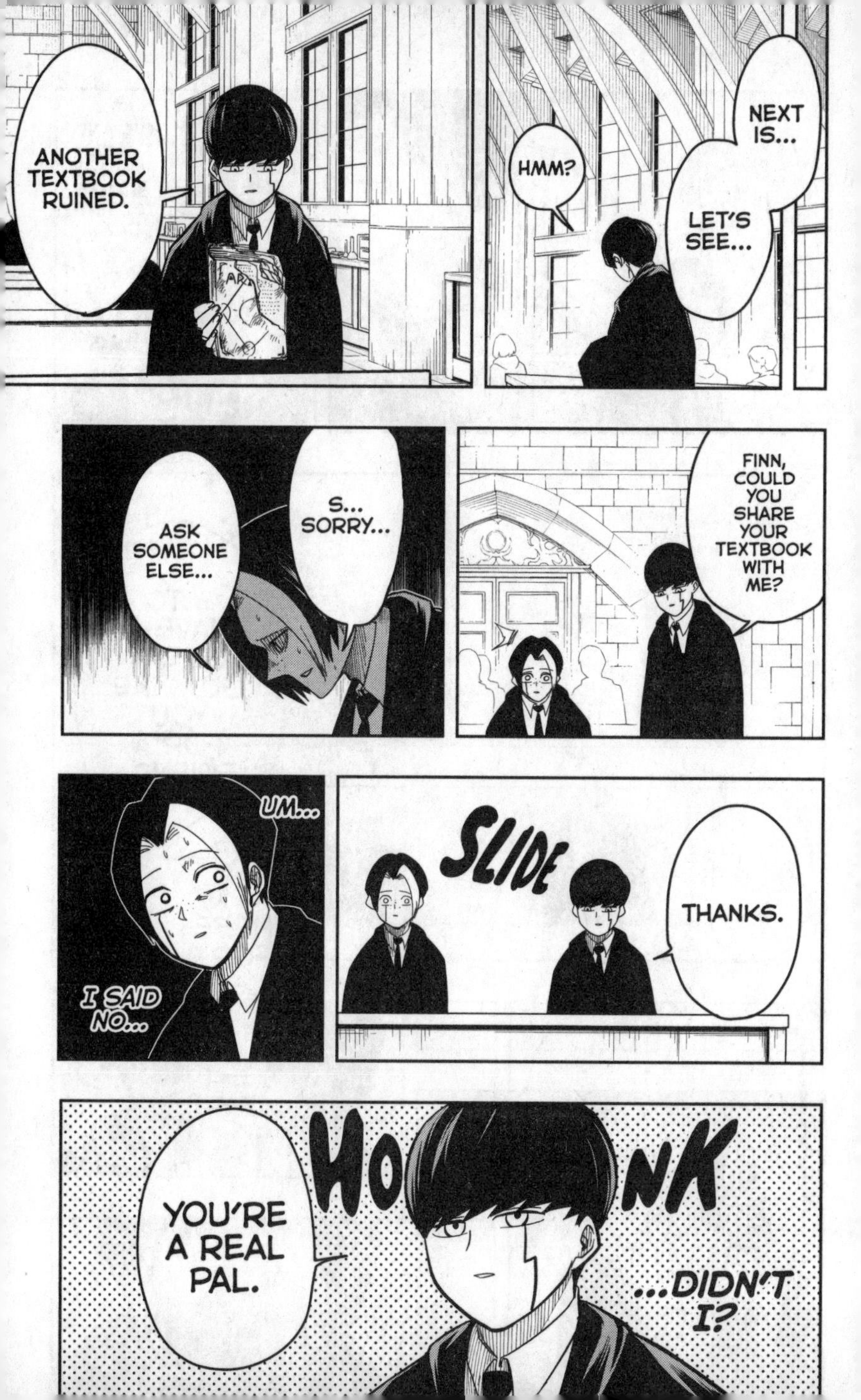
NEXT IS...
LET'S SEE...
HMM?
ANOTHER TEXTBOOK RUINED.
FINN, COULD YOU SHARE YOUR TEXTBOOK WITH ME?
S... SORRY...
ASK SOMEONE ELSE...
SLIDE
THANKS.
UM...
I SAID NO...
HO NK
YOU'RE A REAL PAL.
...DIDN'T I?

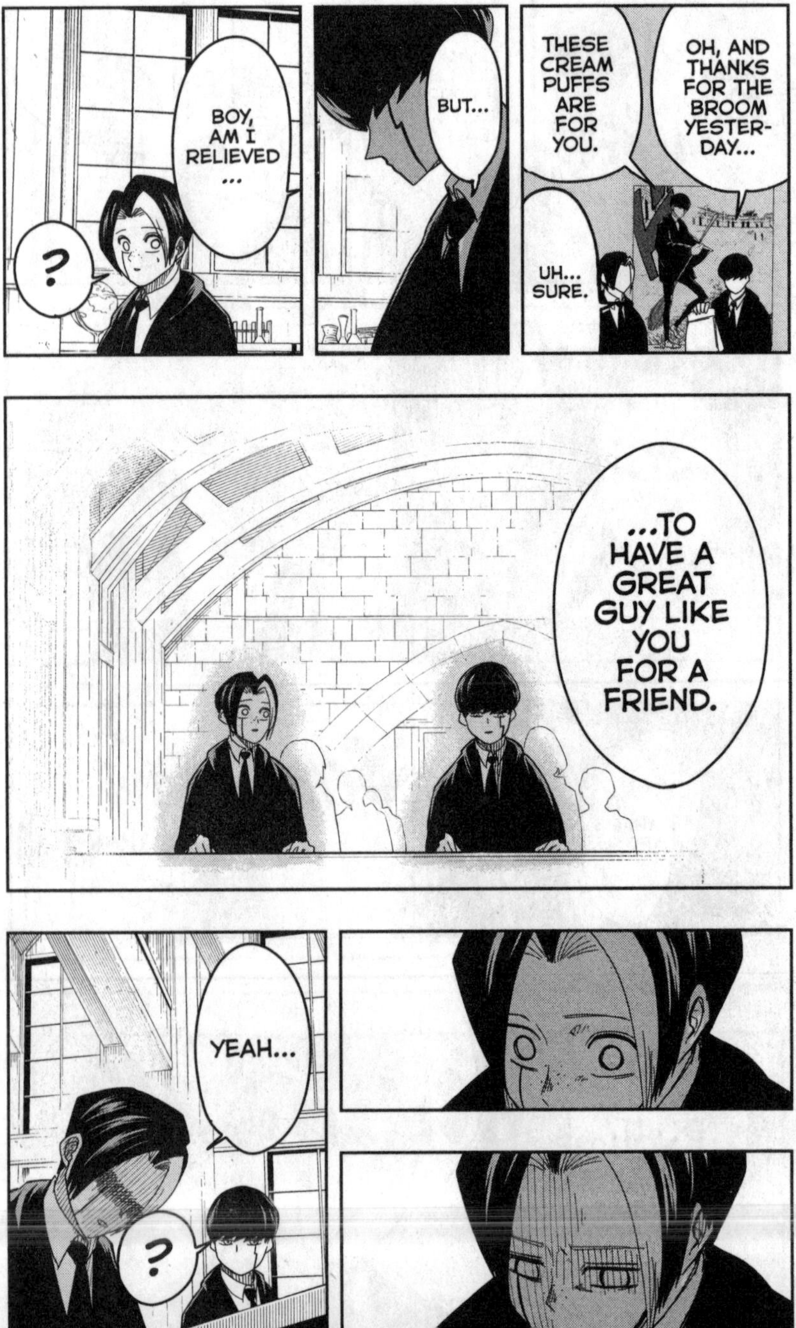
OH, AND THANKS FOR THE BROOM YESTER-DAY...
THESE CREAM PUFFS ARE FOR YOU.
UH... SURE.
BUT...
BOY, AM I RELIEVED...
?
...TO HAVE A GREAT GUY LIKE YOU FOR A FRIEND.
YEAH...
?

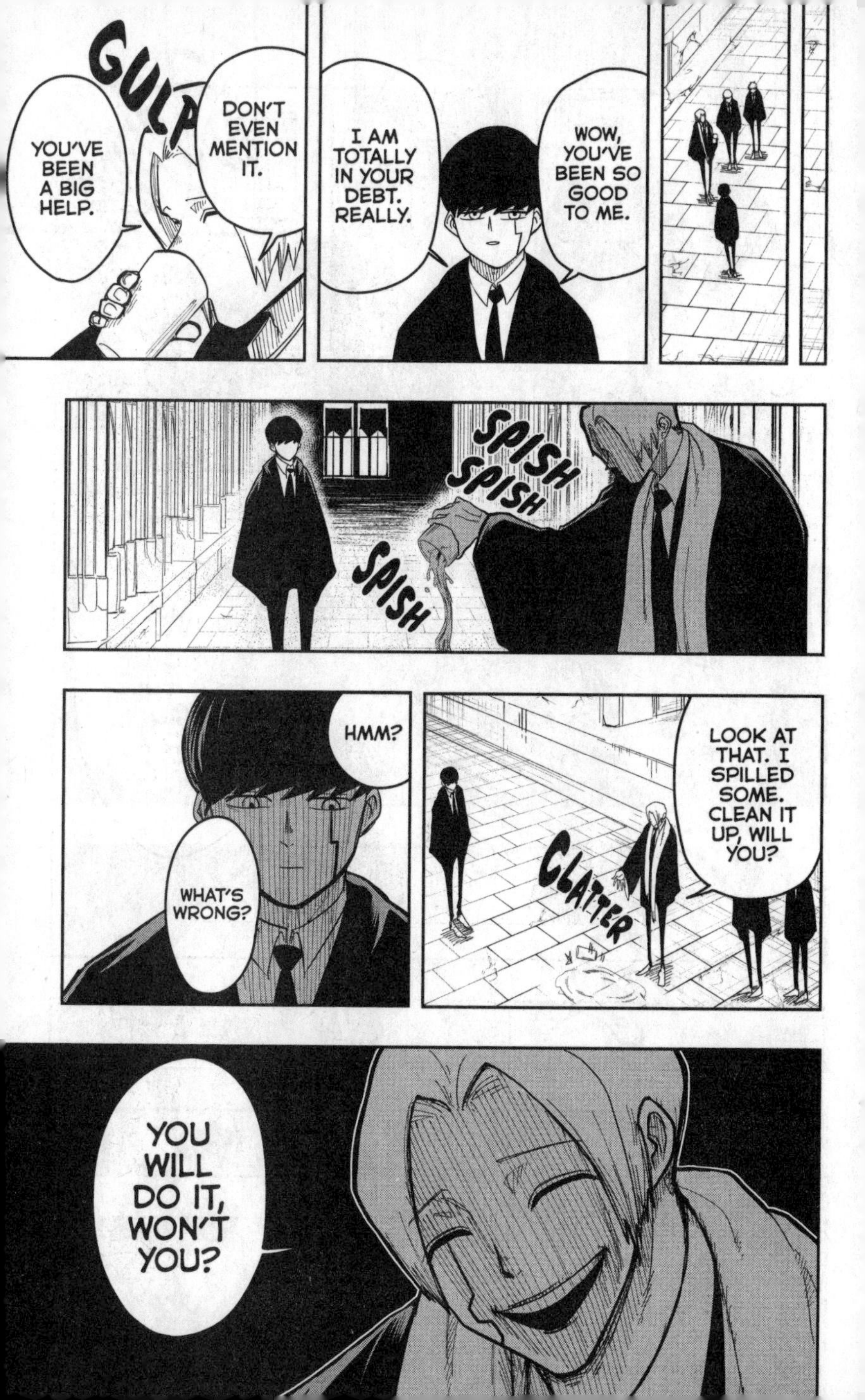
WOW, YOU'VE BEEN SO GOOD TO ME.
I AM TOTALLY IN YOUR DEBT. REALLY.
DON'T EVEN MENTION IT.
GULP
YOU'VE BEEN A BIG HELP.
SPISH
SPISH
SPISH
LOOK AT THAT. I SPILLED SOME. CLEAN IT UP, WILL YOU?
CLATTER
HMM?
WHAT'S WRONG?
YOU WILL DO IT, WON'T YOU?

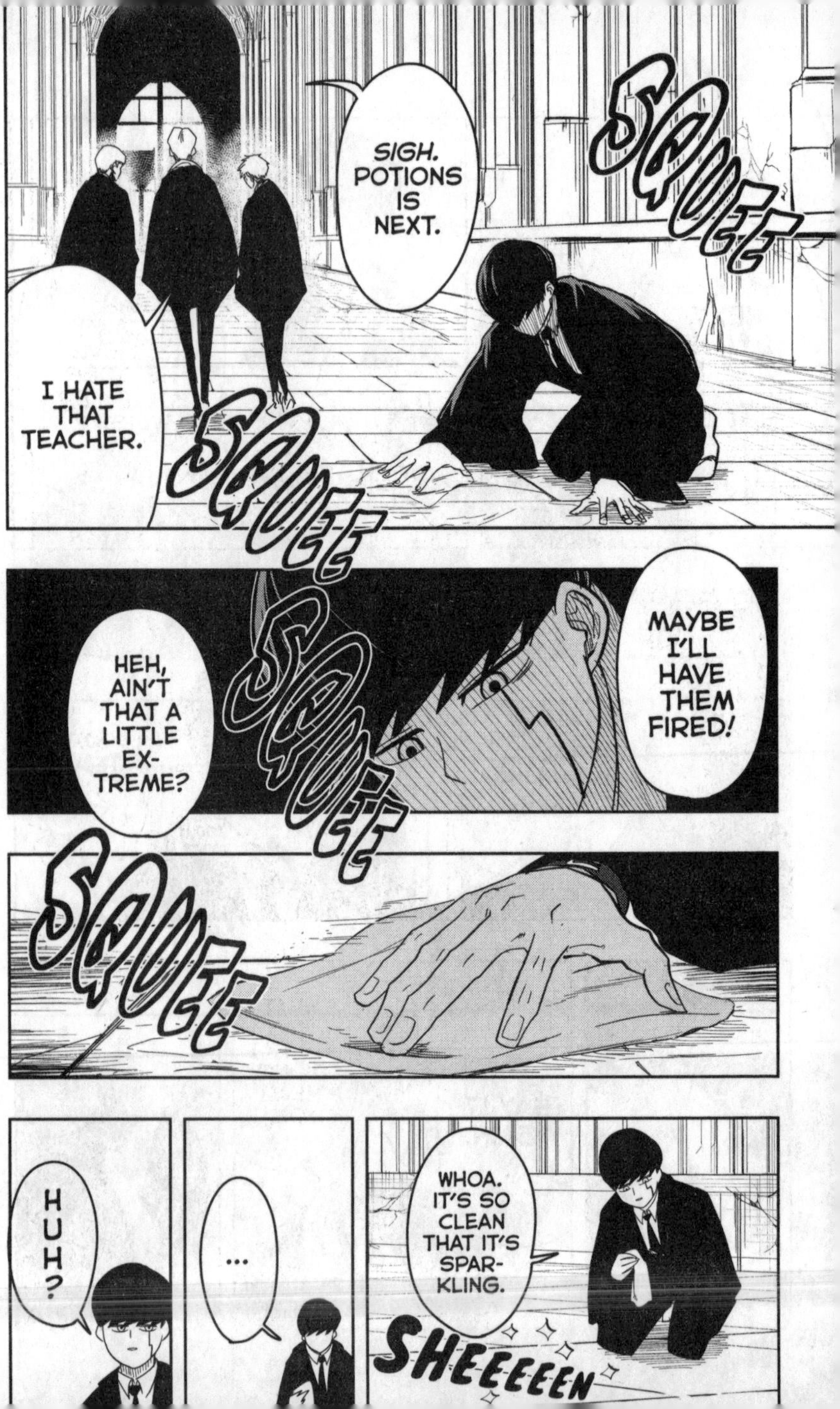
SQUEEE
SIGH. POTIONS IS NEXT.
I HATE THAT TEACHER.
SQUEEE
MAYBE I'LL HAVE THEM FIRED!
HEH, AIN'T THAT A LITTLE EX-TREME?
SQUEEE
SQUEEE
WHOA. IT'S SO CLEAN THAT IT'S SPAR-KLING.
SHEEEEEN
...
HUH?

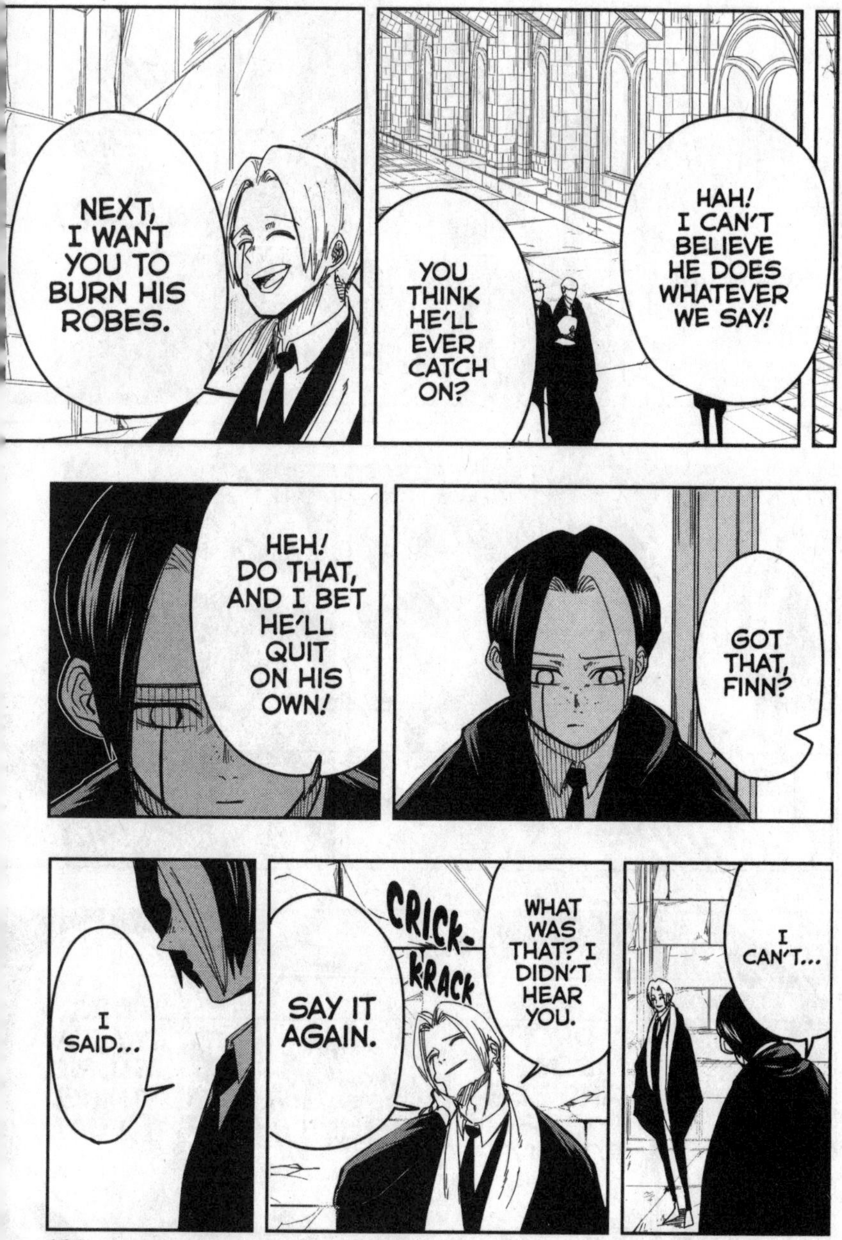
HAH! I CAN'T BELIEVE HE DOES WHATEVER WE SAY!
YOU THINK HE'LL EVER CATCH ON?
NEXT, I WANT YOU TO BURN HIS ROBES.
GOT THAT, FINN?
HEH! DO THAT, AND I BET HE'LL QUIT ON HIS OWN!
I CAN'T...
WHAT WAS THAT? I DIDN'T HEAR YOU.
CRICK-KRACK
SAY IT AGAIN.
I SAID...

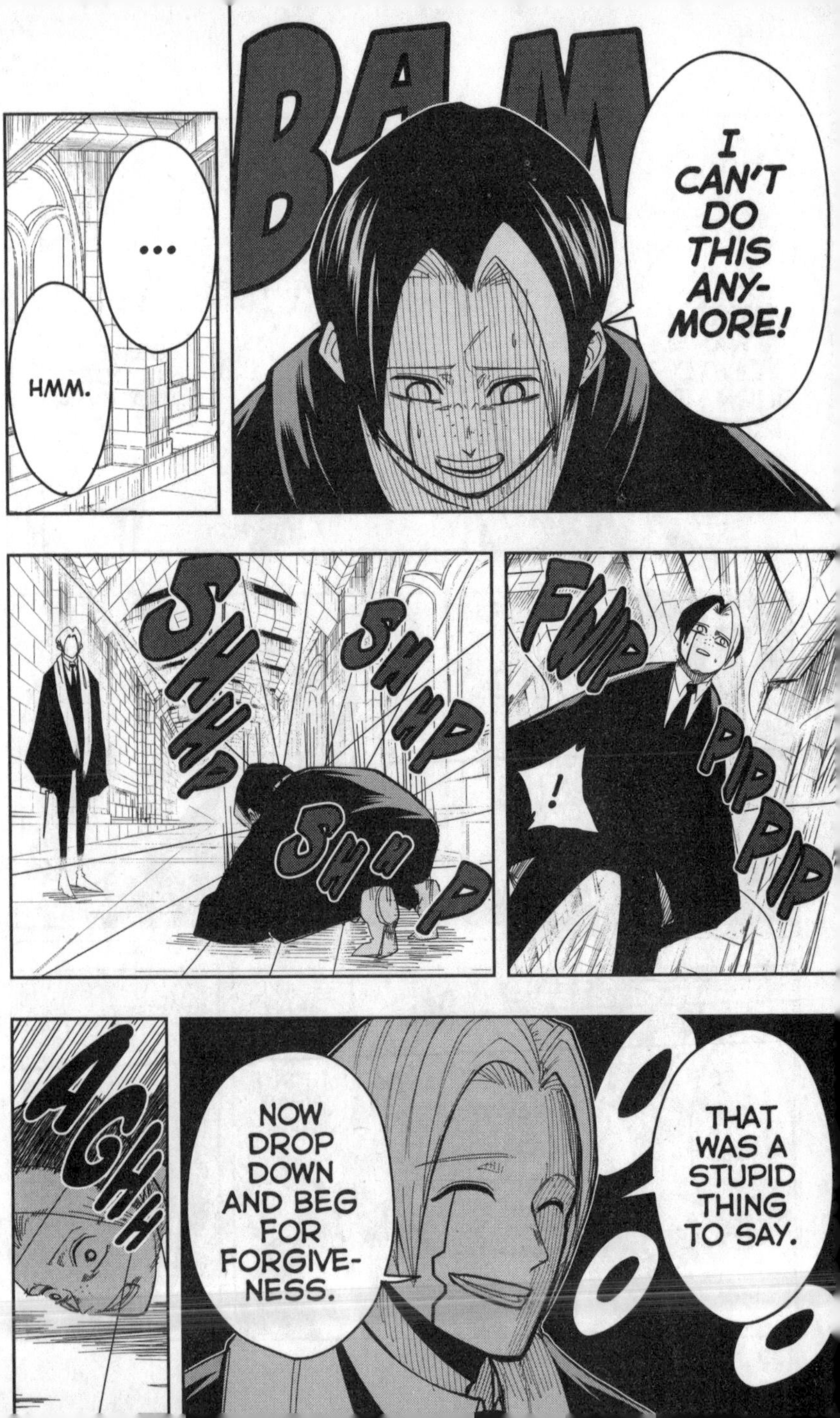
BAM
I CAN'T DO THIS ANYMORE!
...
HMM.
FWIP
!
PIP PIP PIP
SHHP
SHHP
SHHP
THAT WAS A STUPID THING TO SAY.
NOW DROP DOWN AND BEG FOR FORGIVENESS.
AGHH

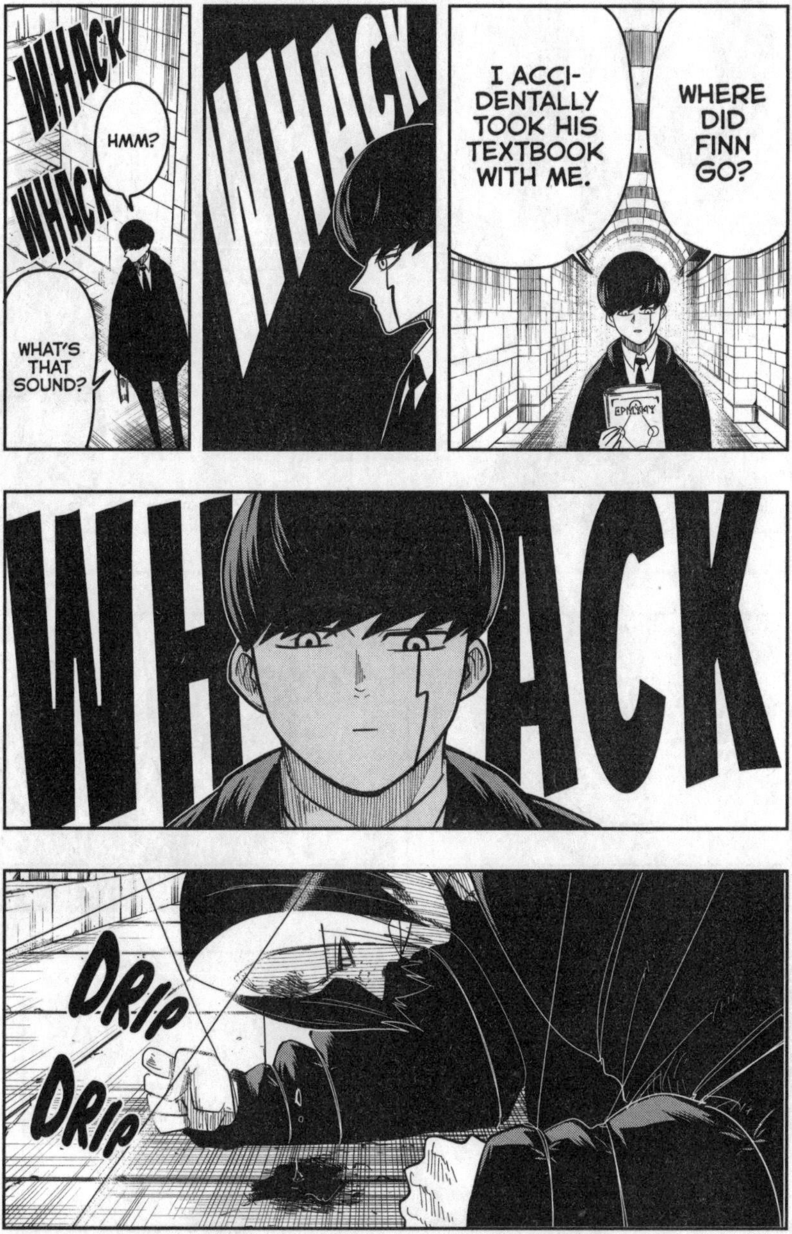
WHERE DID FINN GO?
I ACCI-DENTALLY TOOK HIS TEXTBOOK WITH ME.
WHACK
WHACK
HMM?
WHACK
WHAT'S THAT SOUND?
WHACK
DRIP
DRIP

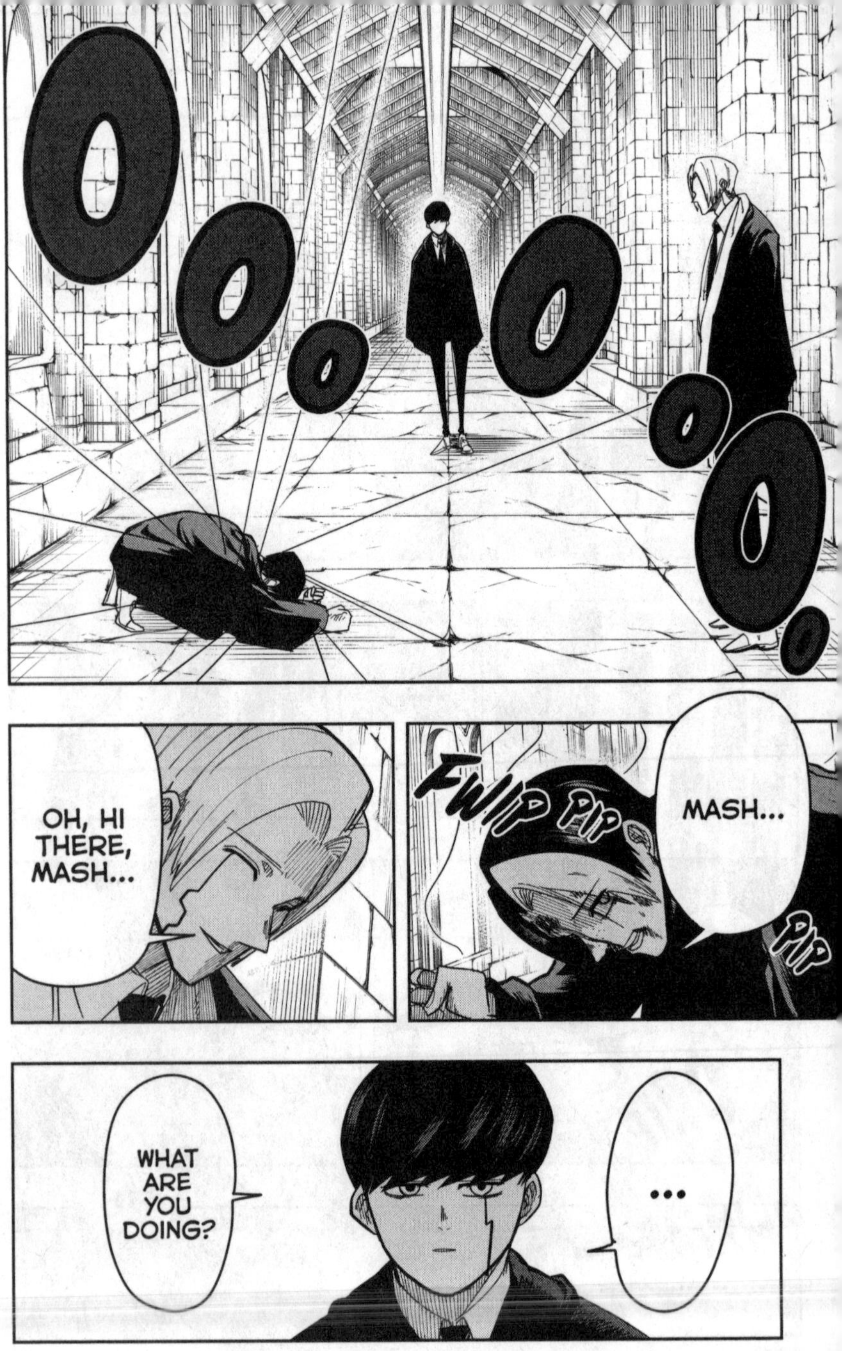
FWIP
PIP PIP
MASH...
PIP
OH, HI THERE, MASH...
...
WHAT ARE YOU DOING?

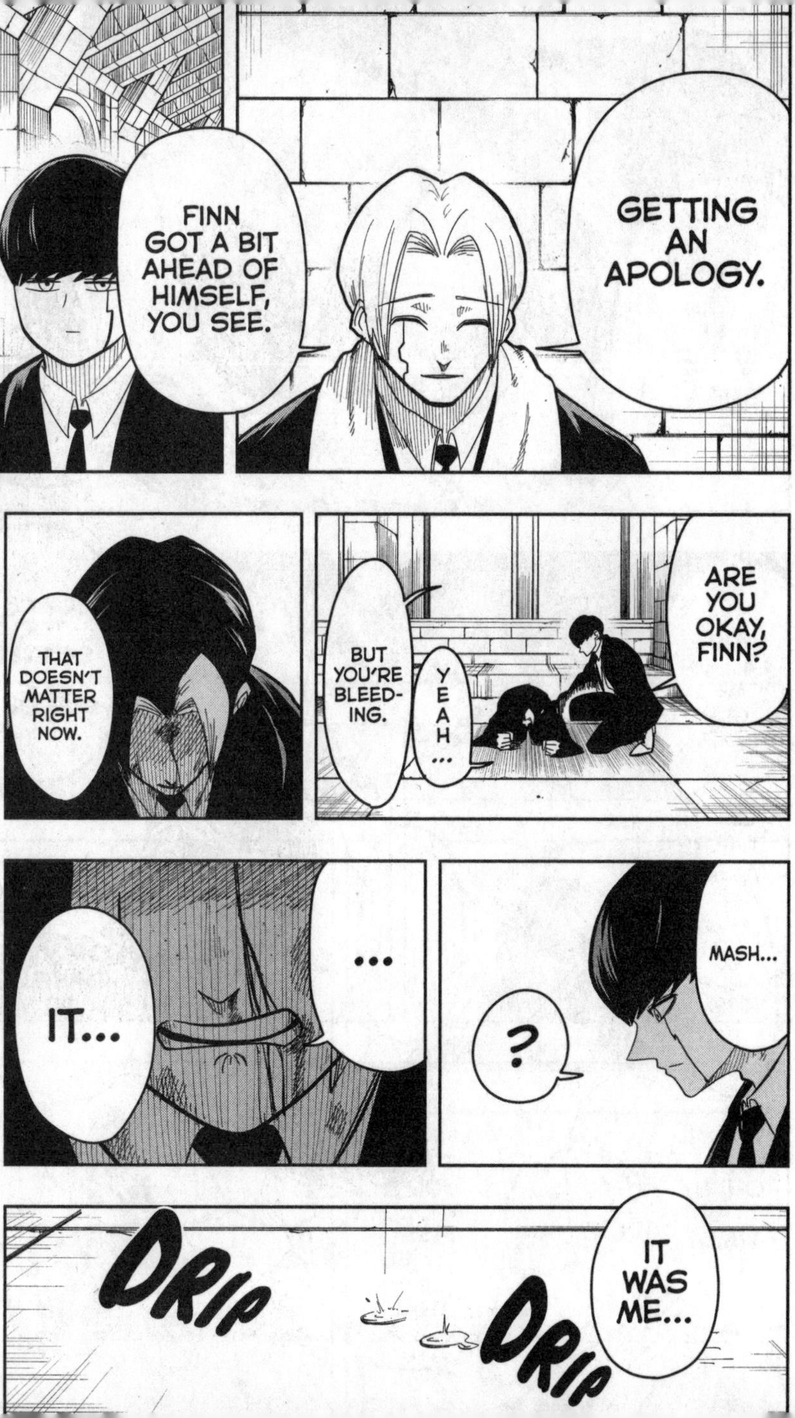
GETTING AN APOLOGY.
FINN GOT A BIT AHEAD OF HIMSELF, YOU SEE.
ARE YOU OKAY, FINN?
YEAH...
BUT YOU'RE BLEEDING.
THAT DOESN'T MATTER RIGHT NOW.
MASH...
?
...
IT...
IT WAS ME...
DRIP
DRIP

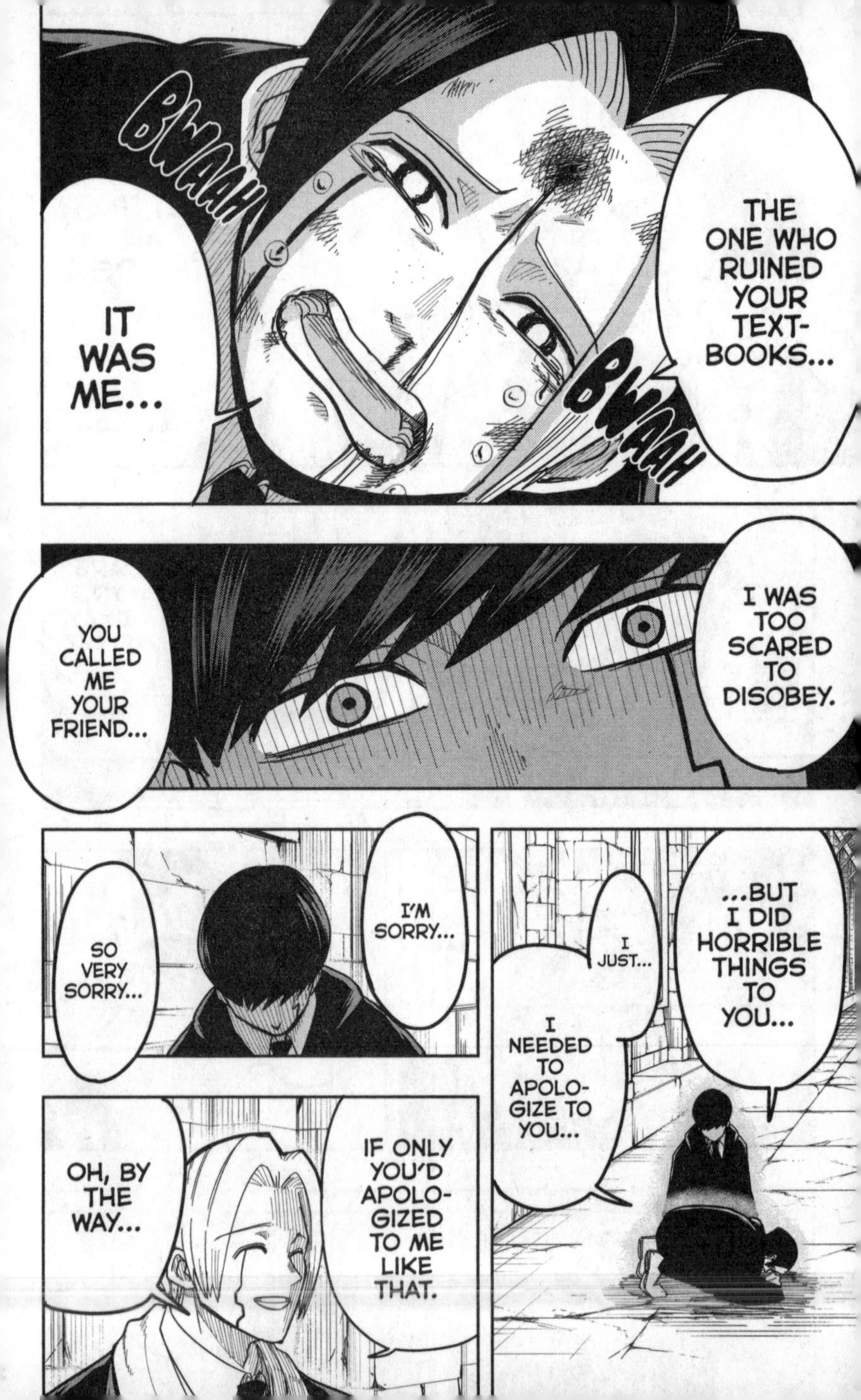
THE ONE WHO RUINED YOUR TEXT-BOOKS...
BWAAH
BWAAH
IT WAS ME...
I WAS TOO SCARED TO DISOBEY.
YOU CALLED ME YOUR FRIEND...
...BUT I DID HORRIBLE THINGS TO YOU...
I JUST...
I NEEDED TO APOLO-GIZE TO YOU...
I'M SORRY...
SO VERY SORRY...
IF ONLY YOU'D APOLO-GIZED TO ME LIKE THAT.
OH, BY THE WAY...

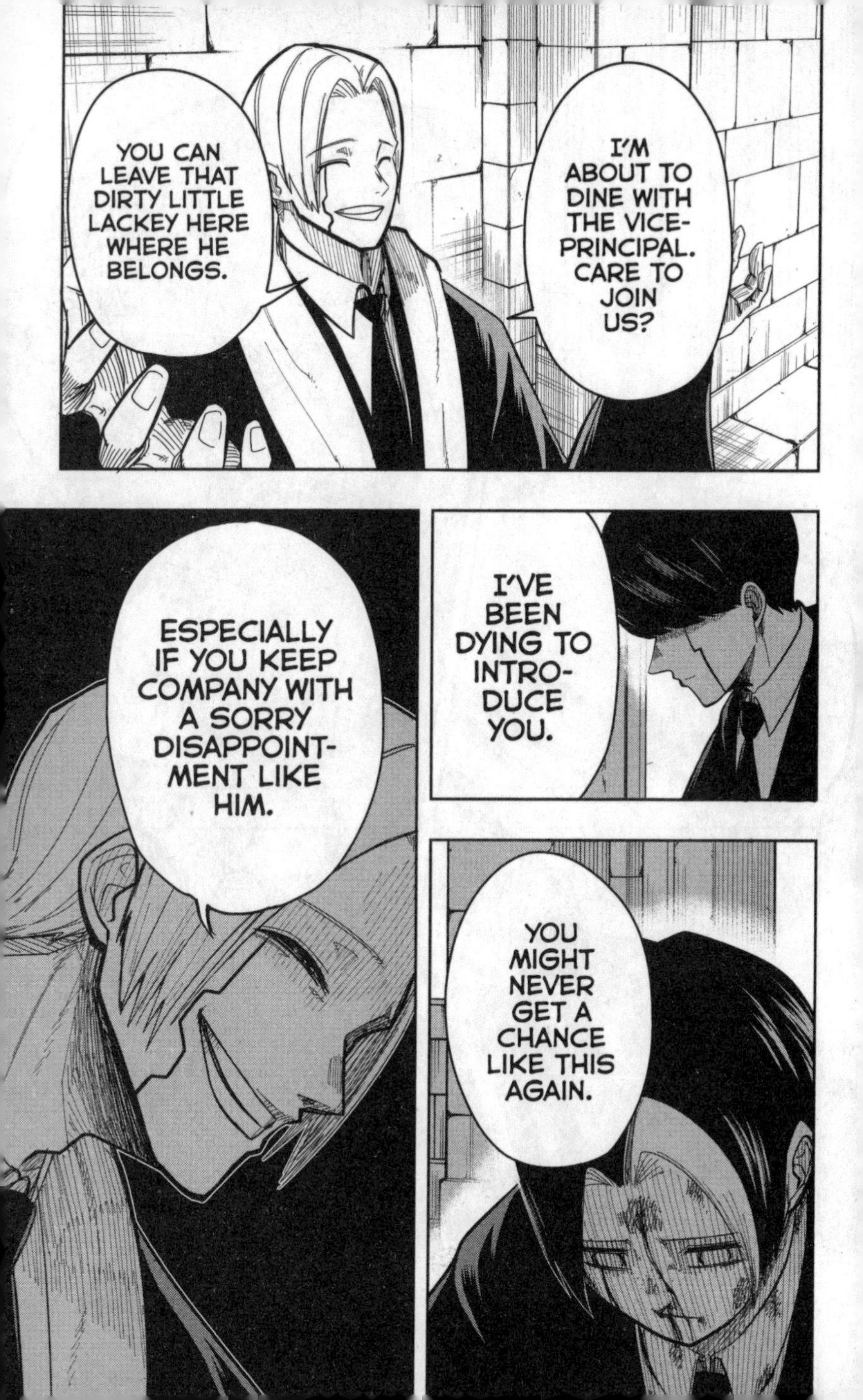
I'M ABOUT TO DINE WITH THE VICE-PRINCIPAL. CARE TO JOIN US?
YOU CAN LEAVE THAT DIRTY LITTLE LACKEY HERE WHERE HE BELONGS.
I'VE BEEN DYING TO INTRODUCE YOU.
YOU MIGHT NEVER GET A CHANCE LIKE THIS AGAIN.
ESPECIALLY IF YOU KEEP COMPANY WITH A SORRY DISAPPOINTMENT LIKE HIM.

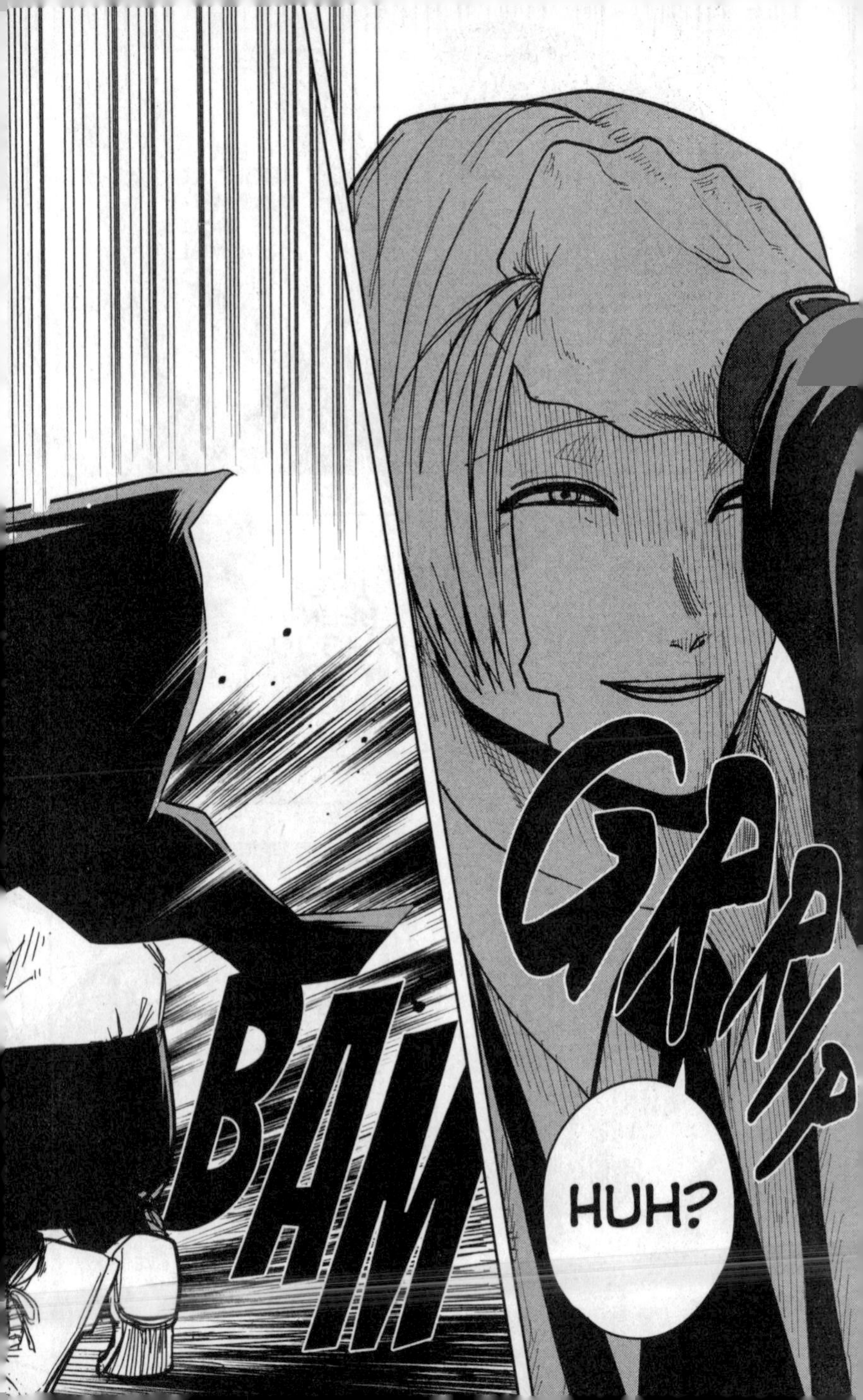
GRAB
HUH?
BAM

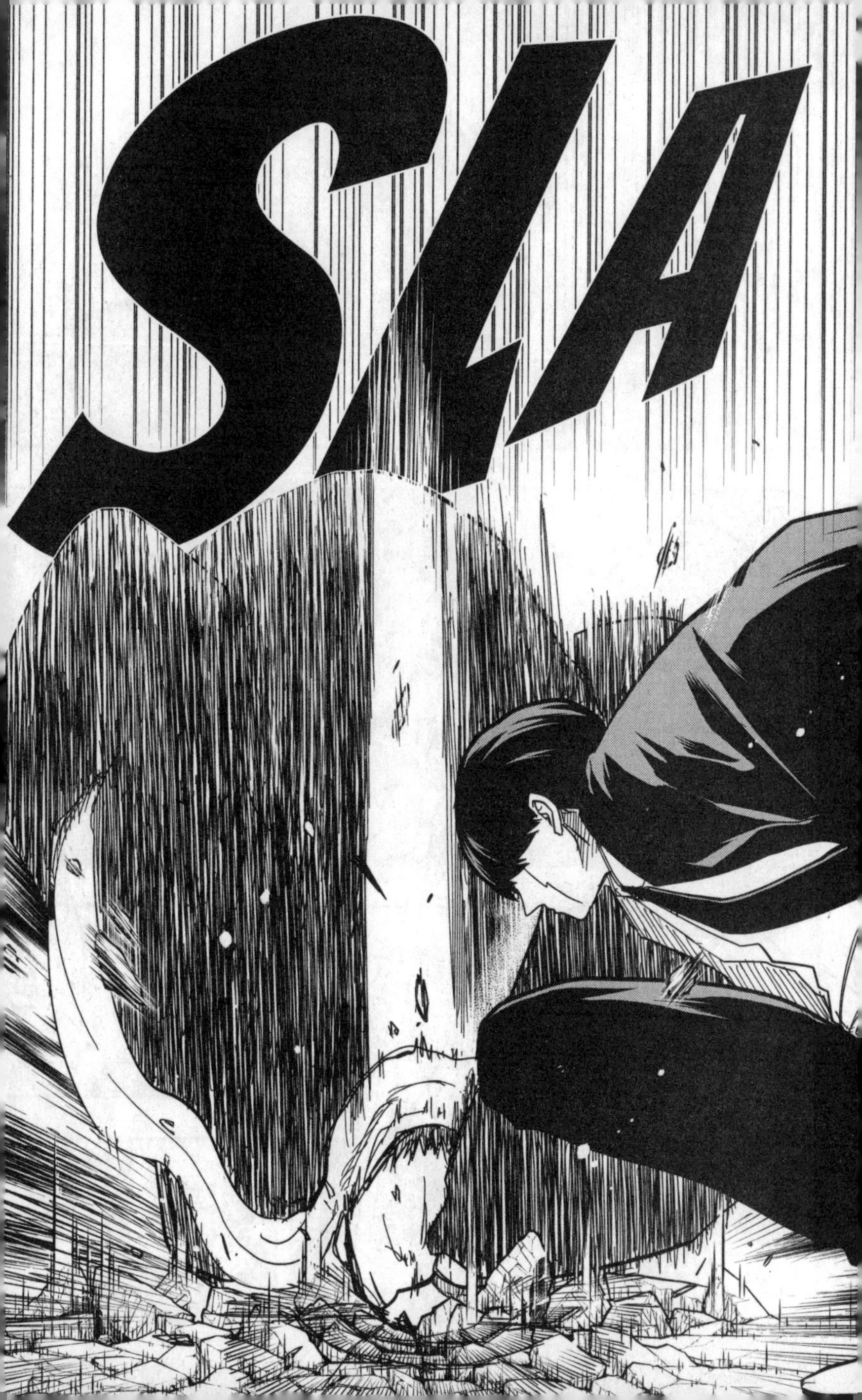
SLA

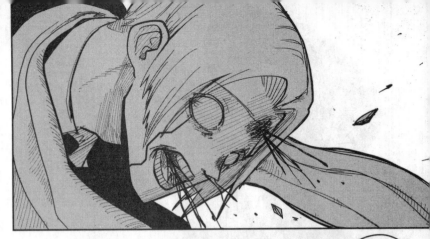

YOU'RE THE ONE...

...WHO SHOULD BE SORRY.

...

TH- THAT'LL GET YOU...

...EX- PELLED...

WUT?

DOUBLE WUT?!

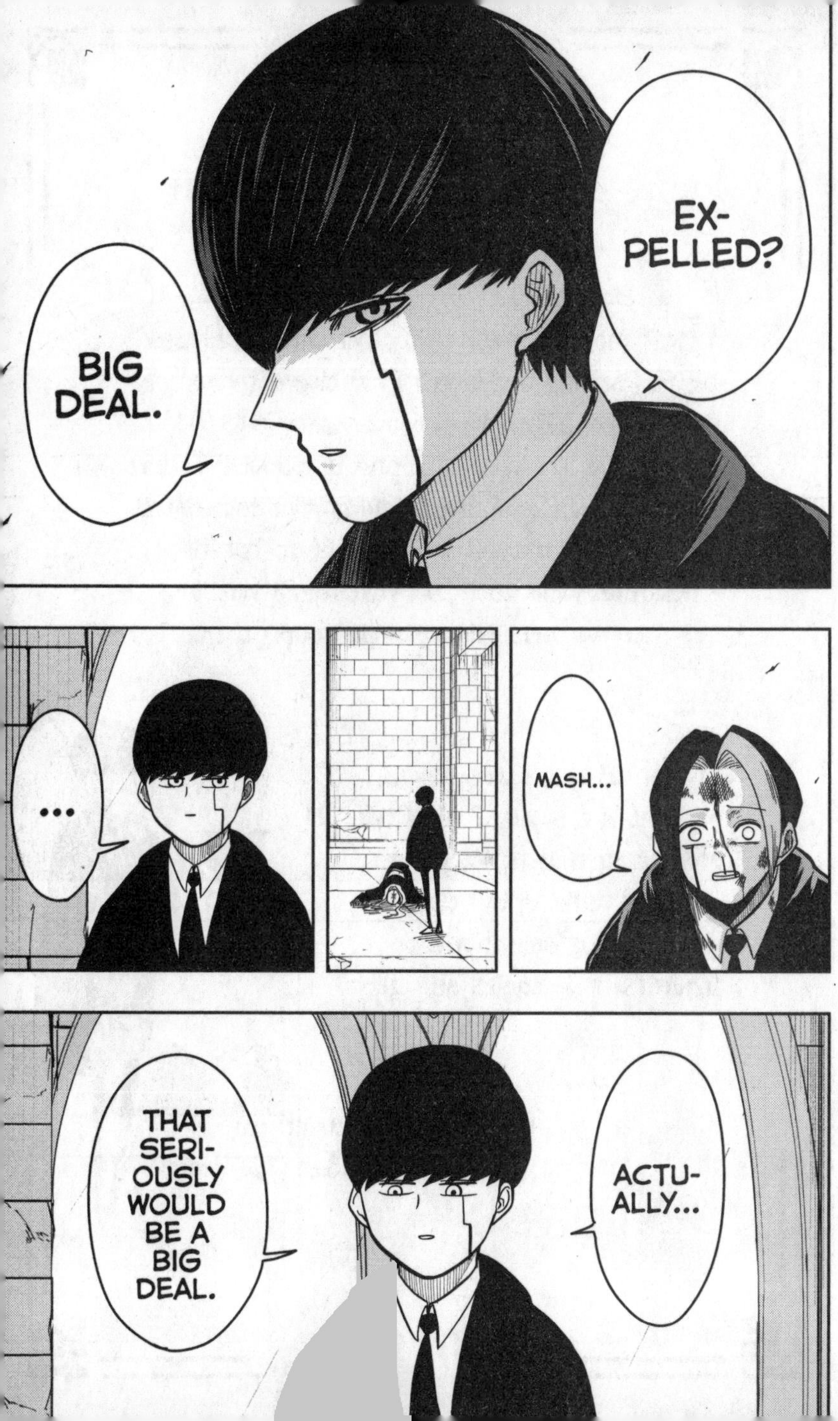
EX-PELLED?
BIG DEAL.
MASH...
...
ACTU-ALLY...
THAT SERI-OUSLY WOULD BE A BIG DEAL.

Mash Burnedead

I first modeled Mash after the main character of my second one-shot. That character was a rude loudmouth. My previous editor said, "You think a guy like that is gonna be popular?! We're trying to put Salisbury steak on the table here! Keep messin' around and it's off to the finger guillotine with you!" So I redesigned him and here we are. Relaxed and droopy eyed.

In fan letters, I was asked, "Does he like sweets?" And the answer to that is, Mash eats almost nothing but cream puffs. But he'll gobble up legumes and veggies as well.

NOM

NOM

THAT SO?

Height: 171 cm
Shoe Size: 26.5 cm

CHAPTER 6: MASH BURNEDEAD AND THE ACADEMY HIERARCHY

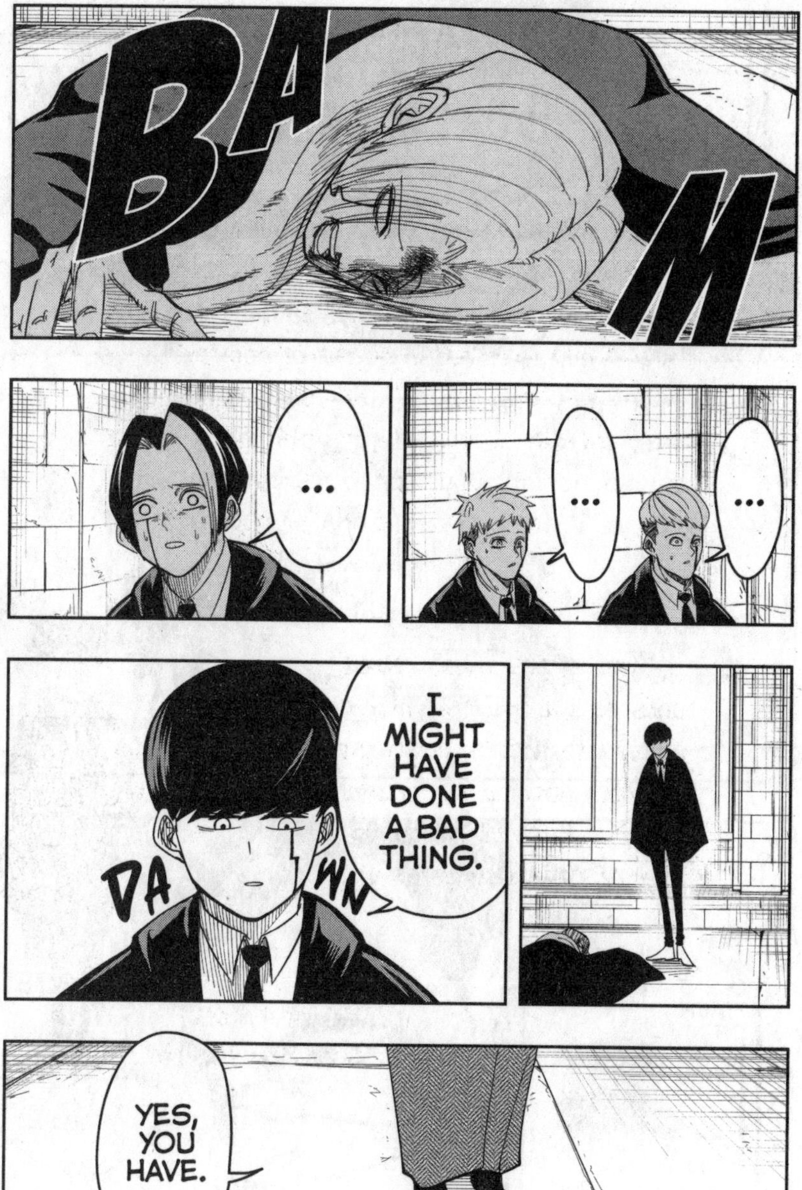
BAM
...
...
...
I MIGHT HAVE DONE A BAD THING.
DAWN
YES, YOU HAVE.

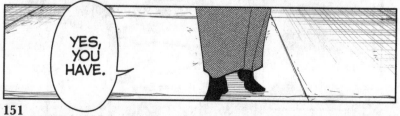

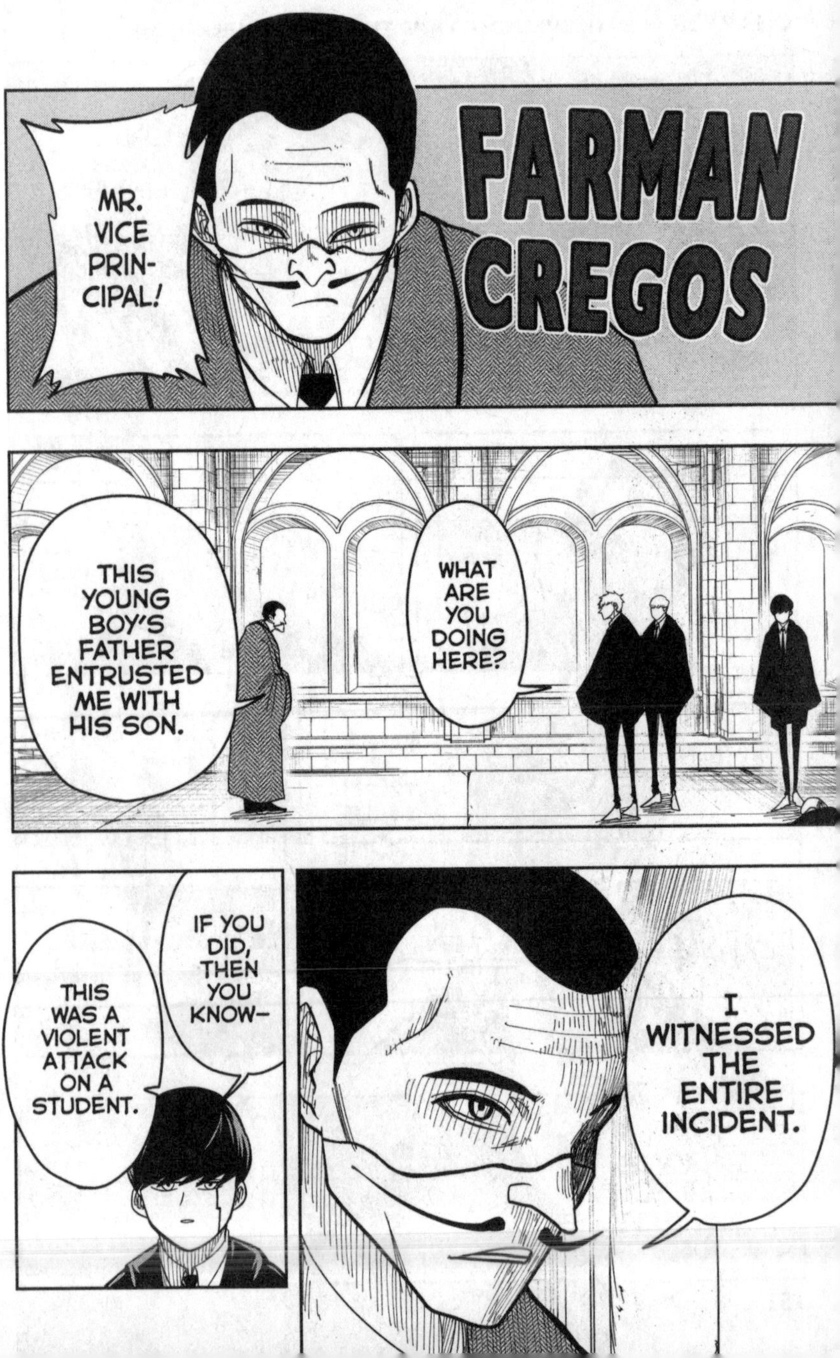
FARMAN CREGOS
MR. VICE PRINCIPAL!
WHAT ARE YOU DOING HERE?
THIS YOUNG BOY'S FATHER ENTRUSTED ME WITH HIS SON.
I WITNESSED THE ENTIRE INCIDENT.
IF YOU DID, THEN YOU KNOW—
THIS WAS A VIOLENT ATTACK ON A STUDENT.

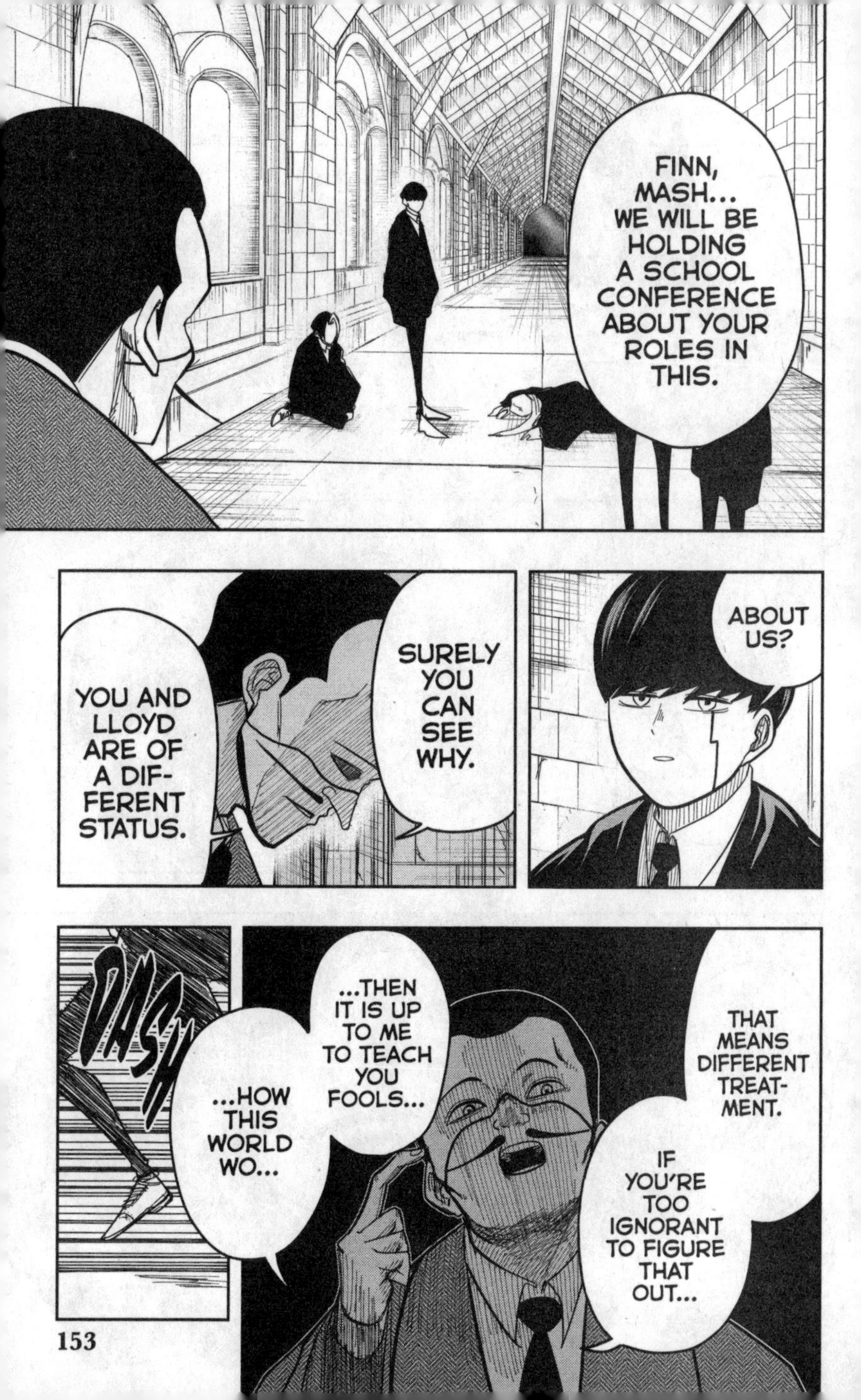
FINN, MASH... WE WILL BE HOLDING A SCHOOL CONFERENCE ABOUT YOUR ROLES IN THIS.
ABOUT US?
SURELY YOU CAN SEE WHY.
YOU AND LLOYD ARE OF A DIF-FERENT STATUS.
THAT MEANS DIFFERENT TREAT-MENT.
IF YOU'RE TOO IGNORANT TO FIGURE THAT OUT...
...THEN IT IS UP TO ME TO TEACH YOU FOOLS...
...HOW THIS WORLD WO...
DASH

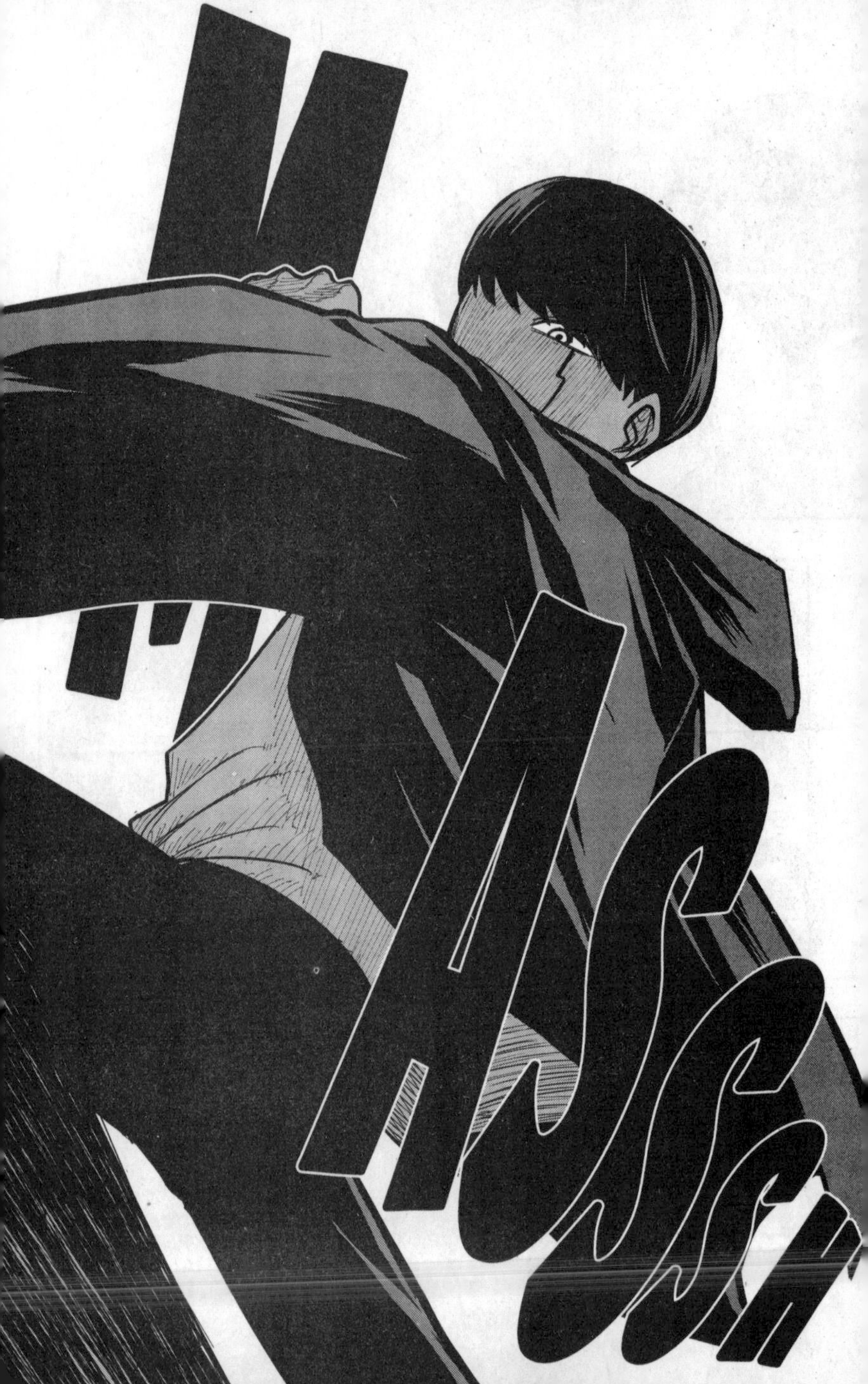
HUSSH

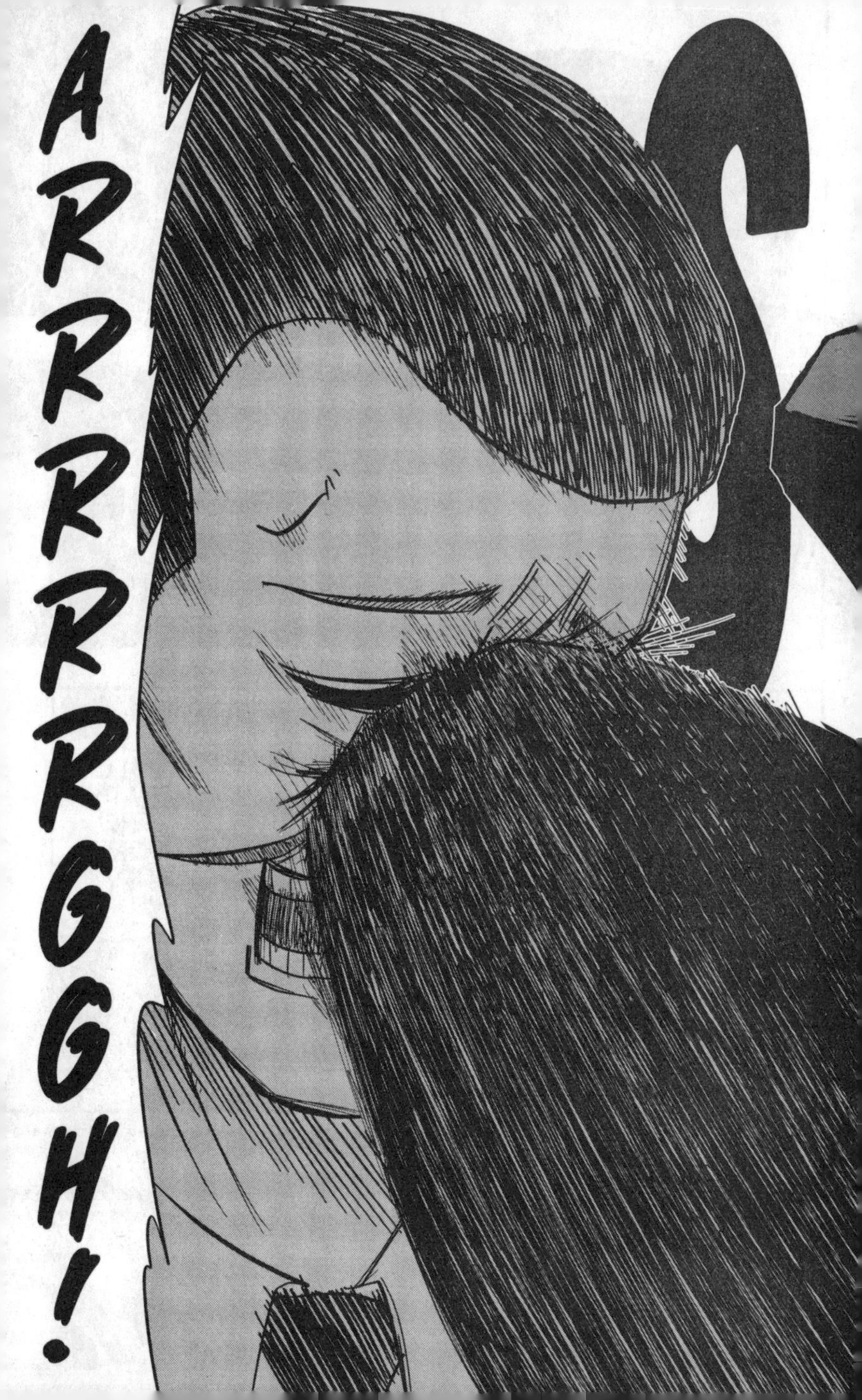
ARRRRRGGGH!

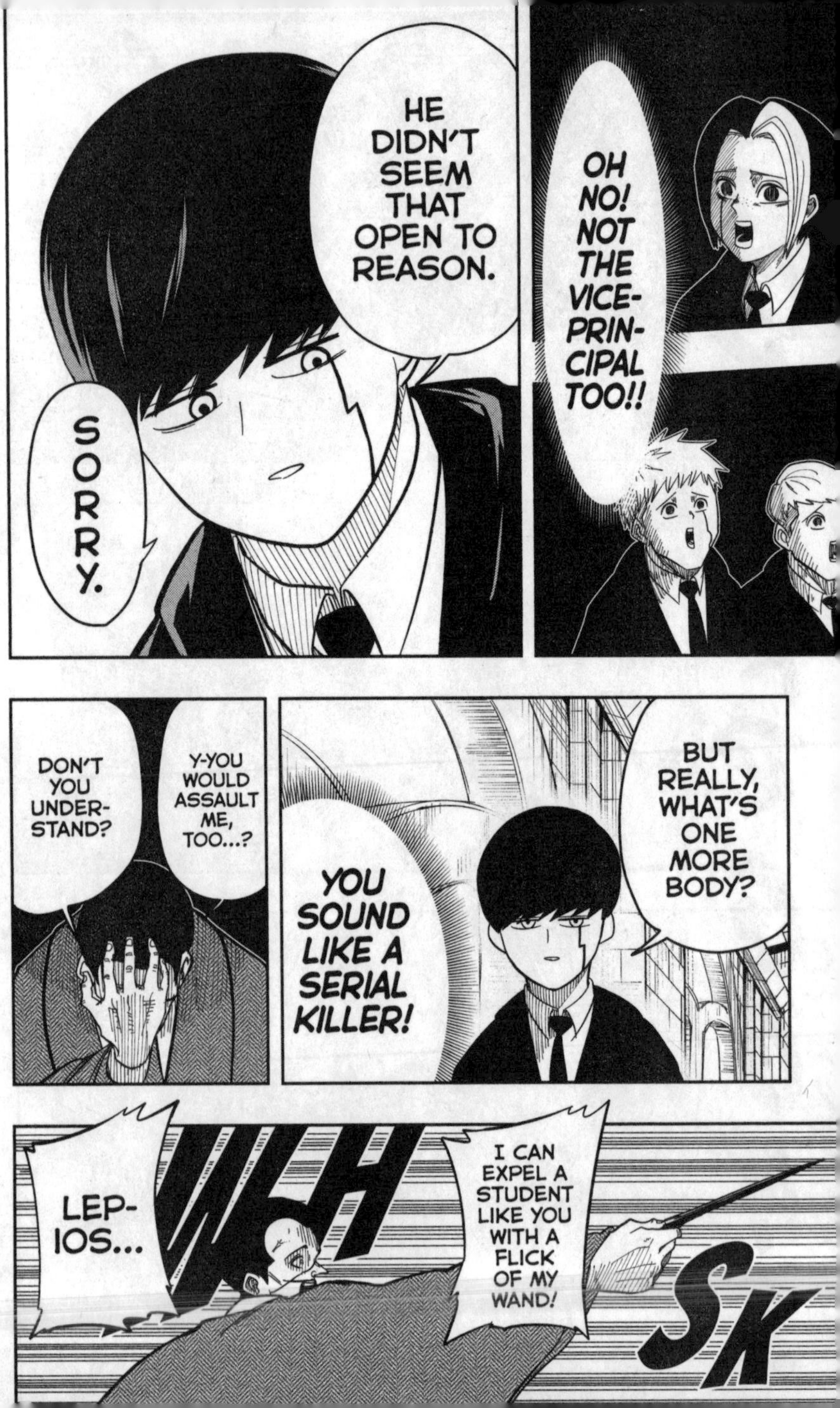
OH NO! NOT THE VICE-PRINCIPAL TOO!!
HE DIDN'T SEEM THAT OPEN TO REASON.
SORRY.
BUT REALLY, WHAT'S ONE MORE BODY?
YOU SOUND LIKE A SERIAL KILLER!
Y-YOU WOULD ASSAULT ME, TOO...?
DON'T YOU UNDERSTAND?
I CAN EXPEL A STUDENT LIKE YOU WITH A FLICK OF MY WAND!
WH
LEP-IOS...
SK

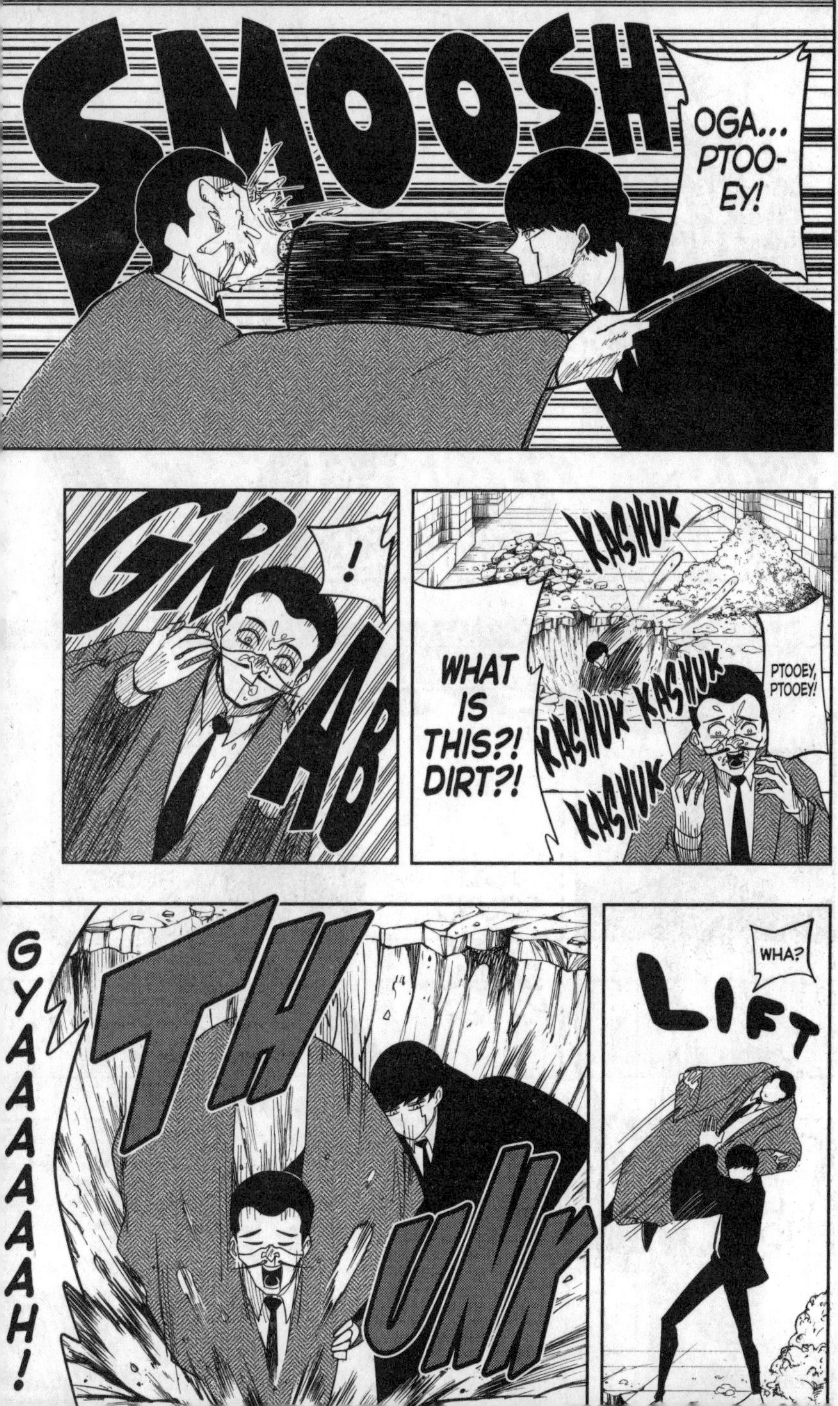
OGA... PTOOEY!
SMOOSH
KASHUK
PTOOEY, PTOOEY!
WHAT IS THIS?! DIRT?!
KASHUK KASHUK
KASHUK
KASHUK
!
GRAB
WHA?
LIFT
THUNK
GYAAAAAAAAAH!

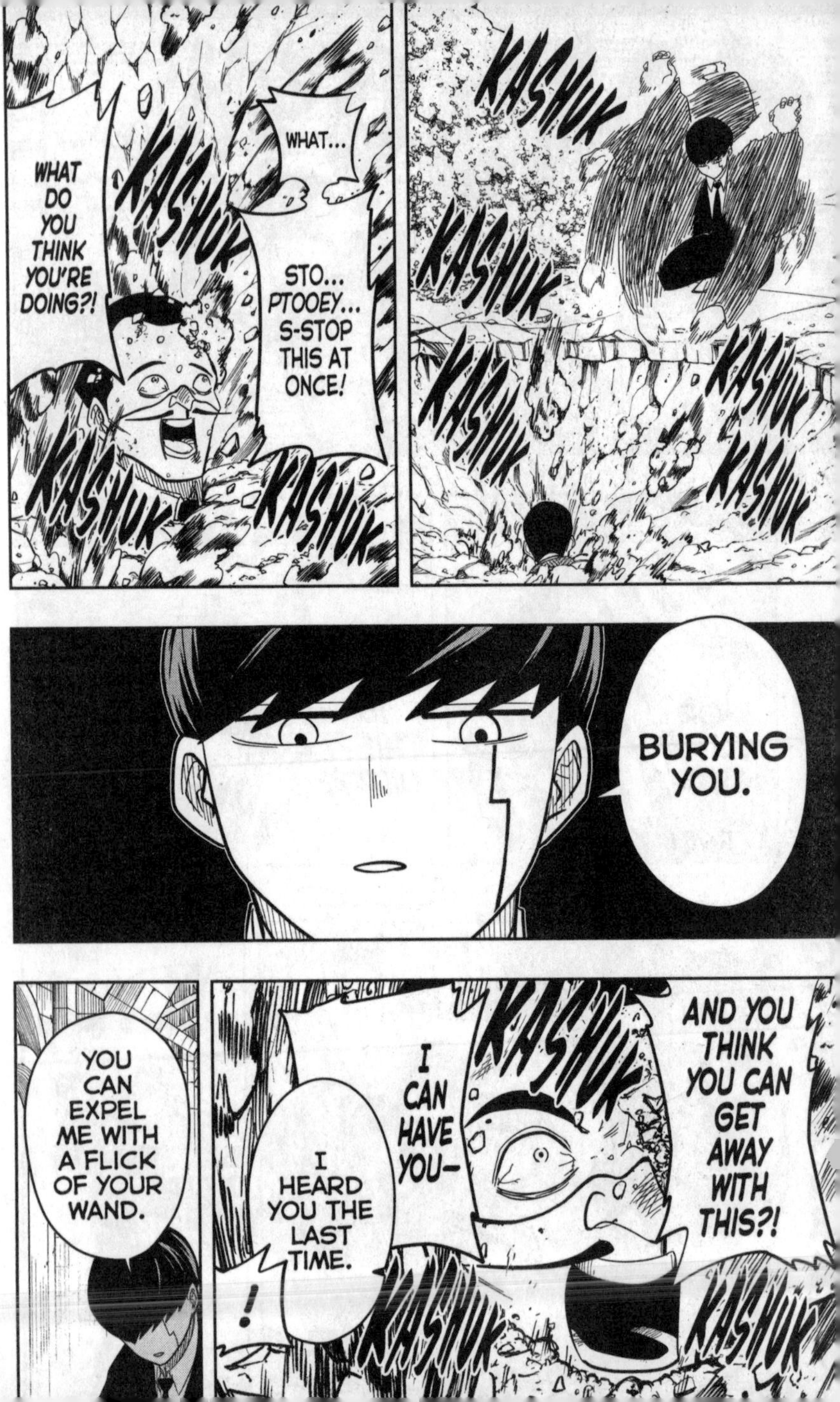
KASHUK
KASHUK
KASHUK
KASHUK
KASHUK
WHAT...
STO... PTOOEY... S-STOP THIS AT ONCE!
KASHUK
WHAT DO YOU THINK YOU'RE DOING?!
KASHUK
KASHUK
BURYING YOU.
AND YOU THINK YOU CAN GET AWAY WITH THIS?!
KASHUK
I CAN HAVE YOU—
I HEARD YOU THE LAST TIME.
!
KASHUK
KASHUK
YOU CAN EXPEL ME WITH A FLICK OF YOUR WAND.

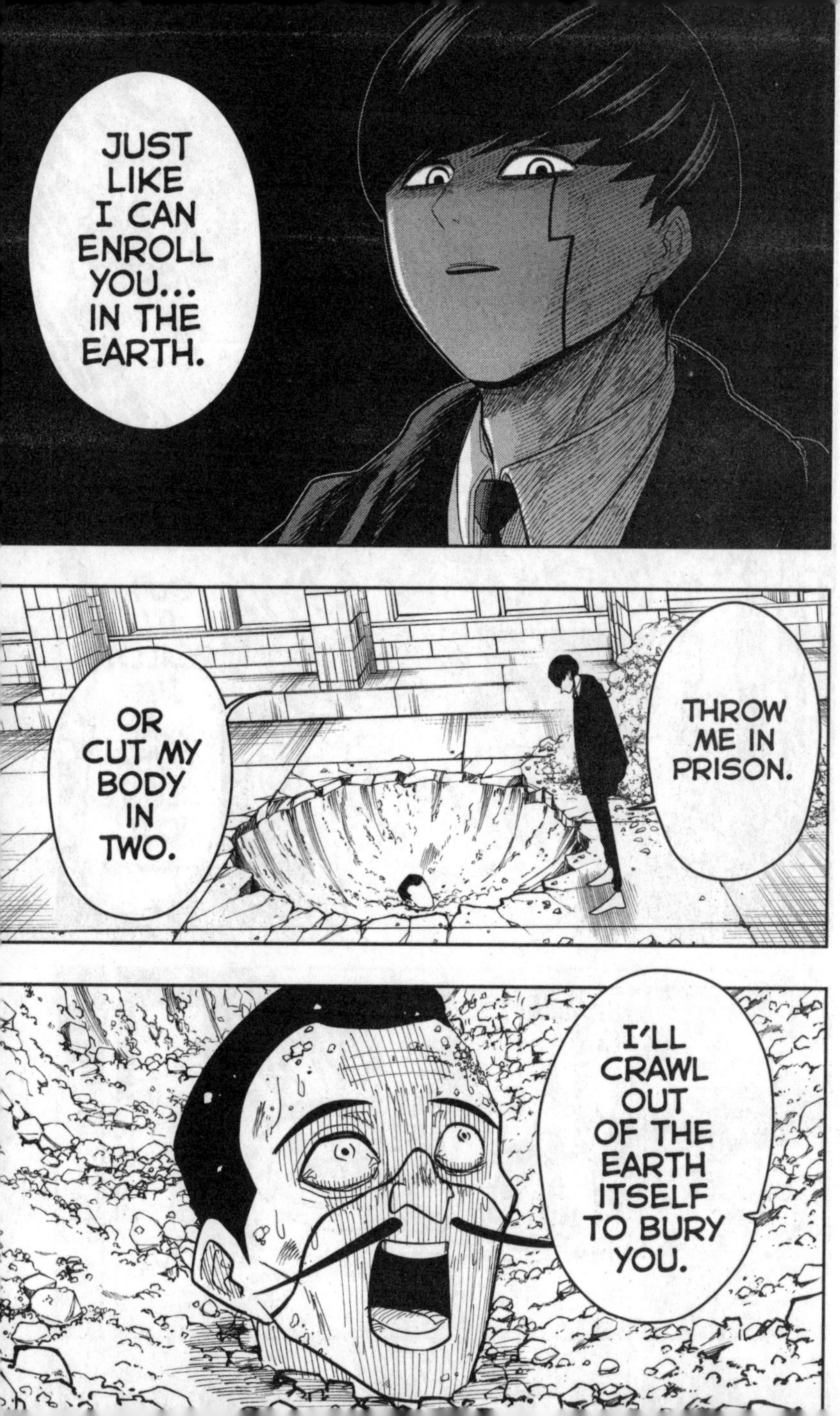
JUST LIKE I CAN ENROLL YOU... IN THE EARTH.
THROW ME IN PRISON.
OR CUT MY BODY IN TWO.
I'LL CRAWL OUT OF THE EARTH ITSELF TO BURY YOU.

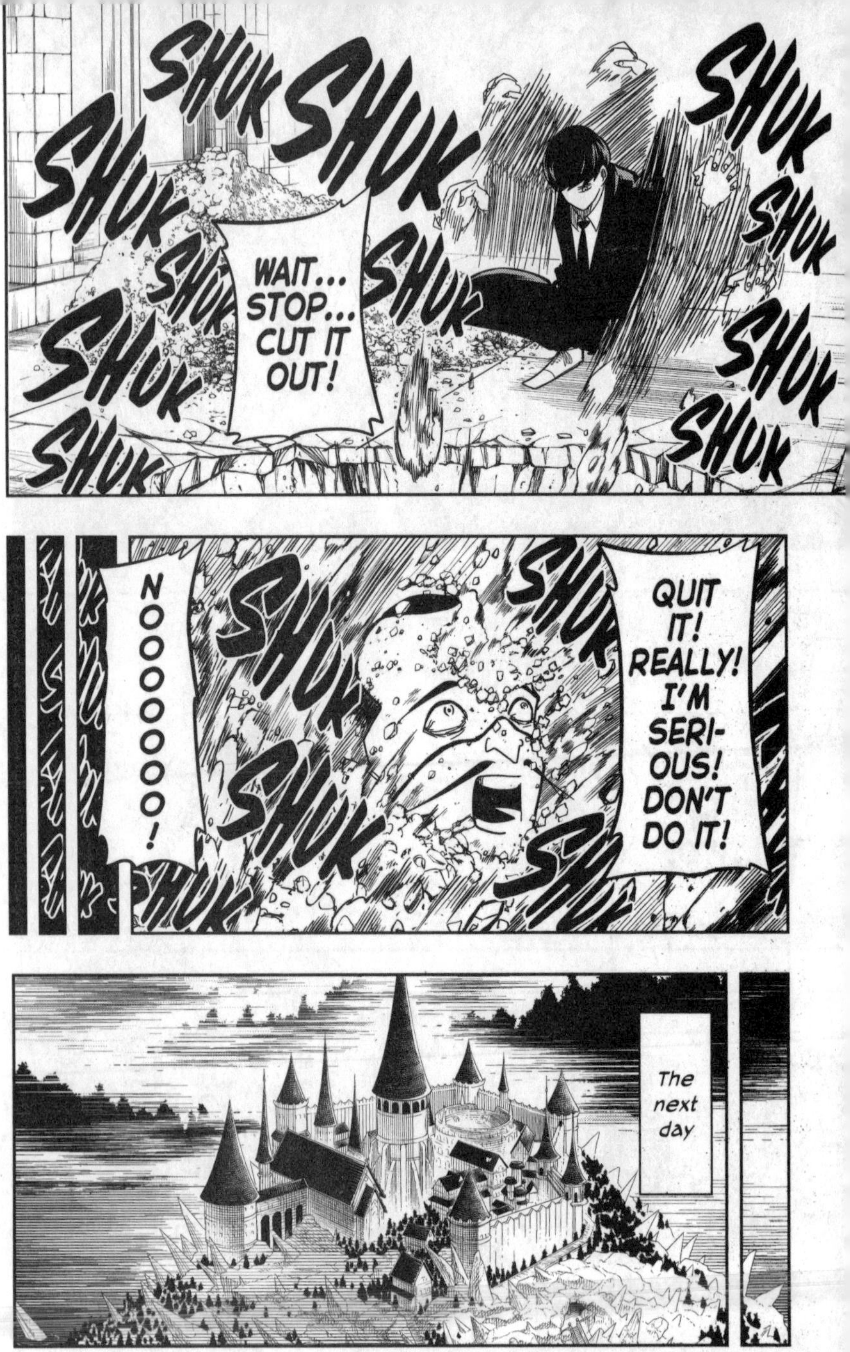
SHUK
SHUK
SHUK
SHUK
SHUK
WAIT... STOP... CUT IT OUT!
SHUK
SHUK
SHUK
SHUK
SHUK
SHUK
QUIT IT! REALLY! I'M SERI-OUS! DON'T DO IT!
SHUK
SHUK
SHUK
SHUK
NOOOOOOOO!
SHUK
The next day

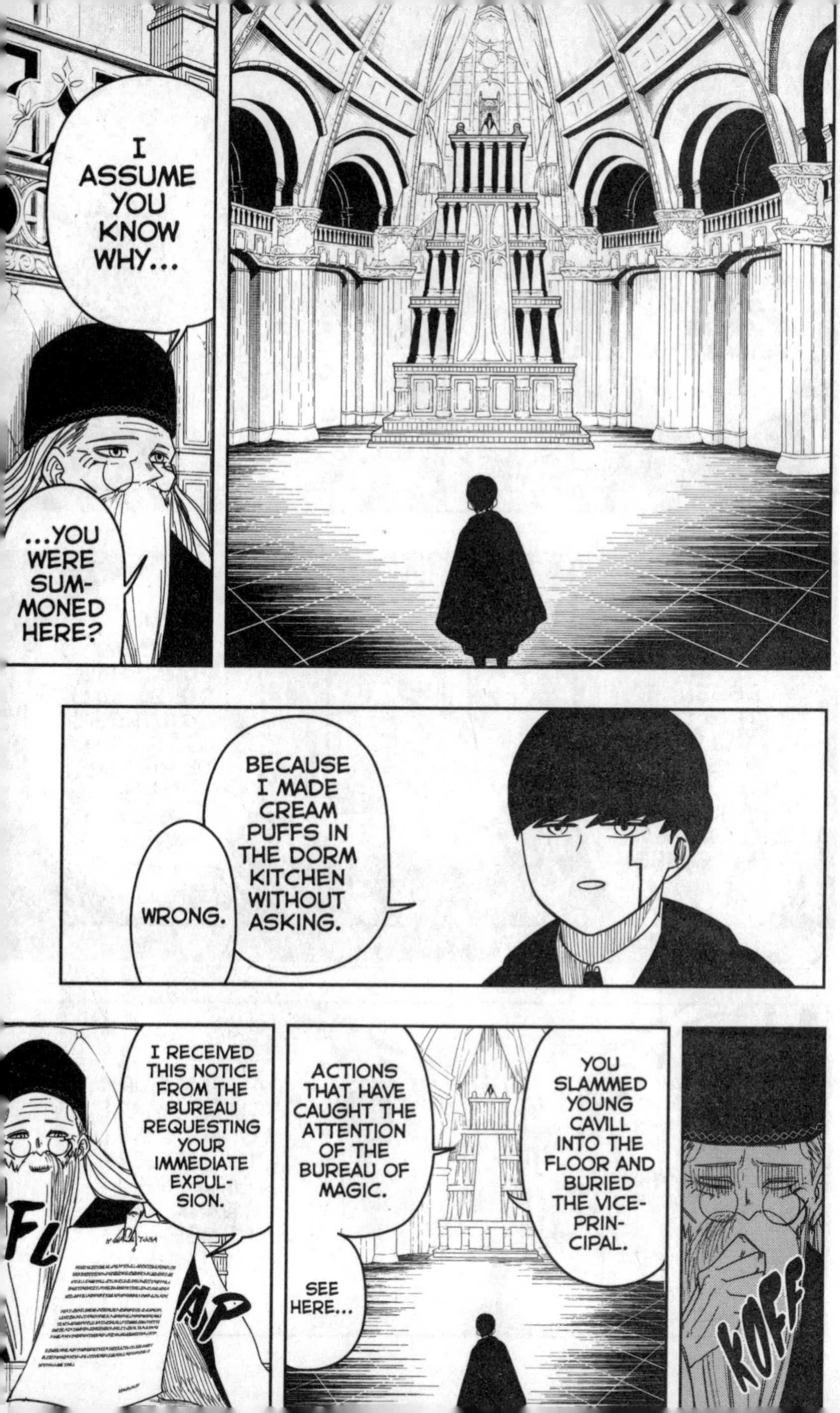
I ASSUME YOU KNOW WHY...
...YOU WERE SUMMONED HERE?
BECAUSE I MADE CREAM PUFFS IN THE DORM KITCHEN WITHOUT ASKING.
WRONG.
KOFF
YOU SLAMMED YOUNG CAVILL INTO THE FLOOR AND BURIED THE VICE-PRINCIPAL.
ACTIONS THAT HAVE CAUGHT THE ATTENTION OF THE BUREAU OF MAGIC.
SEE HERE...
I RECEIVED THIS NOTICE FROM THE BUREAU REQUESTING YOUR IMMEDIATE EXPULSION.
FL
AP

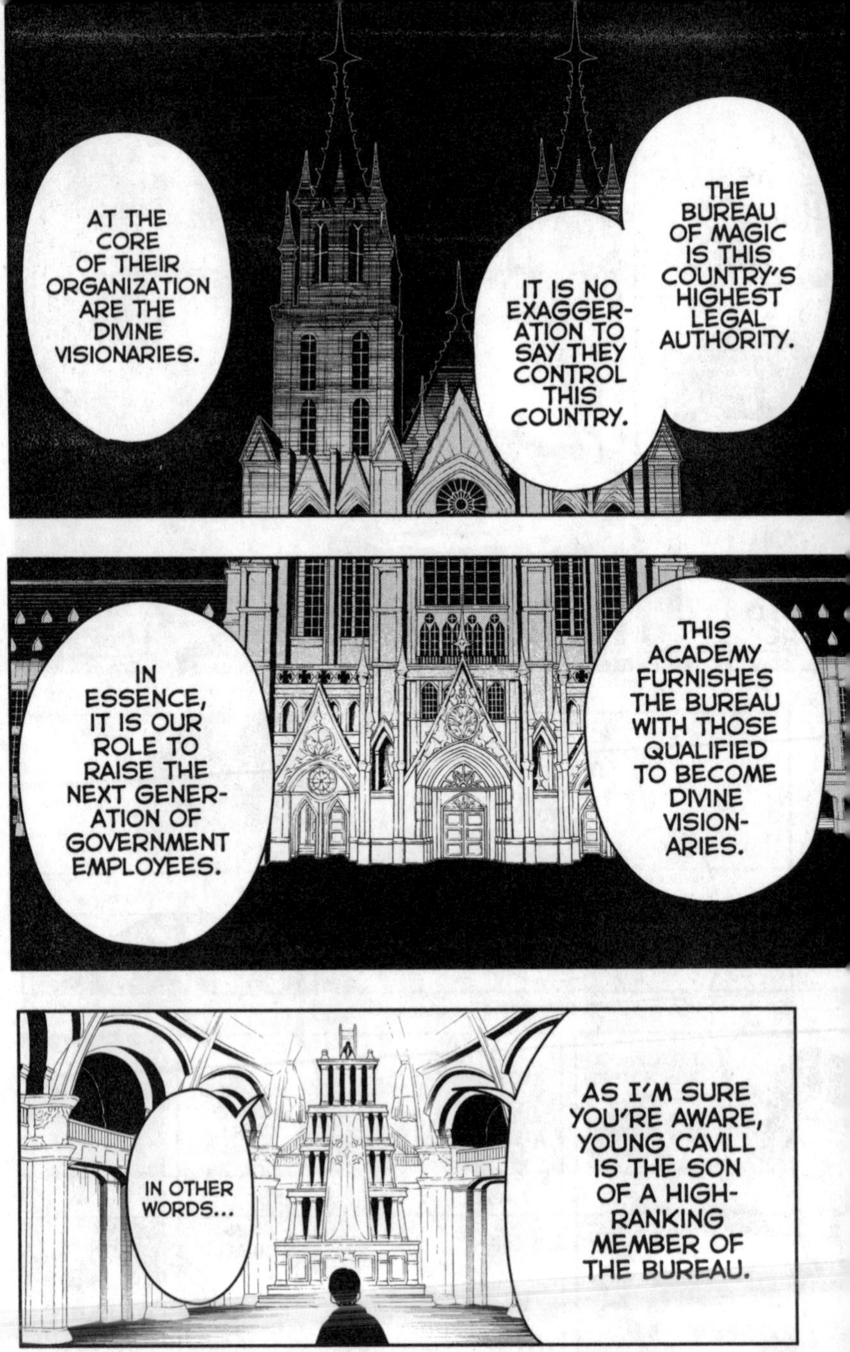
THE BUREAU OF MAGIC IS THIS COUNTRY'S HIGHEST LEGAL AUTHORITY.
IT IS NO EXAGGER-ATION TO SAY THEY CONTROL THIS COUNTRY.
AT THE CORE OF THEIR ORGANIZATION ARE THE DIVINE VISIONARIES.
THIS ACADEMY FURNISHES THE BUREAU WITH THOSE QUALIFIED TO BECOME DIVINE VISION-ARIES.
IN ESSENCE, IT IS OUR ROLE TO RAISE THE NEXT GENER-ATION OF GOVERNMENT EMPLOYEES.
AS I'M SURE YOU'RE AWARE, YOUNG CAVILL IS THE SON OF A HIGH-RANKING MEMBER OF THE BUREAU.
IN OTHER WORDS...

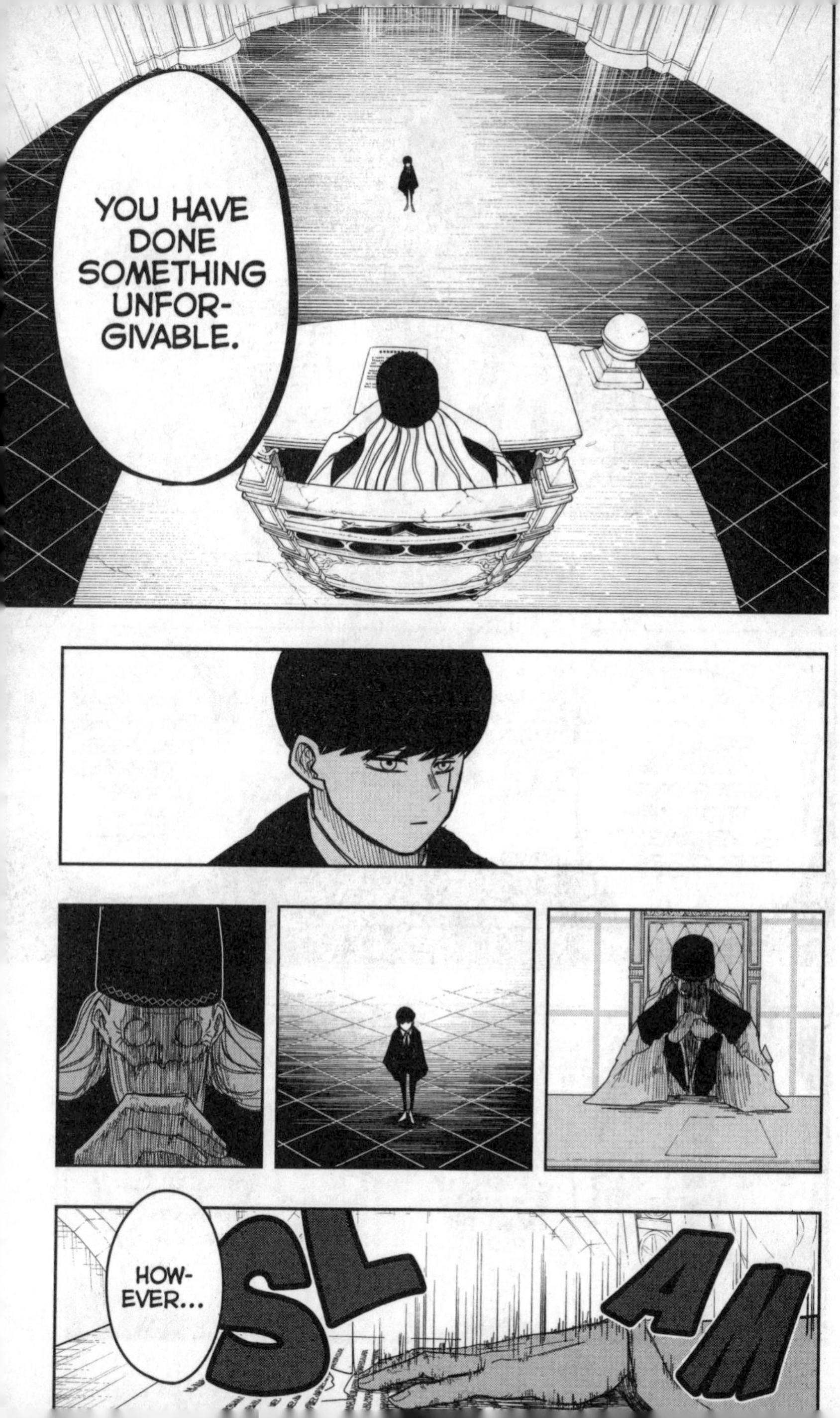
YOU HAVE DONE SOMETHING UNFOR-GIVABLE.
HOW-EVER...
SLAM

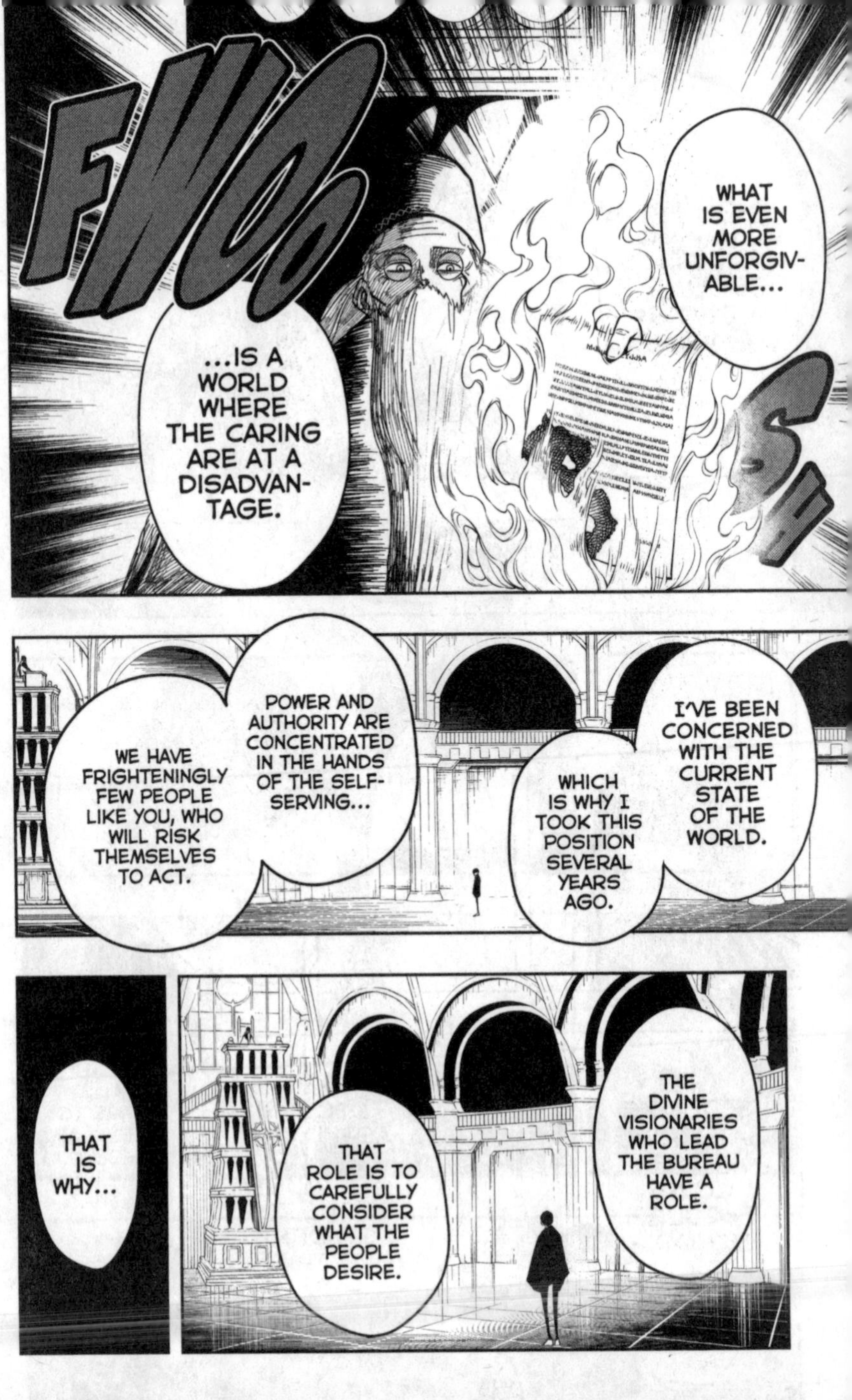
WHAT IS EVEN MORE UNFORGIV-ABLE...
...IS A WORLD WHERE THE CARING ARE AT A DISADVAN-TAGE.
SH
FWOO
I'VE BEEN CONCERNED WITH THE CURRENT STATE OF THE WORLD.
WHICH IS WHY I TOOK THIS POSITION SEVERAL YEARS AGO.
POWER AND AUTHORITY ARE CONCENTRATED IN THE HANDS OF THE SELF-SERVING...
WE HAVE FRIGHTENINGLY FEW PEOPLE LIKE YOU, WHO WILL RISK THEMSELVES TO ACT.
THE DIVINE VISIONARIES WHO LEAD THE BUREAU HAVE A ROLE.
THAT ROLE IS TO CAREFULLY CONSIDER WHAT THE PEOPLE DESIRE.
THAT IS WHY...

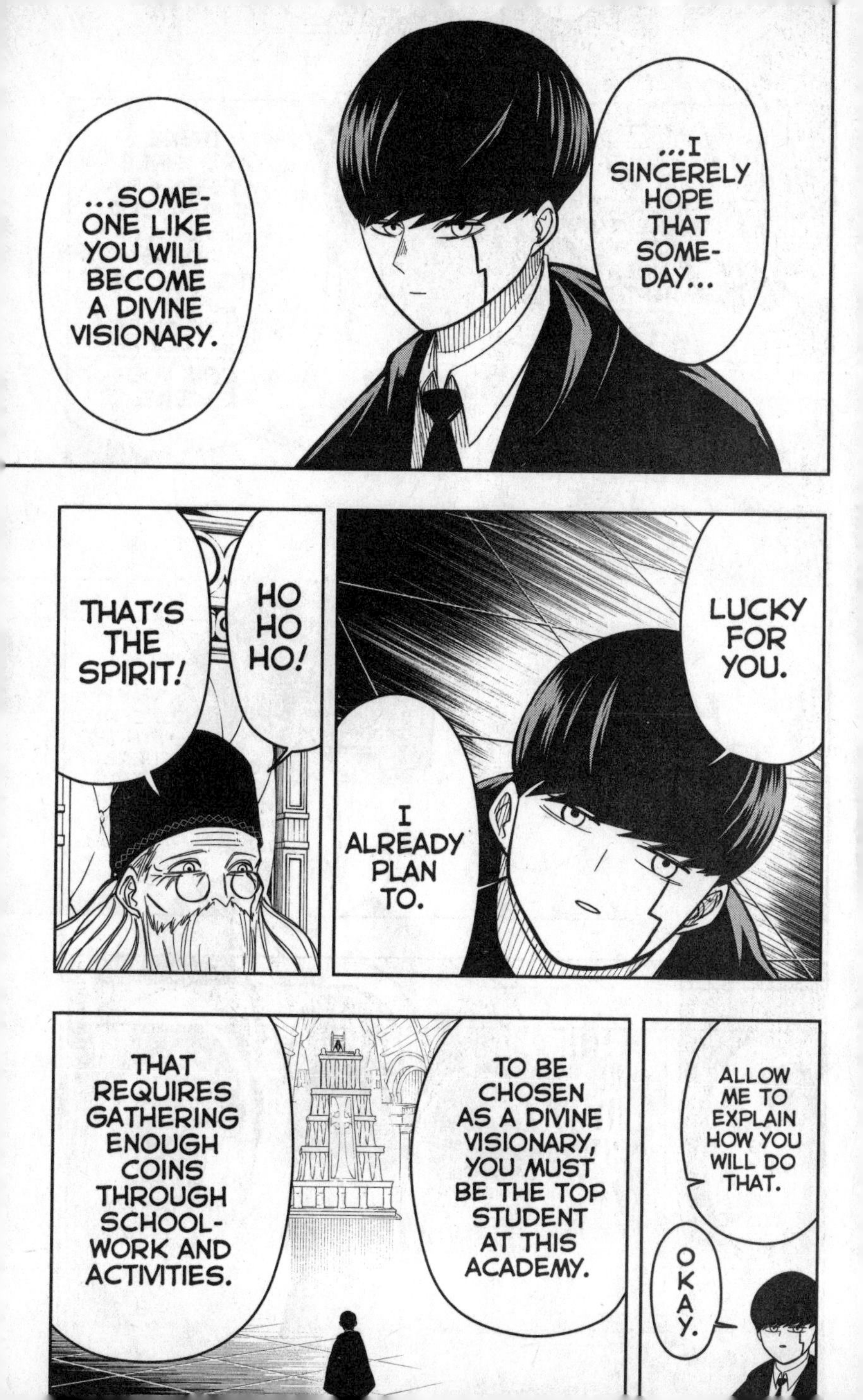
...I SINCERELY HOPE THAT SOMEDAY...
...SOMEONE LIKE YOU WILL BECOME A DIVINE VISIONARY.
LUCKY FOR YOU.
I ALREADY PLAN TO.
HO HO HO!
THAT'S THE SPIRIT!
ALLOW ME TO EXPLAIN HOW YOU WILL DO THAT.
OKAY.
TO BE CHOSEN AS A DIVINE VISIONARY, YOU MUST BE THE TOP STUDENT AT THIS ACADEMY.
THAT REQUIRES GATHERING ENOUGH COINS THROUGH SCHOOLWORK AND ACTIVITIES.

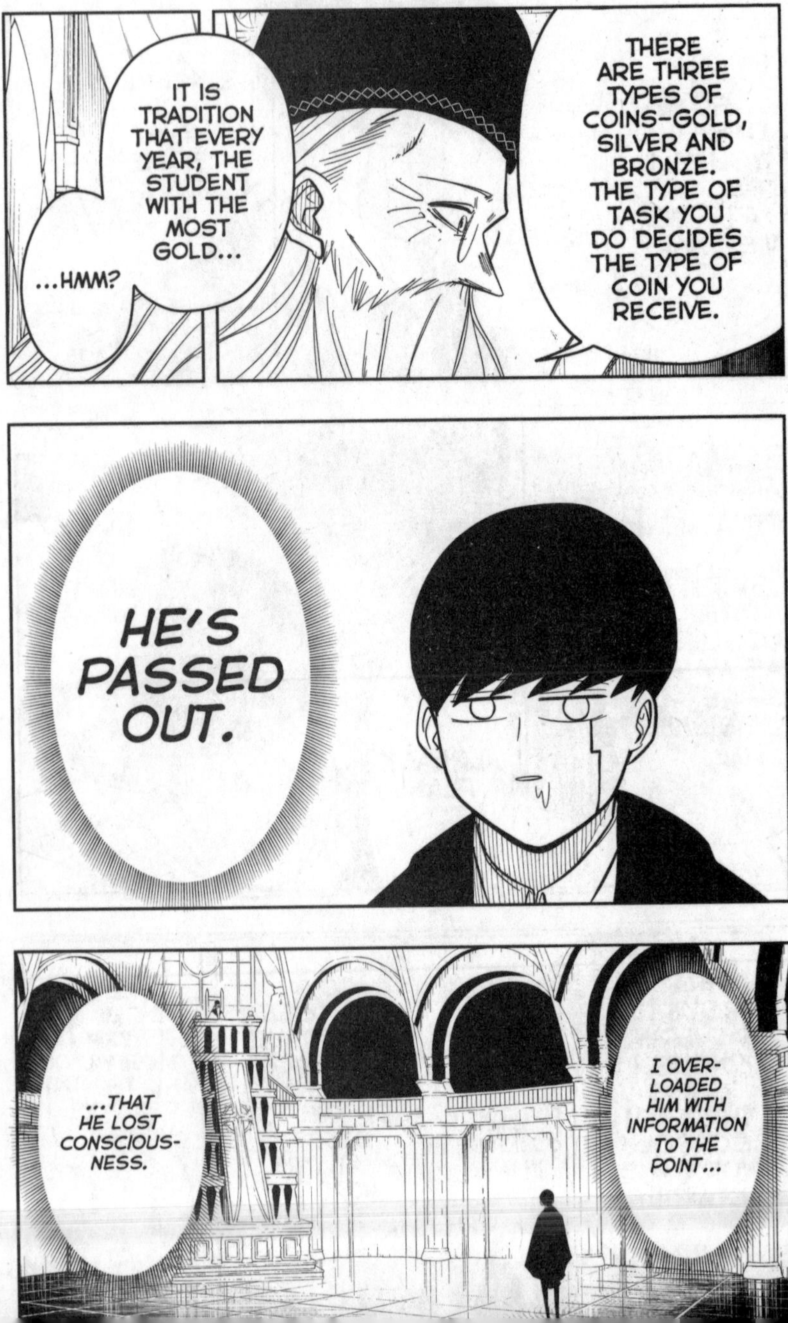
THERE ARE THREE TYPES OF COINS—GOLD, SILVER AND BRONZE. THE TYPE OF TASK YOU DO DECIDES THE TYPE OF COIN YOU RECEIVE.
IT IS TRADITION THAT EVERY YEAR, THE STUDENT WITH THE MOST GOLD...
...HMM?
HE'S PASSED OUT.
I OVER-LOADED HIM WITH INFORMATION TO THE POINT...
...THAT HE LOST CONSCIOUS-NESS.

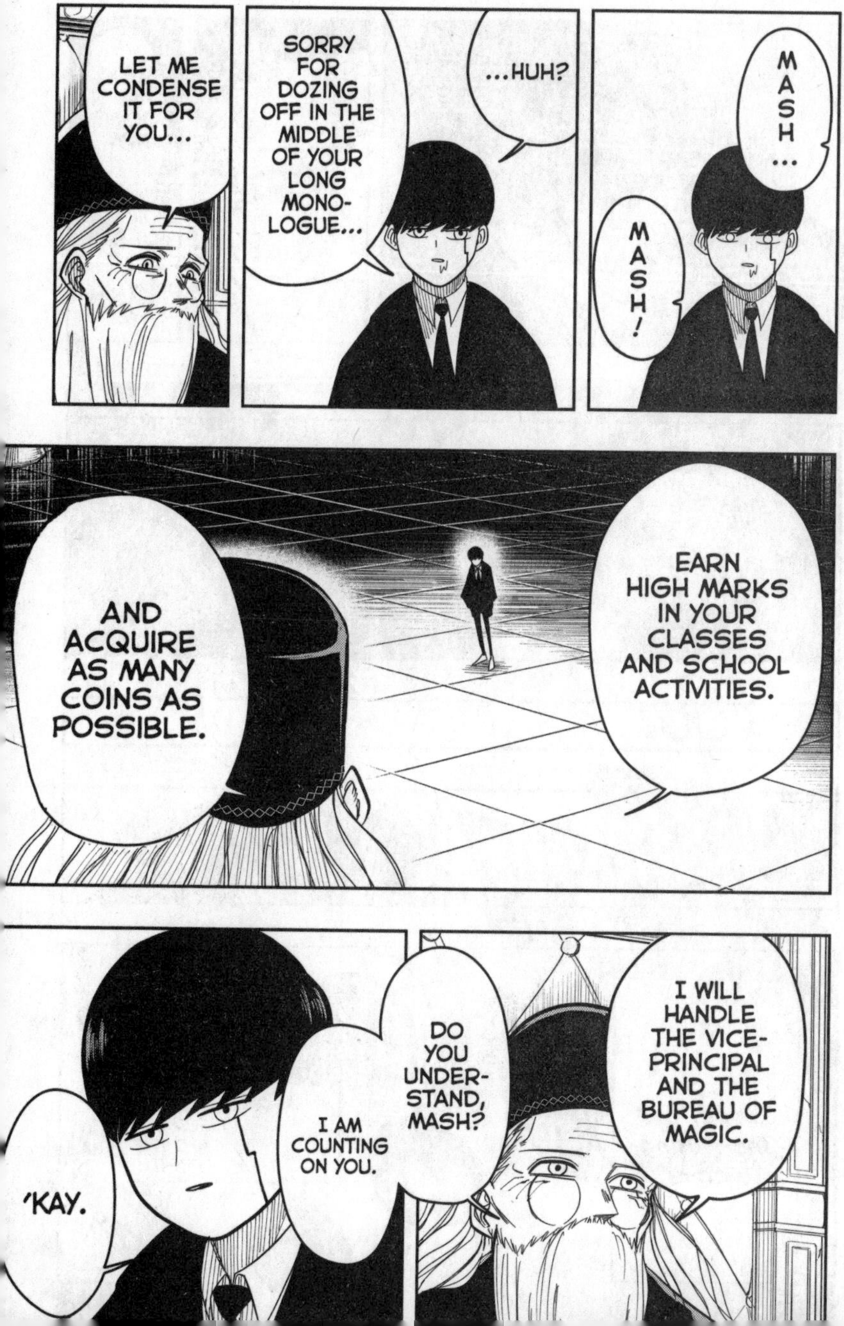
MASH...
MASH!
...HUH?
SORRY FOR DOZING OFF IN THE MIDDLE OF YOUR LONG MONOLOGUE...
LET ME CONDENSE IT FOR YOU...
EARN HIGH MARKS IN YOUR CLASSES AND SCHOOL ACTIVITIES.
AND ACQUIRE AS MANY COINS AS POSSIBLE.
I WILL HANDLE THE VICE-PRINCIPAL AND THE BUREAU OF MAGIC.
DO YOU UNDERSTAND, MASH?
I AM COUNTING ON YOU.
'KAY.

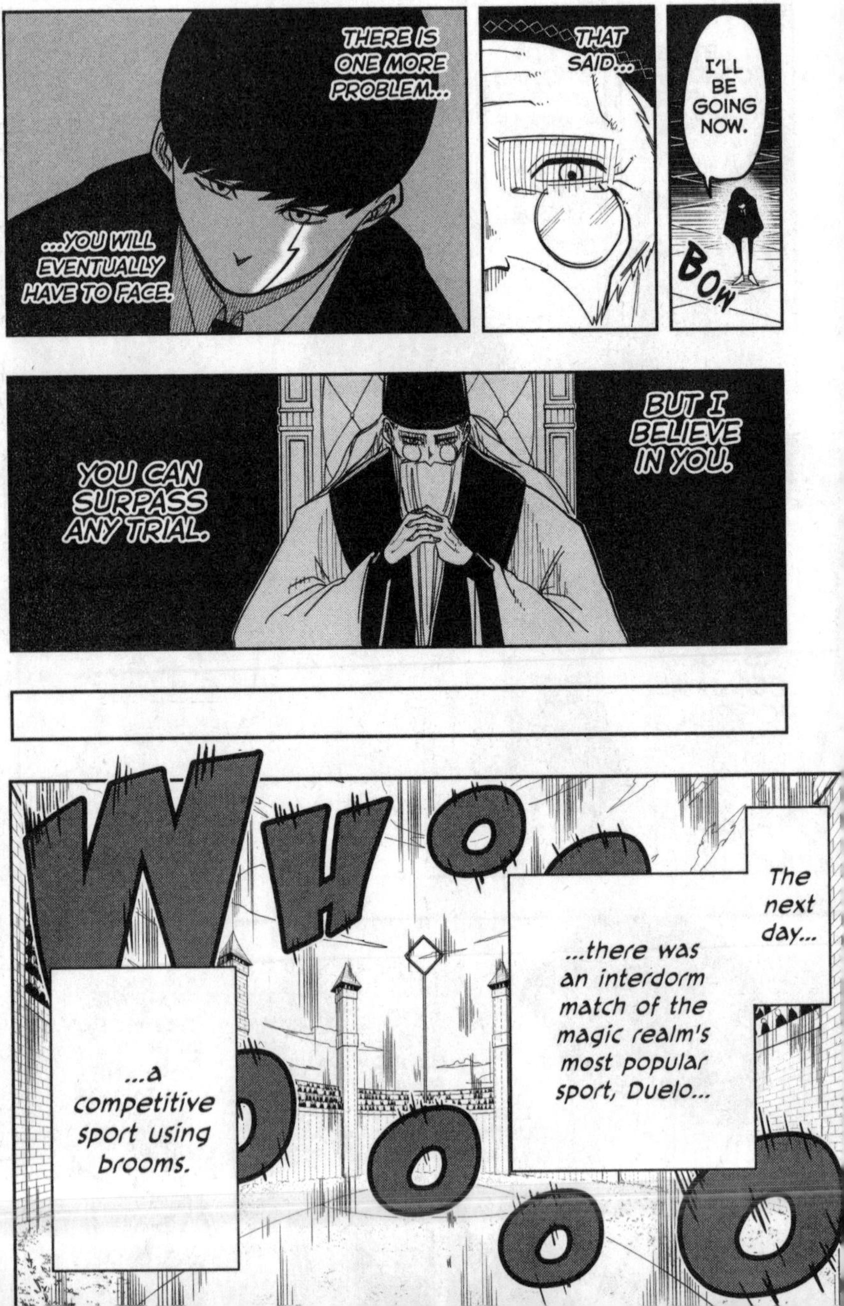
I'LL BE GOING NOW.
BOW
THAT SAID...
THERE IS ONE MORE PROBLEM...
...YOU WILL EVENTUALLY HAVE TO FACE.
BUT I BELIEVE IN YOU.
YOU CAN SURPASS ANY TRIAL.
The next day...
...there was an interdorm match of the magic realm's most popular sport, Duelo...
...a competitive sport using brooms.
WHOOOOOO

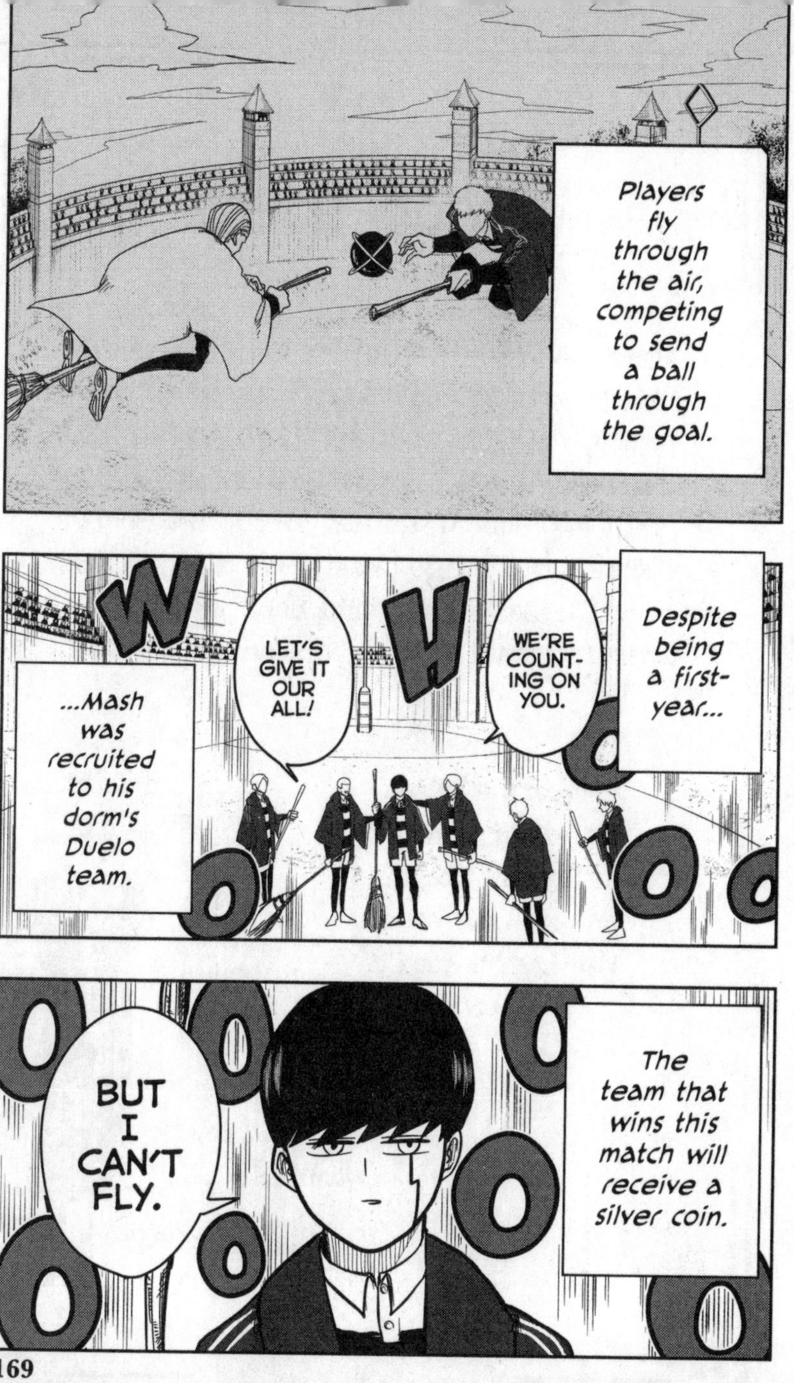
Players fly through the air, competing to send a ball through the goal.
Despite being a first-year...
WE'RE COUNT-ING ON YOU.
WH
LET'S GIVE IT OUR ALL!
W
...Mash was recruited to his dorm's Duelo team.
OOOOO
The team that wins this match will receive a silver coin.
BUT I CAN'T FLY.
OOOOOOOO

Lemon Irvine

Lemon was created when my editor looked over my storyboards and asked, "This story's got a heroine, right?" I'd never drawn girls before, so I was obstinate about not including one at first. But then my editor threatened, "Off to the finger guillotine with you!" So I had no choice but to draw her. She was slightly more unhinged at first, but she's calmed down a lot in her current state.

There's a lot of fan art of Lemon in the letters I receive, so I'm glad I put her in. Her favorite food is strawberries.

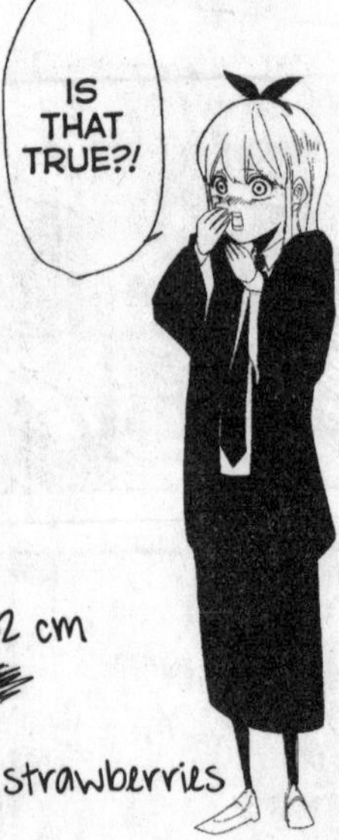
IS THAT TRUE?!

Height: 162 cm

Weight: [redacted]

↳ 3 strawberries

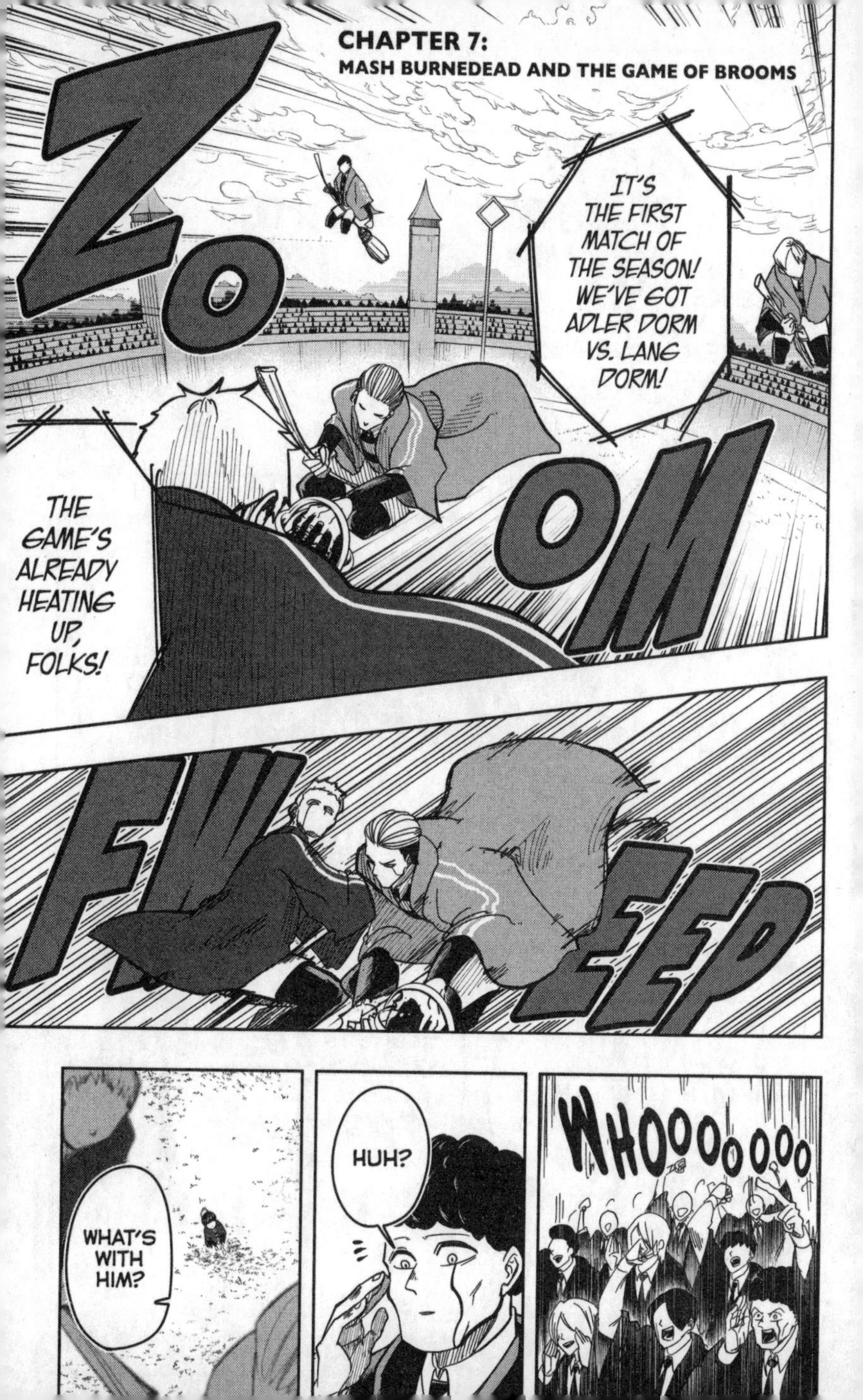
CHAPTER 7:
MASH BURNEDEAD AND THE GAME OF BROOMS
ZOOM
IT'S THE FIRST MATCH OF THE SEASON! WE'VE GOT ADLER DORM VS. LANG DORM!
THE GAME'S ALREADY HEATING UP, FOLKS!
FWEEP
WHOOOOOOO
HUH?
WHAT'S WITH HIM?

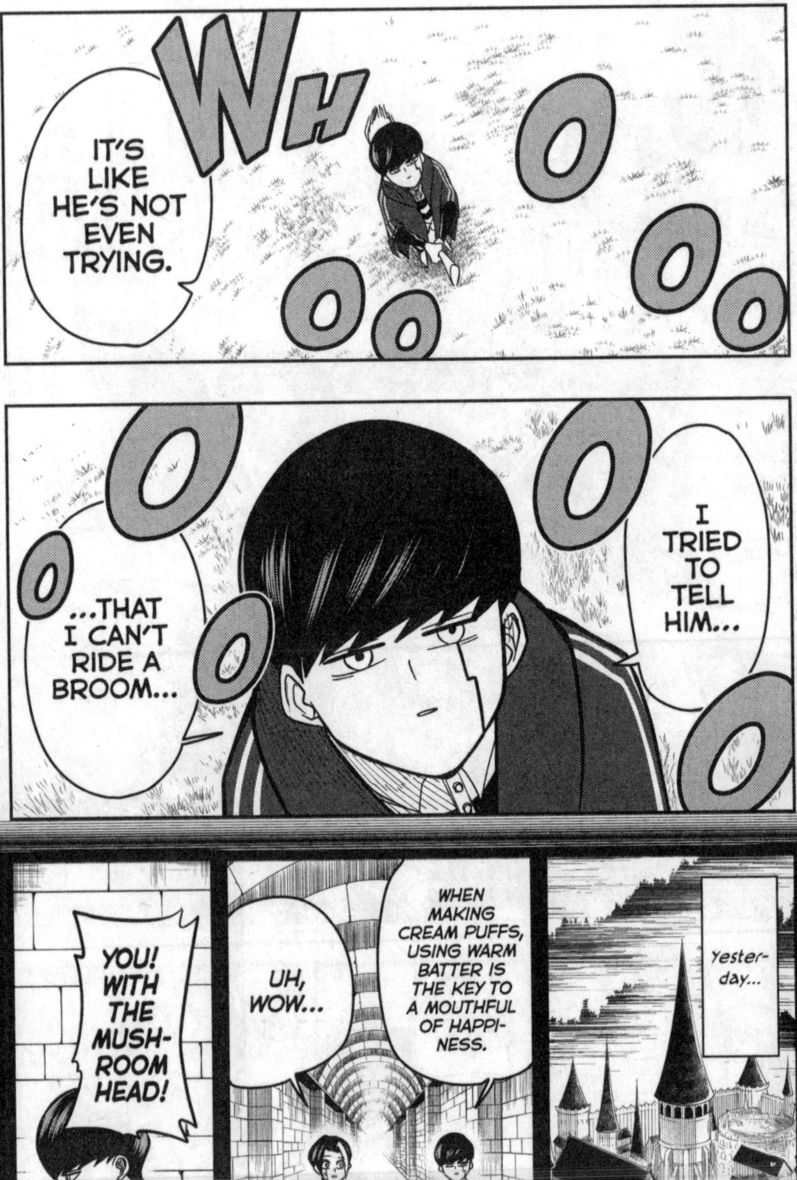
WHOOOOO
IT'S LIKE HE'S NOT EVEN TRYING.
OOOOO
I TRIED TO TELL HIM...
...THAT I CAN'T RIDE A BROOM...
Yester-day...
WHEN MAKING CREAM PUFFS, USING WARM BATTER IS THE KEY TO A MOUTHFUL OF HAPPI-NESS.
UH, WOW...
YOU! WITH THE MUSH-ROOM HEAD!

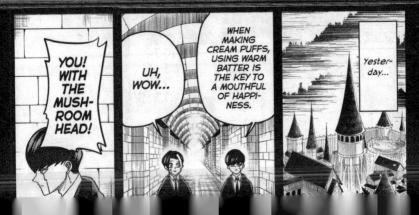

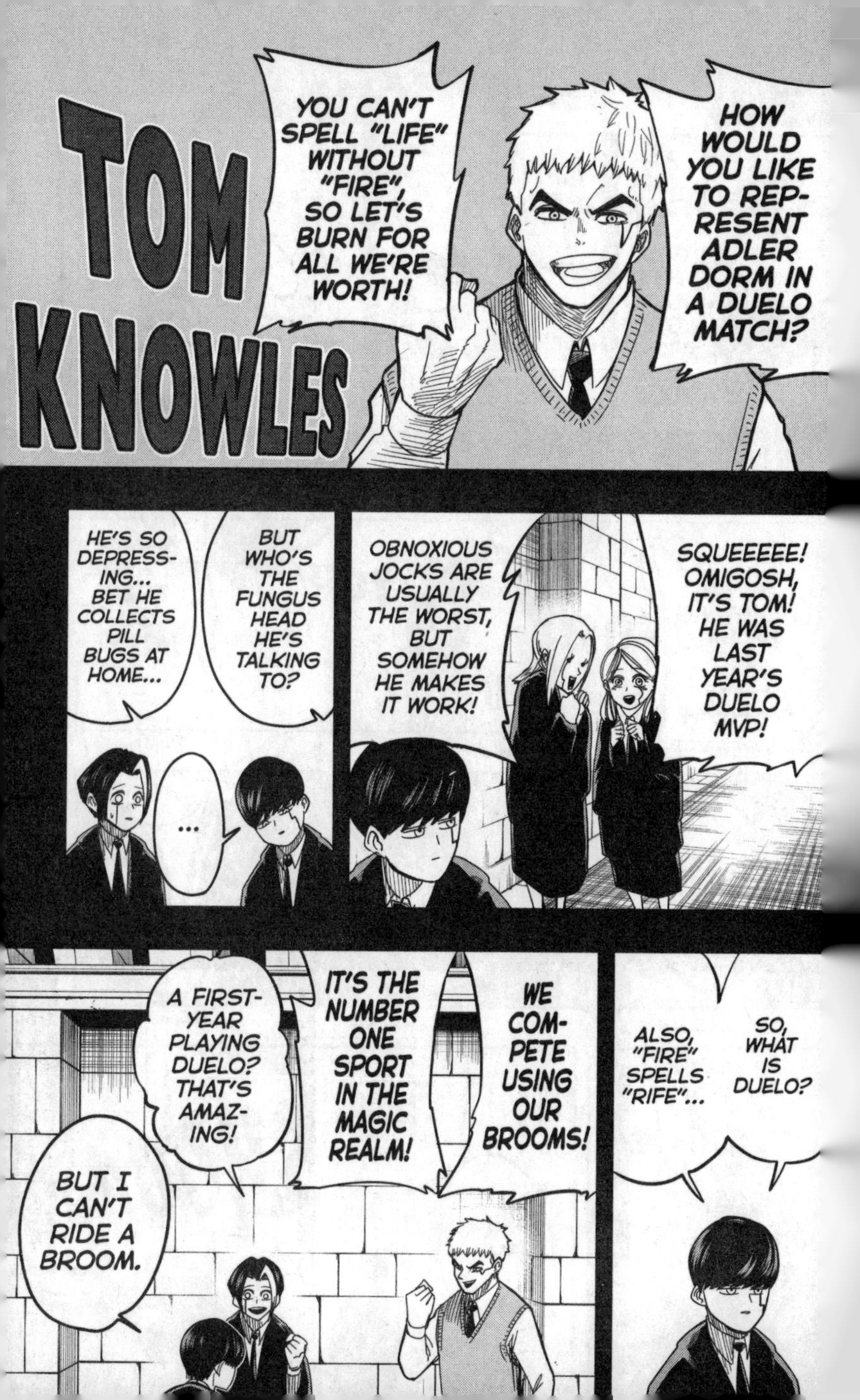
HOW WOULD YOU LIKE TO REP-RESENT ADLER DORM IN A DUELO MATCH?
YOU CAN'T SPELL "LIFE" WITHOUT "FIRE", SO LET'S BURN FOR ALL WE'RE WORTH!
TOM KNOWLES
SQUEEEEEE! OMIGOSH, IT'S TOM! HE WAS LAST YEAR'S DUELO MVP!
OBNOXIOUS JOCKS ARE USUALLY THE WORST, BUT SOMEHOW HE MAKES IT WORK!
BUT WHO'S THE FUNGUS HEAD HE'S TALKING TO?
HE'S SO DEPRESS-ING... BET HE COLLECTS PILL BUGS AT HOME...
...
SO, WHAT IS DUELO?
ALSO, "FIRE" SPELLS "RIFE"...
WE COM-PETE USING OUR BROOMS!
IT'S THE NUMBER ONE SPORT IN THE MAGIC REALM!
A FIRST-YEAR PLAYING DUELO? THAT'S AMAZ-ING!
BUT I CAN'T RIDE A BROOM.

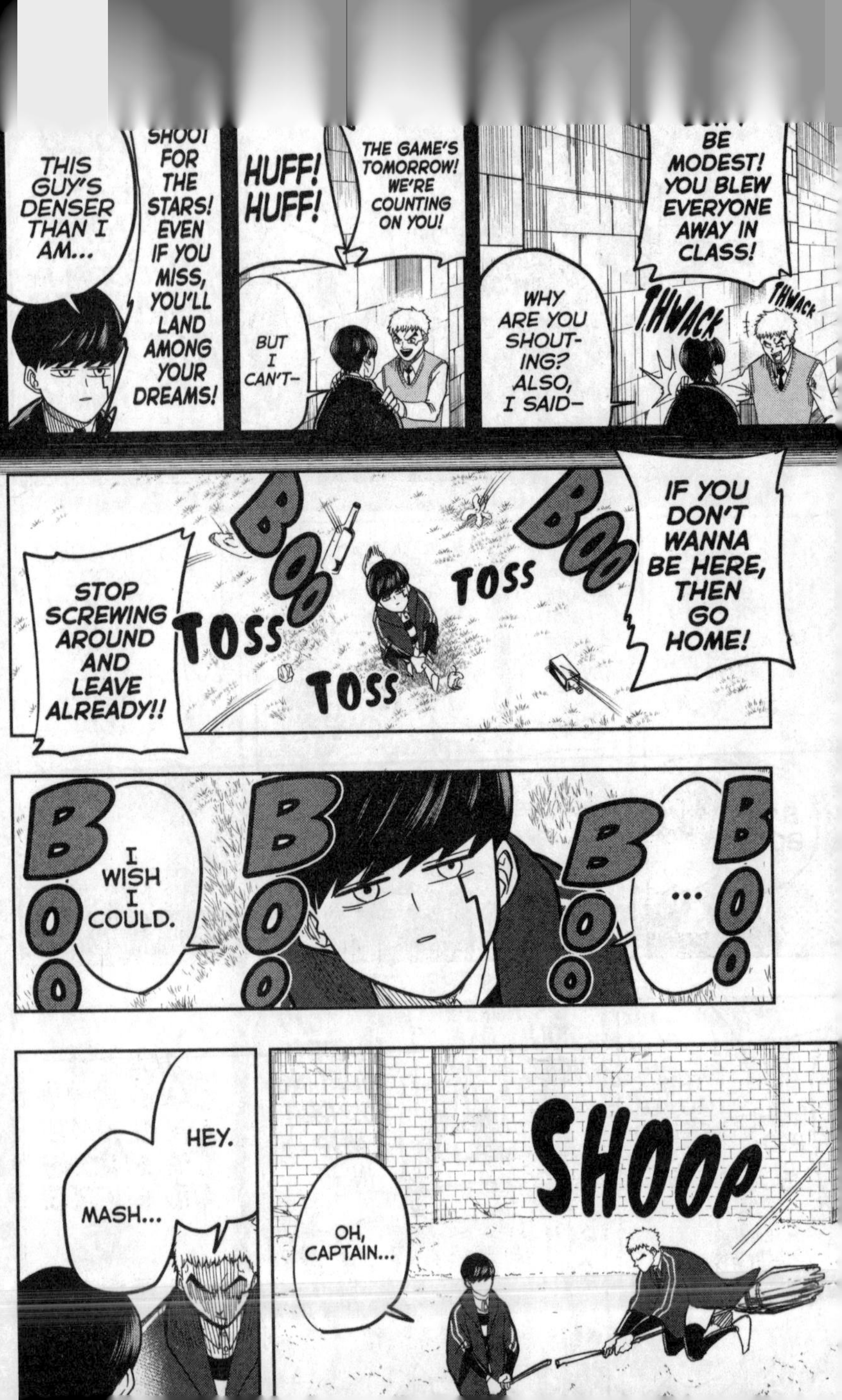
BE MODEST! YOU BLEW EVERYONE AWAY IN CLASS!
THWACK
THWACK
WHY ARE YOU SHOUTING? ALSO, I SAID–
THE GAME'S TOMORROW! WE'RE COUNTING ON YOU!
HUFF! HUFF!
BUT I CAN'T–
SHOOT FOR THE STARS! EVEN IF YOU MISS, YOU'LL LAND AMONG YOUR DREAMS!
THIS GUY'S DENSER THAN I AM...
IF YOU DON'T WANNA BE HERE, THEN GO HOME!
BOO
TOSS
BOO
TOSS
TOSS
STOP SCREWING AROUND AND LEAVE ALREADY!!
BOOO
...
BOOO
BOOO
I WISH I COULD.
BOOO
SHOOP
OH, CAPTAIN...
HEY.
MASH...

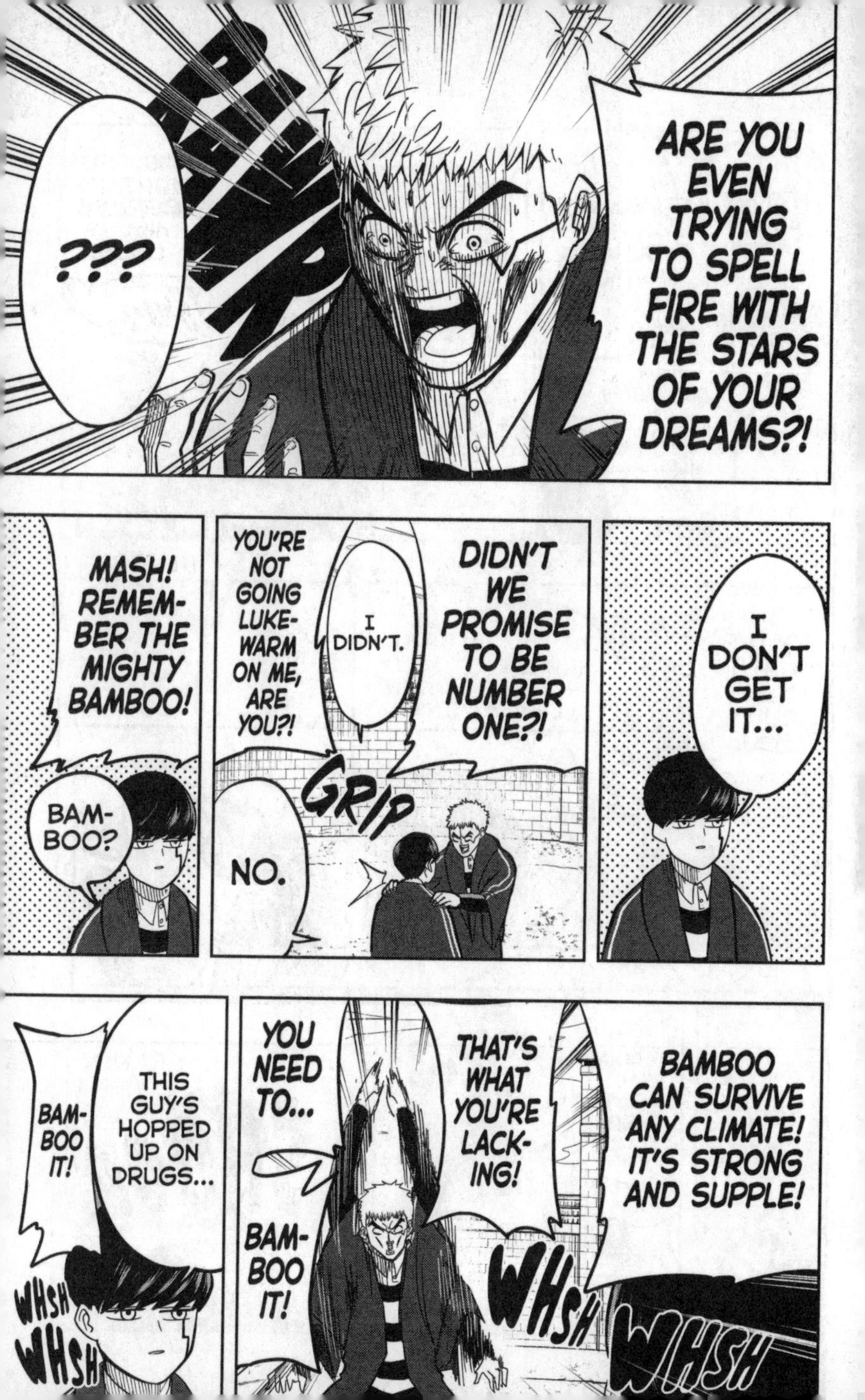
ARE YOU EVEN TRYING TO SPELL FIRE WITH THE STARS OF YOUR DREAMS?!
???
I DON'T GET IT...
DIDN'T WE PROMISE TO BE NUMBER ONE?!
I DIDN'T.
YOU'RE NOT GOING LUKEWARM ON ME, ARE YOU?!
GRIP
NO.
MASH! REMEMBER THE MIGHTY BAMBOO!
BAMBOO?
BAMBOO CAN SURVIVE ANY CLIMATE! IT'S STRONG AND SUPPLE!
THAT'S WHAT YOU'RE LACKING!
YOU NEED TO...
BAMBOO IT!
WHSH
WHSH
THIS GUY'S HOPPED UP ON DRUGS...
BAMBOO IT!
WHSH
WHSH

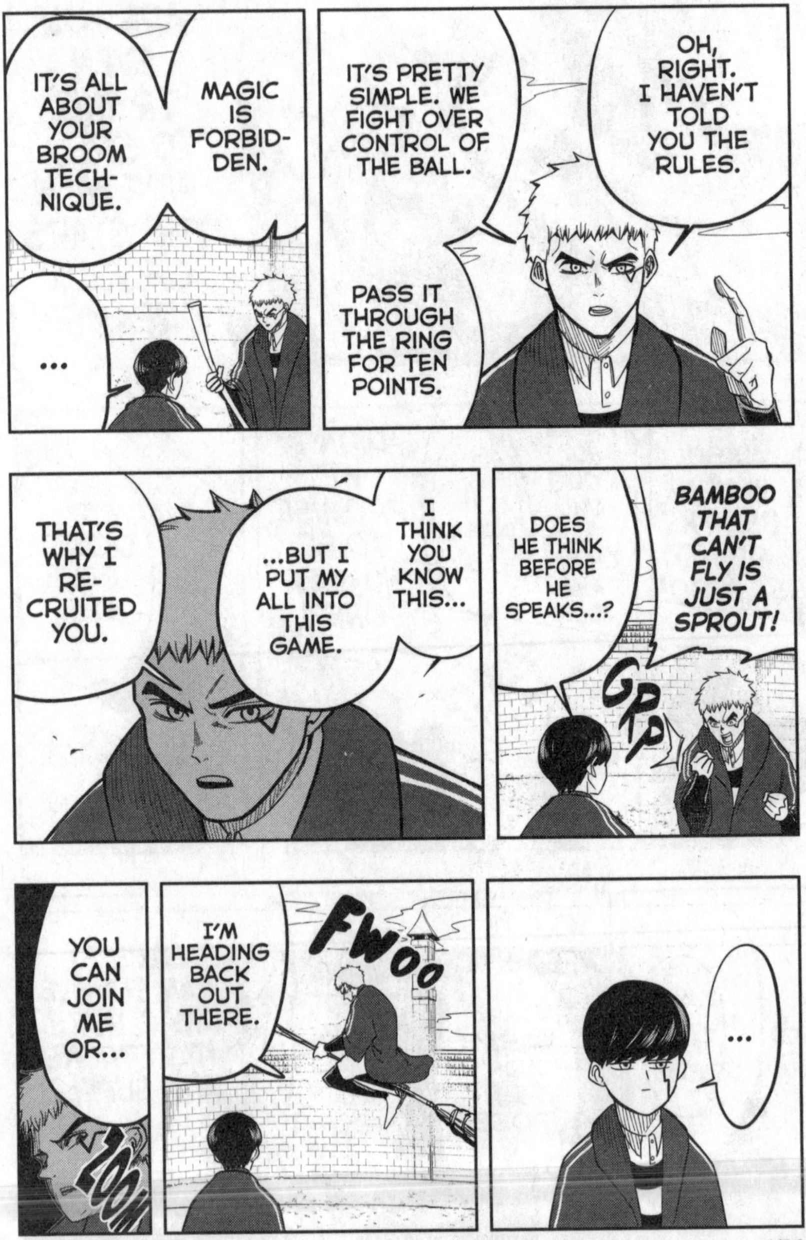
OH, RIGHT. I HAVEN'T TOLD YOU THE RULES.
IT'S PRETTY SIMPLE. WE FIGHT OVER CONTROL OF THE BALL.
PASS IT THROUGH THE RING FOR TEN POINTS.
MAGIC IS FORBIDDEN.
IT'S ALL ABOUT YOUR BROOM TECHNIQUE.
...
BAMBOO THAT CAN'T FLY IS JUST A SPROUT!
GRP
DOES HE THINK BEFORE HE SPEAKS...?
I THINK YOU KNOW THIS...
...BUT I PUT MY ALL INTO THIS GAME.
THAT'S WHY I RECRUITED YOU.
...
I'M HEADING BACK OUT THERE.
FWOO
YOU CAN JOIN ME OR...
ZOOM

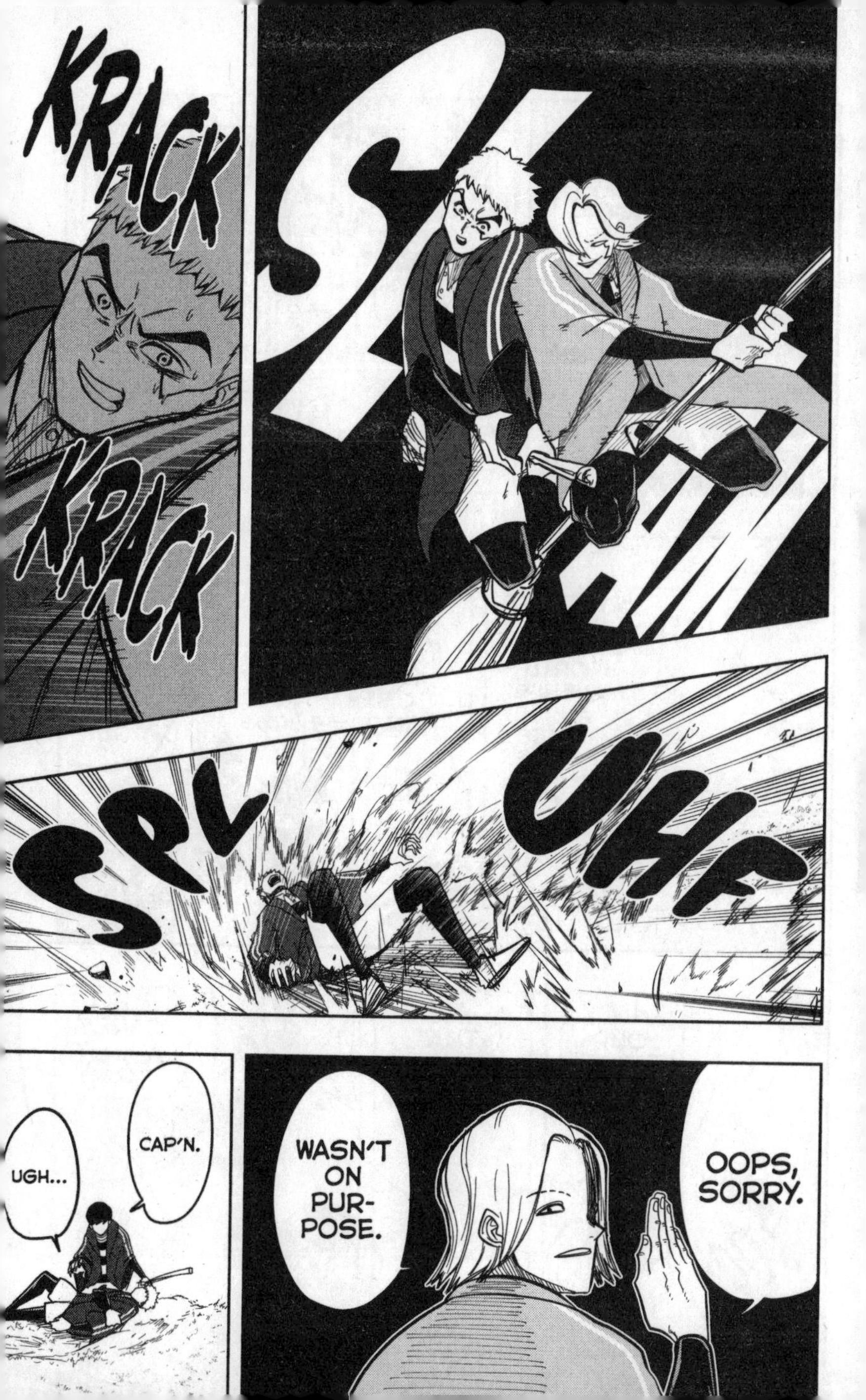
SH
HM
KRACK
KRACK
SPL
UHF
OOPS, SORRY.
WASN'T ON PUR-POSE.
CAP'N.
UGH...

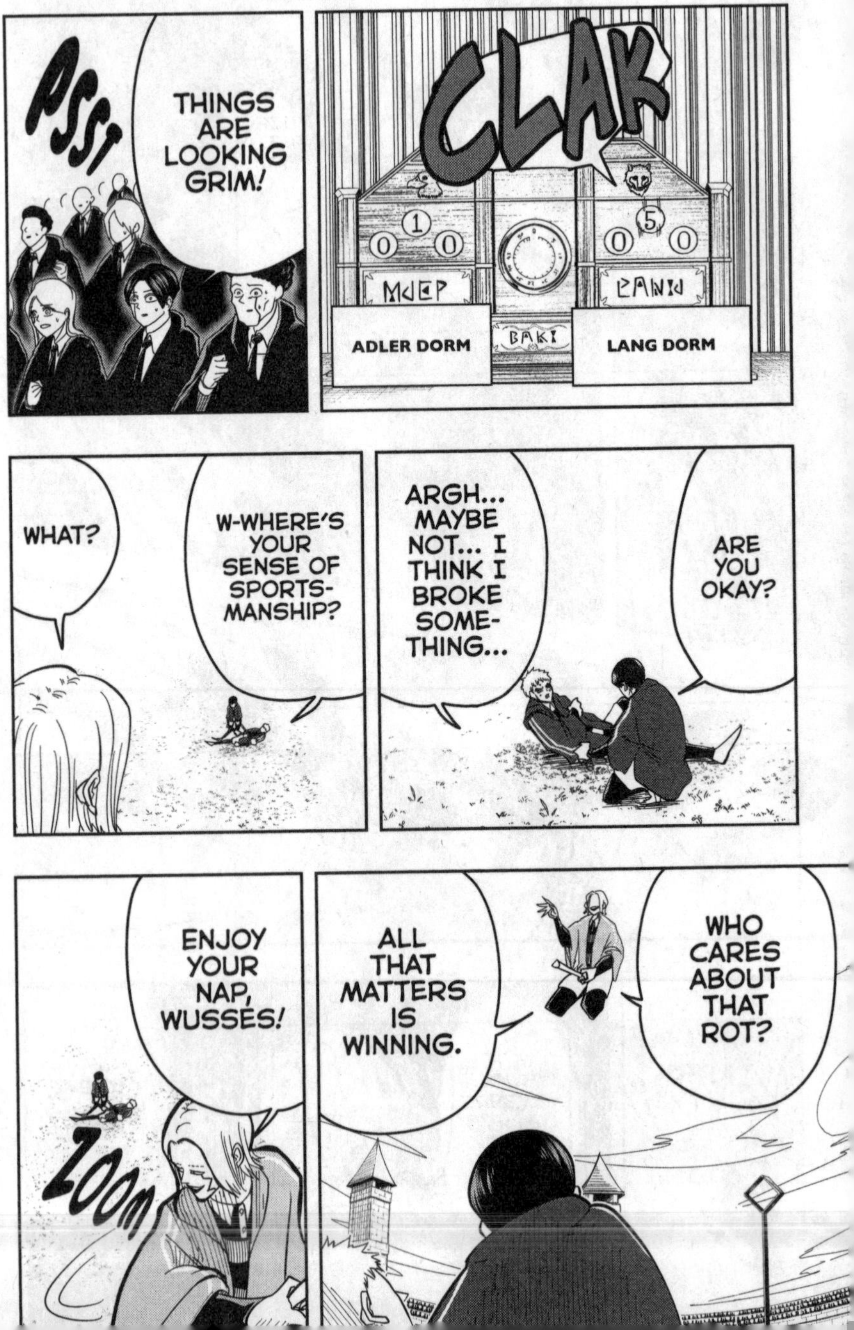
CLAK
100
500
ADLER DORM
LANG DORM
PSSST
THINGS ARE LOOKING GRIM!
ARE YOU OKAY?
ARGH... MAYBE NOT... I THINK I BROKE SOME-THING...
W-WHERE'S YOUR SENSE OF SPORTS-MANSHIP?
WHAT?
WHO CARES ABOUT THAT ROT?
ALL THAT MATTERS IS WINNING.
ENJOY YOUR NAP, WUSSES!
ZOOM

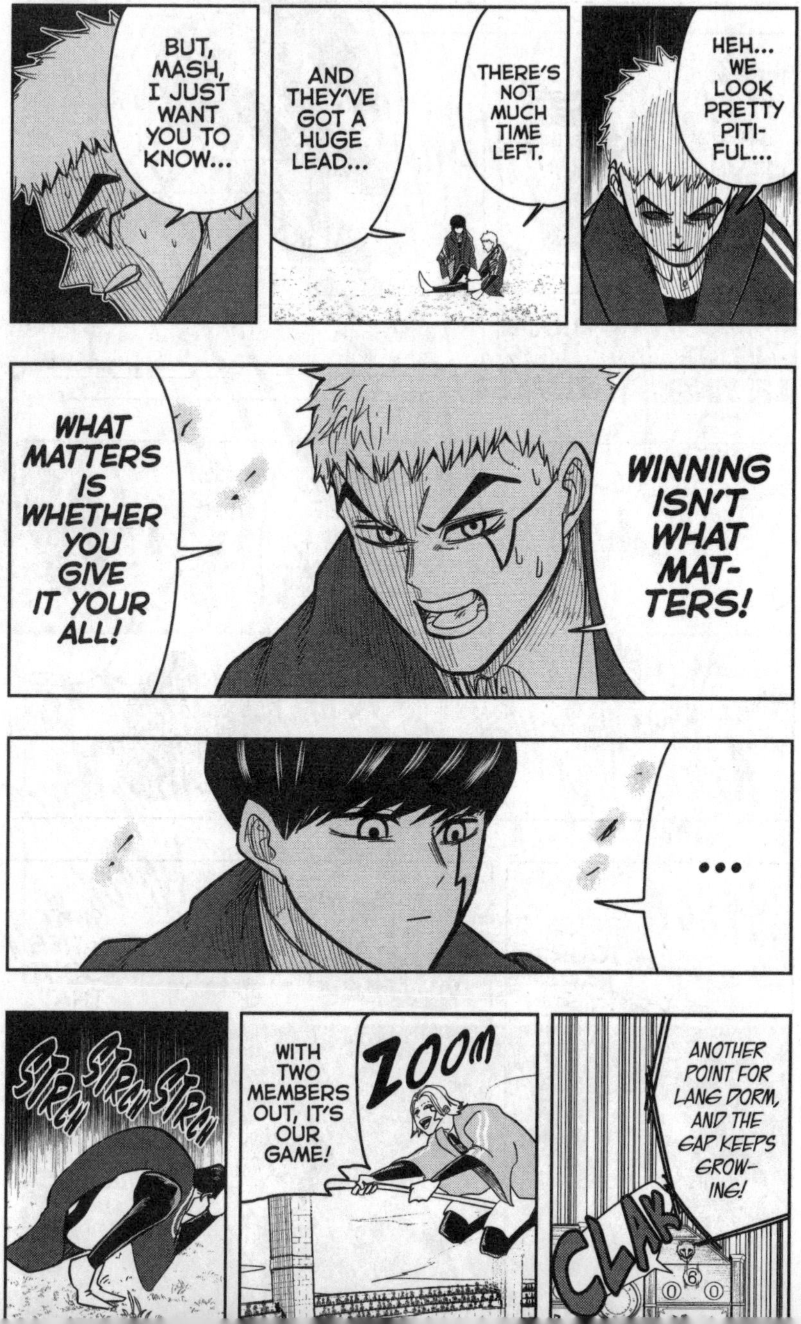
HEH... WE LOOK PRETTY PITI-FUL...
THERE'S NOT MUCH TIME LEFT.
AND THEY'VE GOT A HUGE LEAD...
BUT, MASH, I JUST WANT YOU TO KNOW...
WINNING ISN'T WHAT MAT-TERS!
WHAT MATTERS IS WHETHER YOU GIVE IT YOUR ALL!
...
ANOTHER POINT FOR LANG DORM, AND THE GAP KEEPS GROW-ING!
CLAK
ZOOM
WITH TWO MEMBERS OUT, IT'S OUR GAME!
STRCH STRCH STRCH STRCH

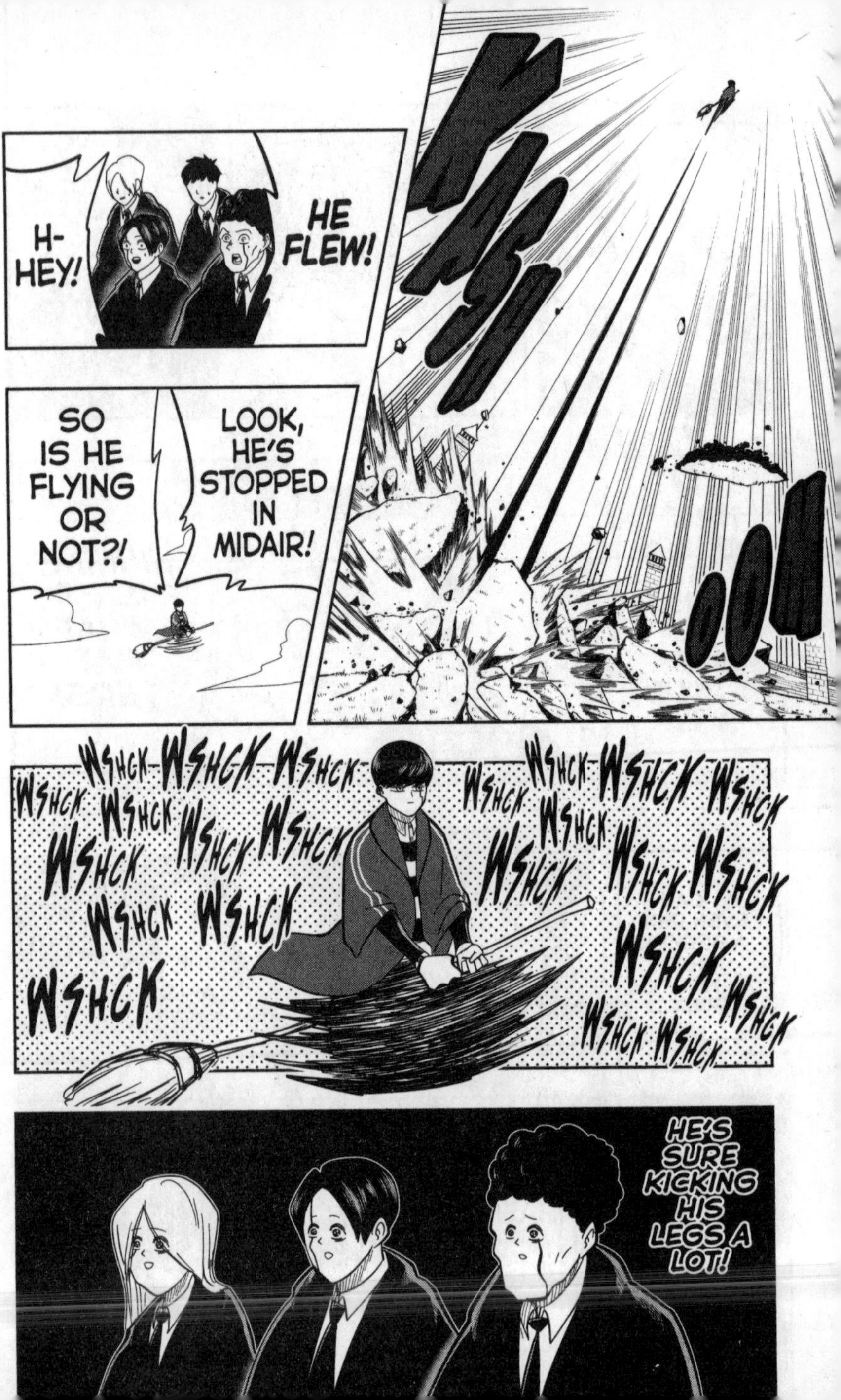
HE FLEW!
H-HEY!
LOOK, HE'S STOPPED IN MIDAIR!
SO IS HE FLYING OR NOT?!
WSHCK WSHCK WSHCK WSHCK WSHCK WSHCK
HE'S SURE KICKING HIS LEGS A LOT!

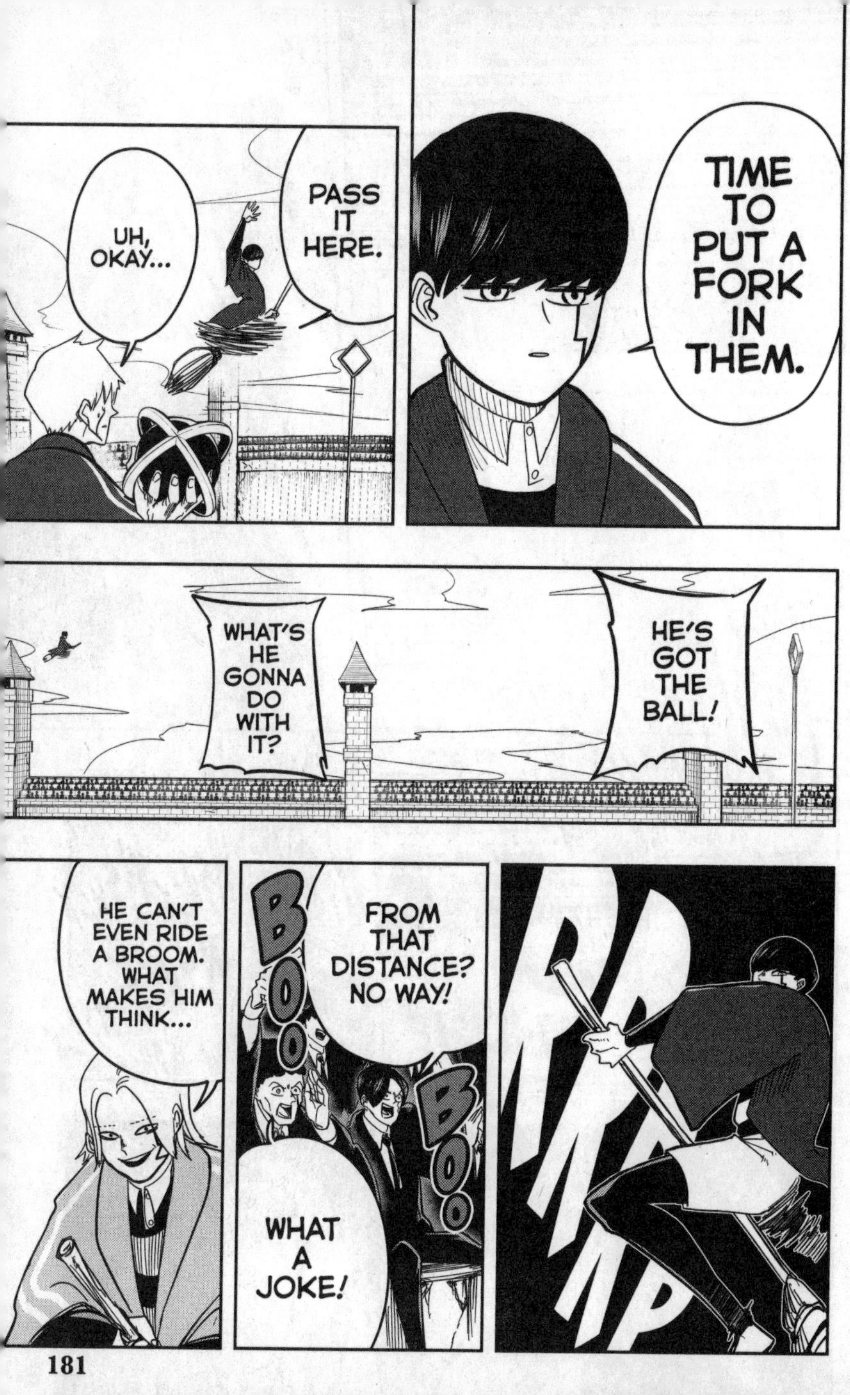
TIME TO PUT A FORK IN THEM.
PASS IT HERE.
UH, OKAY...
HE'S GOT THE BALL!
WHAT'S HE GONNA DO WITH IT?
BOO
FROM THAT DISTANCE? NO WAY!
BOO
WHAT A JOKE!
HE CAN'T EVEN RIDE A BROOM. WHAT MAKES HIM THINK...

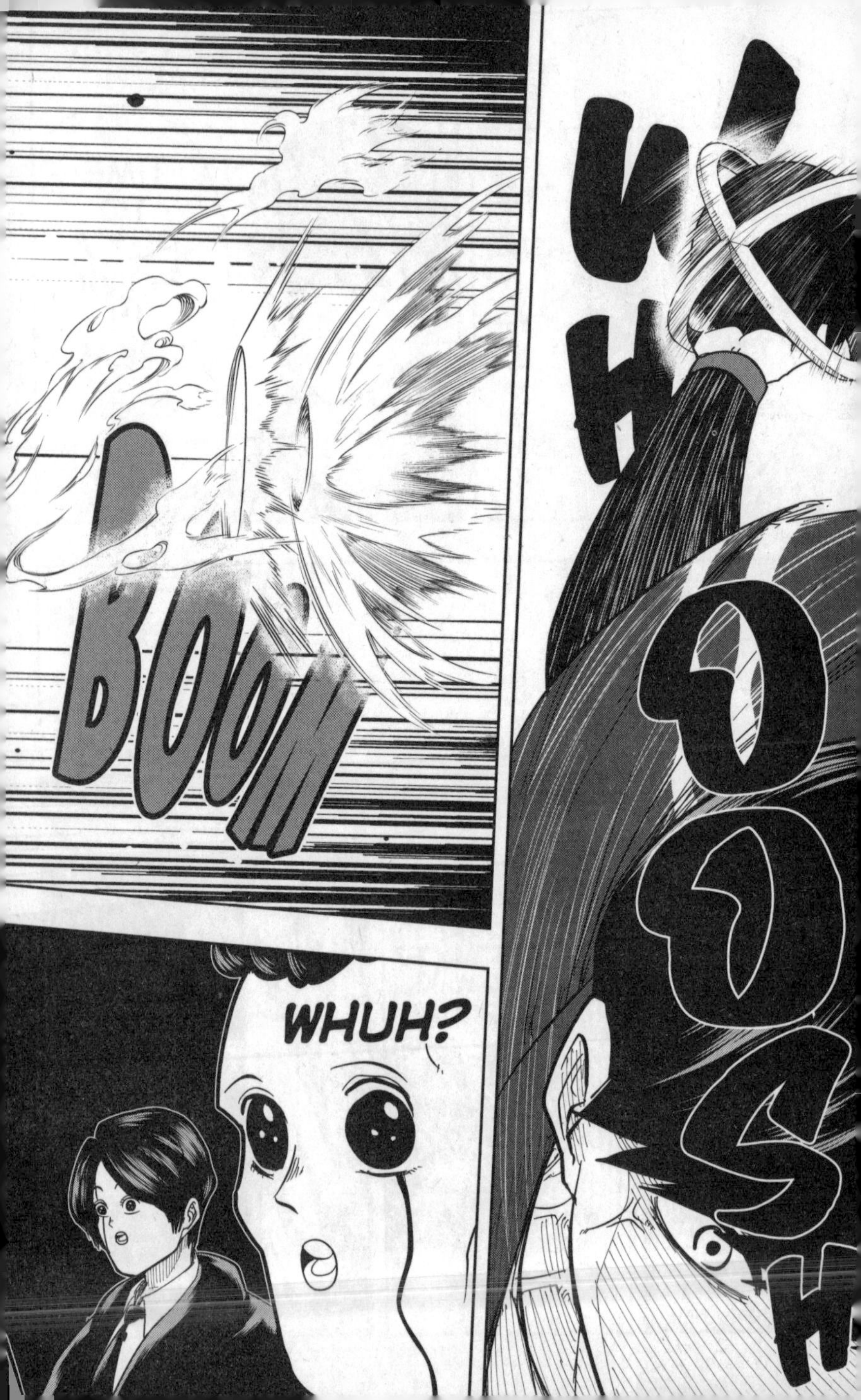
WHOOSH
BOOM
WHUH?

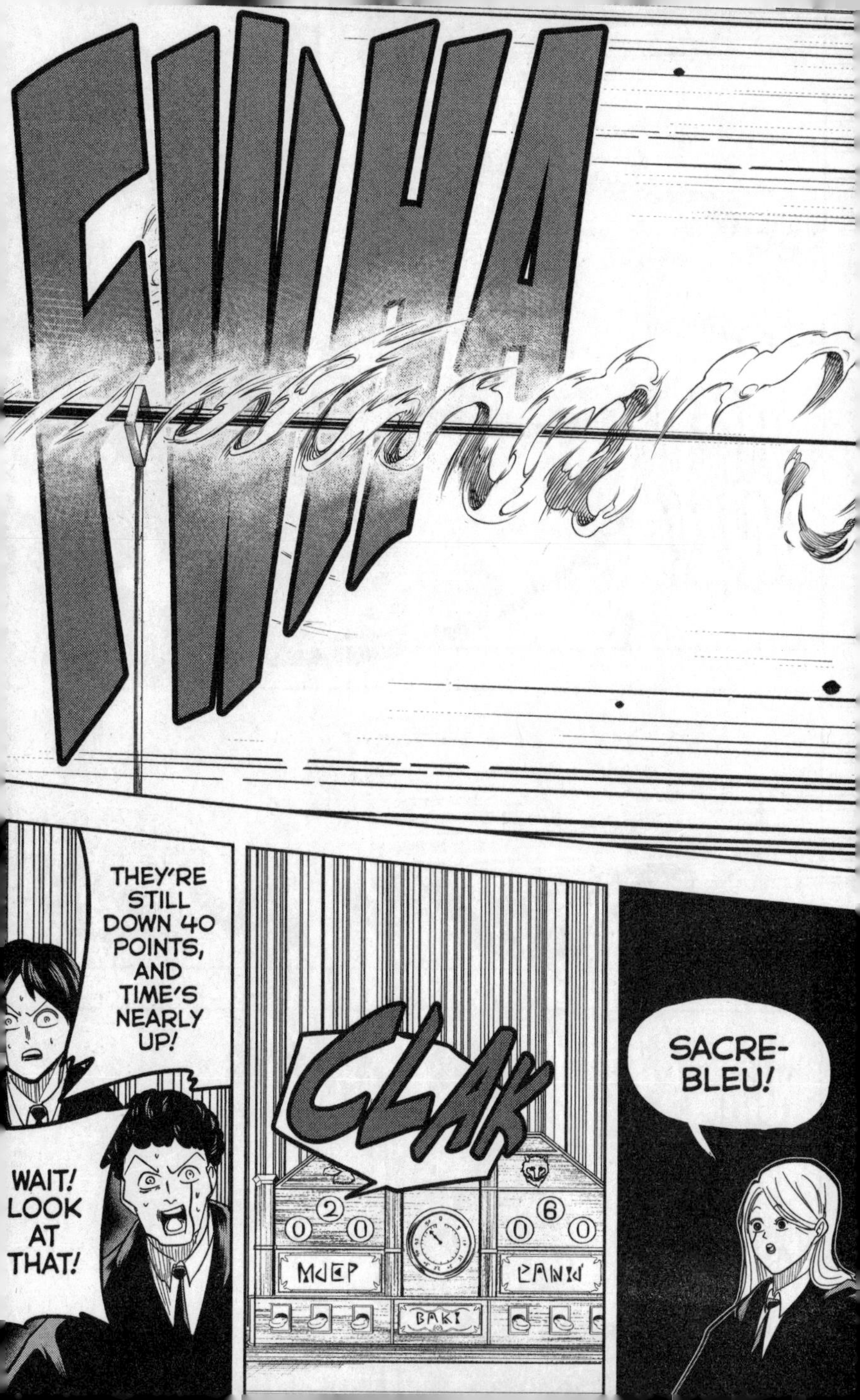
SACRE-BLEU!
CLAK
THEY'RE STILL DOWN 40 POINTS, AND TIME'S NEARLY UP!
WAIT! LOOK AT THAT!

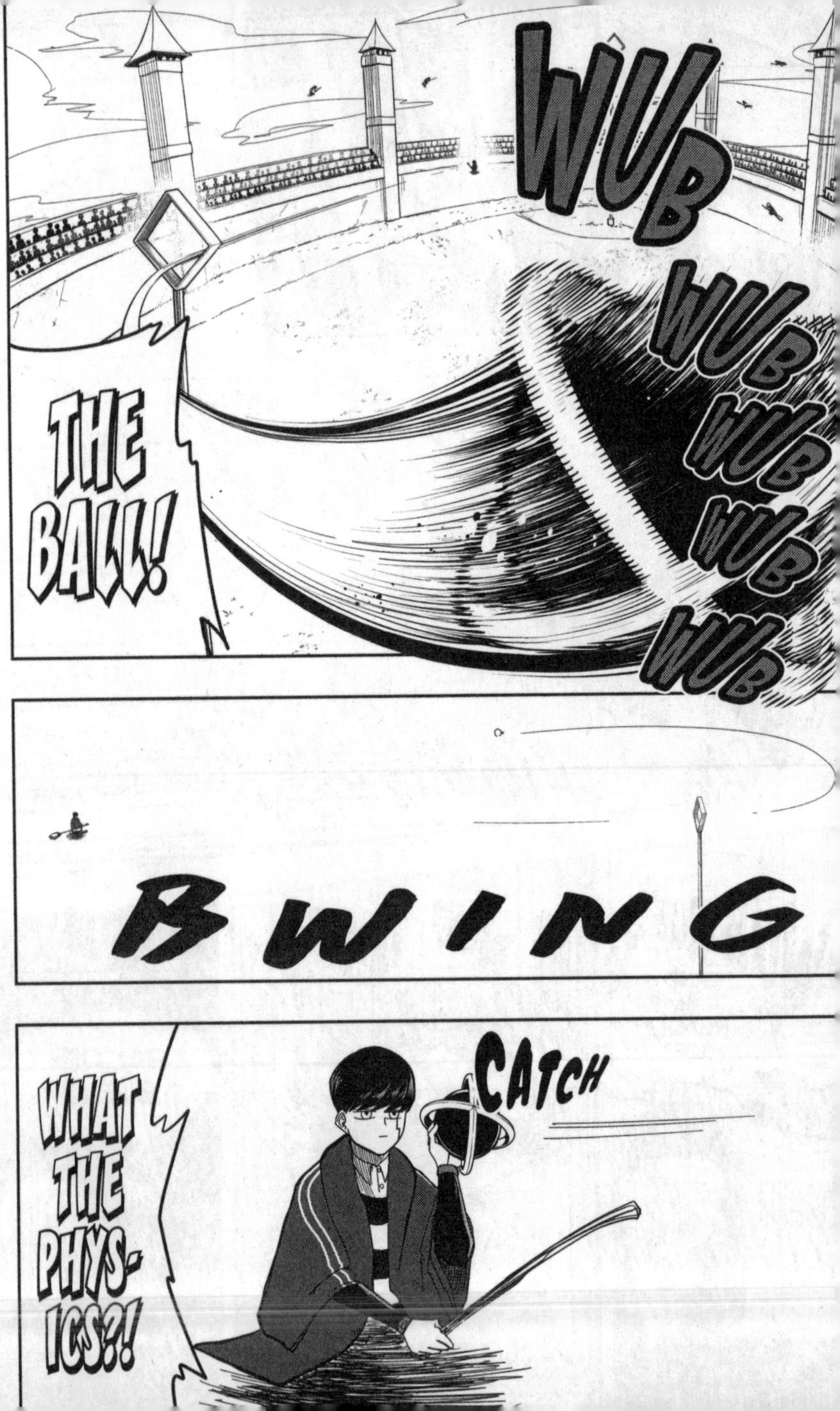
WUB
WUB WUB WUB WUB WUB
THE BALL!
BWING
CATCH
WHAT THE PHYS-ICS?!

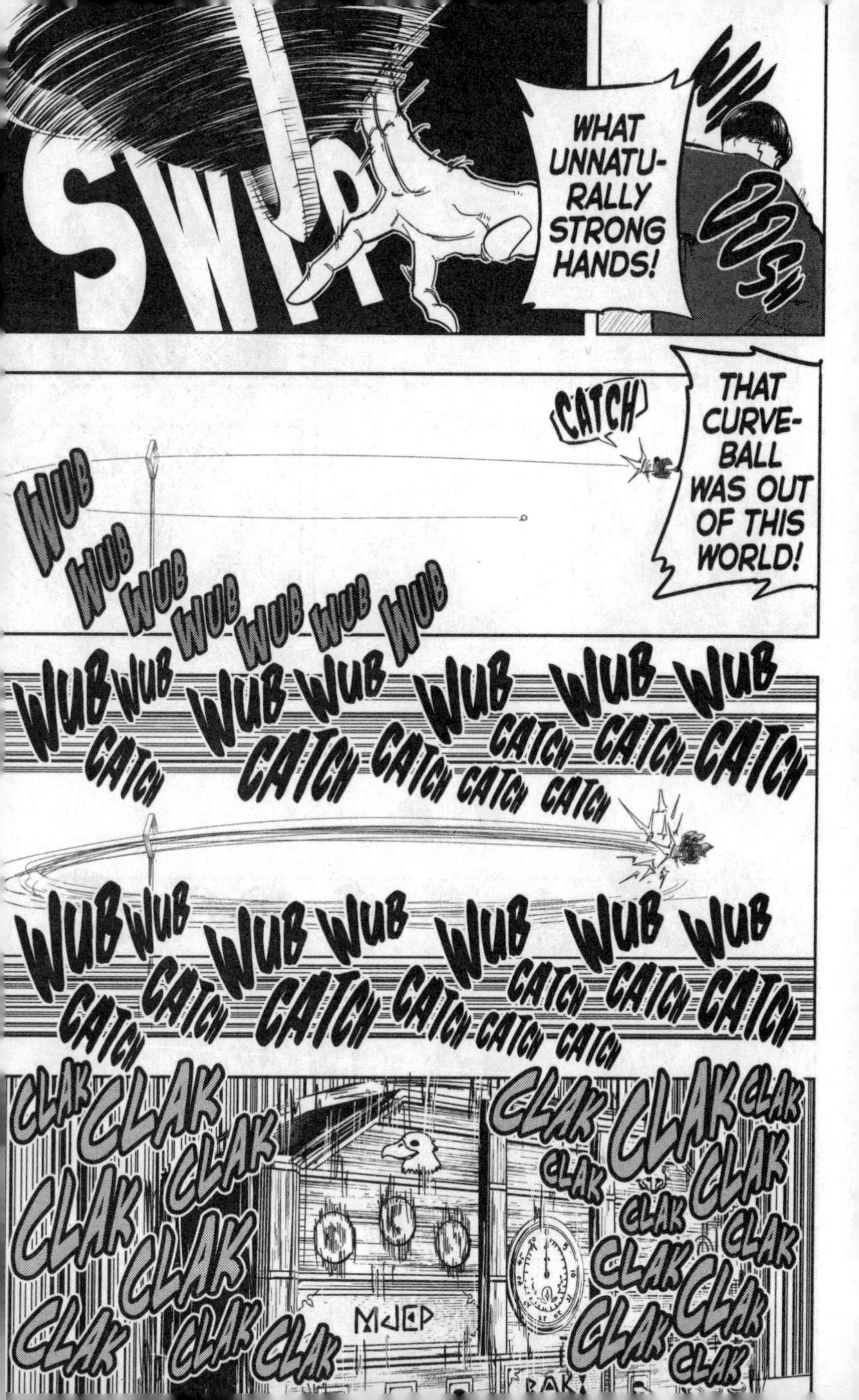
WHOOSH
WHAT UNNATU-RALLY STRONG HANDS!
SWIP
THAT CURVE-BALL WAS OUT OF THIS WORLD!
CATCH
WUB WUB WUB WUB WUB WUB WUB WUB
WUB WUB WUB WUB WUB WUB WUB WUB
CATCH CATCH CATCH CATCH CATCH CATCH CATCH CATCH CATCH
WUB WUB WUB WUB WUB WUB WUB WUB
CATCH CATCH CATCH CATCH CATCH CATCH CATCH CATCH CATCH CATCH
CLAK CLAK CLAK CLAK CLAK CLAK CLAK CLAK CLAK CLAK CLAK CLAK
CLAK CLAK CLAK CLAK CLAK CLAK CLAK CLAK CLAK CLAK

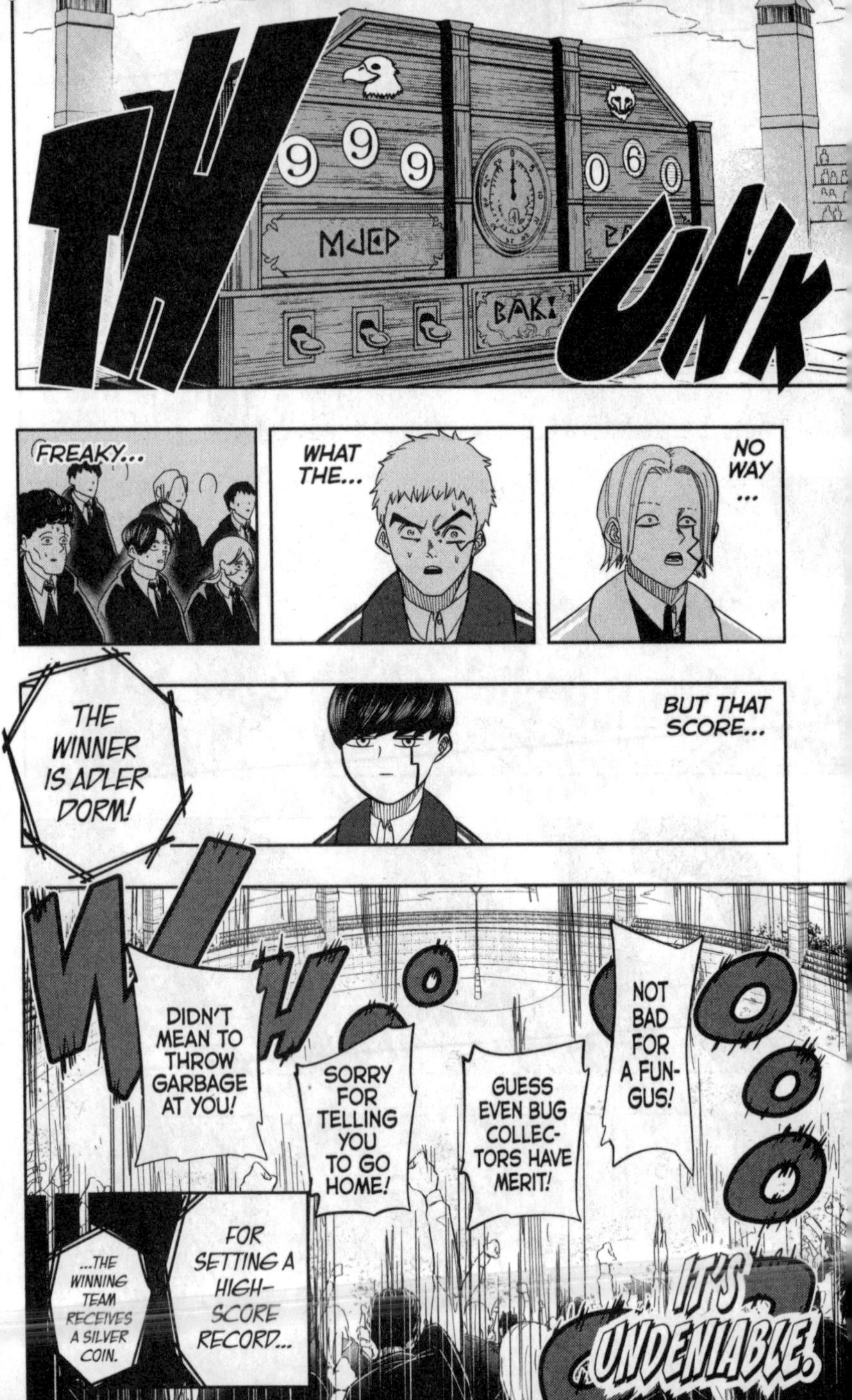
THUNK
NO WAY...
WHAT THE...
FREAKY...
BUT THAT SCORE...
THE WINNER IS ADLER DORM!
WHOOOOOO
NOT BAD FOR A FUN-GUS!
GUESS EVEN BUG COLLEC-TORS HAVE MERIT!
SORRY FOR TELLING YOU TO GO HOME!
DIDN'T MEAN TO THROW GARBAGE AT YOU!
IT'S UNDENIABLE.
FOR SETTING A HIGH-SCORE RECORD...
...THE WINNING TEAM RECEIVES A SILVER COIN.

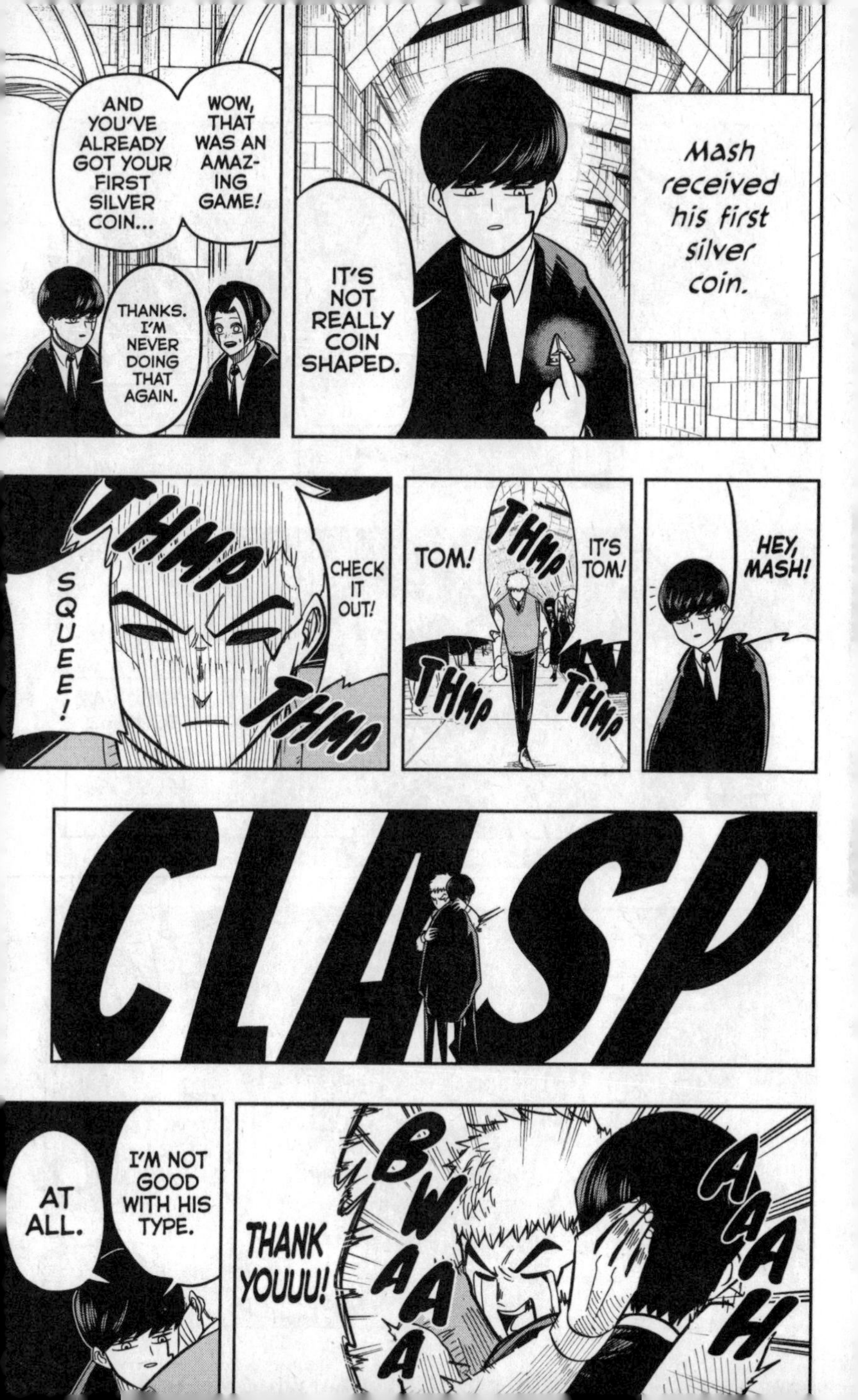
Mash received his first silver coin.
IT'S NOT REALLY COIN SHAPED.
WOW, THAT WAS AN AMAZ-ING GAME!
AND YOU'VE ALREADY GOT YOUR FIRST SILVER COIN...
THANKS. I'M NEVER DOING THAT AGAIN.
HEY, MASH!
IT'S TOM!
THMP
TOM!
THMP
THMP
CHECK IT OUT!
THMP
SQUEEE!
THMP
CLASP
AAAAH
BWAAAA
THANK YOUUU!
I'M NOT GOOD WITH HIS TYPE.
AT ALL.

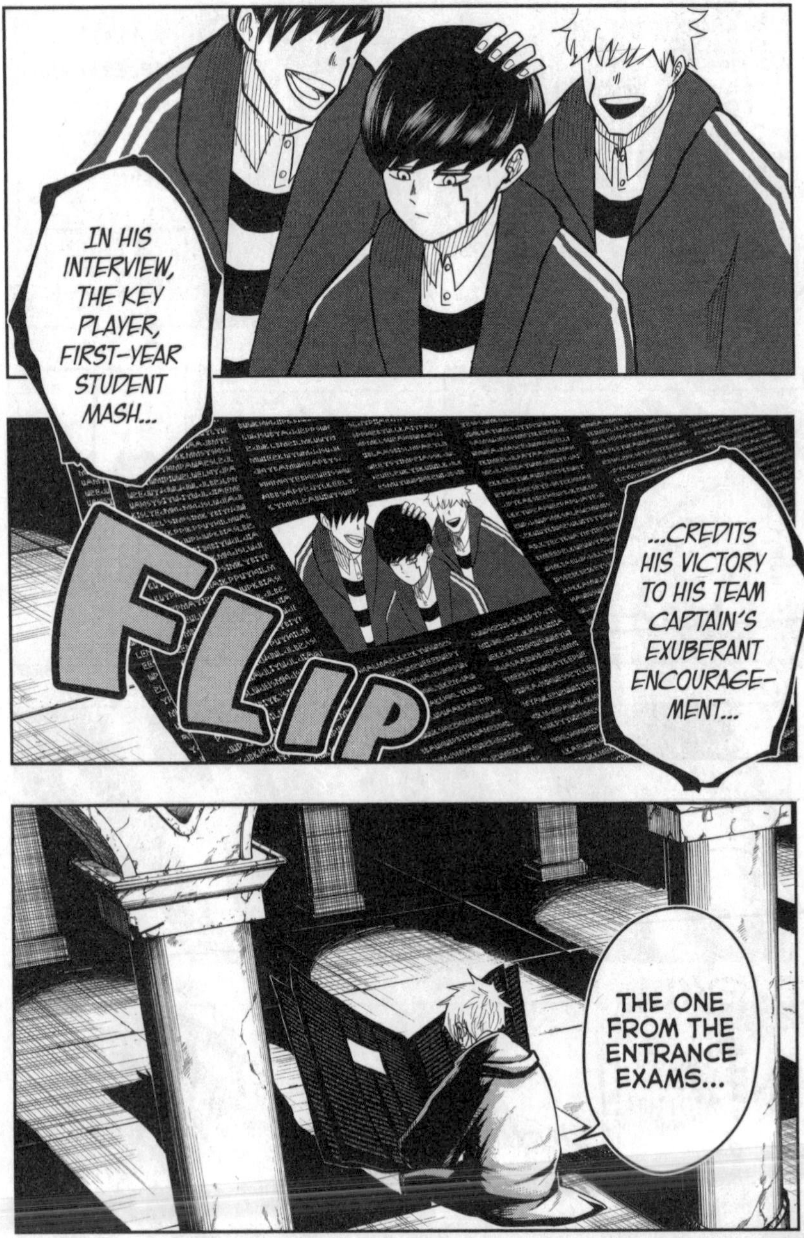
IN HIS INTERVIEW, THE KEY PLAYER, FIRST-YEAR STUDENT MASH...
...CREDITS HIS VICTORY TO HIS TEAM CAPTAIN'S EXUBERANT ENCOURAGEMENT...
FLIP
THE ONE FROM THE ENTRANCE EXAMS...

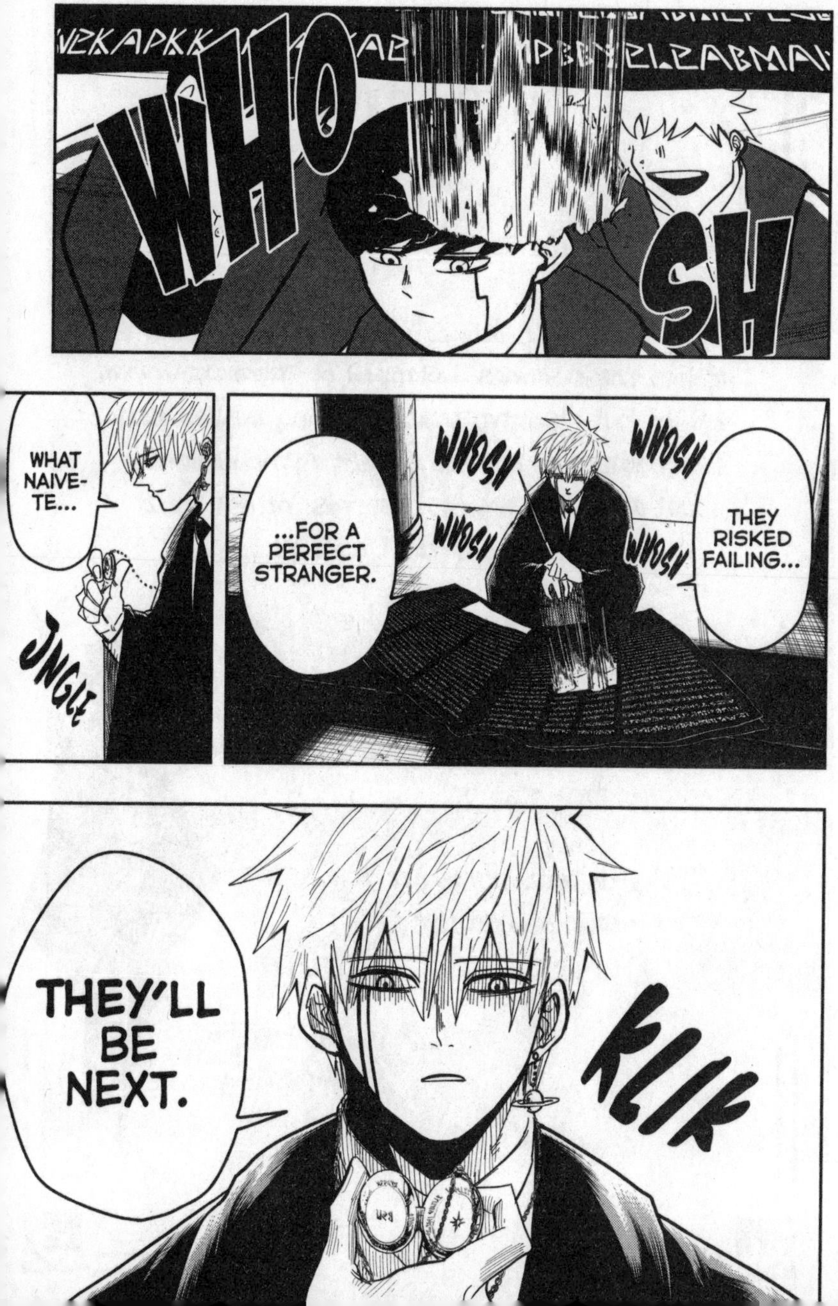
WHO
SH
THEY RISKED FAILING...
WHOSH
WHOSH
WHOSH
WHOSH
...FOR A PERFECT STRANGER.
WHAT NAIVETE...
JINGLE
KLIK
THEY'LL BE NEXT.

Finn Ames

I included Finn as the straight man.

Personally, I feel a likeable character like Finn is vital to these stories. I planned on introducing him earlier, but his intro ended up being pushed back to chapter 4... He was calmer in the beginning, but as I redid the storyboards, he got louder by the chapter. Or did he...?

I really want Finn to become a well-rounded character as the story goes on!!

His favorite words are "peace" and "order."

...

Height: 170 cm
Weight: 52 kg

CHAPTER 8: MASH BURNEDEAD AND THE CHALLENGING MAGIC USER

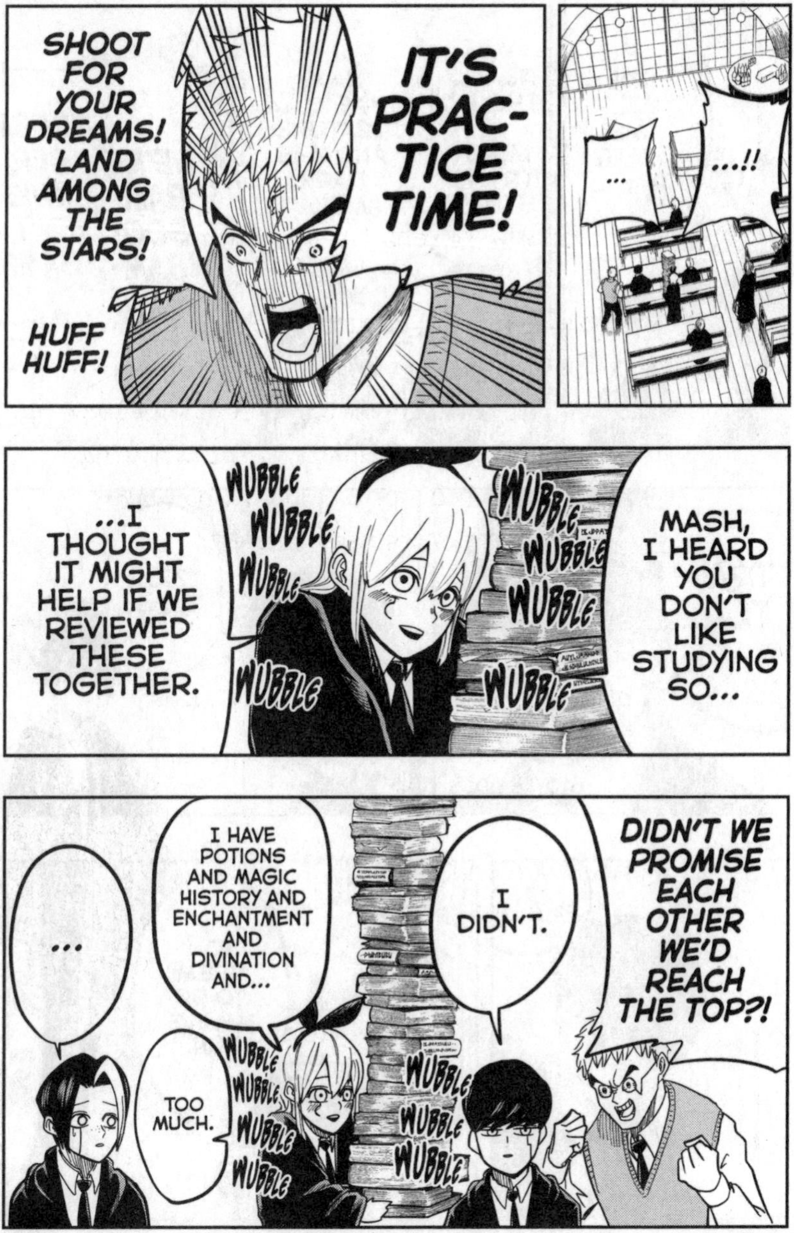
...!!
...
IT'S PRACTICE TIME!
SHOOT FOR YOUR DREAMS! LAND AMONG THE STARS!
HUFF HUFF!
MASH, I HEARD YOU DON'T LIKE STUDYING SO...
WUBBLE WUBBLE WUBBLE WUBBLE
WUBBLE WUBBLE WUBBLE WUBBLE
...I THOUGHT IT MIGHT HELP IF WE REVIEWED THESE TOGETHER.
DIDN'T WE PROMISE EACH OTHER WE'D REACH THE TOP?!
I DIDN'T.
WUBBLE WUBBLE WUBBLE
I HAVE POTIONS AND MAGIC HISTORY AND ENCHANTMENT AND DIVINATION AND...
WUBBLE WUBBLE WUBBLE WUBBLE
TOO MUCH.
...

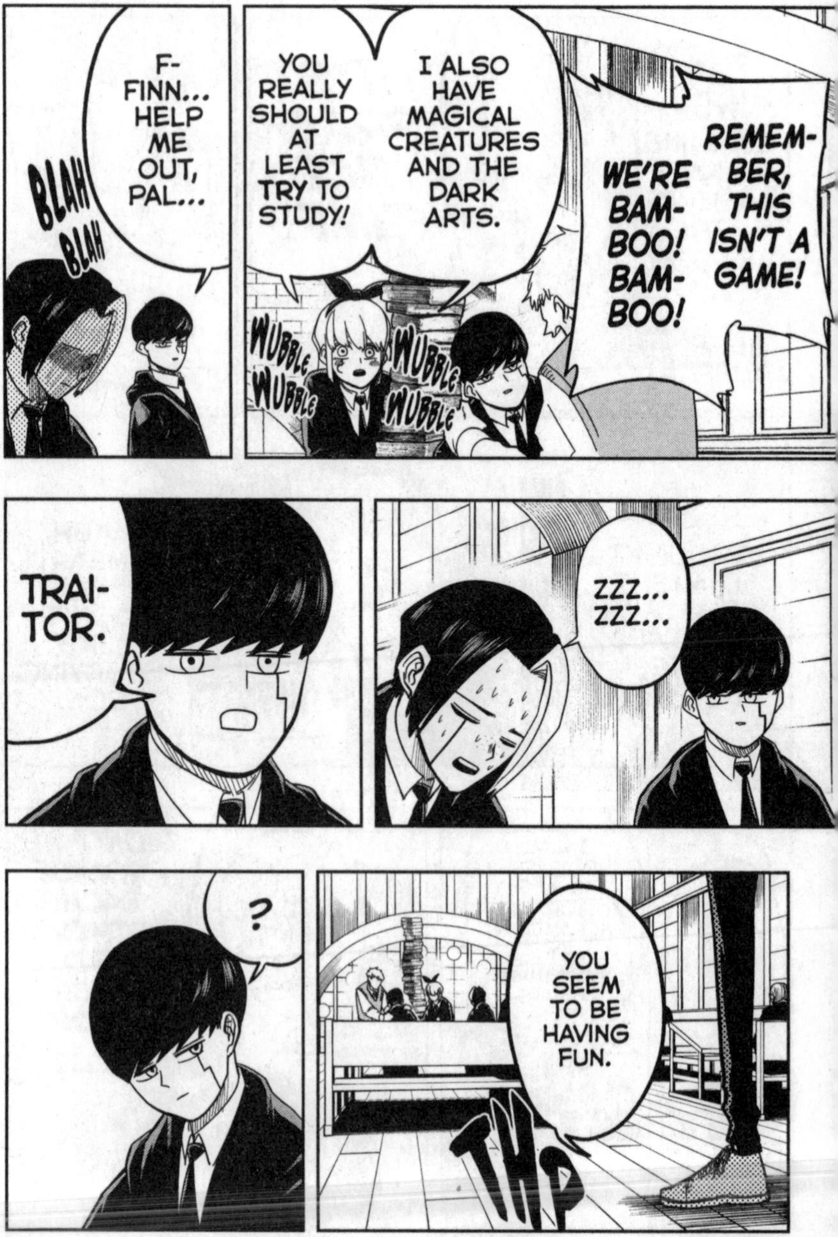
REMEMBER, THIS ISN'T A GAME!
WE'RE BAMBOO! BAMBOO!
I ALSO HAVE MAGICAL CREATURES AND THE DARK ARTS.
YOU REALLY SHOULD AT LEAST TRY TO STUDY!
WUBBLE WUBBLE
WUBBLE WUBBLE
F-FINN... HELP ME OUT, PAL...
BLAH BLAH
ZZZ... ZZZ...
TRAITOR.
YOU SEEM TO BE HAVING FUN.
THP
?

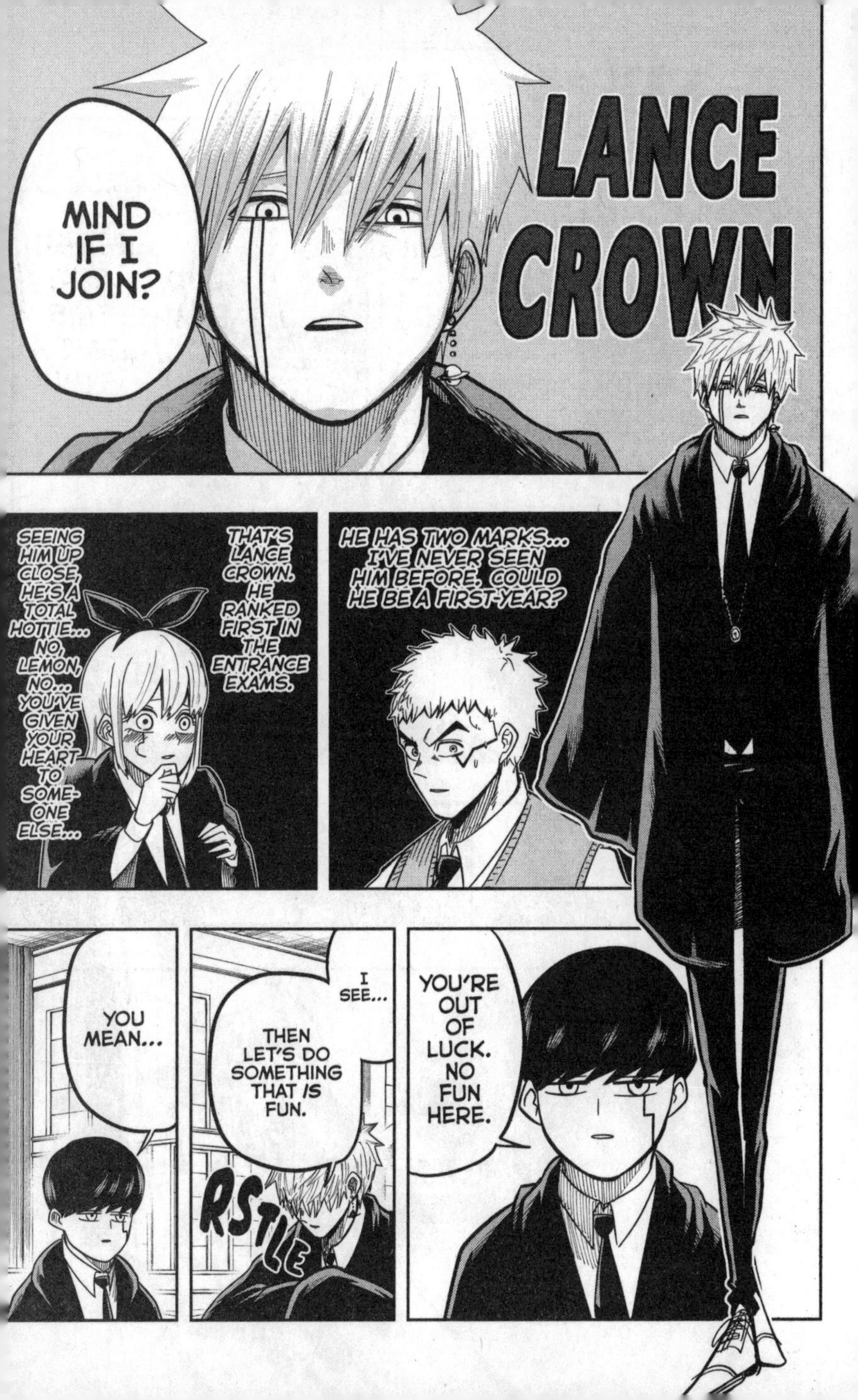
LANCE CROWN
MIND IF I JOIN?
HE HAS TWO MARKS... I'VE NEVER SEEN HIM BEFORE. COULD HE BE A FIRST-YEAR?
THAT'S LANCE CROWN. HE RANKED FIRST IN THE ENTRANCE EXAMS.
SEEING HIM UP CLOSE, HE'S A TOTAL HOTTIE... NO, LEMON, NO... YOU'VE GIVEN YOUR HEART TO SOME-ONE ELSE...
YOU'RE OUT OF LUCK. NO FUN HERE.
I SEE...
THEN LET'S DO SOMETHING THAT *IS* FUN.
RSTLE
YOU MEAN...

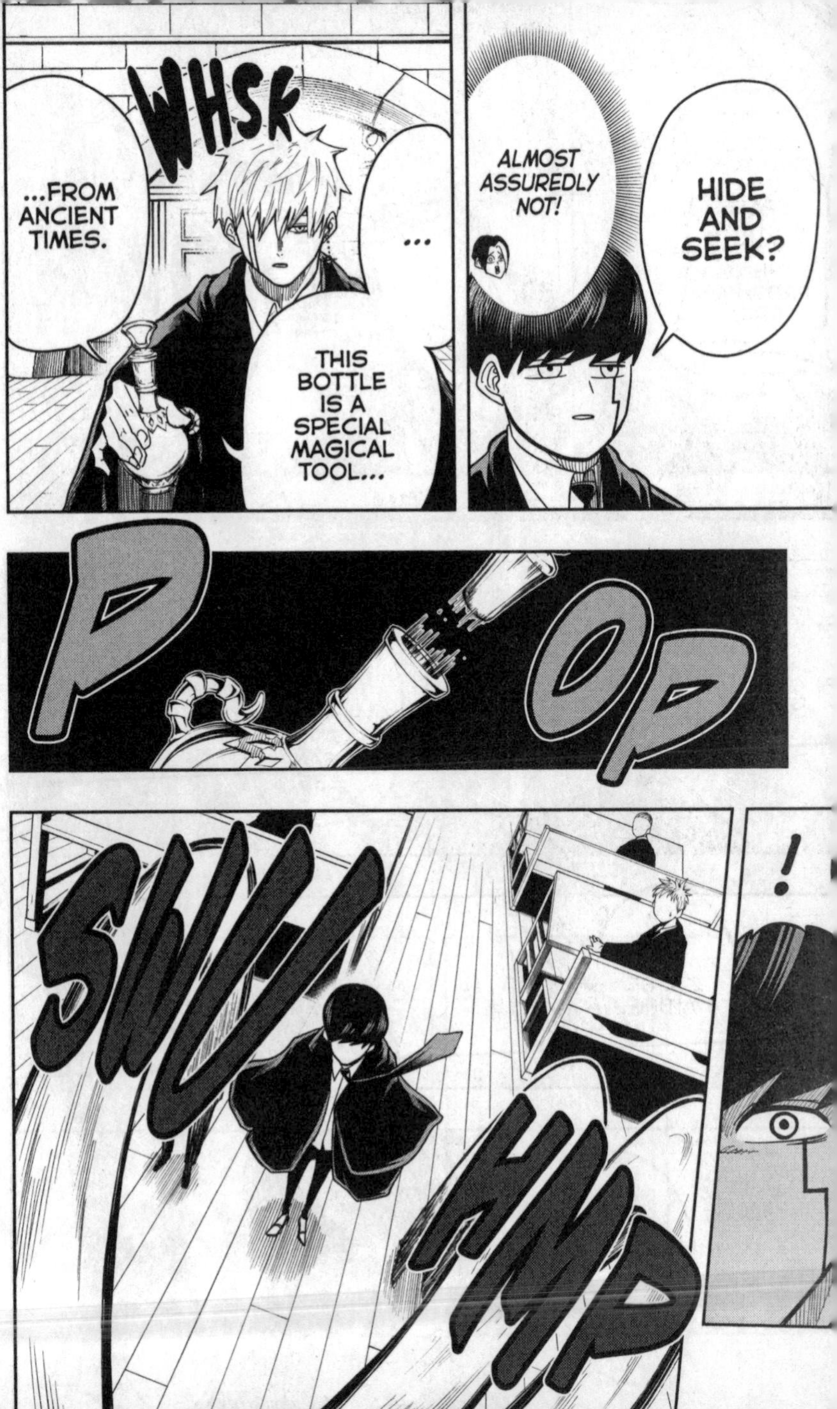
HIDE AND SEEK?
ALMOST ASSUREDLY NOT!
WHSK
...
THIS BOTTLE IS A SPECIAL MAGICAL TOOL...
...FROM ANCIENT TIMES.
POP
!
SWUHMP

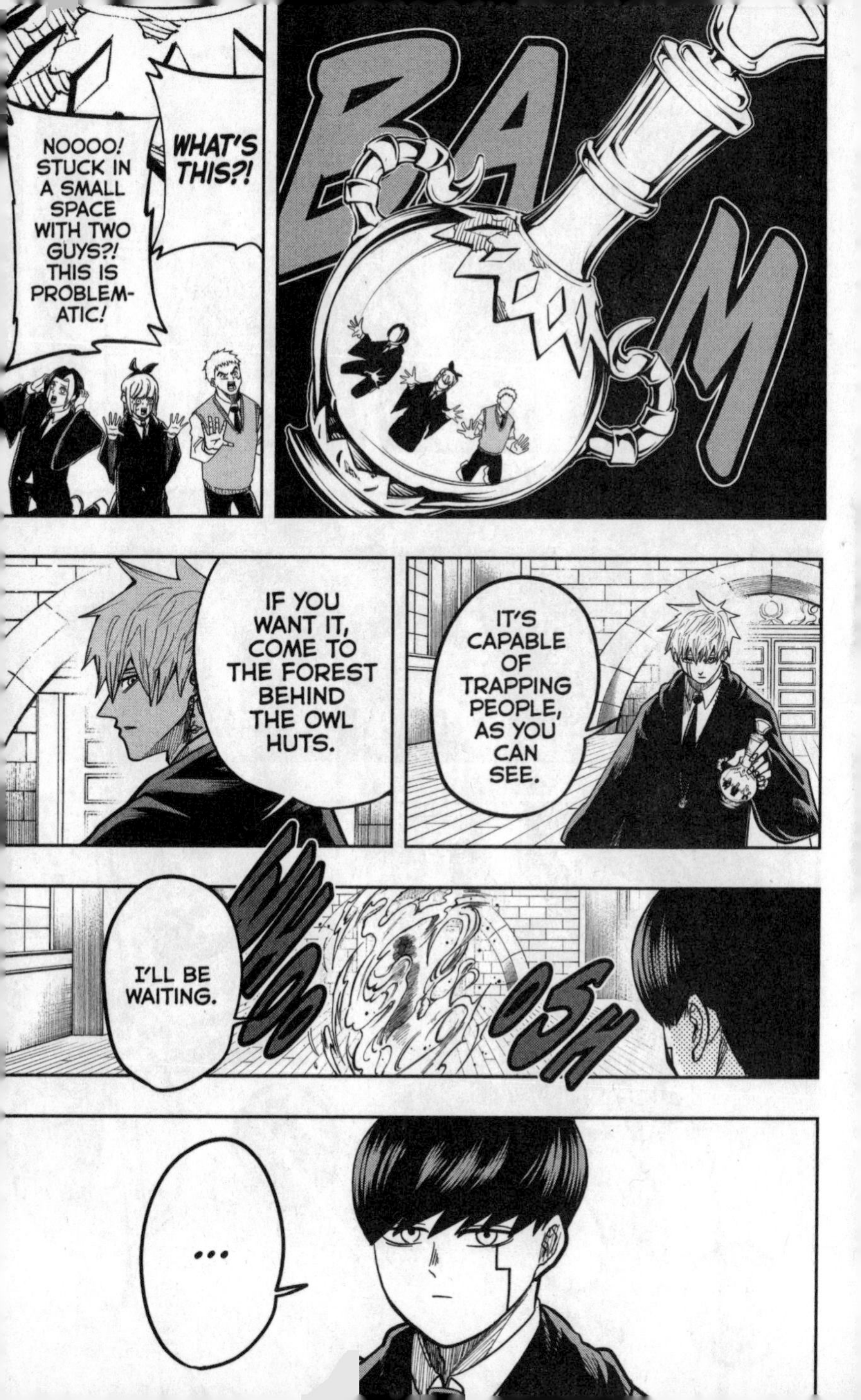
BAM
WHAT'S THIS?!
NOOOO! STUCK IN A SMALL SPACE WITH TWO GUYS?! THIS IS PROBLEM-ATIC!
IT'S CAPABLE OF TRAPPING PEOPLE, AS YOU CAN SEE.
IF YOU WANT IT, COME TO THE FOREST BEHIND THE OWL HUTS.
WHOOOSH
I'LL BE WAITING.
...

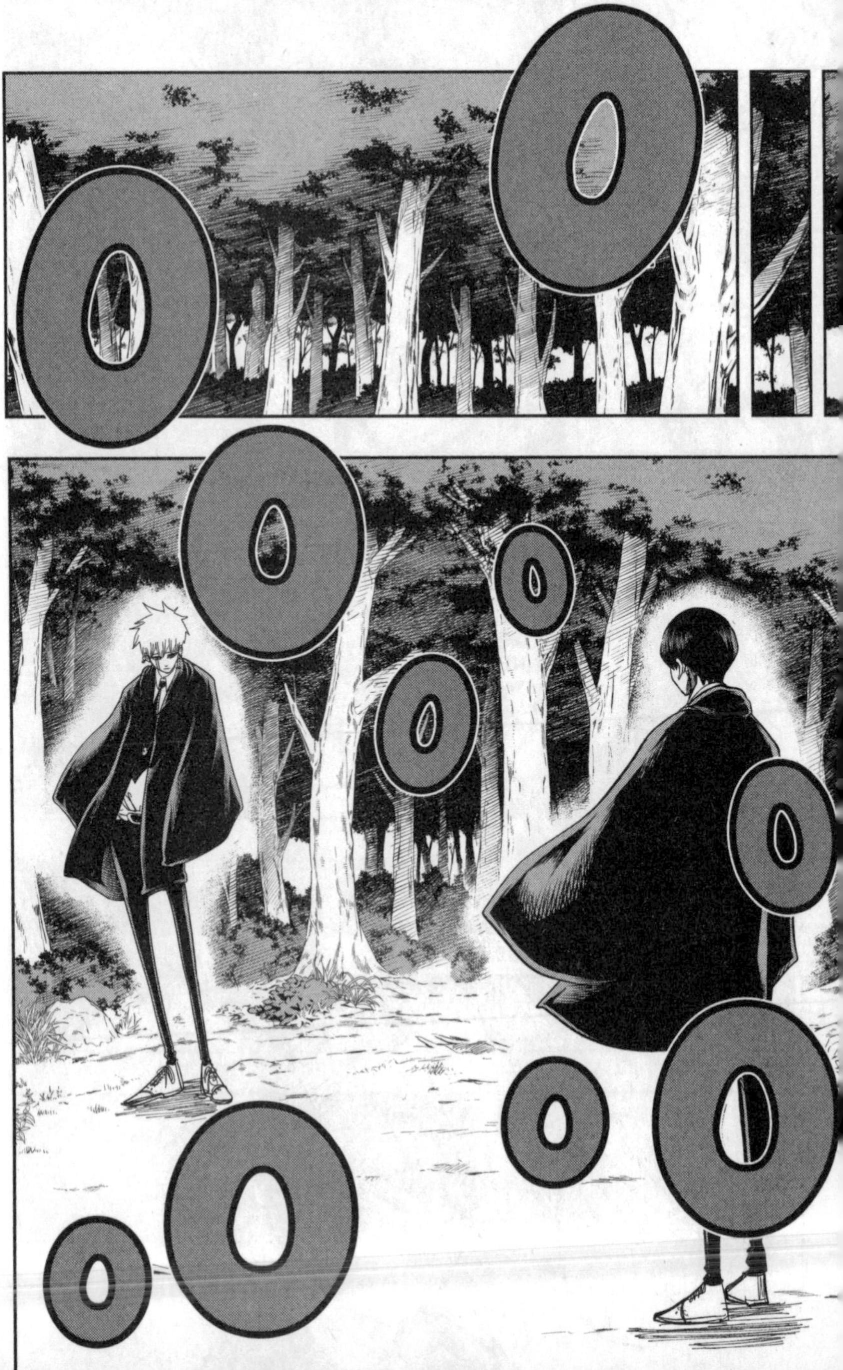

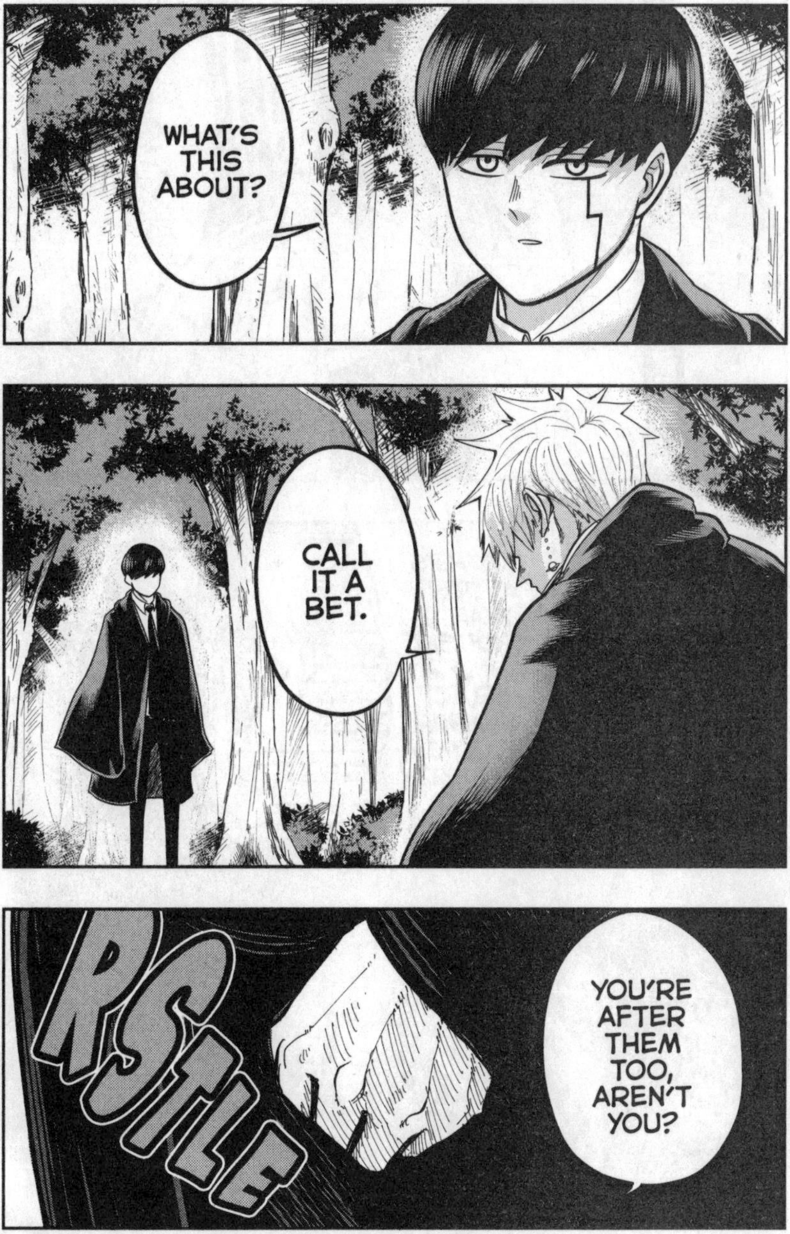
WHAT'S THIS ABOUT?
CALL IT A BET.
RSTLE
YOU'RE AFTER THEM TOO, AREN'T YOU?

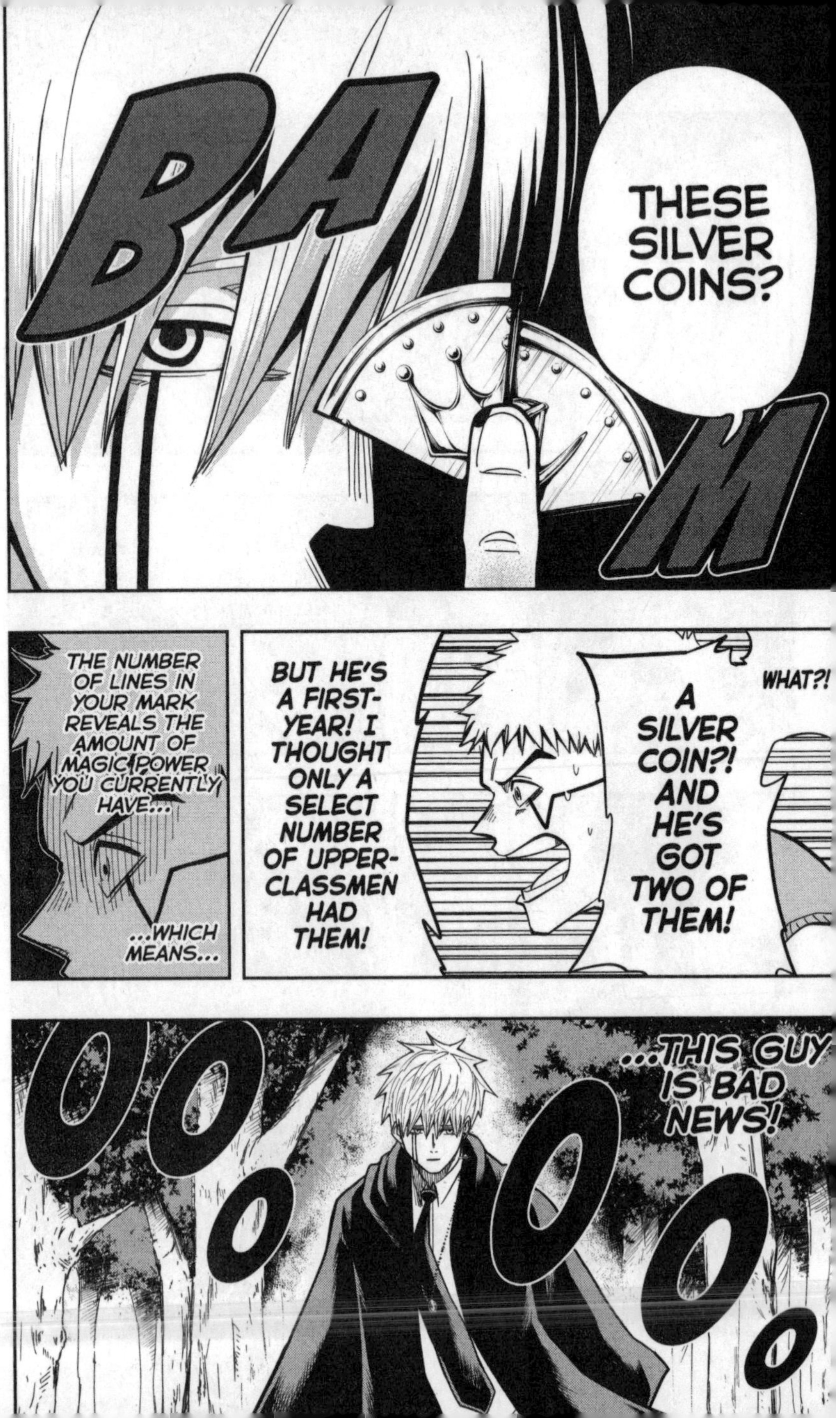
BAM
THESE SILVER COINS?
WHAT?!
A SILVER COIN?! AND HE'S GOT TWO OF THEM!
BUT HE'S A FIRST-YEAR! I THOUGHT ONLY A SELECT NUMBER OF UPPER-CLASSMEN HAD THEM!
THE NUMBER OF LINES IN YOUR MARK REVEALS THE AMOUNT OF MAGIC POWER YOU CURRENTLY HAVE...
...WHICH MEANS...
...THIS GUY IS BAD NEWS!

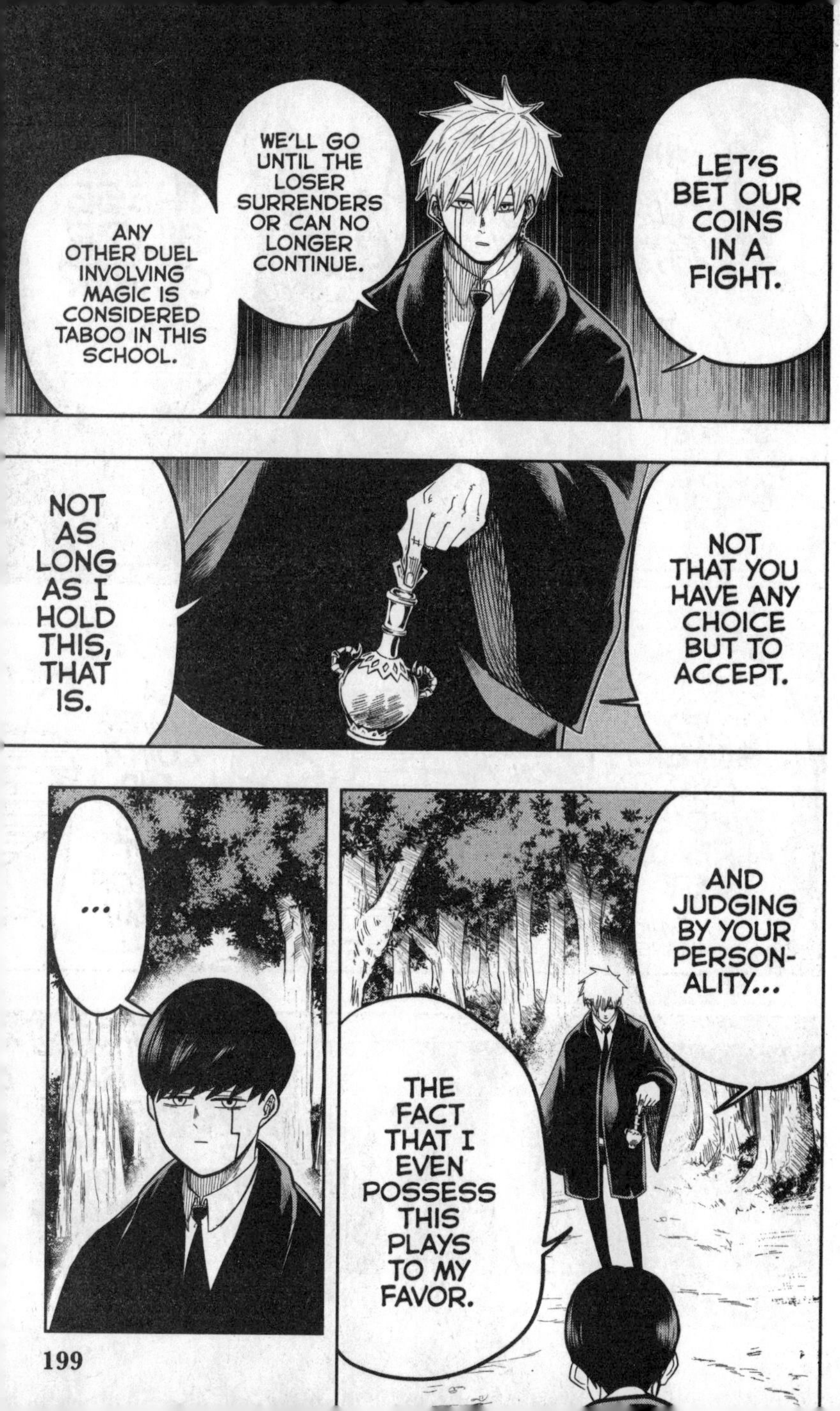
LET'S BET OUR COINS IN A FIGHT.
WE'LL GO UNTIL THE LOSER SURRENDERS OR CAN NO LONGER CONTINUE.
ANY OTHER DUEL INVOLVING MAGIC IS CONSIDERED TABOO IN THIS SCHOOL.
NOT THAT YOU HAVE ANY CHOICE BUT TO ACCEPT.
NOT AS LONG AS I HOLD THIS, THAT IS.
AND JUDGING BY YOUR PERSON-ALITY...
THE FACT THAT I EVEN POSSESS THIS PLAYS TO MY FAVOR.
...

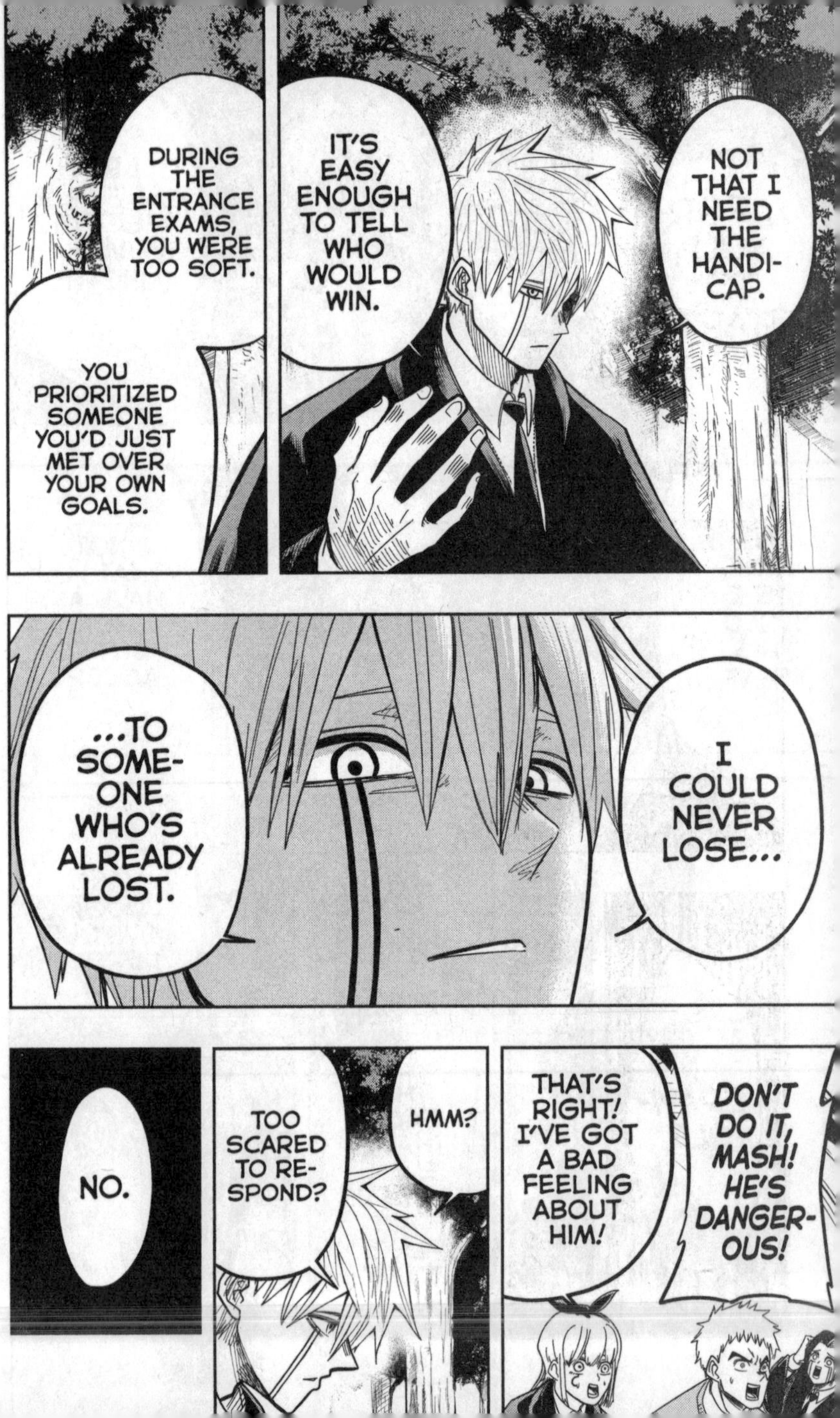
NOT THAT I NEED THE HANDI-CAP.
IT'S EASY ENOUGH TO TELL WHO WOULD WIN.
DURING THE ENTRANCE EXAMS, YOU WERE TOO SOFT.
YOU PRIORITIZED SOMEONE YOU'D JUST MET OVER YOUR OWN GOALS.
I COULD NEVER LOSE...
...TO SOME-ONE WHO'S ALREADY LOST.
DON'T DO IT, MASH! HE'S DANGER-OUS!
THAT'S RIGHT! I'VE GOT A BAD FEELING ABOUT HIM!
HMM?
TOO SCARED TO RE-SPOND?
NO.

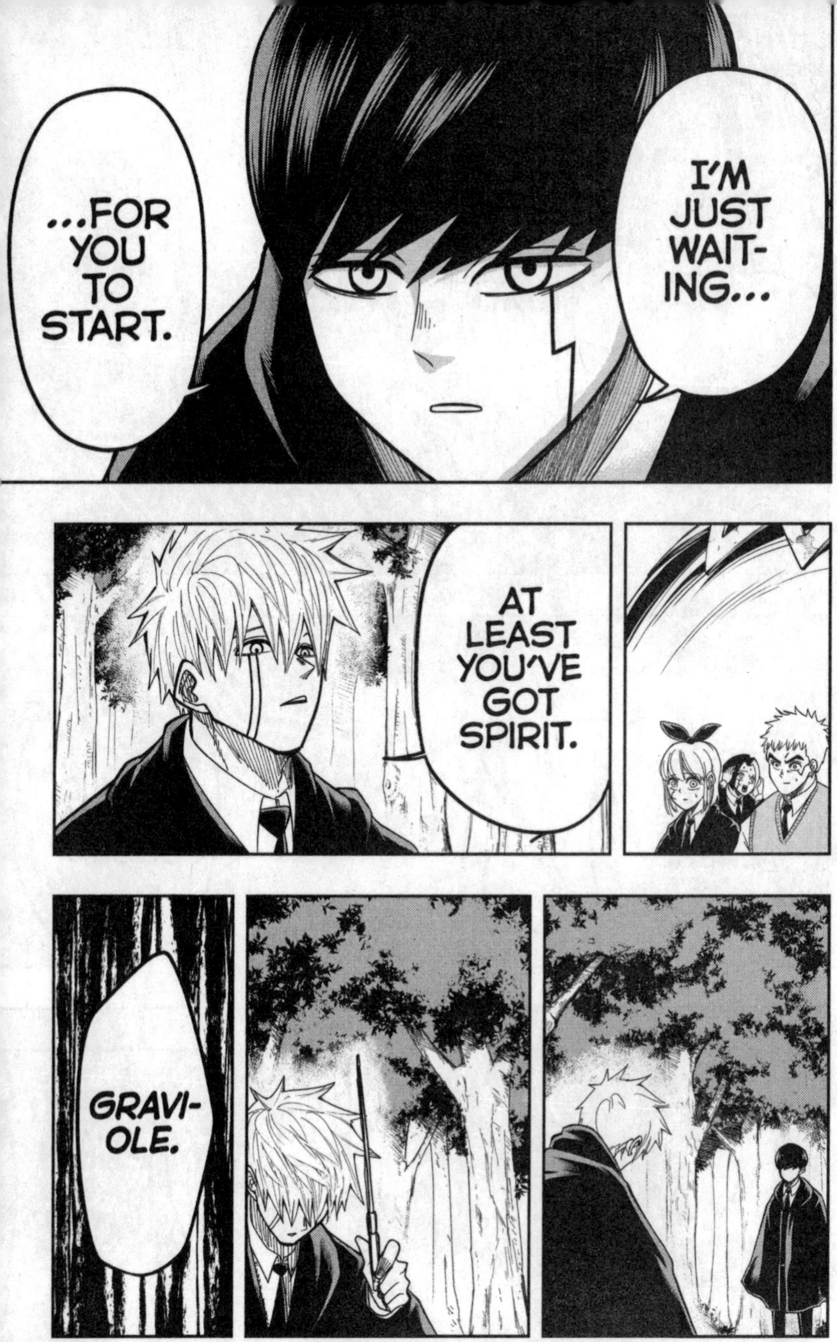
I'M JUST WAIT-ING...
...FOR YOU TO START.
AT LEAST YOU'VE GOT SPIRIT.
GRAVI-OLE.

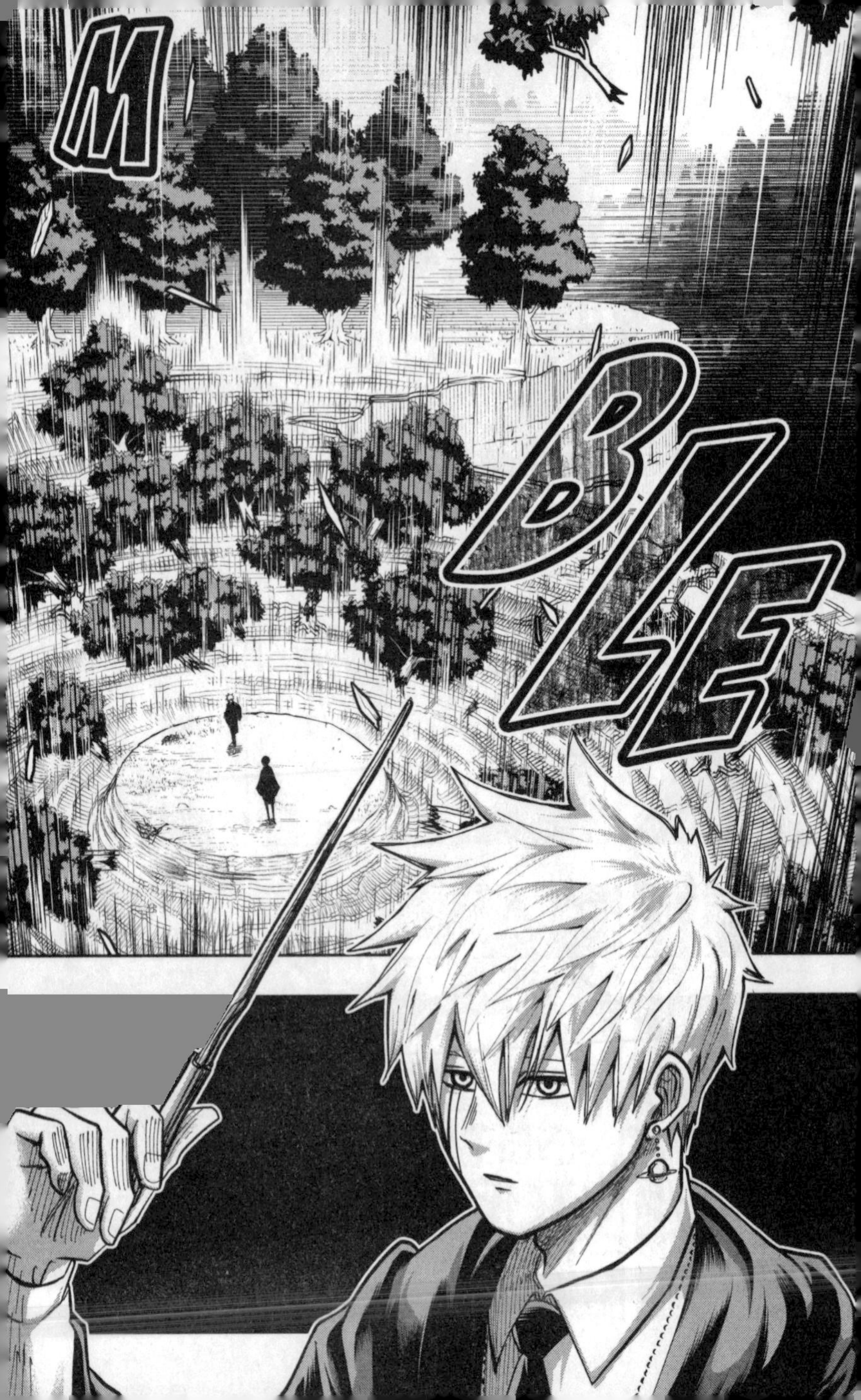
M
BLE

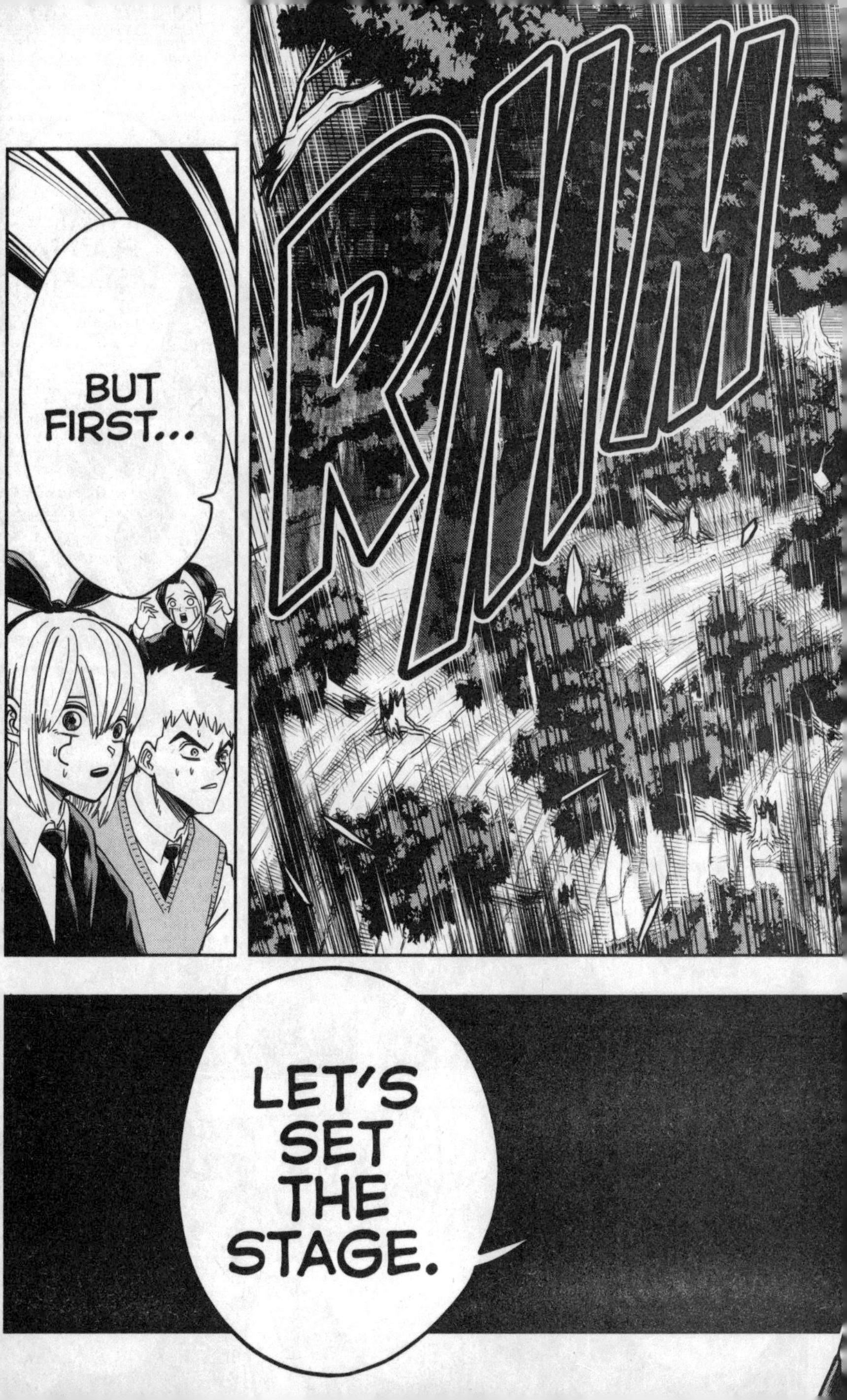
BUT FIRST...
LET'S SET THE STAGE.

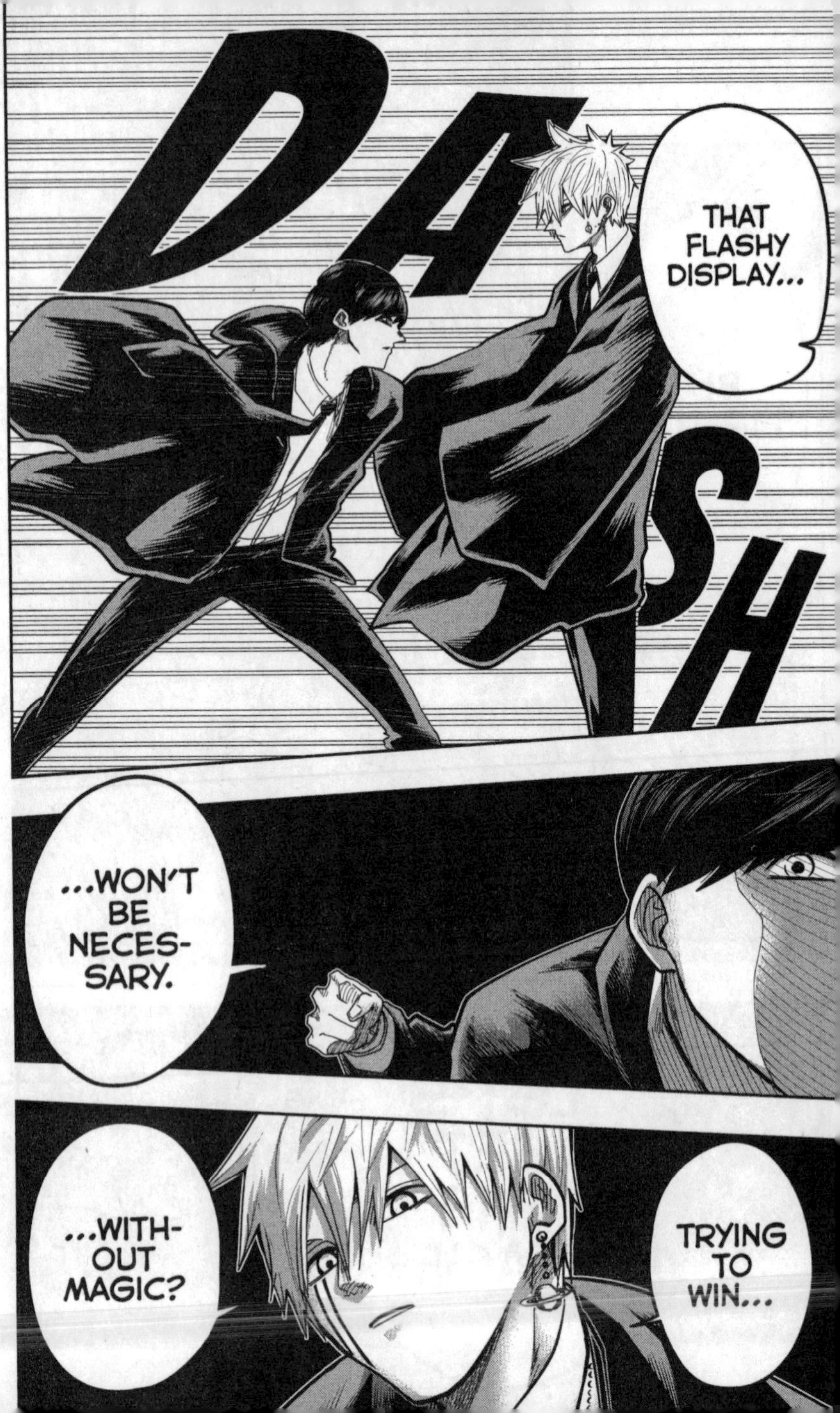
THAT FLASHY DISPLAY...
DASH
...WON'T BE NECES-SARY.
TRYING TO WIN...
...WITH-OUT MAGIC?

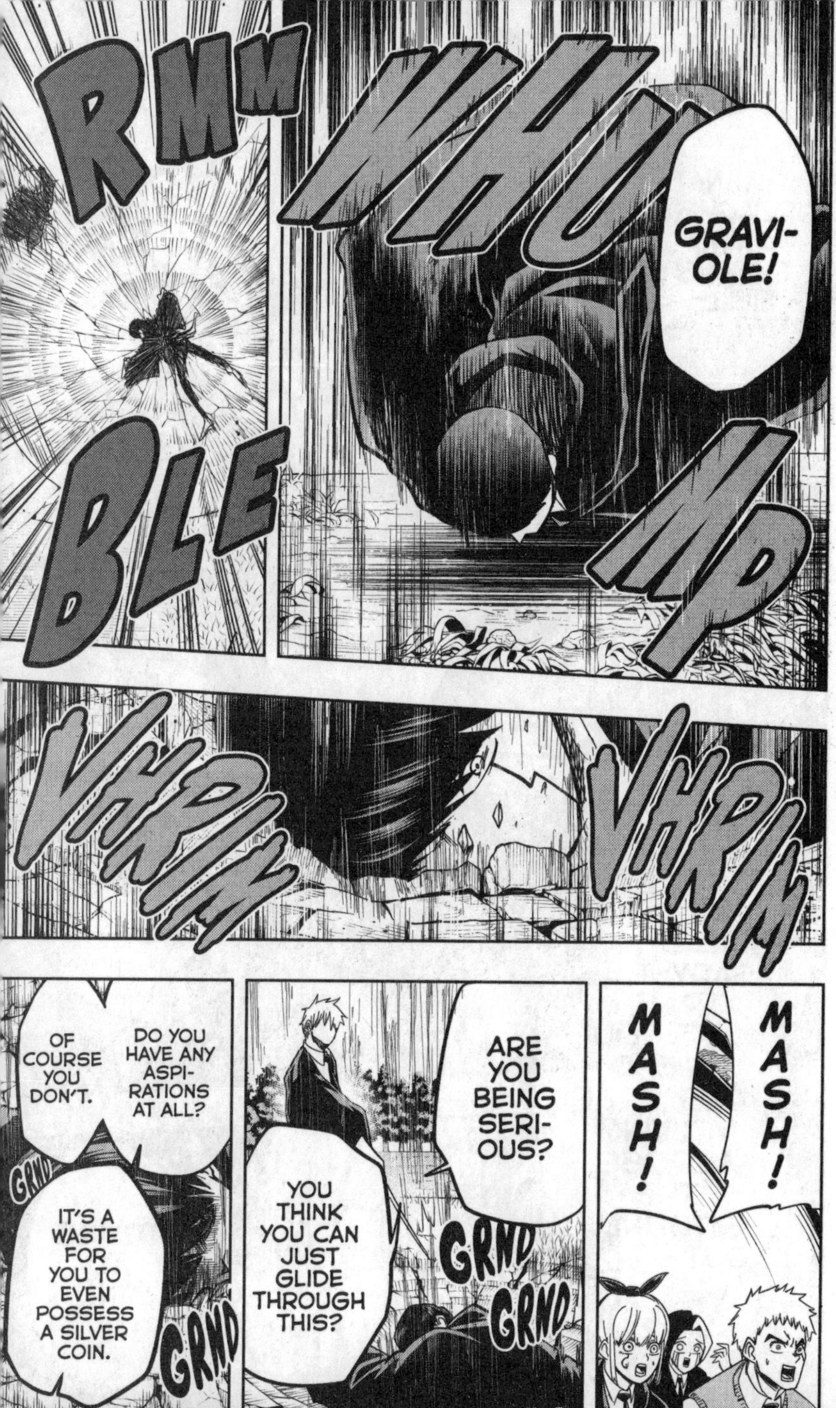
GRAVI-OLE!
WHUMP
RMMBLE
VHRMM
VHRMM
MASH! MASH!
ARE YOU BEING SERI-OUS?
YOU THINK YOU CAN JUST GLIDE THROUGH THIS?
GRND
GRND
DO YOU HAVE ANY ASPI-RATIONS AT ALL?
OF COURSE YOU DON'T.
IT'S A WASTE FOR YOU TO EVEN POSSESS A SILVER COIN.
GRND
GRND

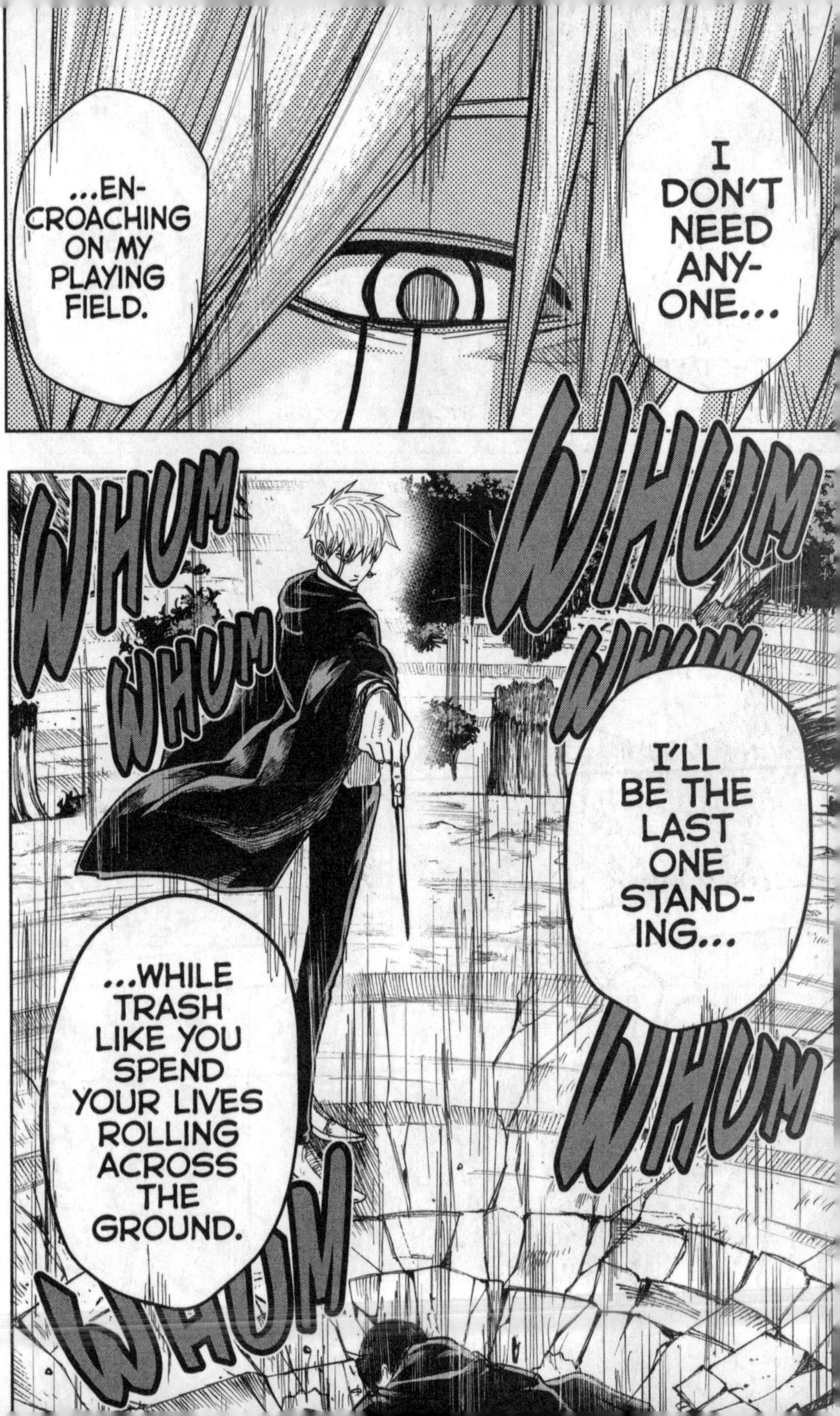

I DON'T NEED ANY-ONE...
...EN-CROACHING ON MY PLAYING FIELD.
WHUM
WHUM
WHUM
I'LL BE THE LAST ONE STAND-ING...
...WHILE TRASH LIKE YOU SPEND YOUR LIVES ROLLING ACROSS THE GROUND.
WHUM
WHUM

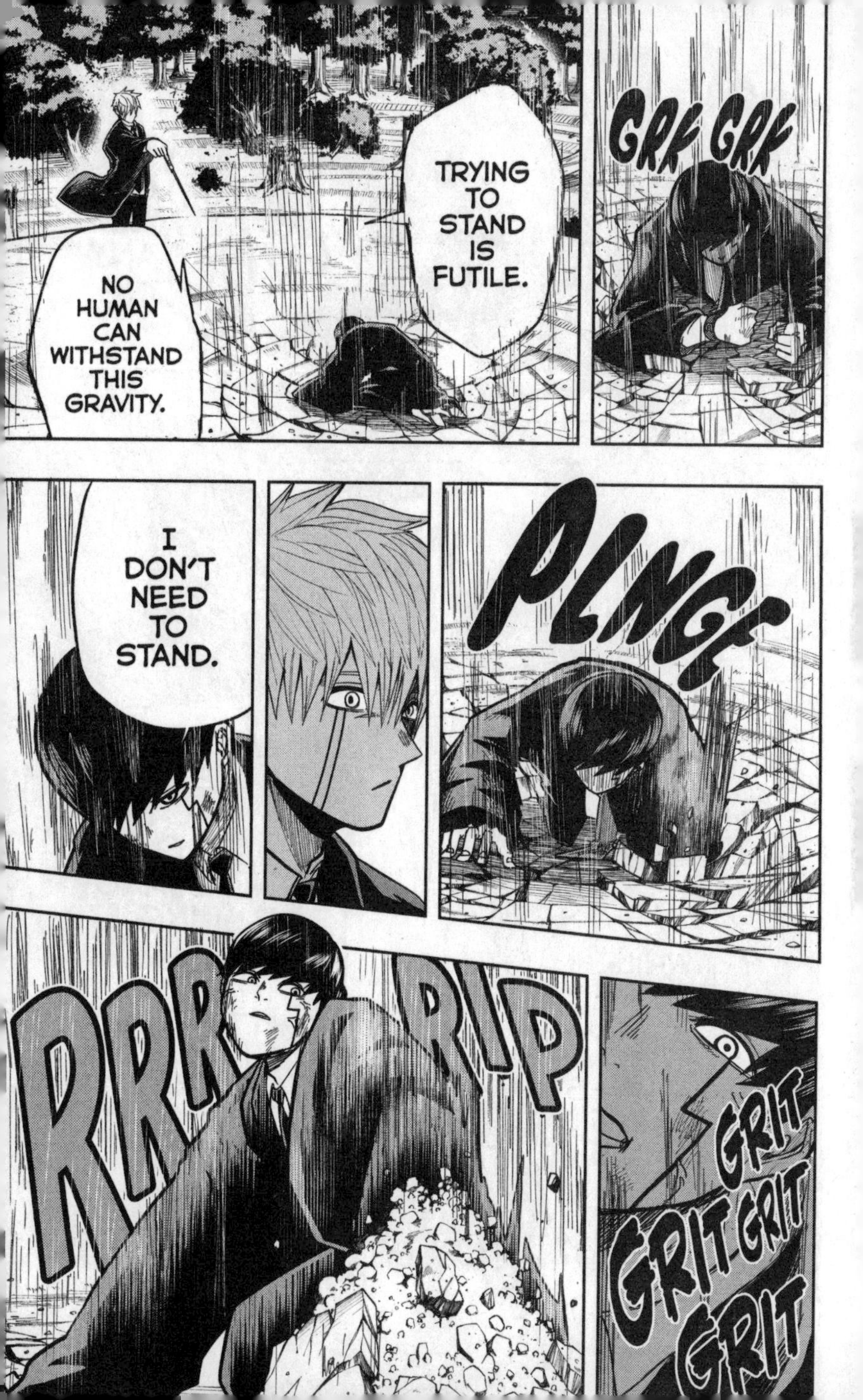
GRK GRK
TRYING TO STAND IS FUTILE.
NO HUMAN CAN WITHSTAND THIS GRAVITY.
PLNG
I DON'T NEED TO STAND.
GRIT GRIT GRIT GRIT
RRRRIP

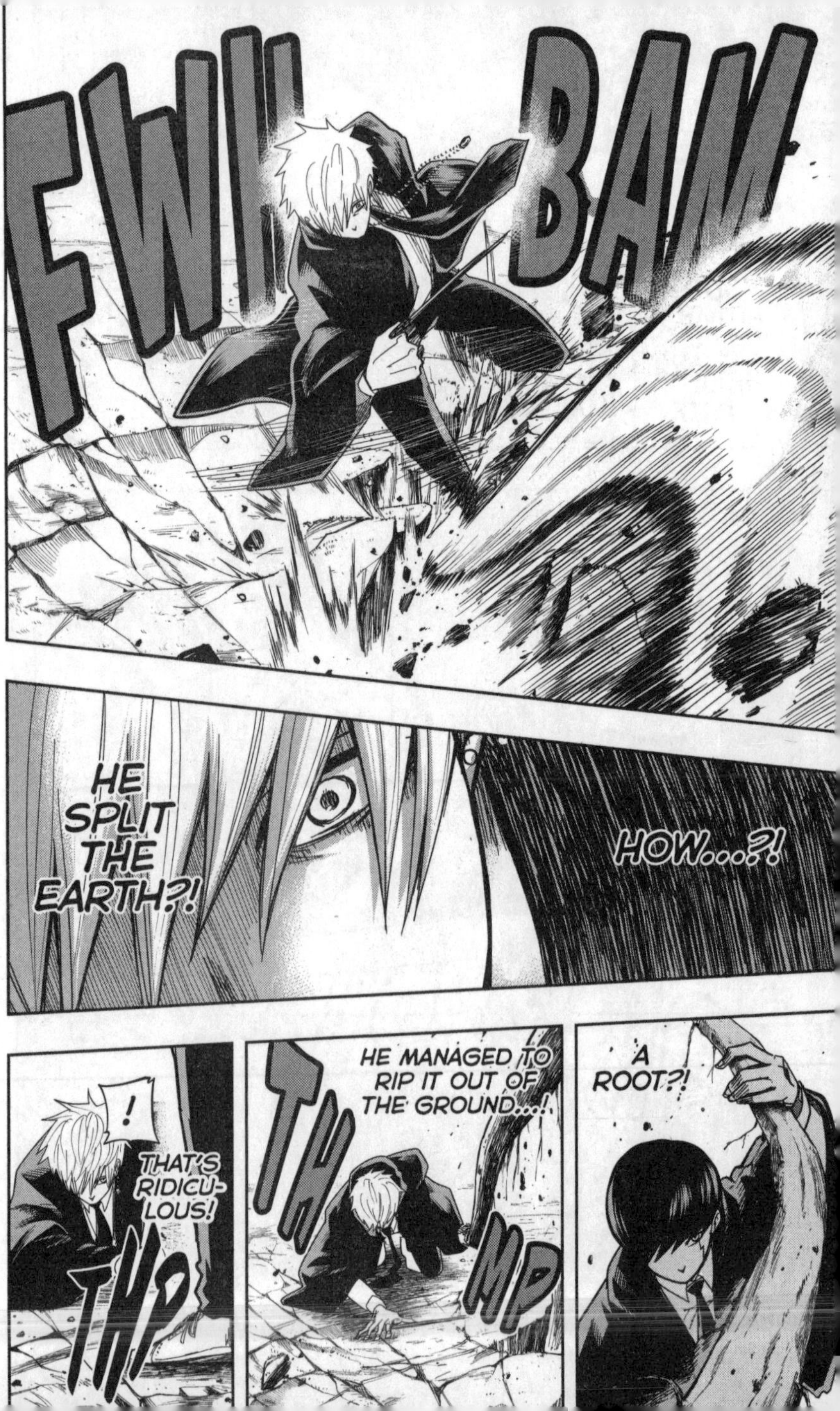
BAM
HOW...?!
HE SPLIT THE EARTH?!
A ROOT?!
HE MANAGED TO RIP IT OUT OF THE GROUND...!
!
THAT'S RIDICULOUS!

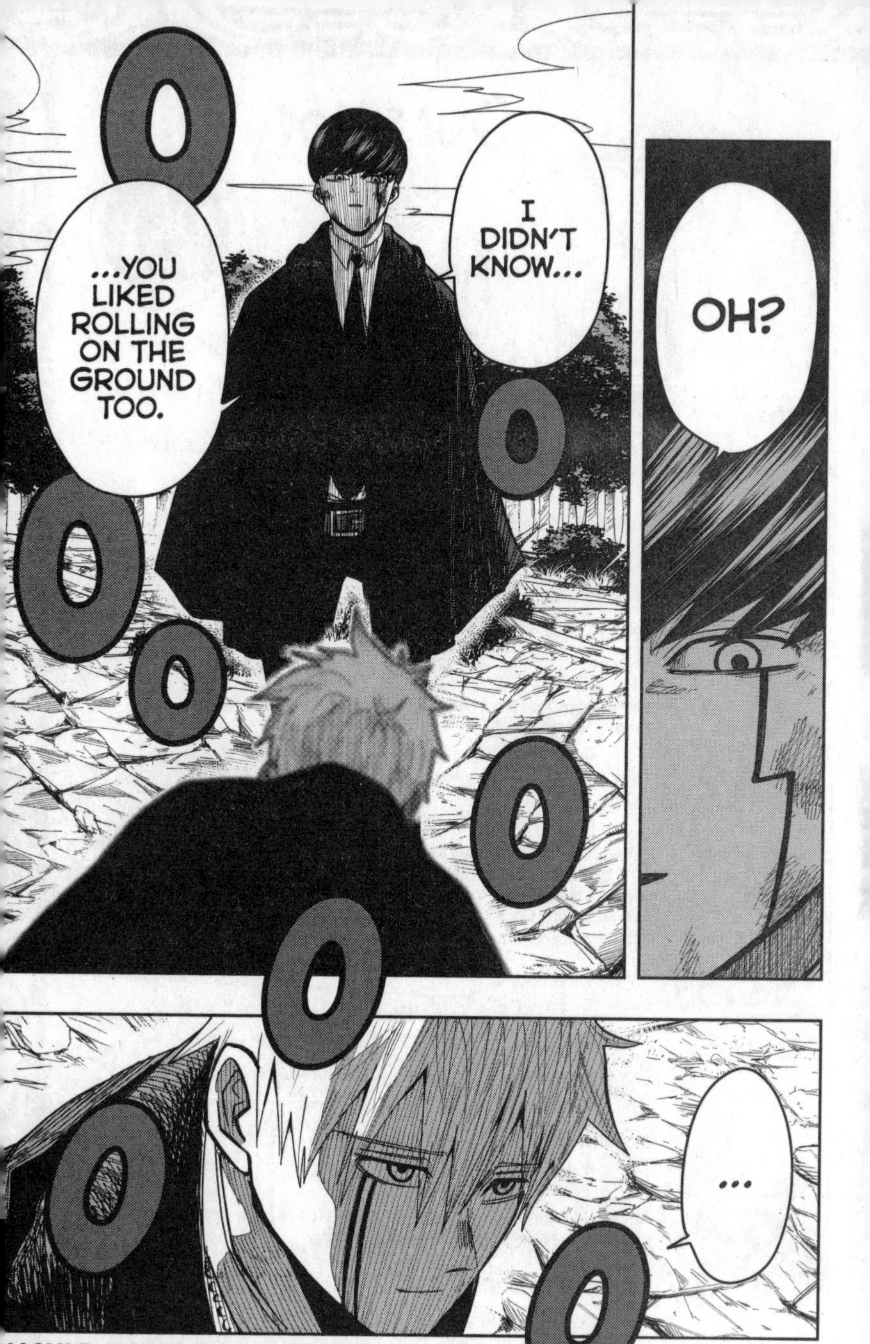
OH?
I DIDN'T KNOW...
...YOU LIKED ROLLING ON THE GROUND TOO.
...

MASHLE: MAGIC AND MUSCLES VOL. 1/END

Question & Answer Corner

Q.1/ ISN'T IT "PUSH OR PULL" NOT "PUSHABLE OR PULLABLE"? (FROM A READER.)

A.1/ Actually, my assistant pointed this one out too, but I kept it because I thought it was easier to understand.

I'm sorry! You're right! "Pullable" isn't a word!

Q.2/ IS A MAGIC USER'S MARK ALWAYS ON THEIR FACE? (FROM A READER.)

A.2/ The first line is always on the face!

Q.3/ IF THE LOCK-OPENING SPELL IS ONE OF THE FIRST SPELLS YOU LEARN, AND EVERYONE CAN USE IT, THEN AREN'T LOCKS USELESS IN THIS WORLD? ARE THERE EVEN LOCKS IN THIS WORLD AT ALL? (FROM A READER.)

A.3/ They have locks.

You could say the lock-opening spell being the first one they learn shows how fancy this academy is— normal people can't use it. But teaching the students how to open all locks would be a pretty bad thing, so the ones they give them in class are simpler than the ones commonly used in this world!!

Q.4/ WHAT HAPPENED TO THE VICE-PRINCIPAL AFTER MASH BURIED HIM? (FROM A READER.)

A.4/ He made the wise decision to avoid Mash and is currently doing just fine.

Q.5/ HOW LONG HAS THE HEADMASTER BEEN HERE, AND WHY THIS PARTICULAR SCHOOL? (FROM A READER.)

A.5/ Let's say it was several years ago that he decided to try and improve things at the school!

Q.6/ THEY HAVE PILL BUGS IN THE MAGIC WORLD? (FROM A READER.)

MAGIC WORLD PILL BUGS.

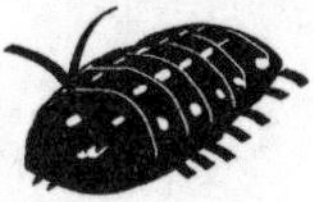

A.6/ Yes, they do...
They hide in groups under large rocks...

Q.7/ PROFESSOR LUCCI SEEMS TO CAST SPELLS WITH LITTLE MORE THAN A SIGH. CAN YOU CAST SPELLS WITHOUT CHANTING THEM? (FROM A READER.)

A.7/ Typically, no.
His spells were abbreviated to make the story easier to read.
He was totally chanting them between panels!! He was!!

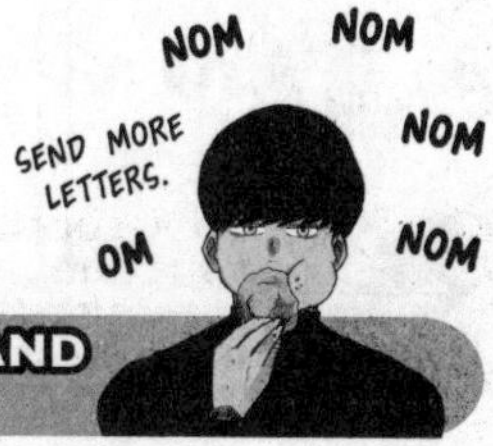
NOM
NOM
SEND MORE LETTERS.
NOM
OM
NOM

SEND US YOUR QUESTIONS AND YOUR MAGIC USERS!

WANT TO KNOW MORE ABOUT *MASHLE: MAGIC & MUSCLES*? HAVE QUESTIONS ABOUT THE WORLD? WANT TO SEE A CERTAIN TYPE OF MAGIC USER APPEAR? SEND EVERYTHING AND ANYTHING YOU CAN THINK OF TO THIS ADDRESS!

101-8050, TOKYO, CHIYODA, HITOTSUBASHI, 2-5-10
SHUEISHA, WEEKLY SHONEN JUMP EDITORIAL DEPT. JC "MASHLE" BONUS SECTION

*BE SURE TO INCLUDE YOUR NAME (OR PEN NAME), ADDRESS, AGE AND PHONE NUMBER.

*SUBMITTED TEXT, IMAGES, ETC. BECOME THE PROPERTY OF SHUEISHA, AND SHUEISHA RESERVES ALL RIGHTS TO REPUBLISH THEM IN DIGITAL OR PHYSICAL FORM. THE EDITORIAL DEPARTMENT MAY MAKE ALTERATIONS TO THE WORK FOR PUBLICATION. ANY RECEIVED ITEMS WILL BE DISPOSED OF AFTER A PERIOD OF TIME. PLEASE MAKE A COPY OF YOUR WORK BEFORE SENDING IT IF YOU WISH TO RETAIN IT. IN ADDITION, PLEASE INDICATE IF YOU DON'T WANT YOUR NAME AND ADDRESS PUBLISHED ALONG WITH YOUR WORK.

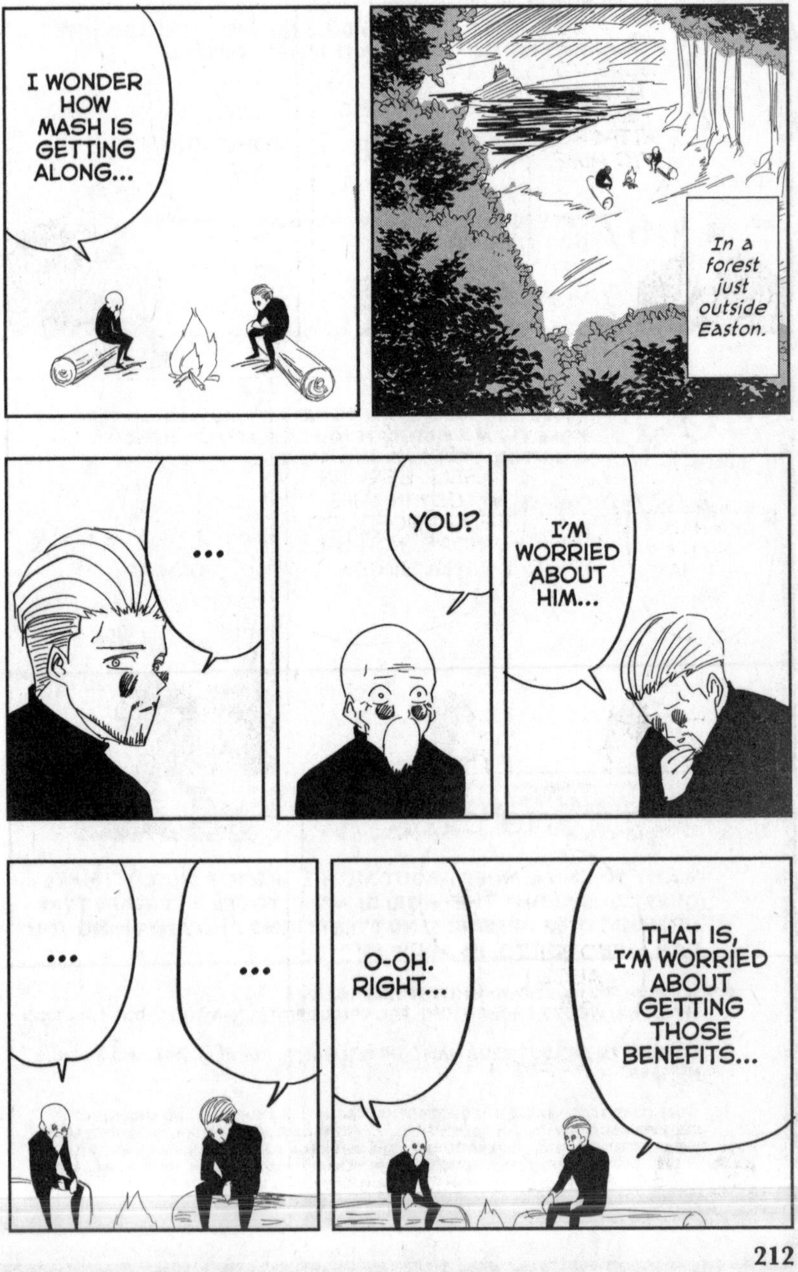
In a forest just outside Easton.
I WONDER HOW MASH IS GETTING ALONG...
I'M WORRIED ABOUT HIM...
YOU?
...
THAT IS, I'M WORRIED ABOUT GETTING THOSE BENEFITS...
O-OH. RIGHT...
...
...

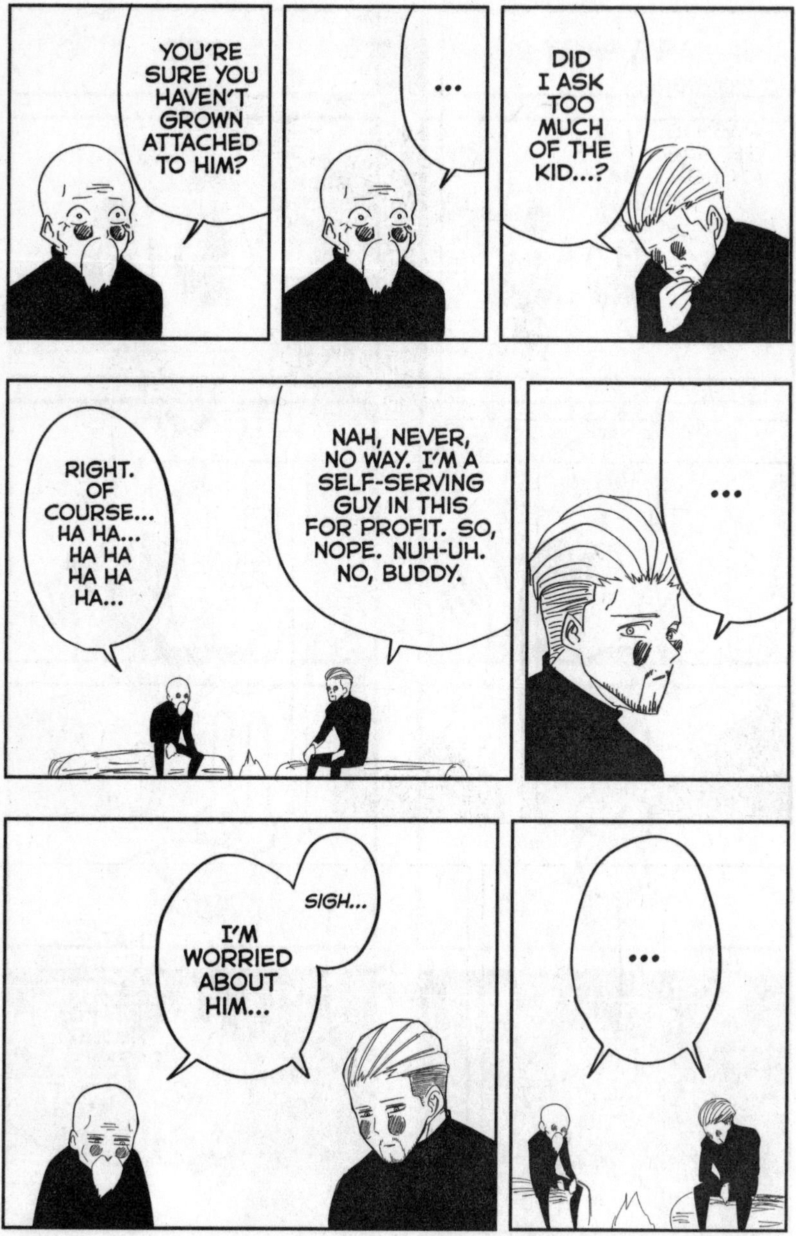
DID I ASK TOO MUCH OF THE KID...?
...
YOU'RE SURE YOU HAVEN'T GROWN ATTACHED TO HIM?
...
NAH, NEVER, NO WAY. I'M A SELF-SERVING GUY IN THIS FOR PROFIT. SO, NOPE. NUH-UH. NO, BUDDY.
RIGHT. OF COURSE... HA HA... HA HA HA HA HA...
...
SIGH...
I'M WORRIED ABOUT HIM...

ART

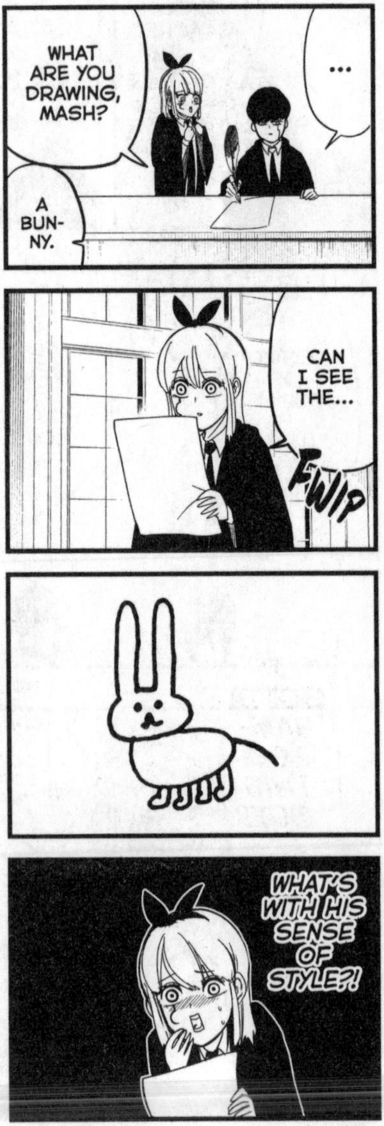
...
WHAT ARE YOU DRAWING, MASH?
A BUN-NY.
CAN I SEE THE...
FWIP
WHAT'S WITH HIS SENSE OF STYLE?!

ART, PART 2

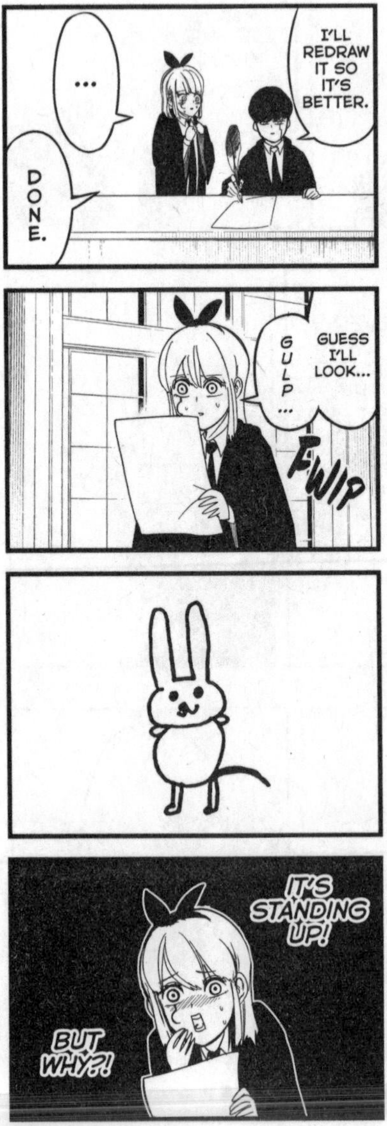
I'LL REDRAW IT SO IT'S BETTER.
...
DONE.
GUESS I'LL LOOK...
GULP...
FWIP
IT'S STANDING UP!
BUT WHY?!

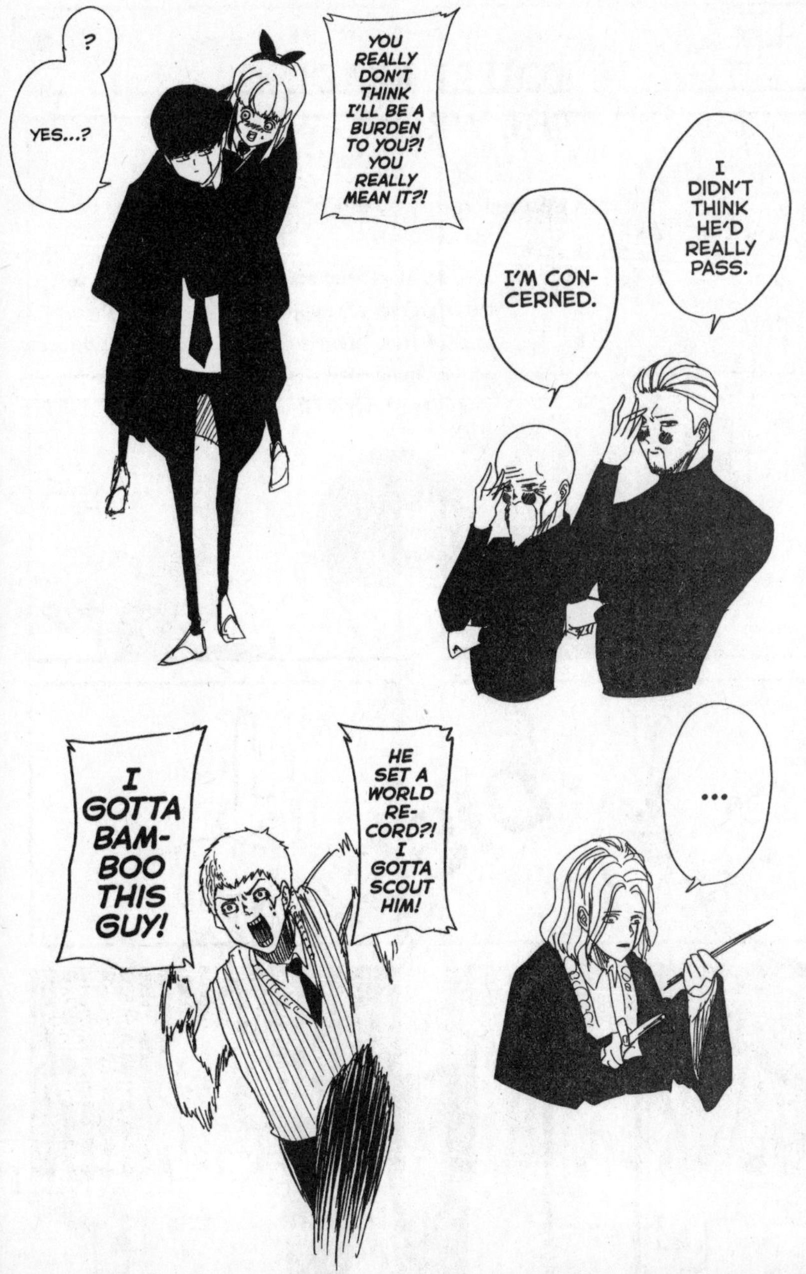
I DIDN'T THINK HE'D REALLY PASS.
I'M CONCERNED.
YOU REALLY DON'T THINK I'LL BE A BURDEN TO YOU?! YOU REALLY MEAN IT?!
?
YES...?
...
HE SET A WORLD RECORD?! I GOTTA SCOUT HIM!
I GOTTA BAMBOO THIS GUY!

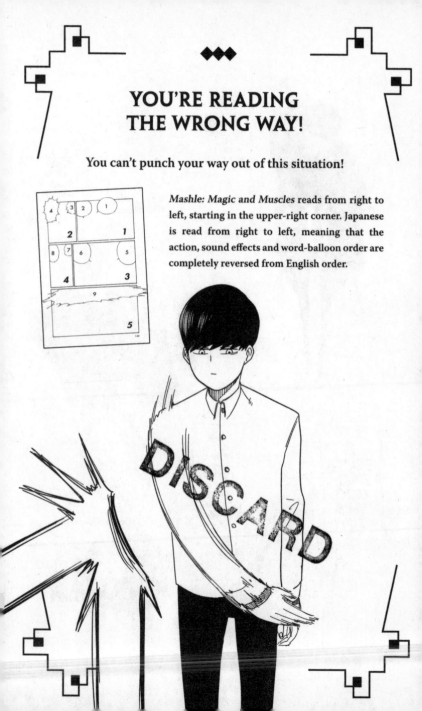

YOU'RE READING THE WRONG WAY!

You can't punch your way out of this situation!

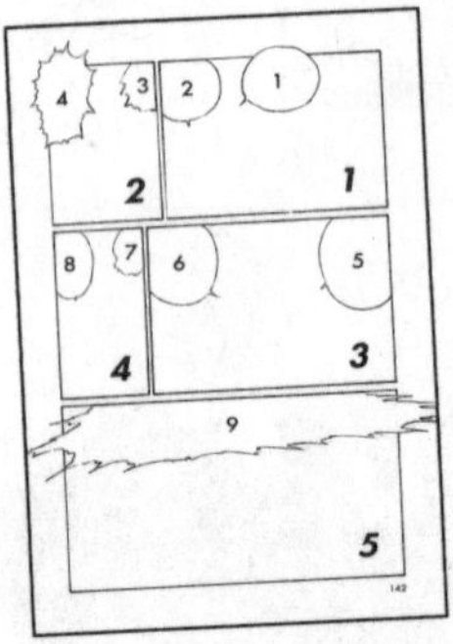

Mashle: Magic and Muscles **reads from right to left, starting in the upper-right corner. Japanese is read from right to left, meaning that the action, sound effects and word-balloon order are completely reversed from English order.**

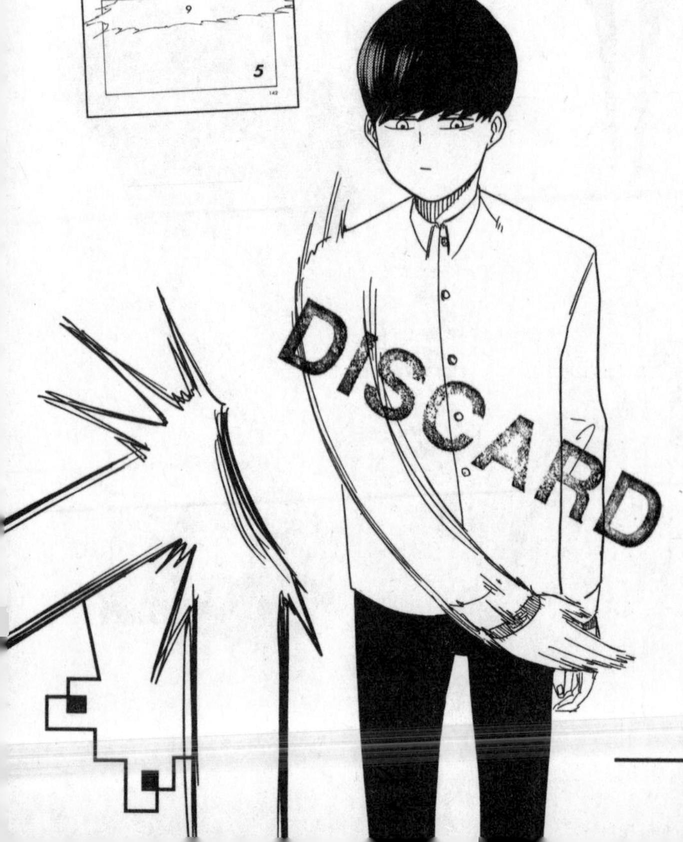
DISCARD